Charlotte Greenwood

Charlotte Greenwood

*The Life and Career
of the Comic Star
of Vaudeville, Radio and Film*

GRANT HAYTER-MENZIES

*Foreword by Brian Kellow
Afterword by William Luce*

McFarland & Company, Inc., Publishers
Jefferson, North Carolina, and London

Library of Congress Cataloguing-in-Publication Data

Hayter-Menzies, Grant.
Charlotte Greenwood: the life and career of the comic star of
vaudeville, radio and film / Grant Hayter-Menzies ;
foreword by Brian Kellow ; afterword by William Luce.
p.   cm.
Includes bibliographical references and index.

ISBN-13: 978-0-7864-2995-0 (softcover : 50# alkaline paper)

1. Greenwood, Charlotte, 1890–1978.
2. Actors—United States—Biography.   I. Title.
PN2287.G677H39   2007   791.4302'8092—dc22   2007000277

British Library cataloguing data are available

On the cover: from left, Charlotte in *Out of This World*, 1950
(Emmett Brennan collection); Charlotte photographed by
Clarence Sinclair Bull, ca 1931 (William Luce collection);
Charlotte as studio drama coach Lola Langdon in *Star Dust*, 1940

Manufactured in the United States of America

*McFarland & Company, Inc., Publishers
Box 611, Jefferson, North Carolina 28640
www.mcfarlandpub.com*

For Les
... shall we dance?

Acknowledgments

It is never easy, after completing a project requiring the kindness of both friends and strangers, to thank everyone involved to the extent they deserve. I must, however, single out a handful of people without whom this book could not have been written, and extend special gratitude to these four: William Luce, my dear friend for 25 years who entrusted Charlotte's papers to me and believed I could not only put her name back in lights, but reveal the real Charlotte Greenwood, and the real Martin Broones, whom he knew and loved. Emmett Brennan, a Greenwood fan and believer in her multifold talents, who encouraged me, informed me, and helped me make this book what it is. Sean William Menzies, superb film editor and brother, whose knowledge technical and artistic helped me understand and appreciate Charlotte's cinematic work. And Les Hayter, my life partner, whose love makes all things possible.

I extend best thanks to the following benefactors, a lucky few of whom had the pleasure of working with Charlotte Greenwood, and two of whom have the pleasure of living in the house where she was born: Dr. Steven Bird; Vicki Calvo; Gary Chapman; Ned Comstock, archivist extraordinaire at the Film and Television Library, University of Southern California, Los Angeles; Carl Reeves Close, the best indexer an author could hope to have; Dr. Dennis Cunniff; Scott Eyman; Jon Finch; George Gaynes; Cyril Hume; Shirley Jones; Brian Kellow; TRH Prince and Princess Michael of Kent; Miles Kreuger, President of the Institute of the American Musical in Los Angeles and national treasure; Vicki Gold Levi; James Mitchell; Alan Mollison; Leo van de Pas; Peggy Rea; Judy Reimche; Mark Trawka; and Gilberto and Dawn Wilson.

Last but not least, I thank my late grandmother, Nina Lewis Strawser, wherever she may be (I have a good idea it's some supernal flower garden). A writer herself, she did not live to see publication of my first book. But from the day she lent her typewriter to her ten year old grandson, she never doubted, or allowed me to doubt, that wishes could become reality.

Table of Contents

⋆ **Part One** ⋆

⋆ **Part Two** ⋆

Foreword
by Brian Kellow

IN THE DAYS OF MY CHILDHOOD, before pay-television, when quality music and drama programs could still be seen regularly on the major networks, CBS inaugurated a tradition that lasted for several years: a Thanksgiving-night showing of the 1955 film version of Rodgers and Hammerstein's *Oklahoma!* Each year, I watched it with my family. It might have been something of a mixed bag as a movie, but at least it had the benefit of an entire cast doing its own singing. And each year, the one who grabbed my attention most was Charlotte Greenwood, who played leathery, sagacious Aunt Eller. I found myself watching for the same bits every year: her lascivious grin in the first scene, with Curly (Gordon MacRae) attempting to spark Laurey (Shirley Jones); her spirited two-step with Will Parker (Gene Nelson) in the "Kansas City" number (at one point, she gives a marvelous high kick as she steps out of the frame); and her touching speech at the end, when she tells Laurey, "You gotta get used to all kinds of things happenin' to you. You gotta look at all the good on one side and all the bad on the other, and say — well, all right then, to both of 'em."

I had no idea at the time who Charlotte Greenwood was or where she came from; for all I knew, *Oklahoma!* had been her only movie. But soon, film had become a passion, and I was soaking up as many old movies as I could find on afternoon and late-night TV. (My parents, who knew a junkie in the making when they saw one, finally limited my viewing to a strict number of hours every week.) I noticed that Charlotte Greenwood frequently turned up in the supporting cast of several of the old musicals and comedies I watched. She seemed down-home and delightful — not remote, like so many of the stars, but the sort of person you might actually have a chance of knowing. If she hadn't been there on your television screen, it was easy enough to picture her as your local postmistress, or the lady who ran the cash grocery.

Later on, I found out that Charlotte Greenwood had also a remarkable stage career, notably in a long series of comedies with intriguing titles (*So Long Letty*, *Linger Longer Letty*), in which she starred as a character with an equally intriguing name, Letitia Proudfoot. And when I was a freshman at Oregon State University, my best friend, Cynthia Peterson, introduced me to the original-cast album of Cole Porter's *Out of This World*. Greenwood's lively and colorful renditions of "I Sleep Easier Now" and "Nobody's Chasing Me" got me through many a pre-finals night of cramming. Maybe this wasn't absolutely first-class Porter, but Charlotte Greenwood made it seem so.

I remember reading that Greenwood had at some point published an autobiography, entitled *Never Too Tall*. I made a concerted effort to find it, but never did, and for a very good reason: it didn't exist. Greenwood *had* written it, but it had never been published. Now, Grant Hayter-Menzies has filled in this gap in American theater and film history with his new book, *Charlotte Greenwood: The Life and Career of the Comic Star of Vaudeville, Radio and Film*.

I first became aware of Grant's work by reading his perceptive classical music reviews in *The Oregonian*. As features editor of *Opera News*, I am always on the lookout for good writers new to me, and I asked him to contribute several articles to the magazine. Perhaps his most notable effort was an astute essay on Tchaikovsky's opera *Mazeppa*. Soon Grant was telling me about the book that occupied his attention for some time. Knowing his wide-ranging enthusiasms as I do, maybe I shouldn't have been surprised that someone who could write so eloquently about Tchaikovsky was also deeply interested in the life of Charlotte Greenwood.

Using Greenwood's unpublished manuscript as the backbone for his own work, Grant has given us a marvelous, detailed look at her colorful life. Like all good biographers, he has provided a wonderful sense of time and place, an illuminating portrait of the American entertainment industry. He covers the American theater of the teens and 1920s and the glory days of Hollywood musicals with equal aplomb and affection.

But in the end, this is the story of a remarkable woman whose belief in herself would seem to have been all but unshakable. Although she was not likely star material, Charlotte Greenwood persevered until she had become one of the theater's national treasures. She was lucky in the sense that the prime years of her career coincided with the first half of the twentieth century — an age of great personalities, an age in which she absolutely belonged.

Brian Kellow is the author of Can't Help Singing: The Life of Eileen Farrell, The Bennetts: An Acting Family, *and a forthcoming biography of* Ethel Merman, *to be published in 2007 by Viking-Penguin. He is also the features editor of* Opera News *and lives in New York City.*

Preface

A FEW MONTHS BEFORE HER DEATH in December 1977, Charlotte Greenwood gave playwright William Luce, then enjoying the Broadway and touring success of his play *The Belle of Amherst*, a large cardboard box. In it was a more or less finished draft of her memoirs, dated to July 1941, along with several earlier drafts and *aides memoirs*, typed and written in Charlotte's handwriting, and that of her husband, Martin Broones, letters to Charlotte and copies of her letters to others, manuscript articles Charlotte had written over the years, and numerous photographs and memorabilia.

Charlotte and her husband, songwriter Martin Broones, had known Luce since the late 1950s. Originally from Portland, Oregon, where Charlotte enjoyed some of her biggest vaudeville successes, Luce came into their lives to write lyrics for Martin's songs; by the end, he was like the son they had never had. After seeing Julie Harris in Luce's first one-woman play, Charlotte seems to have believed her own life, as revealed in her memoirs, was material as capable of holding its own in the theatre as the poetry of Emily Dickinson. Charlotte bequeathed these materials to Luce in the hope that he might be able to use them for a one-woman show. With a nonstop flow of commissions for the stage and screen, Luce had no time to consider the project, and left Charlotte's memoir materials in their box. They were in this state when, having heard of them from Luce, I read and organized them. I realized that though these papers were not publishable in the state in which Charlotte left them, they were still an invaluable glimpse into the origins of one of the great comediennes of the twentieth century, and rich with all the humor one would expect from such a comedy specialist. Yet in significant ways, as I've pointed out in the pages to follow, these memoirs are not just the outline of a successful career in entertainment — they are the baring of Charlotte's soul, and the revealing of a very different person from what generations of movie and theatergoers might have been led to expect.

In Charlotte's papers, I discovered something that may come as a surprise to many who read this book — Charlotte Greenwood did not intend to be a comedian. People remember her for her loony, high-kick dancing, in which she seemed to levitate one long leg and then another toward the ceiling, perpendicular to her lean, lanky body. They remember her throbbing contralto, her high-piled peroxided hair, wide blue eyes and light-up-a-block smile. These people and others will find it curious if not astonishing that this same woman, from her earliest years, had yearned to be an opera singer, a tragedienne, a balladeer who could leave her listeners crying in their kerchiefs. As we all know, she did none of these things. Instead, through an onstage revelation that was at first a devastating one for her, she resolutely donned the clown persona that made her fame and fortune. But she also continued to study singing and acting, and insisted — as did many respected theatre critics — that in the right vehicle, she would prove herself more than just a vaudeville headliner. Charlotte would fulfill that wish on stage, and would luckily also do so on film, a medium for which she ironically had less respect than theatre, where so many of her critically acclaimed dramatic performances went unrecorded. In the 1955 film version of *Oklahoma!*, her unique set of talents, mingling comedy and drama, would be preserved for succeeding generations, and serve as proof that all the critics and, especially, Charlotte herself, were right.

Moved by my enthusiasm, which only increased as I delved into Charlotte's papers, and aware of my background as a biographer and historian as well as reviewer of music, film and theatre, Luce lent her papers to me, encouraging me to use them in writing about Charlotte's life and career.

I have based this book on both the final typescript of Charlotte's memoir, *Never Too Tall*, and the many notes and drafts related to it, included in the collection given to Luce. Though this typescript, under the title *Just for Kicks*, is listed as having been published in 1947 by *The Biographical Encyclopaedia and Who's Who of the American Theatre* (Walter Ridgon, editor, James H. Heineman, Inc., New York), no trace of a book by Charlotte, published under this or any other title, is to be found. (Nor was copyright ever registered by Charlotte, Martin or Charlotte's secretary, Lillian Stransky, who frequently registered Martin's songs for him.) The confusion seems to have arisen from a brief excerpt Charlotte submitted for publication to the annual issue of *Variety* in 1950, with a blurb which described the excerpt as deriving from Charlotte's "soon-to-be published" autobiography. (This two-page excerpt was published by Henry Holt in 1952 in a collection of *Variety* stories called *The Spice of Variety*.) The fact that Charlotte and Martin were still contacting potential publishers as late as the early 1950s makes it clear that the effort to get the book in print far post-dated *Who's Who*'s publication date of *Just for Kicks*. The Greenwood papers in William Luce's possession include a typescript comprising 18 pages from Charlotte's memoirs, written in the third person. Titled *Never Too Tall*, these pages contain notes in Charlotte's handwriting, changing the third-person pronoun to first-person, leading me to believe it is an early version of what became the full-length *Never Too Tall*. These papers also contain an article written by Charlotte during her years in London (roughly 1932–1937), titled *American Days*. Where or whether it was ever published is unknown. But it is clear that even in the 1930s, Charlotte was seeing her life in terms of autobiography.

Many of Charlotte's unused notes for her memoirs reveal more about her and her opinions than what went into the final version, as she tended to cut out any personal observations that might offend people reading the book or strike too close to her family situation — e.g., her conflicted and painful feelings about her father, her miserable first marriage — or color too far outside the lines of the religious faith which, for her, was one of circumscription, discipline and always looking on the bright side of any situation. All of these data I have drawn on extensively for this book, and refer to them *en masse* in the source notes as "Charlotte Greenwood's personal notes" (CGPN).

Introduction

By 1954, WHEN MOVIE LOCATION scouts were seeking appropriate terrain for the filming of *Oklahoma!*, the pristine land which had formed the setting for Lynn Riggs' 1931 play *Green Grow the Lilacs* was far more real in Rodgers and Hammerstein's groundbreaking work of musical theatre than it was in the state admitted to the union in 1907.

Perhaps the fact that Arizona achieved statehood five years *after* Oklahoma gave the human hordes steadily peopling the western United States by the droves a few more years to reach its untouched natural beauties and establish towns, ranches, and roadways. Whatever the case, the decided absence in Arizona of the forest of oil wells that dotted the Oklahoma countryside certainly had much to do with the choice of location — the days when the territory's economy could be neatly divided (if not without argument) between farmers and cowmen were long ago a piece of American mythos. Oil had been king, after all, for half a hundred years, in fact had dominated the landscape ever since Oklahoma had become the forty-sixth state. One thing was clear to Austrian-born director Fred Zinnemann: the only way to recreate the image of a territory not yet despoiled was to leave Oklahoma behind and look elsewhere for the wide open spaces under wide open skies that the lyrics of Oscar Hammerstein II and the music of Richard Rodgers intensely evoked in *Oklahoma!* Those spaces and that sky were found on the other side of Texas, in the San Rafael Valley of Arizona, not far from the Mexican border and Pancho Villa's old stomping grounds.[1]

The preparation for the making of the film was to break as many records — and nerves — as the original theatrical production had done fifteen years earlier, the various contumelies of which would seem to have guaranteed no future cooperation between a hothead like choreographer Agnes de Mille and a confrontation-loathing soul like Oscar Hammerstein II. Yet they all came together again to make what would be, in those pre-*Cleopatra* days, the most expensive film yet made, requiring the construction of an entire farmstead, the dressing up of a local train station to evoke the turn of the century period of the drama, and what Zinnemann called "an army" to carry out everything needed to get the picture off the ground and onto film. "It was like a traveling circus," wrote Zinnemann; "generators, lights, wardrobe trucks, make-up vans, lots of cars for the actors." Like a circus, the film's chaos was of the multiple kind, replete with clowning intended and accidental, and plenty of dangerous moments when a watching crowd might have "golly-gee'd" in breathless unison.

Moving this army across ravines recently carved out by the flash floods that followed the sudden morning thunderstorms was one hurdle to leap over. Another was the electrical by-product of those storms — a member of the production staff was struck by lightning as he leaned against a vehicle, and emerged far luckier than the cattle found electrocuted across the grassy prairie. "Cadillac Gulch" received its name thanks to a unit passenger car that was caught in a flood and washed fifty yards downstream. As with second unit director James Havens, the human lightning rod, the miracle was that nobody was hurt.[2]

In order to have a full stand of corn for when shooting was to begin in mid-summer 1954, regulation corn was planted, the rows laid out at sufficient distance to permit not just cowboy Curly and his horse to amble through the stalks for the film's opening sequence, but also enough space for the cameras that would be following and preceding horse and rider. Two thousand one hundred plants were introduced into land never yet broken by a plough, at an altitude too high, and with no naturally available water, at what Hammerstein estimated to be a cost of almost $9 per carefully nurtured ear. This included the corn not left in the ground — a good deal of it had to be pulled up at peak height and replanted in trays, so as to be easily movable for Zinnemann's spacious dolly shots. It was a lavish care for detail reminiscent of the big-spending ways of David O. Selznick, and proved that even as late as the dowdy Truman era, Hollywood was still capable of bending the world to its own brand of instant magic.

By the time the production's carpenters were finished, a two-story white and yellow farmhouse stood amid peach trees and split-rail fences. Nearby stood a barn, a smokehouse and a windmill to keep it company. As much weathered old wood was used as could be found (from old abandoned buildings in the vicinity), which gave Aunt Eller's farm a stunning authenticity. Yet the magic of verisimilitude had its limits: to keep the fruitless peach-trees looking properly fecund, crew members decorated the branches with fake peaches every morning and carefully denuded them every night.[3]

The character of Curly, the cowboy who seeks the hand of Aunt Eller's niece Laurey, proved as difficult to harvest from the screen test rolls as real Arizona peaches from Aunt Eller's trees: actors as diverse as Richard Burton, Paul Newman and James Dean (none of them trained singers) were considered or tested. Dean, for all his lack of an adequate singing voice, was judged a perfect screen Curly; he made what Zinnemann described as "a sensational test" against Rod Steiger's malevolent Jud in the black-humored duet "Pore Jud Is Dead." But perhaps the actor's already well-known penchant for being unreliable had caused Zinnemann to turn ultimately to the conventional dramatic abilities and sweet baritone of Broadway star Gordon McRae.

From the beginning it was clear that none but silver-toned soprano Shirley Jones (who had auditioned for R & H as long ago as 1952) should play the part of Laurey. Zinnemann had his concerns, which were well founded, as Jones was very much an ingénue. (At the time of filming she was only twenty-one years old, young to be embarking on her first major film role.) But her attractiveness was such that Rodgers and Hammerstein knew they would lose her if she had been allowed to go with the touring company of *The King and I*, for which she had auditioned just as plans were being laid for the filming of *Oklahoma*. Rather than risk not having her available, R&H had her moved to their Broadway production of *Me and Juliet*, so as to keep her in town. As a result, the most perfect Laurey imaginable was added to Zinnemann's fantastic film army.

The rest of the cast was equally well-favored: pert and pouty Gloria Grahame as Ado Annie Carnes, grinning Eddie Albert as the "Persian" peddler Ali Hakim, lithe and dimpled

Gene Nelson as Will Parker, the cowboy who teaches Ado Annie to be a girl who can say no, and brooding Rod Steiger as the unbalanced farmhand Jud Fry, whose presence in this cheery bunch introduces the long shadows of *verismo* tragedy, not to mention a generous helping of Method acting.

For many of these young actors, *Oklahoma!* was a beginning — many, like Jones and Steiger, went on to bigger parts and better things. But for one of the cast, this expensive, difficult, gargantuan musical was the capstone of a career that had already lasted a half century, on stage and screen. She was performing a role originally sketched for her years before but which her film commitments had prevented her from accepting. It was a role which, like Laurey for Shirley Jones, the gods of drama evidently intended for her, and not on the stage, where so much of her art had been admired but lost but on film, because it was the one part with which she would be identified long after her death. That actress was the sixty-five-year-old veteran of vaudeville, comedy and straight drama, silent film and talkies, splashy wartime Technicolor musicals, and a successful stint in radio — Charlotte Greenwood, in the part of Aunt Eller, the wise old farm wife who tends the lives around her with all the stern affection of a woman who has seen it all. And of everyone in *Oklahoma!*'s cast, Charlotte had seen more than most.

From the start of her film career, Charlotte had been gowned by great designers like Coco Chanel and René Hubert, Travis Banton, Yvonne Wood and Adrian; these costumes made for a hilarious ironic backdrop to the klutzy clowning to which most of Charlotte's scripts consigned her. But for her greatest role of all, the camera discovered her not in flamingo satin or emerald tulle but in plain blue gingham dress and a crocheted shawl, sturdily churning butter and flirting as much as an elderly woman dared with the young Curly as he comes to pay court to her uppity niece. In fact, this woman, dressed in nothing but well-crafted characterization, was the real Charlotte Greenwood: some of her greatest successes, as in the role of Abby, the put-upon maid of all work in Sidney Howard's play *The Late Christopher Bean*, or the plain but doughty matriarch in the stage adaptation of Kathryn Forbes' *I Remember Mama*, were decidedly dowdy in outward aspect, the diametrical opposite of the 1940s Hollywood fashion plate she was made out to be. These, too, were the roles to which she had devoted every ounce of her ability, which had been powered since her extreme youth by a yearning to be taken seriously as an actor. And they were the distillation of a woman she really knew, better than she knew any of the eccentric dowagers or man-hungry maidservants that producers' whims and box office receipts dictated she play — her mother, Annabelle, who though she had had to look up at her tall daughter was to Charlotte a tower of unforgettable faith and fortitude.

This gift for being as compelling plain as gaudy — perhaps even more so — and an elemental grounding in the reality of the moment was a part of Charlotte's charm and, indeed, of her genius. "In spite of all her effort to make herself ridiculous and ugly," wrote Rob Wagner in 1936, "Charlotte Greenwood simply can't make the grade. Without a single good feature, and in spite of all the abuse Miss Greenwood heaps upon it, her face is none the less beautiful." It was that inborn grace, which one of her later co-stars, the son of a Russian noblewoman, would describe as "aristocratic," despite the pratfalls and the mugging, that enabled this tall, lanky actress to play everything from society snobs to wisecracking spinsters, vaudeville hoofers and grimacing farm wives; and to bring to each of these roles a facet of experience from her own life — always the touchstone of everything she did on stage or screen — and her own personality that made even her smallest roles somehow unforgettable.

✯ ✯ ✯

It is a commonplace to write of stars that their fame was forged in a hot furnace of repeated failures, that but for the element of a lucky break, or discovery of a gimmick, they might have dragged out lives as anonymous as those who buy tickets to see them on stage or screen. Charlotte Greenwood, however, never stopped being herself, but not like actors held in greater esteem, such as Katharine Hepburn, Spencer Tracy, or Bette Davis, part of whose genius was the ability to fit the masks of various roles neatly over their own faces and yet remain distinctly Hepburn, Tracy or Davis. Something in Charlotte, as noted almost from the start of her career by critics who typically wasted no ink on the less than worthy and by fellow actors in a position to know, was not just *always* Charlotte Greenwood, regardless of the role, but was solidly, warmly, wonderfully *real*. It was a realness that was the same as empathy, that brought depth to otherwise shallow films of silly plot, that made critics like Alexander Woollcott peer beneath the veneer to the solid actor and decry the flimsy material on which Charlotte's energies were wasted.

That this ability to communicate her heart so completely was confined mostly to the ephemeral atmosphere of the stage is not just one of the tragedies of Charlotte's recorded career, but explains why those who do still remember her do so almost entirely from her later films, and thus retain a mere caricature of her, that caricature that Rob Wagner recognized and deplored as representing much less than what was really there. The wartime Technicolor comedies Charlotte made for Twentieth Century Fox are what most people keep in their memory's eye: the gawky height topped with fantastical blonde hairdos; the mile-high leg lifts (*not* kicks, as Charlotte herself was wont to point out), the whirling windmill arms and the scrambling comic antics forced into plots already beyond the pale of possibility. Movie studio heads were so dazzled by Charlotte's ticket-selling horsiness that they cast her repeatedly in films dealing with real horses, right up to the end of her career — an Australian millionaire even named a prize-winning filly "Charlotte Greenwood" after her.

Charlotte took all of this in stride — she had learned to do so the first time she realized that the pleasure her clowning gave people outweighed her pain at being laughed at, and in fact she was known all her life for tossing off remarks that drew attention to these same physical traits that people found so funny. "I'm the only woman alive who can kick a giraffe in the eye," she once claimed. But Charlotte's belief in herself as a serious actor, and her deep desire to prove it, dated back to her earliest days in vaudeville, as a fifteen-year-old greenhorn consumed with ambition: to be a great singer, a great tragedian. Early on, her own body and her often clumsy management of it made her attempts to test her more serious gifts difficult if not impossible. Through trial and error, however, Charlotte learned what she called "the most valuable lesson of my career — that of subjugating self."

What made her role in *Oklahoma!* so unique, among all the parts she had played, was that that subjugation of self could come to its natural end. The role she now assumed, as Aunt Eller Murphy, was not only to provide Charlotte the opportunities she needed to prove herself the talented actor she had always been. It also gave her an unprecedented chance to use everything she was good at, and famed for, in a single, immortal part. One moment we see the slapstick vaudevillian clowning, another the subtler comedian reliant on clever timing, to the point of doing what Charlotte most disliked, that of stealing scenes; we see the dignified bearing that made her entrance something like a royal visitation, and the maternal wisdom that shines from her face like clear sunlight. And those long arms seem to wrap around the entire microcosm of the cast, soothing hurts, putting people in their place, and guiding destinies. In a very real sense Charlotte was the first of the Rodgers and Hammerstein "Earth Mothers," in R&H historian Jeffrey Block's definition, though this was a role for which Charlotte had been preparing all her life, even before she stepped on the stage.

PART ONE

America alone has never produced a folk dance.
I don't know why. Perhaps it is because we are not a folk
in the sense of the word. Perhaps it is because we are still young
among the nations.... It is only in America that a dancer tried to
express his own reaction to life and not a traditional race expression.
And in this sense, Charlotte Greenwood is American to the core. She is
herself and no one else. And her dancing is Charlotte Greenwood's
dancing and no one else's. And, finally she is completely
Charlotte Greenwood only when she is dancing.

— Robert Myron Coates
The New Yorker

✫ ✫ ✫

I was the corporal of the Goon Squad.

— Charlotte Greenwood

1

"I come from a long line of Philadelphia barbers!"

AT A LONDON PARTY IN THE MID–1930S, Baroness Irene Ravensdale, the tall eldest daughter of Lord Curzon, Viceroy of India, and one of the first peeresses to sit in the House of Lords,[1] drew her guests' attention to a tall blonde standing in her Mayfair drawing room.

The focus of Baroness Ravensdale's attention was her friend, the American stage and screen star Charlotte Greenwood, who with her songwriter husband Martin Broones had been the toast of the London theatrical world since the early part of the decade. Forgetting for a moment her democratic beliefs in favor of the unfashionable theory of heredity, Baroness Ravensdale turned to the elegantly gowned Charlotte and said, with as much awe as banter, that a woman as talented as she was surely had to come from a magnificent background. As dancer, singer, clown and actress, Charlotte Greenwood had certainly proven herself rich in talent, from her first burst on Broadway in the Passing Show of 1912 through a variety of turns in vaudeville, straight theatre, and films silent and sound. As a woman who had battled her family background in a way quite different from Charlotte's, but with just as much fervor, and made the most of her handsomely horsey appearance, Irene Curzon knew a winner when she saw one — and as the granddaughter of a self-made American department store mogul, she also knew and benefited from the North American tenets of unremitting hard work.

Charlotte, however, had the last laugh. Though descended maternally from one of the oldest families of colonial America and a distant cousin through an aristocratic Dutch ancestress to Baroness Ravensdale herself, Charlotte quipped: "Yes, I have a wonderful background. I come from a long line of Philadelphia barbers!"[2]

She was indulging in even more irony than Baroness Ravensdale could guess, since the line of barbers extended no farther back in time than an uncle on the maternal side and Charlotte's own father, the handsome, flighty Englishman Frank Greenwood. And though hair, while it lasts, always needs a trim, the Greenwood household in 1890 Philadelphia had been far from secure in that fact long before its breadwinner abandoned it for the lights and diversions of New York City.

But before she had to ponder what she had done to deserve such a husband, on the day of her child's birth Annabelle Higgins Greenwood could not be blamed for assuming that things had gotten about as bad as they could get. It was a sweltering 92 degree Philadelphia summer noon, and she lay in the humid bedroom of her and her husband's red brick row-

Partial view of 1507 Reed Street, Philadelphia, the red brick house where Charlotte was born on a hot day in late June 1890. Courtesy Gilberto and Dawn Williams, current owners of the home.

house home on church-lined Reed Street, struggling — with the assistance of Dr. John S. Pearson — to bear a larger-than-normal child that was also turned the wrong way around in the birth canal.

"I came into the world feet first," that child was wont to explain in later years with pride and good humor belying the dangers associated with her birth. "I was obviously preparing for a broad jump through life."

But being born breach was just one of the hurdles Annabelle's baby, the future Charlotte Greenwood, would have to overcome. Not only would this baby, who came into the world with such difficulty, be plagued for the next several years of her life by bouts of ill health, but within twelve months she would lose her father and such precarious security as his presence had meant to her and Annabelle's household. Until Charlotte began to make her own living on the stage a little over fifteen years later, Annabelle was to be what her daughter described as "both father and mother to me," and the man who had sired her and skipped town would forever remain a stranger, despite her best efforts — and what she insists were his — to rectify the situation.[3]

"Like most of the deserving poor that the philanthropists are forever concerning themselves with," Charlotte wrote in notes for her memoirs, "my parents were inclined to take their poverty for granted and to regard life from its brighter side." (More sardonically, she scribbled elsewhere in her notes: "We had no rich relations and we certainly didn't have any relations we could recognize as poor — we were all in the same boat, and it needed caulking.")

This penchant for optimism was particularly true of Annabelle, who had had to look on life's brighter side from an early age, and would continue to have to do so throughout most of her life. Charlotte, who resembled her mother facially to a startling degree and inherited her regal posture, is inclined to dwell on her mother's descent from faded glory for much the same reason Annabelle refused to admit defeat: it proved that ramrod backbones didn't just spring out of nowhere but rather from the loins of men who had used ramrods in battle and lived to tell the tale. Such is the story Charlotte was told about her maternal ancestry: that Annabelle, though born the eldest daughter of George Rodney Higgins, saloonkeeper of Wilmington and New Castle, Delaware, was a descendant of the Revolutionary War hero and host of Washington and Lafayette, Major Peter Andrew Jaquett of "Long Hook."

While it is true that Annabelle was related to handsome, convivial Major Jaquett, she was not a descendant of his; but being a Jaquett in New Castle was its own badge of colonial aristocracy. It was to Newcastle that the first of the name, Jean Paul Jaquett (born in Nuremberg despite his French-sounding name), brought his wife, Maria de Carpentier, a Dutch lady of blue-blooded antecedents (a descendant of King Henry III of England and King Louis IX, "St. Louis,"

Top: "No matter how much of an effort I made to be filial, it was always like meeting a stranger...": Charlotte Greenwood on her barber father, Englishman Frank Greenwood (shown here ca. 1890), who abandoned her and her mother when Charlotte was one year old. USC collection. *Bottom:* "Equal to all of the Sabine women with some of the Amazons thrown in for good measure" (photograph ca. 1890): Annabelle Higgins Greenwood, a lady whose never-say-die character went far toward influencing her daughter as performer and woman. USC collection.

of France) when he was appointed
Dutch Governor of Delaware colony,
in 1655. Because of her Jaquett ances-
tors' contribution to the early founda-
tion of Delaware, Charlotte understood
herself to be entitled to burial in the
churchyard of Old Swedes Church in
Wilmington, where the Major and
other Jaquetts were buried. However,
"[r]ight now," she asided in her memoirs, with customary mordant wit, "I
can think of better places to be."[4]

Rodney Higgins' wife, Anne, was
"a patient, delicate woman," according
to what Charlotte was told, "silently
suffering from a physical ailment for
many years of her life and finally passing on to her reward, while still young
and beautiful." (A family photograph
album in the Charlotte Greenwood
papers at the University of Southern
California's Film and Television Library
shows Anne as a sweet-faced blonde in
an elegant velvet jacket, under which is
inscribed: "The Belle of Wilmington.")
Annabelle was only 12 when her mother
died shortly after giving birth to her
fifth child, and from that time on she
was mothering her siblings, a husband,
a daughter and many other people,
without having had much mothering herself.

"I was so indifferently equipped with beauty that even
the stork felt a little self-conscious." Charlotte Greenwood at about seven years old. USC collection.

"She took up her duties," Charlotte recalled, "as a matter of course, and maintained them
throughout her life." Annabelle was, Charlotte stated, "a cheerful woman inclined to search
diligently for the silver lining in all passing clouds," which could stand as a thumbnail sum-
mation of all the characters Charlotte played during her long career.[5]

It is possible that Annabelle's strong bond to her siblings brought about her own marriage to Frank Greenwood. Her brother, Jacob Higgins, known to Charlotte as "Uncle Jake,"
was a barber by trade, as was his own brother-in-law, George Clayville, husband of Jacob's
and Annabelle's sister Martha. Not long after his marriage to Annabelle, in Philadelphia's
Church of the Resurrection, on May 19, 1889, Frank Greenwood went into partnership with
his brothers-in-law in a shop located with no small amount of providential proximity across
from the streetcar barns that were to serve an important role in Charlotte's young life.

Whether Frank Greenwood had always been a barber is a matter of conjecture. He was
born in England in 1866, the same year as his wife, and had three sisters, Daisy, Violet and
Rose, who later came to see Charlotte in her Drury Lane triumphs in 1932–34. An English
census record from 1881 seems to show Frank living as a "painter" with his mother Charlotte

(and no father, it should be noted) in Stoke-on-Trent, Staffordshire (he was born in Liverpool, while his mother was born in nearby Hanley). His mother worked as a shopkeeper. Charlotte seems to have been told that in his youth her father had been a champion ice skater (which in Frank Greenwoodese may mean that he was a notch better than the other lads in town). In any case it would have been a short step from one artisanal trade to another, and the vanity of the grooming trade clearly appealed to something self-dramatizing in Frank Greenwood's character — a yearning for theatre that may have been his only bequest to his daughter.[6]

"Father was the type of man who felt that there'll always be an England," Charlotte recalled. "Tall, handsome, with a decided dimple in his chin, my father was the Americans' idea of the typical well-bred English gentleman, who would as soon be found walking down Piccadilly Circus without his trousers as his boutonnière," and had very little concern about anything else not immediately concerning this image or its exploitation. As time would prove, that anything else included his wife and their only child.[7]

2

Illness and Abandonment

CHARLOTTE SEEMS TO HAVE GAINED enough evidence in later years to state that as a baby she "was so indifferently equipped with beauty that even the stork felt a little self-conscious."

She was certainly a long baby, and would continue to get longer: by the time she was in her early teens, Charlotte claims, she had reached her full adult height of 5 feet 10 inches. The average height for contemporary American females is still 5 feet 5 inches, so Charlotte stood out in times when women were shorter than they are today. Charlotte was also an ill baby, afflicted with anemia (perhaps from an inability to keep food down) and with what appears to have been the all too common childhood tubercular disease of the lymph nodes, scrofula, caused by the drinking of unpasteurized cow's milk.

"There were times, I am told," she remembered, "when it seemed that life for little Lottie was held by such a slender thread that the slightest jar would snap it."[1]

Doctors came and went from the Greenwoods' red brick house on Reed Street, and it was their old-fashioned remedy of plenty of sunshine that united Charlotte with a man who was to mean much more to her than her father — who would, indeed, become the father she never had. Streetcar driver John Grace drove his trolley up and down the same street in which Frank Greenwood and Jacob Higgins had their barbershop, and his last stop was right opposite the business. Annabelle had taken to placing Charlotte in a cradle in the bright front window of the shop, where Uncle Jake and his numerous male customers could keep an eye on her as she soaked up the sun, and it was there that the streetcar driver first saw the baby. From that day on, the aptly named John Grace was never far from where Charlotte was, "a staunch admirer who never deserted me, who asked nothing and was willing to give everything."

Lacking family or anyone else, apparently, on whom to spend his considerable warmth of affection, the red-headed, blue-eyed John Grace would pop in during his lunch hour to share a meal with the Greenwoods and to check on Charlotte's state of health, compensating the family every Sunday by giving them free rides to Fairmont Park. After each round, Grace would cross the street from the car barns at the double-quick, poke his head in the door of the barbershop and ask: "Lot has slept four hours, hasn't she?" After being reassured, he would coo over the infant and declare, "She'll grow strong yet! You wait and see!"[2]

Charlotte hints that among her father's peculiarities of character may have been the all too common habit of taking to drink under trying circumstances, but what led to the breakup of the Greenwood-Higgins barbershop and the Frank-Annabelle household can only be conjectured. It is possible that the Englishman's breezy manner and taste for the fashionable grated on the nerves of his staunchly blue-collar brothers-in-law. Whatever the case, by the time Charlotte had turned one year old, Frank Greenwood was off for greener pastures, leaving John Grace to serve as Charlotte's paternal presence and Annabelle the dilemma of having to find work to support herself and her baby. (Since there is no indication in Charlotte's memoirs that her uncle or aunt made any effort to assist Annabelle financially or otherwise, it is possible Annabelle had sided with her husband in the dispute that broke up the barbershop partnership, and had allowed a wedge to be driven between herself and her siblings by a husband who then, maddeningly, fled the scene of the crime.)

"Doubtless there were many strange experiences in my mother's struggles of which I know nothing," Charlotte remembered. In what was clearly a nod to her life's work of always taking care of other people, and perhaps also to her father's profession as saloonkeeper in New Castle, Annabelle went as if by instinct into the hotel business, starting off in the kitchens as the lowest employee on the totem pole.

"While she toiled, faithful John Grace kept his eagle eye on [me]," Charlotte wrote. "I was his self-appointed ward. No steward ever guarded his trust more carefully."[3]

Complicating matters was a health crisis that sent Charlotte to the University of Pennsylvania pediatrics hospital, where surgery was performed on her throat to remove "enlarged glands" (a feature of scrofula). "During my convalescent period," she recalled, "I managed to make friends, child-like, with the entire hospital force; and was allowed full privileges because I was quiet and, in the parlance of the day, 'a little brick.'" She did remember a few moments of terror: when the doctor administering the anesthetic pressed the ether cup too forcefully over her face, and the garb of one Dr. Wood, who in his surgical apron looked to the child like a butcher. "He was really as gentle as a lamb," she discovered shortly thereafter.

Still weak after her bout in the hospital, Charlotte recuperated at home with the help of John Grace and other friends and neighbors of Annabelle's. (Charlotte makes no mention of whether or not Frank Greenwood ever came to see her.) Annabelle had been hired as manager of a family hotel called Bingham House and her responsibilities were increased manyfold. Consulting a doctor who lived in the neighborhood, Annabelle heard from him about the Children's Seashore Home in Atlantic City. He suggested that Charlotte be sent there to recover.

From the start of her account of this period of her childhood, and despite the fact that the Atlantic City organization enjoyed a first class reputation, Charlotte paints the entire affair of the Children's Seashore Home in negative colors, even to giving the Home a pseudonym that is identical with a notorious Atlantic City boardwalk brothel, the "Sea Breeze." An offshoot of the University of Pennsylvania, where Charlotte had had her operation, the Seashore Home was located close to the famed boardwalk and the ocean air then believed beneficial for most bodily and emotional ills. Charlotte insists, however, that the doctor who recommended the Home to Annabelle was little better than a quack, and Annabelle herself too uninformed to make a proper decision. "It was a good deal like advising a man who didn't even know H. G. Wells to take a trip to Mars," she commented dryly.[4]

"I had my first train trip on a fateful Sunday," Charlotte recalled, "and since then I have been one of the best customers the transportation companies ever had — that dream passenger who is constantly on the move." Annabelle packed up her daughter and traveled with her to the Seashore Home, where according to Charlotte she gave the place too quick an inspection before leaving her there and returning to Philadelphia and her job. "I was alone for the first time in my short life," she recalled, "and not at all happy about it."[5]

What exactly made Charlotte so unhappy about the Seashore Home, aside from being left there by her mother, is not clear. Since infancy Charlotte was used to being left in the care of people who were not her mother or even related to her. Whatever the cause, the child quickly disliked the regimentation and retained the impression that the Home was closer to being an orphanage than a rehabilitation hospital. Charlotte also disliked the strict woman who ran the Home, noting that under her supervision the children were treated like miniature servants, with duties to fulfill each day—perhaps evidence that in Philadelphia Charlotte was used to much more pampering than she admits in her memoirs.

"The older children, for example, had to take care of the younger ones," Charlotte wrote, "and my first chore was to wheel the little ones up and down the Board Walk." It was not that she couldn't abide the children, she is quick to add—it was that she was not as old as she looked, and thus the work was hard for a child her age, pushing the carriages of children not much younger than she over the uneven boards and through the throngs of sightseers and touts always crowding the space. She could joke about this years later, when in the late 1930s she saw Douglas Fairbanks Sr. pushing two push-cart boys at the San Francisco Exposition and chided him for suggesting she spell him for a time: "We must always strive to progress," she told him in arch refusal. But at the time, Charlotte cordially loathed her chores at the Seashore Home and desperately yearned for escape.[6]

To make matters worse, she also hated the clothes and the food. "I remember that we all wore the same type of uniform," she recalled, "and that the principal food consisted of applesauce and bread and butter." This, combined with the regimentation and the sudden absence of the spotlight of general concern that hovered over her at home, made for a miserable Charlotte.[7]

Her sufferings, however, were not of long duration. Contrary to the impression given in the final version of her memoirs, that she languished at the Seashore Home awaiting rescue for weeks, Charlotte could not have been enrolled there for more than a week at most. Somehow, whether because Annabelle had sent him to investigate or he had taken the opportunity on his own volition, John Grace showed up one day at the Seashore Home. "There in the center of the room was John Grace—red face, red hair and kindly blue eyes," Charlotte remembered. "It was on his shoulder that I sobbed out my childish woes."[8]

Then John Grace did something that in modern times would have resulted in his arrest: telling the director of the Seashore Home that he was a friend of the family and wished to take Charlotte out for a diversionary walk, he kidnapped her, though in the most disarming and welcome of ways.

The first thing the man and girl did was to go to find the nearest shoe store, "where [John] bought me a beautiful pair of brown shoes," which Charlotte had longed for almost as much as to leave the Seashore Home. "They didn't fit, but I kept tight-lipped for fear the shoe store might not have a pair that did."

"Today the only calluses I have on my feet," she noted, with a certain pride, "are the marks of a tight pair of brown shoes from Atlantic City."

John Grace then took Charlotte to an ice cream parlor and bought her a dish of vanilla ice cream, her favorite flavor. Finished at the marble counter, man and girl then headed not back to the Seashore Home, where Grace was obliged to return her, but to the train station, where he bought two tickets for Philadelphia. "My nice brown shoes were speckled with tears of gratitude," Charlotte remembered.[9]

Whether she cried on seeing her surprised mother in Philadelphia (and whether the overworked Annabelle cried on seeing her) is not known, but Charlotte definitely remembered her mother's incensed reaction on hearing John Grace's tale of the girl's short but woeful time at the Seashore Home. Annabelle sought out the doctor who had advised her to send Charlotte to Atlantic City and read him the riot act, even accusing him of recommending the place because he had a sizeable share in the organization's finances.

"Mama didn't lose her temper often," Charlotte recalled, "but when she did it was in a big way."[10]

Annabelle also had reason to be furious with fate on this occasion, because no sooner had she made what were for her budget expensive plans to have Charlotte cared for at home than she was offered a job to move to Boston to become superintendent of the ground floor of the gargantuan South Station — the biggest concern she had ever been hired to oversee. But the offer was too good to pass up. Leaving her birthplace, and John Grace who had never once failed her, Charlotte began the first of what would be many moves, into many houses, over many years.

3

Near Death in Boston, New Life in Virginia

BOSTON'S SOUTH STATION FIRST opened for business on New Year's Day 1899, and with its great bulk looked a fitting solution to replace the small stations which had previously served the Boston & Providence, Old Colony, New England and Boston & Albany rail companies. As such, of all passenger stations in the country it was by far the busiest. As the person in charge of the ground floor, where all the passengers swarmed as they got off and got on, Annabelle's hands were full.[1]

Very likely because it was less expensive than anywhere else in the building, Annabelle rented the entire top floor of an apartment building at 200 Dartmouth Street where the latter met the Avenue of the Arts in a triangle pointing north to the Charles River. A few blocks to the north lay the famous park, Boston Commons, backdrop for art and literature; while a brisk walk to the south would have brought Annabelle and Charlotte to the Mother Church, Mary Baker Eddy's monument to her belief in the power of faith to heal all ills of body and mind — a faith that was to exert a powerful influence on Charlotte's thought in years to come.

Charlotte remembered the fifth floor rooms at the top of 200 Dartmouth Street, the lower floor of which was rented by an admired older lady, Mrs. Taylor, as "lovely, large, airy ... with plenty of light." Nearby was the Prince Street school where Charlotte would start her education anew that fall.

Meantime, a burning Boston summer had descended on the city, and the building went from airy to oppressive, assisted by a large skylight over the stair landing that allowed the sun to pour in for hours. One day, while Annabelle was still at work, Mrs. Taylor chanced to remark to Charlotte that she would give anything for something to cover the skylight with, as it only made the house "resemble a bake-oven at full tilt." Charlotte watched the tall, angular old lady wipe her brow and immediately took it upon herself to ease her discomfort. "It seemed a shame," Charlotte wrote, "that as nice a person as Mrs. Taylor should be asked to suffer through the heat of a Boston afternoon when it would require only a soupcon of ingenuity and enterprise for a Greenwood to come to her aid." There was a thick blanket in Charlotte's room, and knowing it would not be needed for months, she took it over an arm and began to climb the stairs to the roof.[2]

If the house was hot, the roof was even hotter, and Charlotte had to gingerly pick her way over the burning surface, only one arm free to climb with.

On all fours ... I crawled up the ladder which lay flat on the roof and finally reached my objective. The skylight opening was dangerously near the edge of the building, with a drop of five floors to the hallway in front of Mrs. Taylor's flat. Little shivers began to gallop up and down my spine; little rivulets of perspiration were trickling down my face. Regardless of the tremors, I carried on.

Flipping the blanket over one side of the skylight, Charlotte crawled around to the other side: "Then I made my major mistake." She raised herself up to see how well she had covered the hot glass, and in order to do so inadvertently leaned her full weight on a pane. "Crash! I had fallen through."

What happened next was a kaleidoscope of blood from her gashed arm spurting on broken glass, Charlotte hanging on to the mullion of the shattered pane with several stories of stairwell opening below her dangling legs, and Mrs. Taylor screaming for help. "I was thin," Charlotte remembered, "but I was tough."[3]

Without assistance, she managed to pull herself up through the hole in the skylight, creep back down the ladder, and get into the attic, by which time the clangor of an approaching fire engine was filling the street below and Mrs. Taylor's cries were augmented by those of the other tenants. "I timed my descent with the arrival of the rescue crew," Charlotte recalled, "and fainted. It has been a lifelong regret that I remember nothing of my trip to the hospital."[4]

Though the girl was covered in blood, the doctors determined she had not severed an artery, despite the fact that the gash in her arm was savage enough to leave a scar that would prove all but impossible to cover with stage makeup in later years. But all the child could think of at that moment was Annabelle, who had been informed of the accident and was rushing to the hospital from South Station. Murmuring over and over, as if in delirium, Charlotte kept saying, "I am dead to my Mama ... I am dead to my Mama."

Though Annabelle's job at the station brought her "into constant touch with all types of human unhappiness," this lightning strike of personal near tragedy left her shaken. For years afterward she kept the copy of the *Boston Transcript* issue that gave a graphic account of the skylight accident, as if still unable to believe it had really happened.[5]

By the time school began in the fall, Charlotte's arm had healed, and with the story of her near-death adventure still fresh on her lips, she told it a few times too many: girls who might have been her friends were told by their parents to steer clear of such a rough tomboyish child, and soon her "recitation of the Great Fall" fell on deaf and derisive ears.

A large part of what went toward making this eager-to-please young girl friendless at the Prince Street school was something she could do absolutely nothing about—her ungainly height. It was not enough that Charlotte had trouble with the school work itself, it was that her presence in the school room provoked such cruel mirth that she could not have concentrated on her work even had she been a star pupil. "It is very difficult to be a 'little lady' under such adverse conditions," she wrote later.

Not only is the little lady conscious of the fact that she is inches taller than her school chums, but she does everything in her power to reduce her size and thus becomes more conspicuous and grotesque. Easy enough for philosophers to say that added height can also be the larger container for tolerance, patience and understanding. When you're turning six and look thirteen, those words carry no more weight than gnat fuzz. So the gawk does everything she can think of to reduce her height to the level of her schoolmates. She slinks in her desk inviting permanent curvature of the spine ... [h]er head is held down to hide a swan-like neck—whoever started that fable about swans being lovely, anyway?—she lets her shoulders droop, pulls her arms close to her side, makes pathetic efforts to tie them in knots. [W]hen she leaves her desk for a stint at the blackboard, her feet catch on the sides, her arms knock innocent victims on the head, she falls up the aisle tripping over her own feet.... Worse, teachers forget that she is merely "big for her age" and persist in treating her like the village idiot. Wherever she goes, she leaves a wake of titters.[6]

Long after she had been a star of stage and screen and the toast of two continents, Charlotte could still conjure up the stuffy Boston schoolroom where her daily sufferings took place unabated: the pot-bellied stove in one corner, the scratched wooden desks and the smudgy blackboard. To make matters worse, in winter Annabelle saddled Charlotte with what to the Boston children probably came across as a smelly bit of countrified preventive medicine, by making her wear around her neck a bag of the foul-smelling herb asafetida, which was believed by frontier doctors to ward off disease. A few other children had to carry these putrid bags, but Charlotte's was always the most generous because "Mama was never one to do things by halves."

Considering her daughter's almost constant illness since birth and her recent flirtation with violent injury, Annabelle could be forgiven for turning back the clock and seeking help in folk remedies. In fact, Annabelle had reason for concern, because after living in Boston for two years Charlotte was not improving health-wise; it cannot have escaped the watchful mother's attention that her daughter was also miserable at school. The doctors Annabelle consulted gave the advice usual to the period — to send the ailing child away for a climatological change, in this case not to the ocean but to the warmer temperatures of the south.

Unlike the experience with the Children's Seashore Home, however, this advice proved worth its weight in gold. With characteristic fortitude and optimism, Annabelle "made up her mind to lift anchor and set sail for Old Point Comfort [in Virginia] where she could find some place for me and get herself another job with Colonel Hull Davidson," her first employer in Philadelphia.

"It was a move," Charlotte penciled in her memoir notes, "that led to some of the happiest days of my life."

Colonel Hull Davidson was an entrepreneur who owned and managed a network of hotels and inns along the Eastern seaboard, and seems to have taken a personal interest in Annabelle's welfare. He first hired her to be manager of the Hygeia Hotel in Old Point Comfort, where Annabelle and Charlotte lived in the beginning of their Virginia stay. "It was a small, country hotel, conducted along very simple lines," Charlotte recalled. But the demands there on Annabelle, which increased when she was appointed cashier, grew to a point where she could not do her job and look after a child. Through friendship with a girl named Lacey Engleburt who had been hired to work at the hotel, Annabelle was able to board Charlotte with Lacey's parents, who lived on a farm near Phoebus, a dozen or so miles from Old Point Comfort and therefore close enough for Annabelle to check on Charlotte with some convenience.

"It was my first taste of farm life," wrote Charlotte, who till that time had known nothing but the hot streets of Philadelphia and Boston, "and I liked it enormously."

Mr. Engleburt did all the farm work and our milk, meat and vegetables were fresh. Also, since Phoebus is located on Chesapeake Bay we had plenty of fish, oysters and clams. Before long I was able to tread clams with my toes like the natives.... I was turned loose on the farm, taught to swim, allowed to run barefoot in the fields ... I learned a lot of things, consumed gallons of cream, dozens of freshly gathered eggs, scads of rich butter and cheese, oatmeal by the pound.... After a short time I could climb trees monkey fashion; eat large, juicy mulberries right off the trees, bugs and all; row boats in the quiet coves off Old Point Comfort, ride a pony bareback, the while I imagined I was a circus queen; squiggle happy notes to my mother; spend all my waking and sleeping hours in the open [and] grew like a weed.[7]

Not only did the Engleburts' farm go far toward restoring Charlotte to the robust good health that she would enjoy the rest of her long life, but it also gave her a certain ideal life to aspire to, which would find fulfillment a dozen years later with her beloved farmhouse on Long Island.

Farm life also gave her an experience of life-as-farce, which would inspire her comedy routines of the future — an experience which enabled her in later years to say to an astonished trustee, during an entertainment she was engaged to give at Sing Sing Prison, that she, too, had once been railroaded into jail.

"It had started as a perfectly innocent errand," Charlotte explains in her memoirs — one which, it would appear, she and young Chris Engleburt, son of farmer Engleburt, undertook without communicating their intentions to the proper adult authorities. A farmer neighbor was experiencing a constant loss of fowl from his henhouse, due either to human or animal means, and had asked Mr. Engleburt to retrieve the remaining chickens to the safety of his own property until measures could be taken to repair or move the hens' dwelling. The tall girl and the small boy "sallied forth on this errand in high spirits, armed with sacks and a little grain as lure for the birds."

Getting the birds together into the henhouse was easy enough, but as Charlotte recalled, "then the trouble started. Like many humans, the chickens were perfectly willing to eat our food but when it came to reciprocating by getting into our sacks, they suddenly developed conscientious objections." The feathers began to fly in earnest, all from the two dozen hens crowded into the small space, none wanting the least to do with the sack-armed human invaders. "The din could be — and was — heard for a mile."[8]

"We succeeded in trapping one languid hen," remembered Charlotte, "and impounding her in the sack when the constable arrived. I think that must have been the origin of the old vaudeville joke, 'There ain't nobody in here, 'ceptin' us chickens.'" A neighbor had heard the commotion in the henhouse and, no doubt having heard the rumors of suspected thievery from the farmer, assumed that a heist was taking place and had called the police. Unfortunately, the children were not just dirty and hot from their tussle with the hens, but were so startled by the appearance of a man in uniform they couldn't explain that they were there on a pre-arranged errand, and began to cry, rendering themselves unintelligible. "My dress was a wreck," she remembered. "I had pin feathers in my ears as well as a ribbon askew on my pigtail. Chris didn't look any better, but boys aren't supposed to be little ladies anyway."

"So we were led, two unhappy children, bewildered and screaming toward the lock-up," recalled Charlotte. "We were certain that we would be executed at dawn." The squawking hen, taken as evidence, only added to the noisy trip to the town jail.[9]

By the time the key was turned in his and Charlotte's cell door, Chris Engleburt had summoned enough reason to tell the constable that his father had an agreement with the chicken farmer to move his hens to the Engleburt farm, and that the police had only to reach him to get an explanation. Since the Engleburts had no telephone, however, the next best person to bring into the fracas was Annabelle, whose telephone at the hotel rang shortly thereafter.

"In phoning Mother, however, the constable made a slight error," recalled Charlotte. "Mama was not inclined to be helpful. She was, on the contrary, outraged, and when Mother became outraged she was equal to all of the Sabine women with some of the Amazons thrown in for good measure."

She was also a woman to whom it must have seemed that life was forever throwing messes for her to clean up — her enraged response to the news of her daughter's arrest is understandable. Annabelle descended on the police station, "prepared to take it down brick by brick," and demanded to see her daughter at once.[10]

"Mama's voice filtered through the cell block and [Chris and I] chorused in reply," Charlotte remembered. "I screamed at the top of my voice, Chris' wails were ranging from baritone to falsetto, the hen added to the din; the constable wished aloud he had never been born and vowed that he would never run for re-election; Mama was assuring him that if he escaped a term in the state penitentiary he could consider himself born under a lucky star."

Before long, the station was full of additional cast members for the unfolding jail farce: Mr. Engleburt arrived in a cloud of dust, driving his horse and buggy at top speed from the farm; the neighbor who had caused the alarm also came hurrying in; the hens' owner soon showed up, furious; and various friends and extended family came to see what was going on. "Some said there was a horseless carriage in the caravan, too," Charlotte recalled, " — probably a tourist!"[11]

"When the explanations were finally made, Mother departed in a huff," Charlotte in tow — and as in Boston, after the news of her escapade with the skylight filtered into the schoolroom, Charlotte was avoided for a time by all but the Engleburt children. As usual, she chose to find a heroic explanation for this sorry state of social affairs: "I was a convict," she gloried. "That was something of which they couldn't boast."[12]

4

"Show people were my people"

Annabelle's share in adventure of one kind or another, each one predictable in timing if not in character, was shortly to be augmented by another upheaval: in a fire that raged too fast and furious to save the building, the Hygeia Hotel burned to the ground.

Brave as ever, Annabelle had stayed in the flaming hotel long enough to retrieve from it as many of the financial records as she could carry. She emerged from the ruins without a place of work but with the even greater admiration of her employer, Colonel Davidson. Accordingly, Davidson found a place for her at another of his hotels, this time the Atlantic in Norfolk.

For the second time, Charlotte had to be uprooted from people she loved: first John Grace, now the Engleburts. But because Annabelle worried, as she had done with the Hygeia, that the Atlantic was not the best place for her daughter to live with her, and because she would rarely see her anyhow, Charlotte was boarded with another family and enrolled in a school that would both prove to be the first rung up the ladder that led her to a career on the stage: Charlotte was boarded with the jovial Ferriers, and went to a school in Ghent, near Norfolk, that had on its staff a teacher who shortly would become Charlotte's inspirational muse.

"The next twelve months were at once the happiest and the unhappiest of my life," Charlotte remembered. "[H]appy at home with Mrs. Ferrier and her carefree tribe, unhappy at school ... where they were not interested in my prowess as a roof climber, nor in my adventures as a clam digger, nor even in my experiences as a chicken thief." The Ferrier children — Doda, Alma and Ross — did their level best to "sell" Charlotte to her fellow students. "It might have been easier if I had been a good student, but I ran to legs, not brains."[1]

She also missed her mother terribly, and for the first time began to realize that "[Annabelle's] was a life of unending toil." Sitting hunched over at her desk at school or quiet amid the laughter and games at the Ferriers' dining table, Charlotte indulged in dreams not only of how she might help her mother, but of what sort of career she should follow in order to do that. Practicality in one so young — she was just 13 — fused with the day-dream world of what-if: because it was at this time, Charlotte wrote, that "[a]s fantastic as it may seem, my secret wish was to become an actress.... I was mortally afraid that people would laugh, yet my day dreams found me a great singer with the world at my feet — perhaps a second Calvé or a Melba or, on second thought, a Bernhardt or a Charlotte Cushman. They were only names to me but I read feverishly of their exploits."[2]

"I might have gone on wishing for the moon," she added, "had it not been for Miss Emily Newman."

> Today the laughter of the theater audiences is my meat and drink, but I can remember vividly when laughter cut me to the quick. My dreams were haunted by guffaws that took on a diabolical shrillness and left me trembling [and] weeping on my pillow.... Laughter seemed to follow me everywhere in school — when no one could reach my examples on the board, when, if sent on an errand, I would either drop [what I was carrying], spill it or fall down. The teachers saw in me only a backward drip who looked more like a college sophomore than a seventh grade student. Everyone laughed but Miss Newman.[3]

Emily Newman, in fact, had a plan for how to build up this skinny, withdrawn young girl's self-esteem. A primly neat woman who wore her hair in a pompadour with a braid wrapped around it and shirtwaist with tie, Miss Newman realized that Charlotte had a powerful natural contralto voice, a gift unusual in a girl so young. Annabelle seems to have recognized this gift even earlier, pointing out within Charlotte's hearing to visitors that her daughter had "a voice," though Charlotte was never sure whether she meant it as a compliment or a comment on how loudly her daughter was capable of crying.

"It was the practice in those days for members of the school board to make frequent trips of inspection," Charlotte recalled. "They would come in a body, separate and then swoop down individually on the various rooms. It was on those occasions that I would constantly disgrace the class by ridiculous answers [to questions put by the visitors]. Miss Newman made other plans. Instead of sending me to the blackboard to display my incredible ignorance, she suggested that I provide the board with a bit of entertainment, by way of a song. I fell in with the project without a second thought."

> In time Friday afternoons were holidays for me. On that day I became Miss Big. Let the board pay a surprise visit to Room 3 and quick like a flash, Lottie Greenwood was on her feet singing "The Holy City"; let them move to Room 5, and I stumbled down the hall making a magnificent entrance, often on all fours, chanting the virtues of "Old Heidelberg" or "The Palms" or even something topical such as "Over the Garden Wall," "Red Wing" or "In the Shade of the Old Apple Tree." I even had a comedy routine, "The Man Who Broke the Bank at Monte Carlo" which I sang in costume — that is, high hat and a cane.... Between my long arms, unaccountable legs and the cane it was inevitable that I would knock the flower vase from teacher's desk, slip in the water and get a good bump on the floor going down in a welter of arms and legs — but still singing.... Unwittingly, I was mastering the first principles of knock-about comedy — learning the hard way, the Greenwood way.[4]

As word spread of Charlotte's talent, she was asked to sing outside the school precincts — requests which even the ever-supportive Ferriers tried to dissuade Charlotte from accepting, but which Emily Newman urged her to take on. "She was certain," Charlotte wrote, "that the day would come when I would trade my awkwardness for poise, my shyness for assurance."

Miss Newman arranged for Charlotte to take piano and voice lessons, as well as lessons in a small dancing school in Norfolk, which she loved despite her awareness that any young man paired with her faced "the prospect of dancing with a moving Eiffel Tower." While pursuing these activities passionately Charlotte continued to sing, despite the laughs she drew through unwonted awkwardness. The snickering bothered her intensely, but as she gained experience of performing and was able to lean on knowledge picked up from her music lessons, she made a discovery. "I didn't care [about the laughter] while I was in the midst of my act," she explained. "I was learning to regard Lottie Greenwood the entertainer objectively and quite apart from Lottie Greenwood the Norfolk dunce."[5]

While Charlotte was making these discoveries about herself and her gifts, Annabelle was preparing for yet another move, this time to New York City. She had been hired to take over management of the Royal Arms Hotel in Times Square, which abutted the famous Hammerstein's Victoria Theatre on 42nd Street and Broadway. That Charlotte saw in her mother's transfer to New York and her proximity to fabled Broadway a sign that she herself was on the right track is clear from her own account. "I dwelt on my preparations for [my] first vacation to New York," she wrote. "I had been counting the days until I would get my school holidays.... I had something very, very important to take up with Mama — the matter of a career!" She had learned as much from the freedoms and the frustrations of life in Virginia as she needed to face the new ones awaiting her on Manhattan Island.[6]

✳ ✳ ✳

"There was no brass band to welcome me to New York," Charlotte wrote of her move to that city in 1905. "I didn't need one. My heart was thumping louder than any bass drum and my brain was throwing off a crescendo of music illustrative of the best efforts of George Gershwin, Ferdy Grofé and a wheezy carousel."[7]

Musical accompaniment she hardly needed: the city of over four million souls into which the tall, taffy-haired fifteen-year-old aspiring actress stepped for the first time had since a few seasons before enjoyed an unusual bumper crop of musical shows, which continued to inspire the productions lighting up Broadway on Charlotte's arrival — some of these, indeed, were to inspire future performances for the young comedienne. Two years before, in 1903, well over a quarter of the theatrical entertainments in the city and on tour from there were musicals — thereafter billed as "musical comedies" — and with several of these shows and their performers Charlotte would develop a close professional and personal relationship in a few years. L. Frank Baum's adaptation of his book *The Wizard of Oz*, with piquant lyrics written by the author, was playing, with David C. Montgomery and Fred Stone playing the Scarecrow and the Tin Man respectively — in another decade, Charlotte would be playing the role of Queen Ann Soforth in Baum's musical adaptation of *The Tik-Tok Man of Oz*. Another musical that season that would have appealed to children was *Mr. Pickwick*, with De Wolf Hopper, whose fourth wife, Hedda, would become a life-long friend of Charlotte's after both had made their way to Hollywood.[8]

The theatre season of 1905, the year Charlotte came to New York and got her first foot in show business, has sometimes been called the Year of George Bernard Shaw, since no fewer than four of his plays were premiered there that year, and several of his older plays were revived. It was also the season of Maude Adams' most famous role, in James Barrie's *Peter Pan*. Metropolitan Opera singer and comedienne Fritzi Scheff, with whom Charlotte would co-star in the near future, played her most successful role in the 1905 season in the Victor Herbert operetta *Mlle Modiste*, as well as making Herbert's song "Kiss Me Again" a smash hit. A then slender black-bearded young juggler named W. C. Fields would perform in the vaudeville standby *The Ham Tree* (and would later teach Charlotte something about keeping several objects in the air). The grandiose New York Hippodrome opened that April, its huge space replete with a swimming pool which was frequently employed in the extravaganzas produced there.

Though the *New York Times* had opened its new office complex at 42nd Street and Broadway and that phenomenon known as Times Square was on its way to full frenzied maturity, the Square that Charlotte first knew still lacked the electric lighting effects and the commercial venues that would characterize it by 1911. Even so, there was plenty to dazzle a young girl from Norfolk, Virginia.[9]

Seeing herself very much as "a young woman with a mission," Charlotte walked up 42nd Street, with its brand-new subway station (the Interborough line), the steps up from which concealed till the last minute a sudden exciting view of angled stone buildings, bustling traffic, waves of pedestrians and the still-miraculous electric signs and standards. Charlotte emerged from below ground in the middle of this parade, a slightly battered straw hat on her head and a straw-covered suitcase in her hand, as full of joy in her mission as she was under absolutely no illusions about her physical appearance.

"From the waist up I was a ravishing beauty," she recalled dryly, "— by contrast with the rest of me. Those hands of mine, dangling from my thin spindly arms like a pair of five-finger fern fronds on a string — and those long narrow feet, like the roots of a sapling tree.... I might just as well have been walking on skis."[10]

None of these physical drawbacks concerned a girl who had learned to become another person during her amateur performances, whose mother managed a hotel near Times Square which catered to variety stars, whom — who knew? — she might very well meet in the lobby that day. In fact it was hard for Charlotte to decide, she remembered later, which she wanted to see more, the stars at the hotel or her mother who managed the desk; and so fixated was she on both, as well as on the big subject she would be discussing with Annabelle — that of her aspirations to a stage career — that she stepped into 42nd Street without looking, "oblivious to the shrieking of the cop's whistle and the squealing of automobile brakes and the groaning of the auto horns of that era."

Such was her state of excitement that on reaching the Royal Arms, Charlotte rushed straight through the glass doors and met a potted rubber plant head on.

"Every time Gracie Fields sings her famous song about the biggest aspidistra in the world," Charlotte recalled, "I am reminded of that rubber plant in the lobby of the Royal Arms and what happened to it."

If Fields' aspidistra, per her song, grew stout on regular doses of Guinness beer, it could be forgiven for falling over on its own; but the Royal Arms' rubber plant had no such excuse. Had Charlotte merely knocked it over, her entrance might not have seemed quite so mortifying to Annabelle, who was standing behind the check-in counter watching the farce unfold. As Charlotte would jot in her memoir notes years later, "You could hide a single buckshot in a ballroom the size of Buckingham Palace and Greenwood would not only find the shot but use it as a springboard for a hundred yard non-stop slide."

"[T]o even things up I had to trip over the corner of the rug," Charlotte remembered, "sending my sailor straw skimming in one direction and my straw suitcase catapulting in another. Mama made a desperate effort to get from behind the desk to intercept me before I destroyed the hotel."

Thrilled to see her mother again after so many months, Charlotte got up from the rumpled, earth-strewn rug and threw herself at Annabelle, kissing her with a "resounding smack." Veteran of many such an emergency, Annabelle gathered her dignity and lectured her daughter about the unsuitability of such public displays of affection. Then she turned to the lobby full of staring and smiling guests and said, "Folks, this is Lottie, my little girl."

"And nobody laughed," Charlotte recalled, "— nobody in the whole lobby." Not only that, but a small, compact woman with a generous bust and vivid smile walked toward her, carrying the battered straw suitcase in an elegant white hand. "Here's your bag, my dear," said the woman. She then turned to Annabelle and "added in what I thought was the most wonderful speaking voice I had ever heard, 'Hasn't she lovely eyes!'"

Charlotte's Good Samaritan was none other than the comic actor Eva Tanguay, who in a few years would be dubbed "the Evangelist of Joy" for her high-energy dancing and singing. In 1905, Tanguay was "the toast of Broadway, the idol of America," as Charlotte had read in her constant perusals of newspaper theatre columns. Despite her pudgy cheeks and turned up nose, she was also one of the first sex symbols of the American stage, mostly due to her risqué songs delivered with a carefree sensuality. Charlotte just knew Tanguay was a star, and she remembered thinking in awe, after receiving her bag from her: "She had given me my first kind word in New York and had done me my first service."

"It was then that my resolution was made," Charlotte wrote. "Show people were my people — people with heart and understanding. Like the Biblical Ruth, I would never leave them."[11]

Given her daughter's clumsy entrance before such witnesses as Eva Tanguay, Annabelle cannot be blamed for taking Charlotte's frenzied desire to go on the stage with more than a grain of salt. "She was not in sympathy," recalled Charlotte, but Annabelle's objection had as much to do with her concern for her girl's ability to make her way in the world armed with a proper education as with the feeble likelihood of so gangling a young woman making anything like a success in the theatre. Annabelle pointed out that the Higginses and Jaquetts had been educated people, "and here I was proposing to leave school in the seventh grade." What good was a girl without education except as a chambermaid, which in Annabelle's world of hotel management was the lowest of the low.

"No, Mama," Charlotte told her — "drawing myself up to my full height, and threatening to thrust my head through the ceiling" — "I am not going to be a chambermaid. I'm going to be an actress."

> Even Mama thought that was funny, but her laugh was gentle. Neither of us knew that three of my biggest roles in after life were to be the maid in *Wild Violets* at Drury Lane in London; the maid in *The Late Christopher Bean* in San Francisco; and the maid in the film *Moon Over Miami*. [She also played a maid in *The Man in Possession*, opposite Robert Montgomery, and a nightclub singer turned housekeeper in *Tall, Dark and Handsome*.][12]

Regardless of Annabelle's gentle laugh, before treading the stage Charlotte first had to enroll at P.S. 148 Manhattan, an act that must have made her drag her large feet most reluctantly out the door every morning. In her spare time she had to make do, at Annabelle's insistence, as substitute switchboard operator at the Royal Arms. Before long she had mastered the many plugs, cords and buzzers of the monstrous machinery, with a rapidity at least partly due to the proximity the switchboard put her to the stars dwelling on the floors above. When the regular operator returned to her job, Charlotte had to find another position.

At a nearby hotel, the Lincoln, which also catered to the theatre trade, Charlotte found herself another switchboard job, and again became enmeshed, if from the other end of miles of telephone cord, in the lives of actors she had only read about.

> I remember that my first chore each morning when I checked in at 7 A.M. was to answer a call from the room occupied by Thomas Q. Seabrook, the star.
> "It's on its way up," I would say as the red light flashed on.
> "Thank you," Mr. Seabrook would reply.
> I never met the man but I knew his habits. He awoke at seven A.M. no matter how late he retired and he wanted without delay one absinthe frappe. I have met many actors who religiously started their day with a bottle of beer; and many who had their eye-openers of bourbon before they dallied with their morning coffee; but Thomas Q. Seabrook alone was individual in his matutinal tastes.[13]

Not only Charlotte's age but her fascination with colorful entertainment and her desire to be a part of it went toward losing her this job and her inside scoop on the drinking habits of famous actors:

The Fourth of July brought forth its usual quota of noise and before long Eighth Avenue was a battle ground. I stood it [at the switchboard] as long as I could. Then I began to dart away from the board to look out the lobby door. Before I was well aware of it, I was in the midst of the fire cracker brigade. Meantime bedlam was occupying the Lincoln. The switchboard was clogged with calls. The management was in a frenzy. I don't know what inspired the manager to look out in the street but when he saw me, he became articulate enough to yell that I was fired.[14]

She was out of work, and "I didn't want to go back to school," Charlotte remembered later, "— any school. I could visualize myself standing in the center of Hammerstein's [Victoria] stage, receiving baskets of flowers, hearing the enthusiastic plaudits of the crowd, reading the glowing newspaper notices in my luxurious suite, being acclaimed the newest toast of Broadway," things which were to happen to her soon enough.[15]

None of this enthusiasm convinced the gun-shy Annabelle, however, and several days of renewed debate took place. For starters, it was like trying to convince a child in a candy store that sugar was bad for her teeth. "[M]any of the greats of that day lived in my mother's hotel," Charlotte recalled. "Gertrude Hoffman and her husband, Max; Stella Mayhew and Billie Taylor; James Richard Glenroy who was known as 'The Man with the Green Gloves'; Charlie Aldrich; Eva Tanguay and others." Because the Royal Arms was adjacent not only to Hammerstein's Victoria but to the famed celebrity restaurant Considine's, those stage stars who did not live at the Royal Arms were often to be found lounging in its lobby or laughing their way through it on their way to post-performance celebrations.

Forgetting for the time being the mother whose toiling she had so worried about while in Virginia, Charlotte could sit for hours in Annabelle's apartment, from which she had a front row seat on the alley separating the Victoria from the hotel. Through the dressing room windows that gave onto the alley Charlotte looked longingly on the enchanted lives of the show people temporarily ensconced there. "People laughing, someone singing, another playing a banjo or tuning it," she recalled. "Once a monkey got loose from the theater and came over to the hotel, brushed all the toilet articles off the dresser and just generally wrecked the room. He was sitting in front of my mirror powdering his face when the attendant finally arrived to retrieve him."[16]

Eventually, Charlotte's campaign — and perhaps her relentless mooning over the theatre across the alley — broke down Annabelle's defenses. "She was always on my side," noted Charlotte, "and in the end I won her nod."

> If, she said, I would wangle my way into the theater, she would offer no objection. On the other hand I was not to expect any help from her. As a matter of fact, I am satisfied that she spoke to Max Hoffman before I did, because, come to think of it, [when I finally did meet with him] he seemed fully aware of what I was trying to say before I got the first halting sentence out...[17]

Max Hoffman was a Broadway composer and music director who had begun his career by providing music for the 1903 hit, *The Rogers Brothers in London*, and was especially known for his ragtime rhythms. His wife, Gertrude Hoffman, was famed as a dancer, particularly of the so-called "Salome Dance," which used veils and allusive movements — in 1907, she would be arrested on charges of indecent dancing, after a performance rigged by Oscar Hammerstein II's producer father, Willie Hammerstein, achieved the desired publicity for his theatre. (Richard Strauss' *Salome* made its American premiere at the Metropolitan Opera that same year and was closed down on grounds of indecency after a few performances: New York City might have been a sink of every vice, but in Edwardian America it just didn't do to flaunt it, even in the make-believe world of the theatre.) Gertrude Hoffman was also a respected choreographer who used powerful muscular movements and acrobatics in a way reminiscent of Isadora Duncan and, later, Martha Graham and Agnes de Mille. Perhaps more pleasing to the vice squad was her invention of the polite social dance known as the "Hoffman Glide."

Obviously, getting to know Max and Gertrude Hoffman and gaining their friendship and enthusiasm for her talents was a good part of the battle Charlotte had ahead of her in gaining the stage and making it a career. Charlotte did so by waiting for Max in the lobby of the hotel, till he arrived home after his latest show. Her first reaction to seeing him was to begin crying. Between sobs,

> I told him how I would look out of our windows and see the people in the Victoria laughing, singing, playing banjos and having fun.... The music, the rhythm, the activity, the excitement — that's where I wanted to be working. More, I wanted to be of some material help to Mama. I wanted to be earning money.
> As I rattled on I confided that my height was humiliating, that my various ailments and our constant moving had retarded my schooling. That here I was almost 13 [sic: she was 15], big enough to be a help to my mother and only in the seventh grade.
> Max listened quietly, told me to quit crying and blow my nose, and started to talk. If I really wanted to go on the stage was I prepared to start at the bottom? Did I realize that life in the theater was not all that it seemed to be looking across the alley way? Did I realize this and that?
> I did, and I still wanted a chance! ... [Hoffman] was an intimate friend of Ned Wayburn who was at that time producing a musical play called "The White Cat." Wayburn, it seemed, owed him a favor; and he would collect it through me.[18]

Later on, as Charlotte stood shaking but happy beside the desk in his and Gertrude's Royal Arms apartment, Max Hoffman grabbed for something to write on and scribbled a brief introduction to Ned Wayburn on a rectangular piece clipped from a brown paper bag:

> Dear Ned: This will introduce you to Lottie Greenwood of whom I spoke to you Saturday for "The White Cat."
> Sincerely, Max Hoffman

"I have collected a great many personal mementos in my lifetime," Charlotte recalled, "and many have been lost as I moved from place to place. But I have never lost a bit of brown paper bag. It was my passport into paradise."[19]

5

The White Cat

IN THE MIDDLE OF THIS maelstrom of hopes, dreams and fears, a handsome figure from a past so distant Charlotte could not even place it in memory emerged from the many faces of New York City and stood solidly in the middle of Annabelle's apartment.

"Lottie," said Annabelle, drawing Charlotte closer to the stranger, "I want you to know your father!"

"I had never seen Frank Greenwood," Charlotte jotted in notes for her memoir that were never used, "nor did I know that my mother had invited him to the hotel.... I adored her so much [that] this meeting meant very little to me, and I could never bring myself to love my father for which, in later years I was extremely sorry and really made the effort."

Despite the fact that Frank Greenwood had his barbershop within the same neighborhood as the Royal Arms — what Charlotte remembered as "a very exclusive barber shop in the McClure Building on 34th Street" — and attended to the grooming needs of many of the young actors who played on Broadway (typically making them over in his own British bachelor-buttoned image), there was no way this man who had left Annabelle and their infant daughter to their own devices fourteen years earlier could become part of their lives again, however much he or Annabelle might try.

"No matter how much of an effort I made to be filial, it was always like meeting a stranger...," Charlotte recalled. On first meeting Frank, Charlotte had even tried to curtsey to him, succeeding only in falling at his feet. He lifted her up, a tear on his cheek, which for Charlotte "fascinated without rousing any emotional surge in me."

> "Didn't hurt yourself did you?" he asked in the clipped accent of the Britisher. I shook my head and ran into the bathroom where I eavesdropped on the conversation. I couldn't understand it. Mama seemed to be asking his help in something; he was saying, rather sadly I thought, that he was afraid it was too late for him to be of any service.

"[A]fter I achieved some distinction on the stage, [Frank Greenwood] used to make it a point to visit me regularly"— a point that cannot have sat too easily with a woman who had needed this father much more as an anonymous little girl than as a famous vaudeville headliner.

That Charlotte made so much of an effort at all had much to do with what some theatre friends of hers once told her, on being apprised that Greenwood was trying to make amends. "[They] told me that when David Warfield was playing 'The Music Master' in New

York, my father went so often to the performance to see a single scene that the box office men used to pass him in free," she recalled. "The scene was not unlike a chapter from his own life, relating the incident of a father seeking to reclaim the affections of a child he has deserted." (In Charles Klein's 1904 play, an Austrian conductor searches for the daughter taken from him by his first wife, who had left him for another man — an ironic reverse of the real-life Frank-Annabelle scenario, in which the husband and father deserted the mother and child.)

"My father was very proud of me," Charlotte adds in the brief portion of her memoirs she devoted to the subject of Frank Greenwood, then crossed out with thick strokes of her pencil. "[I]t must have been a dreadful situation for him, particularly when his luck turned and he knew that the money Mother was secretly supplying him came from the earnings of the baby he had left to shift for itself."

> I never loved my father, although in later years [I tried to]. [We] met first as strangers and later as casual acquaintances. It seems to me unjust that anyone should be permanently penalized for a single ungenerous act. As a child, of course, I had [had] no such philosophy. He was a person who had hurt my mother, who had abandoned her with a baby and no visible means of support. It wasn't until much later that I realized how pathetic he was, how pathetically proud of me, how eager to share a little in my life. He used to visit my dressing room on opening nights when I reached musical comedy and fairly beamed when I would introduce him to the usual corps of well wishers as "my father." ... [But] he had destroyed the bond on that summer day in Philadelphia years before, when he had strolled out of our house and life.[1]

With Max Hoffman's brown bag note in her hand — "my precious scroll" as she called it — and the self-absorbed obsessions of a normal teenaged girl set against a backdrop of towering ambition, Charlotte wasted no time pondering what might have been where Frank Greenwood was concerned. She left him and his clumsy guiltiness behind, heading straight for the New Amsterdam Theatre, newly built jewel in the theatrical crown of Klaw and Erlanger, where Ned Wayburn's rehearsals for *The White Cat* were getting underway, and where all that mattered was one untried chorus girl's glorious future.

A native of Pittsburgh whose first connection with the theatre came when he worked as an usher, Ned Wayburn was a curious mix of multi-faceted talent, super-human endurance, and over-weaning addiction to the super ego, exemplified nowhere better than in his 1925 self-published book, *The Art of Stage Dancing*.

This limited edition tome, bound in green leather and filled with photographs of dancers, actors, singers and clowns in whose discovery or training Wayburn believed he had had some part (Charlotte is featured in this array, despite the fact that his manner of training her seems to have consisted mostly of shouting at her), and grandly autographed and numbered by the author, is a cross between an autobiography and what must be the most expensive advertisement for a dance studio ever put to print. By turns self-congratulatory and rich with the testimonials of those whose lives were changed forever via contact with the "Wayburn Method," *The Art of Stage Dancing* is a fascinating glimpse into what sort of regimen a high-powered producer/manager/director like Wayburn expected his theatrical soldiers to know.

Fond of placing his distinctive monogram "NW" on everything he touched, including the breast of a collegiate-looking sweater he wore when presiding over rehearsals, Wayburn insisted that any performer under his tutelage know exactly who they were and what they had to offer, and that they offer what they had with at least 150 per cent of their energies or give up their show business dreams as a lost cause.

Information on various dance tempos, advice on dancers' proper diet, a management chart of who's who in a given theatre, down to the merest stage-hand, how to tell good contracts from bad, even what makeup to use (a photograph of "The Ned Wayburn Professional Makeup Box and Outfit," replete with box prominently printed with "Ned Wayburn Studios of Stage Dancing, Inc., 1841 Broadway [Ent. on 60th Street]," is given a full page of its own); and the thread that holds it all together, through line drawings showing ingénues approaching distant temples of art marked with the inevitable "NW" and repeated exhortations, is Wayburn's overbearing obsession with bringing out the success he assumes to be latent in everyone. "There is no such thing as an untrained successful dancer; there never has been; there never will be," declared Wayburn. Beyond that, the only thing preventing a dancer from the "glory and the gold" of Broadway was purely the performer's own gifts and initiative.[2]

As time would tell, the only thing Ned Wayburn had to teach Charlotte Greenwood — thereby guaranteeing her a place in his book's pantheon of those deserving of "glory and gold" — was not so much how to dance as how to project her total energy in the act

Even without his coach's whistle and what Charlotte described as his "rah-rah boy sweater," Broadway dance instructor and choreographer Ned Wayburn still looks ready to muster theatrical troops. He gave Charlotte her first job as chorus girl in 1905 and prodded her to become a star.

of performance; and it is likely that had she known how brutal his technique would be in going about coaching her, she would have run back to the Royal Arms and signed up for the next year's high school term. She was to learn the Wayburn Way the hard way — or, as she termed it, "the Greenwood way."

Charlotte waited in the New Amsterdam's anteroom while the stage manager, through a lower intermediary, took her "precious scroll" back to Wayburn, and was thrilled when it was returned to her, stamped "Engaged — Ned Wayburn." The stage manager looked as puzzled on his return. "Accustomed to the vagaries of producers," she opined, "he probably realized that Wayburn was stark, staring mad, hiring a chorus girl sight unseen." It was true, she had to admit, that the waiting room was filled with several hopefuls like herself, beautiful as she was not, and he did not know which one was which.

"Which one of you is Greenwood?" asked the stage manager, regarding the faces of the lovelies and looking through Charlotte's flushed features as if they didn't exist.

"'I'm Greenwood!' I gurgled and stumbled toward him, tripping smartly over my feet."

"The man virtually fell in a faint. You could see — even I could see — his whole world tumbling around him. Here was Wayburn, forerunner of Earl Carroll as the picker of the world's most beautiful women, hiring this scarecrow for the chorus not only without a second thought, but without a first look."

The man eventually recovered, and crisply ordered Charlotte to follow him out to the stage, where a kind chorus director handed her notes containing the lyrics she was to sing and advised her to watch the other girls to pick up the dance steps.

"There was a great deal of excited whispering among the beautiful ladies of the chorus," Charlotte recalled. "They were unable to decide offhand whether someone was playing a practical joke on Wayburn — a very dangerous practice — or whether he had completely lost his mind ... or whether I was a comedienne in disguise or a laundress who had wandered into the wrong hall."

Not that Charlotte could hear most of what the girls said — her teeth were chattering, her head ached, she dripped perspiration: "[A]nd I was radiantly happy." She moved through the rehearsal in a daze of bliss, unable to believe that she was actually in a theatre, on a stage, under hot lights. Even the annoyed murmurs of the tough dressmakers who fitted her for her costume, criticizing Charlotte's lack of a figure and bemoaning the difficulties of making her costume fit, meant nothing to her. "I was an actress," she told herself proudly, like a holy mantra, "a member of the Wayburn company in the cast of 'The White Cat' at the New Amsterdam."[3]

For the first few weeks, Charlotte saw Wayburn, but for reasons she was never to understand, he did not see her. Only 31 and working hard on what was just his second show (his first, *In Newport*, had lit up the Liberty Theatre for a mere twenty-four performances), and caught up in the typical tempests over costumes, book and lyrics, bookers and backers, Wayburn could be forgiven for the oversight, if not necessarily for the way in which he finally did catch Charlotte in his sights.

"It used to take months to put on a big production in those days," Charlotte recalled, "and there were times when it seemed as if it would take years to get the curtain raised on 'The White Cat.'" *The White Cat* was indeed a complex show to mount, being what Gerald Bordman refers to as a "Drury Lane pantomime-spectacle," a descendant of Elizabethan masques, heavy on spectacle and short on plot. These were already out of fashion on Charlotte's side of the Atlantic but were to find something of a reincarnation a few decades later in the spectacular Broadway revues.

While the show was being teased into shape, Charlotte wasted no moment of her time. With a steel-trap memorization technique that was to be both her strength and her weakness all of her life, Charlotte imprinted all the dance steps, all the chorus' lines and those of some of the principals, on her eager memory. The one thing that continued to distress her, of which she had been largely ignorant until then, was the matter of her matchstick figure. Where many girls are filling out at fifteen, Charlotte was decidedly slim: "I was as 'flat as a pancake' in all the places where, according to nature, there should have been bulges," she recorded in notes for her memoirs. After some soulful discussions with Annabelle, Charlotte found what seemed an ideal solution: the stage padding then known as symmetricals, used not just by women but by men to fill out thin legs and upper body mass. (When he played his acclaimed Hamlet on Broadway in 1922, John Barrymore resorted to symmetricals to beef up his skinny calves.)

The first shock following this happy solution came right away: the $9 Annabelle paid for the symmetricals turned out to be the last cash she had. "Colonel Hull Davidson had sold his chain of hotels," Charlotte wrote, "and the new management had ideas on its operation that did not include Mama." Annabelle and Charlotte had to leave the charmed precincts of the Royal Arms and move to an apartment at 245 West 42nd Street; for all that, they still had the pleasure and, for Charlotte especially, the useful professional connections, of Max and

Gertrude Hoffman, who lived across the street from them. "I was glad I had forced the issue of leaving school," Charlotte remembered. "Mama needn't worry any more" because once the show got going, Charlotte would be earning $15 per week in the city and $18 on the road — a princely sum to those who have had to part with their last $9 for a pair of symmetricals.

Just prior to Annabelle's leave taking from the Royal Arms, Charlotte seems to have approached the staff of the Metropolitan Opera to see about an audition, a fact she does not record in her memoirs or notes for them, but which she confided to a reporter later in her career. Though her formal musical training had been brief, according to Charlotte, after applying to the opera company "I got an audition.... The man said, 'Bring that voice back to me in 10 years.' But I had no money and felt I should earn and take care of my mother."

Work on the Great White Way was, then, for Charlotte a practical means to a practical end, replete with the sting of unattained hopes: she was not to abandon her aspirations toward high culture and her certainty that she would achieve success in it, either as an opera singer or concert artist, for many years yet. The career she made such a success in was, in fact, very much a compromise wrung from her at the price of personal pain and for the gain of professional maturity.[4]

6

A Wayburn Girl

"FINALLY THE GREAT DAY CAME—the day of the dress rehearsal!"

I started toward the theater with a song in my heart and a tune on my lips. Wouldn't Mr. Wayburn be glad he had engaged me! Wouldn't Max Hoffman be delighted he had recommended me! Wouldn't Miss Newman, my old school teacher, be proud if she could see me now! Wouldn't the kids in Phoebus and Boston and Norfolk envy me! Me, a Broadway star.[1]

Clad in her costume and symmetricals, Charlotte adjusted both in the reflections of store windows on her way down the street. "From the waist down I was now something pretty snug. The symmetricals gave me a sort of Mae West flavor from hip to toe." In her hurry to the New Amsterdam, Charlotte hardly had the time or the concentration to really study how she looked in all her padding; even the chuckles of the other chorus girls, when they beheld her enter in her getup, didn't send her instantly to a mirror for a good cold look.

"How was I to know," she wrote later, "that I was goon from the waist up, glamour from the waist down?"

The stage manager called the chorus and out they marched to the stage, smiling in their tights, right up to the footlights, where Ned Wayburn, in his prominently monogrammed sweater with the silver whistle around his neck and fierce dark eyes studying everything, sat in the front row of the empty theatre.

"Suddenly, the whistle shrilled," Charlotte wrote; "the curtain stopped in its ascent; the music paused in mid-air; the chorus came to a halt. Wayburn's eye had fallen on me and he bellowed: 'What in the name of God is THAT?'"

All Charlotte remembered was reflexively looking around to see what Wayburn could be talking about. "I was in the limelight for the first time, the cynosure of all eyes—in a very loose manner of speaking."

Then Wayburn went on a tear. "Where did it come from?" he demanded of the empty seats around him. "What is it anyway? Why does everything happen to me? Will somebody kindly explain this grotesque practical joke?"

An assistant rushed to the great man's side and whispered in his ear. "Hoffman!" Wayburn shouted, letting fly a string of profanity.

"Finally, he ran out of oaths and I was dissolved in tears," wrote Charlotte, who now knew she was the "that" to whom Wayburn was referring. "It is no fun being a protégée when your patron is being excoriated as a fool, a villain, and a blithering idiot."

"Take her out of there," Wayburn said at last, pointing straight at the weeping Charlotte. "Put her in the Japanese number."

"And so I made my debut on Broadway, divested of my symmetricals, equipped with a monumental black wig and garbed in an Oriental robe that reached to the floor," Charlotte recorded. "Even Mother had difficulty recognizing her daughter in the disguise. But it was all the same to me." "Hashimura" Greenwood (as Charlotte called the character she played) might have been the tallest Japanese in America, but "I was a professional," she reassures her reader and herself.

She was also learning to behave like a professional, and learning how to do so, as usual, the hard way. "For a long time, [even] in my salad days," Charlotte recalled, "I used to have a recurring nightmare having to do with a long legged girl frantically trying to catch the tail of a moving train. I didn't need Freud to explain the nightmare to me; it was based on an actual happening." Though she now knew New York almost like the back of one of her long, slender hands, and considered herself a well-matured "Wayburn Girl," Charlotte was still given to all the nerves of a typical teenager, and while walking toward Pennsylvania Station the morning the production set forth for tryouts in Syracuse, Charlotte realized the crew was leaving from Grand Central Terminal. "With horror, I realized that I hadn't the vaguest idea where Grand Central was located."

Charlotte took to her heels and ran back up the street to Gertrude Hoffman's apartment, where to her poundings on the door an astonished Mrs. Hoffman opened and beheld a young woman on the brink of panic.

"Where," Charlotte wailed, "is Grand Central?"

"Gertie hit the ceiling," Charlotte remembered. "The air was blue with profanity, but she gave me the directions. It was drawing closer and closer to 10 A.M.— trains didn't wait; not even for Wayburn girls." What followed was a real-life preview of the crazed physical comedy that would endear Charlotte to film audiences in another two decades' time:

> I made a picture no artist could paint galloping across town. Grand Central was its usual beehive of activity when I bolted through the doors, slid along the marble floors and managed to squeeze through the appointed gate just as it was closing. I raced along the ramp onto the runway. The train was slowly moving away. On the rear platform was the stage manager whose job included the checking of performers onto the train. Telling me to run faster, he held out his arms. Believe it or not, I outran the train, reached the rear platform and was hauled bodily over the railing, completely exhausted. That experience cured me once for all. I have never missed a train, or even nearly missed a train, since.

She also found yet another life experience to use in what would become a formidable arsenal of comedic weaponry.[2]

No sooner had *The White Cat* closed, after what Charlotte charitably calls a successful run (46 performances — at least it had nearly double the life of Wayburn's first show), than she was hired by Max Hoffman himself and, certainly through his good offices, by the popular dialect team of Gus and Max Rogers, known as the Rogers Brothers, "whose shows always had a new location — 'In Panama,' 'In Ireland,' 'In Zanzibar.'"

Hoffman had composed music for three Rogers Brothers shows already (*In London, In Paris* and *In Ireland*), and would have had sufficient pull to get Charlotte into *The Rogers Brothers in Panama*. Possibly to see how she would hold up on tour, he hired her for the cast of a "vacation tour" show in 1906 that traveled through Southern cities and towns featuring Gertrude Hoffman and two girls who were to become good friends of Charlotte's and icons of the Jazz Age, Hungarian twins Jenny and Rosie Dolly.

"The Dollys came along with their mother," Charlotte recalled, "a beautiful Hungarian woman who spent all of her waking hours sewing red ruffles on their dancing costumes. As children the Dollys couldn't dance for sour apples, but they were so attractive that audiences never bothers about the missteps. That was Mrs. Dolly's problem, for after each performance their blunders had ripped yards of ruffling. Yet with all their reputation for great beauty — and they were lovely creatures — the Dollys were but a mild reflection of their mother's beauty. She was the most exquisite bit of Dresden china I have ever seen."

During this brief tour Charlotte was to see what happened when a performer famed for one kind of act attempted to take on another. While Max was back in New York attending to business, Gertrude Hoffman talked Charlotte into helping her add a bit of "emotional acting" to her well-known dance to "Spring Song." "I was to stand in the wings with a sheet and, as she danced toward me ... I was to toss it to her," Charlotte remembered. "She would do the rest. She certainly did. Catching the sheet in mid-air, she draped it around her shoulders and barged into a recitation of [William Cullen Bryant's famous 1814 poem] *Thanatopsis* in the grand manner. Fortunately for her, the famed hospitality of the Old South stood the test, and Southern courtesy and chivalry held under the strain. When Max heard what had happened, he was apoplectic. After that sortie into the realm of higher art, Gertie stuck to her dancing." Charlotte's most cherished memory of this night was of standing in the wings tittering with the Dolly Sisters as Gertrude struggled to make a dramatic impression, but she was to find herself very much in Gertie's shoes in the not so distant future.[3]

The Rogers Brothers' concept of zany American travelers' crass and confused dealings with the inhabitants of the foreign countries in which they found themselves was an early forerunner of the Bob Hope/Bing Crosby *On the Road* films, and was immensely popular not only because the Rogers Brothers were a solid comedy team but because the formula had been tried before with even greater success by the ethnic stereotyping comedy duo of Lew Weber and Gus Fields. As famed for their stars as for their shows' content — they built several productions around the glamour of 1890s singer and actress Lillian Russell — which relied heavily on spoofing whatever or whoever was the current theatre hit, the Weber and Fields comedies lit up Broadway till they phased out in 1908, the years after the Rogers Brothers show that became Charlotte's next chance to tread a stage.

What made this second performing opportunity as amusing for Charlotte as her first had been tear-stained was the fact that again she was obliged to dress up in a costume wildly at variance with her height and coloring. This time she became a gypsy — a very tall gypsy — named Lola (a name that would reappear in her first film for Twentieth Century Fox 33 years later), wearing a black wig, hoop earrings, trailing scarves.

But the great thing was that the Rogers Brothers, far from yelling at her as Wayburn had done, realized her stage potential and made the most of it by giving her a solo of her own. In *The Rogers Brothers in Panama* (1907, 71 performances), Charlotte stepped out of the chorus and sang a ditty that she jotted in her memoir notes as:

> 'Twill do no harm, to cross my palm
> With silver, pretty maiden.
> To you I'll state, if future fate
> Be fair or sorrow laden.

"Curiously," Charlotte remembered, "the few lines always brought applause because I had unwittingly introduced an innovation in singing."

In that day of coon shouting[4] it was customary to lift the voice at the end of a song and "sell it." I purposely reversed the process and lowered the key. The transition came as a surprise and proved pleasing to the audiences. Something of the same technique years later came into vogue with torch singers. Alice Faye used it with great success on the screen.[5]

In the cast list of *The Rogers Brothers in Panama*, evidently assuming her childlike nickname was only too appropriate for a player of chorus parts, Charlotte is listed as "Lottie Greenwood." A publicity shot of the chorus line up, pasted into one of Charlotte's scrapbooks, shows her at the far left end of the row, wearing a wide hat fringed with pom-poms and a dirndl blouse vaguely suggestive of the show's Panamanian setting.[6]

Charlotte was, however, already part of the grown-up world of being responsible for another person, as her mother had been responsible, at a similar age, before her. "I was beginning to turn over my entire envelope to [Annabelle];" Charlotte wrote, "when I went on the road, I held out $10 a week for living expenses. This meant some pretty close budgeting but in time I knew every theatrical boarding house from Maine to Omaha.... I allowed myself $7 or $8 a week for room and board, which left me a full $2 to squander in riotous living."

It was not always easy, or even healthy, living in this manner. Once, during a freezing Boston winter, a shivering Charlotte finally broke her budgeting rule and spent five times her weekly allowance on a $10 coat that was too thin "but it served. Strange how you don't feel the cold when what you need has to meet what your purse holds." Expecting Annabelle to praise her for her shrewdness, Charlotte remembered showing the coat to her mother, disavowing the cold she had just survived, and watching her mother burst into tears.[7]

Perhaps it struck Annabelle, as with many parents when their children reach adulthood, that the traditional roles had been reversed; perhaps, too, she was already sending some of the money Charlotte forwarded to her to the impecunious Frank Greenwood, unaware that her daughter was raising this money by braving the Boston snows in a coat too thin for winter. If so, it is clear she continued to send Frank money. As the breadwinner who knew all along where some of her hard-earned cash was going, yet continued to provide it, Charlotte was far more adult already than her mother knew.

From the very beginning of her efforts to get on the stage (as evinced by her dogged attempt to get into opera), Charlotte saw in herself the makings of a serious performer — a true chanteuse, whose rich contralto voice could hold the stage and audiences spellbound as she emoted her way through popular songs of the day. That people like Max and Gertrude Hoffman also seemed to take her as seriously as she did herself merely fed this belief.

Charlotte was not a lone comedian seeking to let her true Duse come out. Comedian Eddie Cantor, who would perform in many of the same vaudeville houses and with many of the same producers as Charlotte, and would star with her in the successful 1931 comedy *Palmy Days*, had had a similar set of aspirations. Like Charlotte, once Cantor's voice and theatricality had been discovered at school he was trotted from room to room to entertain visiting dignitaries. He, too, in trying to show his dramatic prowess had drawn laughter from a crowd. As he noted in his memoirs, "[V]ery much to my dismay I was hailed as a great comedian," not the tragedian he'd hoped for. Like Charlotte, once he got into theatre shows he made a point of learning all the roles and was called on to fill in for absent performers. "I learned one of the basic lessons in the delivery of comedy," he wrote in *My Life Is in Your Hands*, "and that is to never consciously point one's fun, but do one's comedy very seriously, almost grimly, and let the audience pick the laughs itself." This could have been Charlotte's comedic credo. Charlotte's aspirations are certainly echoed in his statement, never fulfilled, of what he hoped to accomplish: "It is my hope ... to enter the producing field and perhaps appear in my first straight play where I will not have to depend on singing or dancing or clapping of hands to get my effects, but upon my simple ability of acting, which maybe I have, after all."[8]

Charlotte was also intent on attaining and demonstrating that "simple ability." She continued singing lessons, studying art song as well as operatic literature — Brahms' songs would remain a life-long favorite, and the book of opera arias across which she scrawled a huge "Property of Charlotte Greenwood" includes penciled check marks beside such famed mezzo-soprano arias as the *Habañera* and *Seguedilla* from Bizet's *Carmen*. As anyone who has heard Charlotte's singing can attest, she had a big voice made for belting big tunes but lacking in the lyricism and subtlety necessary for opera or art song. In this she bore a resemblance to Nora Bayes, a famous comic singer whose work Charlotte admired (among Charlotte's records was a 1920 Columbia 78 of Bayes singing two of her better known songs, "Sally Green the Village Vamp" and "The Argentines, the Portuguese and the Greeks"). Bayes' voice, while not as flexible as Charlotte's, was also a colorful contralto — an honest voice, delivered without artifice and, thus, strikingly spontaneous.

Charlotte had a comfortable top of F natural above the treble clef, and perhaps with full-time training she might have developed into a respectable operatic contralto, possibly extending to a lyric contralto. She was certainly equipped to create characterful *comprimario* or supporting roles. But it was to be her speaking voice in the theatre and in films that displayed all the nuances and colors, in comedy and in serious drama, that her singing voice lacked.

What makes Charlotte's situation all the more interesting — and poignant — is that while she evinced absolutely no illusions about her physical persona, and played on its exaggerated imperfections like cadenzas on a battered but tuneful violin, she maintained her intention to one day take the concert stage, well past the point where it was clear that her greatest qualities lay elsewhere. "I'd never try singing opera in public," she told a reporter as late as 1941, "although I'm not bad, my husband says" — which is, indeed, something her husband Martin Broones would have said.[9]

What followed the closing of *The Rogers Brothers in Panama* served as one of the first of life's attempts to show this ambitious young woman just where those gifts were, if she would only open the door and let them out into the limelight.

After Charlotte had gone the rounds of the managers' offices, proud of her earnings history — "$20 in New York and $22 on the road" — she discovered that the actor/director Sam Bernard, with his Kaiser Wilhelm-style upturned mustache, was casting for a new show.

"He wanted, among other things, a tall chorus girl to use in a measuring sequence," Charlotte recalled. "I rushed over to the office and emerged with a new contract. I was not only tall, I was thin and he expected to have a lot of fun at my expense."

The planned sketch was part of a musical show called *Nearly a Hero*. Bernard, as Ludwig Knoedler, the almost-hero of the title, was to play a tailor working in a theatre costumer's studio. He would be measuring a bevy of beautiful young women, among whom Charlotte was to serve as the unbeautiful comedy relief. As a stout small man, Bernard was the first of the short male sidekicks who would serve as comedic foil to Charlotte's towering height. He would also become the first of these little men to engage in violence with her as part of a popular comedy routine.

According to what Charlotte told Kyle Crichton of *Collier's Magazine* in 1938, one night Bernard got a little too rough with her during the measuring scene, so she pushed him; he pushed back, and she reacted by shoving him to the other side of the stage—an accident which was assumed by the audience to be a gag, and which the ever-resourceful Bernard decided to include.[10]

Regardless of what he asked her to do in his show, Charlotte was thrilled to work with the successful Bernard, and shortly afterward he came to see that the seventeen-year-old Lottie Greenwood was a decided asset in terms other than her amusing height and skinny arms. "[H]e had heard of my proclivities as an understudy," Charlotte remembered, which as usual meant that she had learned not only the parts of the stars in the show but all the rest of the parts as well, "and appointed me to that chore. It didn't increase my salary but it gave me prestige. And there was always the possibility that someone would become ill enough to miss a performance—a rare occurrence in that day and age in the theater."[11]

The star of the touring company of *Nearly a Hero* was the beautiful but flighty songstress Grace La Rue (probably playing the part of musical comedy queen Angeline DeVere, created by Ethel Levey in the Broadway production). One of the big attractions of the Ziegfeld Follies of that year (1908) and the next, La Rue had just made a success in operetta (*The Blue Moon*), and would continue as a Broadway attraction well into the early 1930s. (She popularized the song "You Made Me Love You [I Didn't Want to Do It]" in London in 1913.) What no one knew about Grace La Rue was that she was carrying on a romance with producer Byron Chandler, monikered "The Candy Kid" of Broadway, who before La Rue divorced him would produce an original musical (*Betsy*) for her in 1911. When the *Nearly a Hero* company was about to go on tour, La Rue up and eloped with Chandler, and then announced she and Chandler would sally forth on an extended honeymoon. To Bernard's fury, *Nearly a Hero* was left without its star.

"He decided to close the show," recalled Charlotte, "when I spoke up from the chorus that I knew Miss La Rue's songs and would gladly volunteer. I think Bernard accepted in the beginning in the hope that he might shame Miss La Rue into remaining with the company rather than have an awkward chorus girl take her place. She didn't react that way. She was genuinely in love, she was tired of the role, and she was eager to give someone else a chance." And besides, as Charlotte pointed out, "[S]ince Cupid can laugh at locksmiths, he can also laugh at stage managers."[12]

Living up to her name, gracious Grace stayed around long enough to show Charlotte where all her elegant gowns were and offered the services of her maid. One of the gowns, a confection in blue with a train "draped with festoons of coral beads," was the centerpiece of a show-stopping song the wistful lyrics and meaning of which would be a stock-in-trade of Charlotte's repertoire in years to come—*Gee, I Wish That I Had a Beau.*

"I donned Miss La Rue's beautiful wardrobe with definite misgivings," she remembered. "To begin with, the clothes didn't fit. Her proportions were generous, along the Lillian Russell style; mine were scant to the point of abject poverty." If there was ever a time when Charlotte could have used her infamous symmetricals from her Ned Wayburn days, this was it. But there was another problem to surmount—managing the heavy draperies and trains of La Rue's costumes. "She used to sweep onto the stage wearing a long train to her blue gown," Charlotte recalled. "As she reached the center of the stage, she would gracefully kick the train aside. I had seen her do it night after night, so I knew the business perfectly—unfortunately, I didn't know the technique."

On Charlotte's night as La Rue's stand-in (she does not state in her memoirs where this performance took place), she strode out to the middle of the stage, smiled at the audience and the conductor, and remembered everything Grace La Rue would do:

I kicked, too, a lusty kick-back, and things immediately began to happen. The train caught between my legs; I stooped to disentangle it and lost a string of beads; I tried to recapture the beads and my hat fell off. As I stooped to retrieve my hat, another string let go and rolled all over the stage. To me, the noise was deafening. The theatergoers remained deadly silent. Then the orchestra leader, seeking to cover the affair, went into the song. Not to be outdone, I came in on cue, despite the fact that I was still in a crouch. "Gee I wish that I had a Beau, like the Other Fellows Have," I chanted and the house went hysterical. This was [just] the beginning. As I tried to stand erect I discovered that my heel was caught in the bottom of my skirt and the garment was raised above my knees. I kept on singing; the orchestra continued to play; the audience shrieked with laughter; and Sam Bernard stood in the wings tearing his hair out by the roots and losing weight by the minute. He couldn't decide whether to ring down the curtain or not. If he had, it undoubtedly would have hit me on the nape of the neck. Finally, I reached the last line and stumbled toward the wings and the choleric Bernard, pausing midway to look back ruefully at the shattered string of beads. Curiously enough, I wasn't thinking of the mess I had made of my big chance so much as of the mess I had made of Miss La Rue's dress.

Then it happened — what Charlotte afterward called "the miracle." The audience burst into loud applause. Torn between Bernard screaming at her from the wings and a theatre full of appreciative patrons, Charlotte stepped back on stage for a brief curtsey, losing more beads in the process; then felt Bernard's hand reach out and pull her toward the backstage darkness.

"The applause became tumultuous," remembered Charlotte. "Then [Bernard] had a great idea. He seized my arms and went back with me for my bows, as if to reassure the audience that the comedy had been planned. He improvised ... picking up the beads, while I stood helpless. Every time I bowed I lost a fistful of coral."

The pair was called back to the stage several times. Charlotte offered another chorus of the song before finally escaping to the chorus dressing room, where she sat in the ruined dress before a mirror, makeup and tears running down her face.

"Here was my first big chance and I had muffed it," she recalled. "I would never be a star!"

Then Bernard came knocking at the door, and she was sure it was to announce that she was fired. She was to be surprised all over again. "'Crying?' he said in amazement," remembered Charlotte. "'What about? Don't you realize you took as many encores as La Rue on that number. You were great.' ... I couldn't answer him. It had been the second memorable event in my theatrical career. I had been spoken to with kindness by Eva Tanguay, and I had won praise from Sam Bernard."

Nearly a Hero had made a stage hero, and a stage personality, of Charlotte Greenwood. Not the serious chanteuse she had dreamed of being, but an elegantly dressed clown who tripped over her hem and sent her expensive hat sailing through the air. Yet it would take Charlotte another few years to understand that in comedy she had found her fame and fortune. As usual, Charlotte could only learn the hard way, especially when it came to learning from herself.[13]

This experience also gave Charlotte and another chorus girl from *Nearly a Hero* an idea for an act that was to carry them like a charge of electricity across the grid of the vaudeville circuit, from east coast to west and back again. Not only would they become one of the highest paid vaudeville duos in the nation, but once again, in the unpredictable crystal ball of the live stage, Charlotte would discover something about herself that she didn't know before, and this time she would follow where the flashing signs wanted to lead her.

7

Two Girls and a Piano

"Producers took every precaution to please every type of tired business man [and] sought to cater to all tastes in feminine pulchritude," Charlotte explains in her memoirs. "Chorus girls in those days were divided into three distinct classes — tall, stately showgirls; plump vivacious mediums; and small dancing girls, called 'ponies.'" Among the mediums was a woman named Eunice Burnham, eleven years Charlotte's senior, who besides being as plump and vivacious as a medium was supposed to be, also played the piano well.

"Like me," Charlotte adds, "she was consumed with ambition."

Whenever she wasn't on stage, Eunice was backstage practicing: "I would hear her after the performances on her way out of the theatre, when she stopped at the practice piano ... to play. Often, if I happened to be ready at the same time, I would join her and sing. We struck up a close friendship [and] finally we decided to fix up an act for ourselves." It would be "a vaudeville act, a serious act with classical music and ballads."[1]

Charlotte and Eunice went straight to a man whose life and career were already a big part of Broadway history — Fred Fisher, born Frederick Fischer to American parents in Cologne, Germany in 1875. Like Charlotte, Fisher had started on his life path quite young, with sketchy education and enormous ambition. A thirteen-year-old runaway to the German navy who later served in the French Foreign Legion, Fisher fetched up in Chicago at the turn of the century, and began to learn the piano from a tavern musician there. When Charlotte and Eunice approached Fisher in 1908, he was a Tin Pan Alley song composer who had yet to change his last name from Fischer to Fisher, and had still not scored the major song successes of his long career — "Come Josephine in My Flying Machine," "Peg o' My Heart," and "There's a Broken Heart for Every Light on Broadway" were still to come.

Clearly, had Fisher been as famous in 1908 as he was to become in a few years, he would not have had the time for these two obscure chorus girls with a need for an act but no idea how to form it. But with his help and some of his songs, "we worked out a routine, selected material and prepared between seasons to try our stuff," Charlotte recalled. "We called ourselves the Fisher Sisters, for no particular reason unless it was in compliment to our master, Fred Fisher."

Though not yet under the wing of an agent, the Fisher Sisters opened at the Dewey Theater on 14th Street, and something of the fare they offered can be seen in bit of routine Charlotte remembered and inserted into an early version of her memoirs. "The act went well enough [there]," Charlotte wrote, noting however that the Dewey Theatre patrons were not the most exacting sort. But the structure of the patter exchanged by the two women — pointing up Charlotte's height, for the most part, and her other physical characteristics — would become part of the Greenwood legend:

> BURNHAM (AT THE UPRIGHT PIANO): You've got something there.
>   What price your bleached blond hair?
> GREENWOOD: This hair cost me $2.98.
>   Bought and placed it there. [*At which point* CHARLOTTE *would begin pulling off blond pin curls and tossing them into the audience*—that they and, by extension, CHARLOTTE, *were* blonde is interesting of itself, since she did not go platinum full-time until the mid–1920s]
> TOGETHER: Scandal, scandal! What do you think of that?
> GREENWOOD: I used to think some time ago
>   That you were quite petite.
> BURNHAM: I'd like to say the same of you
>   But I chanced to see your feet.
> GREENWOOD: Leaving off the jest, my dear,
>   Of something else we'll talk
> BURNHAM: But if you left off your feet,
>   However would you walk?
> TOGETHER: Scandal, scandal! What do you think of that?[2]

After securing the services of agent Joe Wood, the Fisher Sisters, who after a while had changed their name to "Two Girls and a Piano," began to work every small circuit that would book them, their only prop an upright piano. "It was the beginning," wrote Charlotte, "of a long, arduous and often heartbreaking apprenticeship." They played "Western vaudeville, Butterfield time, Independent houses, Pleasure Bay for Joe Schenck [later head of Metro-Goldwyn-Mayer], Junior Orpheum — three and four shows a day — trying new songs, changing arrangers."

When Charlotte got word from Joe Wood that he had been able to book the duo at what to her was the holy of holies, Hammerstein's Victoria on Broadway, she was speechless. "Remembering how I had looked from our rooms in the Time Square hotel right into the dressing rooms at Hammerstein's — I wondered if I would perchance have the same room. It all seemed too easy now, the hard work was over. 'Two Girls and a Piano' had definitely arrived."[3]

With all the optimism that had once sent her walking toward Grand Central Terminal without knowing where it was, Charlotte engaged elegant and fashionable actress/modiste Clara Bloodgood, who showed off great style if not acting in the light comedies popular at the time, to make gowns for herself and Eunice.

Bloodgood also gave Charlotte some lessons that she never forgot in what sort of fashion statement works best for the tall woman: "Tall girls should use plain fabrics instead of patterned materials; but if they must have patterns they should be large ones — flowers and figures." Anyone who has studied the costumes made for Charlotte by top designers for films can see that more than a little of Clara Bloodgood's wise advice was part of every outfit they made for Charlotte Greenwood.

Even before they were worn, the gowns Bloodgood made for Charlotte and Eunice received plaudits. "Eunice chose grey and silver," recalled Charlotte, "and I picked blue and gold.... When they were finished, Joe Wood hung them up in his office to impress his other acts." On one occasion Wood had sent the gowns over to the office of high-powered female agent Jennie Jacobs, who harangued much better known clients by pointing to the gowns and saying: "If you two could get a wardrobe like this, perhaps I could get you some decent book-ings. These girls have brains."

In clotheshorse terms, a new era in Charlotte's career had begun. But like one of her characters, she suffered the sad comedy of being all dressed up with no place to go.

> We went to the [Victoria] well ahead of curtain time. I was hoping that we might be assigned one of those dressing rooms into which I used to gaze across the alley from the Royal Arms. It would provide a sentimental bridge across the years. We stopped in front of the theater to examine our billings and had our first shock. There was no mention! Back stage, Big Mike Simon, the stage man-ager, explained that it wasn't the practice to bill try-out acts. This was the second blow. Joe Wood had neglected to mention that we were doing a try-out. He had taken it for granted that we knew.... There was no thought of rushing home in tears, however. Two years had taught me a great many things. I now knew how to take the thorns with the roses. The show must go on, and so did we, first on the bill!

On Sunday, September 26, 1909, "Two Girls and a Piano" performed in the least respectable place on the bill, at the very top, before a Victoria Theatre full of mostly empty seats — one per-formance was all a try-out was entitled to. They were followed by singer Gracie Emmett (con-sidered something of a star), the comic William "Billy" Gould, and dancer/singer Pat Rooney and wife Marion Brent (Rooney's big hit was a song called "You Be My Ootsie, I'll Be Your Tootsie"). In short, Charlotte and Eunice were quickly got out of the way.

After it was over, the young women "oozed out of Hammerstein's Victoria and got con-veniently lost in the 42nd Street crowd." Yet going back to the small time gigs proved far more valuable for Charlotte than any number of performances at the Victoria would have done. She didn't yet know it, but the Victoria had rejected her not because she was not yet ready for the big time houses but because she had not yet discovered herself. This process of revelation would come, as usual, in the public sphere of small theatres scattered across the country, as two girls and their traveling upright realized they had a jewel tucked down inside their battered luggage.[4]

After playing Chicago's Majestic for one performance before being refused by its man-ager, Lyman Glover, on the basis of what he considered "risqué" lyrics, Charlotte and Eunice were booked into an obscure house in Wichita, Kansas; and during the performance Char-lotte did something half-unconsciously that would have enormous ramifications for her career. "I forgot the advice I learned as a chorus soloist with the Rogers Brothers and accidentally tossed in a gesture with my long arm during a sentimental song." At almost six feet in height, Charlotte was not only taller than her partner, Eunice, but as tall as or taller than many men in the audience. Her long face, long arms and long legs made her appear when in motion, as one critic would later put it, like "an animated Beardsley drawing." Clothing all these lengthy appendages in elegant gowns only pointed up their comic length. But caught up in her song, Charlotte could not be expected to observe a dignified stillness.

"When the audience saw that long, spindling wing of mine swing upward like a pump handle," she recorded, "they laughed!"

> Humiliated, I quickly brought my arm down again and stood through the rest of the performance as stiff and firm as a stalk of asparagus. We made our exit to more than the usual amount of applause, but in our dressing room I collapsed in tears. Somehow this seemed the last straw. Not only were we failures but I was right back where I started from. People were laughing at me again. Eunice took

a different viewpoint. We had covered about all the territory available to as, in the words of Balieff of the Chauve Souris, "sinkers of sat sonks." If audiences wanted to laugh at us, she argued, why not encourage them? I finally agreed. Why not? We had nothing to lose.

"In that decision," Charlotte wrote, "I had learned the most valuable lesson of my career — that of subjugating self. I was ready for a career as a clown."

The newly remade "Two Girls and a Piano" as comic act caught on quickly. "It was something new for audiences to see two girls come out for a pianologue of quiet dignity only to find that the tall one was awfully funny when she waved her arms in sentimental gestures.... At once we began to get better reports from the managers and, as a consequence, better bookings and more money."

"Some of my best bits of comedy came about through accident," Charlotte wrote. Another intimation that the clownish god of comedy was knocking at the door of Charlotte's dressing room came at the Heilig Theatre in Portland, Oregon, an elegant house at Southwest Taylor and Broadway rumored to have the biggest stage west of Chicago.

"Two Girls and a Piano" was billed right after an animal act called "Fink's Mules," in which the animals were put through various routines, wearing costumes and other gear to ratchet up the laughter. By this time, Charlotte had incorporated some dance steps of her own into her act, as well as some impromptu arm swinging, which took her away from Eunice and the piano toward all parts of the stage.

"[E]verything was too ducky for words when I started to go into my high kicking dance," she recalled. "Suddenly to my horror, I realized that one of the mules had been untidy; I also realized that I was on the floor with what folks used to call a crick in my back." No one, even Eunice, seemed to realize that Charlotte was almost paralyzed with pain (and probably lying in mule urine); everyone was laughing uproariously, believing the fall part of the act, just as the audiences had done when Grace La Rue's beaded gown had gone out of control.

> As the laughter mounted, I wondered how I could get off the stage without disclosing that I was really hurt. Finally I crawled off with mock dignity, virtually dragging myself to the wings. This was the introduction to the "Camel Walk" that eventually became a Greenwood trademark.[5]

Charlotte was to refine the "Camel Walk," which basically was nothing more than a straight-legged crawl with hands and feet flat to the floor, at New Jersey's Pleasure Bay, run by Joe and Nicholas Schenck, again as a quasi-graceful escape from an accident. Because the stage was surrounded by water, on which boats were always running in the passage between the audience and the outdoor stage, "[I]t was imperative that the actor exaggerate his every gesture. I was in my element."

"In making my leaps in the song called 'The Kangaroo Hop,'" Charlotte remembered, "I misjudged my distance, overstepped myself and landed in a heap. Fortunately, I wasn't hurt." Recalling the incident at Portland's Heilig Theatre, Charlotte blended the mishap into the act. "The audience welcomed the stunt with open arms, and by the time I finished I had worked in the splits and 'Two Girls and a Piano' had definitely turned into a comedy act." In one newspaper photo preserved in Charlotte's scrapbooks at USC, she is shown doing the splits, in her Clara Bloodgood gown, atop Eunice's upright piano, Eunice winking up at her — very different from the way the act had started out.

Charlotte was learning to accept the inevitable. As she wrote later:

> I was fully acquainted with the nettles that go hand in glove with the roses. I decided that if I were to be a clown, I would create the character and let the character speak for itself — not the freak. So I set

about the mastering of countless details and the elimination of false notes, premature entrances, elaborate gestures, inappropriate inflections, bad timing — the many eliminations that make up theater technique.[6]

Charlotte concentrated with Eunice on making "Two Girls and a Piano" the best show it could be; soon they were asked to replace a poor act at New York's Fifth Avenue Theatre, where they played to acclaim. "We were a sensation," Charlotte recalled. "'Mike O'Shea, the vaudeville king of Upper New York State and Eastern Canada, who always had his eye out for new material, promptly booked us at $350 a week ... the highest price ever paid for a sister team at that time. Things were beginning to break," she added.

What Charlotte might have said was that things were beginning to break for her rather than for Eunice. Having rejected an offer from A.L. Erlanger to play in the London company of *The Pink Lady*, being less willing to break up the act than to part with Eunice, Charlotte continued with Two Girls and a Piano until it became clear that the duo had done as much as it could.

"[W]e finally reached our decision at Henderson's on Coney Island," remembered Charlotte. "The piano fairly swirled around in an ocean of tears at our last performance. Vaudeville had taken us both out of the ranks and expanded on our individual talents"— but it was clearly Charlotte's talents that needed more room to expand. After Eunice went her own way, eventually setting up in another duo with Charles Irwin,[7] Charlotte was left without even the support she had had when she first got her foot on the stage.[8]

"I was almost as much a stranger in New York as I was on that fateful day when I checked in from Norfolk," she wrote. Her mother had remarried (to James Reilly, a bartender from New York) and had moved to another state. "I didn't even have Max Hoffman and Gertie at my side. I began to think in terms of another partner when I was saved the trouble, and from a very unexpected source."

A call came one morning from Lee and J.J. Shubert, who with brother Sam held ownership of over one hundred playhouses and had booking connections at over a thousand theatres across the United States. The sons of poor Jewish immigrants, the Shubert brothers were what Charlotte respectfully calls "theatrical powers," noting that when she arrived at their offices in response to the telephoned summons, both Lee and J.J. were waiting for her. "They were friendly and courteous," she writes, somewhat carefully. "There was nothing of the ruthless czars in their attitude."

Politenesses over quickly, the Shuberts got down to business. They told Charlotte they admired her work and would like to hire her, if she were free. Charlotte, who had never been freer than at this moment, listened while they asked her "would I be interested in 'The Passing Show of 1912?'"

> Needless to say, I walked back to my hotel on eggs and indulged myself in a good cry. At last I had come to the end of the long road toward success. The Holy Grail of Broadway acclaim was finally at my fingertips.[9]

8

The Passing Show of 1912

"THE YEAR OF 1912 was destined to be a red letter one for me," Charlotte wrote. "Max Hoffman had been right — the theater was proving a more exacting master than school had been, but the rewards were sweet."[1]

For the New York theatre world as a whole, 1911–1912 had been something less than the red-letter variety, with but two dozen new American production mountings and a little over half dozen as many imports from abroad. As it does today, under such conditions Broadway fell back on revivals, of which the operettas of Gilbert and Sullivan made a particularly healthy showing.[2]

But the Shubert brothers, as usual, had something up their sleeves. In 1911 they built the theatre which, in Charlotte's words, introduced them and their new venue to the theatre world in a typically big way. Located between 50th and 51st Streets and Broadway, the Winter Garden, seating over 1,600 people, was "devoted to novel, international, spectacular and musical entertainments" in an elegantly appointed atmosphere:

> During the intermissions the audience is invited to make use of the spacious promenoir in the rear of the theatre and the lounging spaces and White Room, which are on the balcony floor.... The White Room, with accommodations at table for several hundred persons, overlooks Broadway and Seventh Avenue. It is a veritable summer garden, in that all sides are open. Here one may pass the interval quaffing a refreshing drink while listening to the Lounge Orchestra, which plays there only during intermissions.

For those unwilling to crease their gowns or reduce their fullest possible social exposure by sitting at the marble-topped tables in the White Room, the Shuberts had provided an area where drinks and "dainty" edibles could be partaken. In addition, "girl attendants" served lemonades in the balcony and orchestra areas during intermission.[3]

As for the "novel, international, spectacular" shows promised by the Shuberts, the Passing Show of 1912 was indeed of a grandiosity matching their new theatre. Eighteen years before, George Lederer's Passing Show, produced at the Casino in 1894, gave birth to the first American revue, which the *New York Times* described as "a kind of entertainment little known in this country.... It is a review, in dramatic form, of the chief events of the past year — political, historical and theatrical."

In his Passing Show, with its cast of 100, Lederer had poked fun at a pair of recent Pinero plays; in one sketch, "Round the Opera in Twenty Minutes," he grouped characters from operas of Wagner, Bizet, Leoncavallo and others in one manic ensemble; in others, news and celebrities of the day were spoofed without mercy. The concept caught on immediately, and the show had a long run; a lengthy tour followed its closing.[4]

The Shuberts' Passing Show, while built along similar lines to Lederer's "review," was not connected, being more inspired by the brothers' grudging admiration for the success of Florenz Ziegfeld's Follies and by their dislike of Ziegfeld himself, whose connection with producers Klaw and Erlanger, the Shuberts' inveterate enemies, they could not forgive. The Shuberts' show featured a two-part program. Part I, called "The Ballet of 1830," was what was then called a "mimo-dramatic ballet in three scenes," which had played London's Alhambra Theatre for eight months and had a light plot involving Bohemians in early 19th century Paris. Among the characters were an Henri Murger-like male character named Rodolphe, a female named Mariette, the inevitable slumming Baron, an operetta-like character called The Vampire Girl, and various "Painters, Midinettes, Members of the Wedding Party, Flower Girls, Etc.," all against the telling settings of "The Studio," "Restaurant de Nuit," and "Jardin des Amoureux."[5]

The evening's second half brought in a whole gang of players, both the famous, the infamous, the to-be-famous and the never-famous, in two acts set against the harsher background of "Pier of the S.S. Cleveland," "Greeley Square, New York," "The Harem of Sewer-Man," and "The Bought and Paid for House," in risqué spoofs of current and past plays and comedies.

The show swayed dizzily from highfalutin *La bohème* references in Part I while Part II displayed much in the tradition of Weber and Fields with a dash of Follies glamour thrown in: elegantly (when not naughtily) costumed young chorus girls, a scene set in a harem, another on the liner *S.S. Cleveland*, a wedding set to ragtime music. Charlotte was cast throughout Act I (as Fanny Silly to Sydney Grant's Jimmy Gilley and Maid of the Harem to Grant's Chief Eunuch) and in two scenes of Act II (again as Fanny to Grant's Jimmy). She sang "Girlish Laughter" and "The Kangaroo Hop" (a hold over from her act with Eunice Burnham), replete with hops, kicks and Camel Walk, and performed two duets with Sydney Grant: "Modern Love" and "It's All Over Now." Charlotte had perfected the high kick (what she termed "leg lift") for which she would become so famous, because she is depicted in the program lifting a leg as daintily as her white lace gown would allow her to do — which was pretty high for a New York which had just (in May) witnessed a great parade of suffragettes showing not the slightest hint of ankle beneath their crisp white gowns.[6]

No life of Charlotte Greenwood would be complete without some discussion of how and when her famous "kick" became part of her act, and thanks to *San Francisco Chronicle* critic Ralph E. Renaud, who interviewed Charlotte and Eunice in 1912, we have the kick's genesis in Charlotte's own words and the best description of it that I have ever read. "All good vaudevillians search for an act with 'a kick in it,' as they express it," wrote Renaud in February 1912. "The act concocted by Charlotte Greenwood and [Eunice] Burnham has a kick in it that, so far as any recollection of vaudeville is concerned, has never been approached on O'Farrell Street."

This kick, like the whole family of kicks, starts at the floor, but instead of displaying the family trait of swift aspiration into the air, it rises quietly and carelessly until the leg is level, then continues to mount upward with the same easy assurance until the toe is poised somewhere in the upper atmosphere over Miss Greenwood's head. "Tell me, Miss Greenwood, how you developed that kick?" "Well," she responded, "we have a line in our opening song about 'then you touch the scales.' I used to raise my foot a little, just for some kind of gesture. Somehow or other it kept getting higher and higher, until finally — well, I'm all up in the air. People said I couldn't do it without being suggestive — but I can."[7]

Charlotte starts a career of high kicks in this illustration from the opening night program of *The Passing Show of 1912*. The program shown here was Charlotte's own copy. William Luce collection.

As with the Camel walk, accident, experiment and a remarkably limber set of joints and tendons went into the kick that was to become Charlotte's trademark until her mid–60s, and the highlight of a performance style that Russian Realist Constantine Stanislavsky might have been describing when he defined theatre of the grotesque as "vivid, external, audacious justification of enormous inner content ... so all-embracing as to verge on exaggeration."[8]

The Winter Garden's magnificent curtain would rise on the Passing Show on July 22, 1912, a few days before Charlotte's twenty-second birthday, and even as the show itself and the theatre it inaugurated would make history, so was the occasion the real beginning of Charlotte's professional career. (Luck also played a part in getting the Passing Show of 1912 off the ground: because Ziegfeld's show *A Winsome Widow* was doing so well, Ziegfeld opted to hold off till the fall to bring out a new Follies, which gave the Shuberts the summer opening they needed.)[9]

"At last I was in important company," Charlotte wrote in her memoir notes. "Jobyna Howland, William and Eugene Howard, Oscar Schwartz, who subsequently won fame under the name of Oscar Shaw, Trixie Friganza, Hilarion Ceballos who later shortened his first name to Larry and made history as a producer; Ernest Hare who, teamed with Ernie Jones, wrote a colorful chapter in the annals of radio as 'The Happiness Boys'; Sidney [sic] Grant who was to be my comedy team-mate in a great many plays."

During the rehearsal period Charlotte saw none of her co-stars. In a dozen or more rehearsal halls scattered across town, each of the big numbers was blocked and rehearsed by an army of assistant directors, with the Shubert brothers poking their heads in every day. When the general rehearsal finally arrived and everyone was gathered at the Winter Garden, Charlotte looked out at the empty seats and saw one of them filled with a familiar figure — Ned Wayburn, "still wearing his ornamental sweaters, still bedecked with his silver whistle." Wayburn himself had come a long way since the days of *The White Cat*, and had been tapped by the Shuberts to stage their monster production.

For her part, Charlotte was in a daze of bliss for the first few days and happy to be working again with Wayburn, his past enormities toward her forgotten. "The veterans were kind to the youngsters," she remembered, "as veterans in the theater invariably are, and we were one large happy family. We practiced incessantly, rehearsals starting early in the morning and continuing until all hours. Costumes were fitted, songs were arranged, comedy routines manufactured and altered, and the clocks drove us relentlessly toward dress rehearsal."

"By this time," she remembered, "it was [Wayburn's] habit to perch in the topmost peak of the gallery during rehearsals and watch the show. He felt that if he could see and hear everything from this pinnacle, he had done his best by his customers; and he was a stickler for clarity of speech."

As I finished my first song, feeling very well pleased with myself, the whistle shrilled. It sent icy shivers down my spine and in a twinkling I was back at the New Amsterdam as that tall Japanese in "The White Cat." There was deadly silence for a moment. I strained my eyes to see what was happening in the gallery. Wayburn, who had a fine sense of the dramatic, was making a leisurely descent to the lower floor.

You could hear his feet in a measured clump-clump tread. Each footfall crushed me. Finally he reached the last row in the orchestra section and came slowly and majestically forward like an avenging god bent on the destruction of a muddling mortal. With each leisurely step, he hurled imprecations at me.

"I don't know what you're here for," clump-clump. "The Shuberts are intelligent men." Clump-clump. "They evidently had some idea that you could do something." Clump-clump. "They must have been told you had talent." Clump-clump. "Else you wouldn't be here." Clump-clump. "Or be getting this salary." Clump-clump. "But I don't know how the public is going to find out unless they can hear you."

As he stood directly in front of Charlotte, Wayburn added, "I can *see* you all right MISS Greenwood.... But that is not quite enough, MISS Greenwood. I'll be damned if I can *hear* you, MISS Greenwood."

"With that," Charlotte recalled, "he turned and stomped back into the dark of the auditorium again, leaving me dissolved in tears. They dripped onto my blouse as I stood there frozen in my tracks."

The conductor tapped his bow on the stand and the music started. Charlotte sang her song again, several times, crying more with each repetition, and with each repeat "from the cavern in front came the single bellow: '*Louder!*'" When Wayburn was satisfied that Charlotte could be heard from the very top of the gods, his whistle shrieked and the company was dismissed.[10]

Charlotte was devastated. "I shrugged off the comforting pats of the older members of the company," she remembered, "avoided the eyes of my erstwhile comrades in the chorus, and went blubbering home to my hotel. I was through in the theater! All that I had worked and slaved to accomplish was being tossed overboard. My life as an actress had begun with Wayburn and it was ending with Wayburn."

Then the anger began to build. As she walked along the dark streets, barely cooling after a hot July day, Charlotte stopped slumping and started stamping. "I was almost home now, nearly in the haven of my own room," and it was all she could do not to turn around and march back to the theatre, where Wayburn was surely still barking orders to the production crew, and show him how little she could be pushed around.

> Who was this Wayburn to humiliate me in front of the entire company? ... The more I thought of it, the snappier my imaginary retorts became. Before I was through mulling the question, I had the mighty Wayburn groveling in the dust before me, abject in his apologies, rather appealing in his humility, begging me not to report his insolence to the Shuberts — my intimate, personal friends! Cold rage was replacing hysterics. I'd show this whipper snapper with his tin whistle and his rah-rah boy sweaters! ... Why, the ears of the gallery gods would be ringing when I finished my number. Day after tomorrow, I'd be the toast of Broadway; critics would write paeans of praise about the lovely young vocalist who had such clarity of speech and tone.

"And to my utter astonishment," added Charlotte, "that's exactly what happened."[11]

After opening night, Charlotte hurried to find the critics' notices in the papers — she was never one of those performers who disdained reviews or reviewers, from the beginning of her career till its end — and there found herself "singled out from all that cast of important people for special mention."

> The critics liked "The Poor Working Goil." They liked the willowy blond who sang it. There was talk that she was a new "find" and Wayburn, of all people, was publicly congratulated for discovering her. Later, some of the critics, spurred on by the canny A. Toxen Worm, chief press agent of the Shuberts, recalled that this Greenwood had made her first Broadway appearance in Wayburn's "The White Cat." So I was heralded as a Wayburn protégée who had been carefully groomed for a surprise appearance on Broadway. Interviewers called to see me; old friends looked me up; the company shared delightedly in my success; and I began to be invited to parties. Life was opening up for me and only one hand was withheld from me. Wayburn never mentioned the incident of the rehearsal and appeared to take my minor triumph for granted.

Wayburn can't entirely be blamed for wanting to share a little of the acclaim that came Charlotte's way, particularly when it was as enthusiastic as what one critic [probably the distinguished Henry Taylor Parker] wrote in the *Boston Evening Transcript*:

> The one person, very much out of the ordinary, was lanky Charlotte Greenwood, of the long limber arms and those marvelous legs which she raises and lowers in great stiff sweeps like solemn semaphores. When the end came, with a racing shadowgraph of the whole company behind a white curtain, Miss Greenwood's shade stood pensive as a stork and waved us a sad farewell in a characteristic manner.[12]

Charlotte did have something to thank Wayburn for, however, despite his abuse of her at the general rehearsal. "In all the years that have passed," Charlotte noted, "no theatergoer has ever complained of being unable to hear or understand anything I ever said on the stage, with or without the use of a public address system. And I had the good grace," she added, "from the first to be thankful rather than resentful to Ned Wayburn for a most valuable lesson."

In fact, Charlotte was to finally come face to face with Wayburn in later years and express those thanks to him, only to be shooed away, though with better humor than his past behavior had given her reason to expect.

> "I didn't have time to take you aside and discuss the matter quietly," he chuckled. "I had to drive it home the hard way and in a hurry. I knew from experience that if I made you mad enough, you'd deliver...."
>
> Instead of being my Nemesis, Wayburn was really my Mentor. Critics today may be privileged to say that I'm not "good," but they never can justly accuse me of not being "loud." The Wayburn incident also taught me a valuable lesson in the judging of people. How often we make that same mistake in life, failing to understand something that is done for our own good, resenting the help that is offered to us, brushing aside the well-intentioned because their advice doesn't suit us at the moment.[13]

Charlotte also eased into trust of her fellow performers — the veterans who had tried to comfort her, the chorus girls who had tactfully looked away when she had turned tear-filled eyes to them. Trixie Friganza became not just a friend but in the near future became Charlotte's neighbor on Long Island; but it was Jobyna Howland, sister of Olin Howland, with whom Charlotte would costar in future productions, that Charlotte took to most closely and knew the longest.

Part of the attraction was Jobyna's height: "She was a giant of a woman, given to heavy makeup and the grand manner, and her constant companions were two small griffin dogs, so small that together they didn't make one dog." A strikingly fashionable woman said to have been illustrator Charles Dana Gibson's original "Gibson Girl," Jobyna also shared with Charlotte the same reverence for actress Lillian Russell: when the latter's "intimate personal belongings, jewelry, laces, handbags, furs" were put up for auction, both actresses were there, Jobyna buying "a lot of 63 small baroque pearls with gold linked chains" for the not inconsiderable sum of $180, according to the *New York Times* of December 16, 1922.

"She was a grand person with a great sense of humor and, like most large people, a slave to sentiment," Charlotte recalled. When Charlotte and Olin Howland were performing several years later in *Linger Longer Letty*, Jobyna came back stage after the curtain had fallen on what Charlotte describes as "a particularly sticky sentimental scene. Tears had caused her mascara to run down her jowls: 'Children,' she cried, 'you were magnificent — simply magnificent! The theater has two great artists.' Fortunately neither Olin Howland nor I were duped by Jobyna's enthusiasm."

Charlotte was to see the great lady again many years and a continent's breadth later, "sweeping through the Westmore cosmetic shop in Hollywood, the two little griffins or their counterparts trailing her. I said, 'Jobyna, shouldn't you watch out for those puppies?' 'My dear,' she fluted, with a grand gesture toward her canine escort, 'following me is a protection.'" Anyone who has seen Charlotte's ocean liner-like society hostesses or other such magnificent women of leisure can assume that more than a little of grandly draped Jobyna Howland went into the ever resourceful Greenwood storehouse of characterizations.[14]

9

The Birth of Letty

"IT IS EXTREMELY DIFFICULT to follow a hit with a hit," Charlotte wrote; and in her case, she followed the hit of the Passing Show of 1912 with two quite tame successors. After 136 performances, the first Passing Show closed down and Charlotte was hired for the cast of Franz Lehár's new operetta, *The Man with Three Wives*. Produced by the Shuberts, the show opened in January 1913 at the Weber and Fields Music Hall and closed 52 performances later, without making much of a splash — so much for Charlotte's first foray into the almost-opera of operetta, a failure she significantly does not address in any detail in her recollections.

Exactly a year after the first Passing Show had put Charlotte's name on everyone's lips and party invitations, six months after the Lehár premiere she went into the Passing Show of 1913, and from the very beginning, at least to Charlotte, the production gave every indication "that it was destined to be a dud," she wrote in her memoirs. "Nothing went right — the songs were mediocre, the jokes didn't ring true; the sketches were dull.... We opened under the most harrowing difficulties. It is still a sort of nightmare to me."

Possibly what most irked Charlotte about this Passing Show was its bald effort at dropping all pretense of "culture" and aiming straight for more traditional means of entertaining its audiences — meaning that it relied heavily on burlesque and on a story line derivative of a real hit show, *Peg o' My Heart*, in which Peg sets sail for American shores to learn how to dance the Turkey Trot. Charlotte still held to aspirations for herself that did not exclude the art song and the recital stage, and the newest Passing Show would have seemed to her especially childish and awkward after the style and cultural allusiveness of the first.

"Wayburn was producing," she recalled, "but I was not longer afraid of him"—he was, in fact, struggling with the material at hand as much as Charlotte was and just as worried about whether it would succeed. Charlotte had also just joined Actors Equity, as one of its charter members. Founded on May 13, 1913, the labor union for stage performers was intended to prevent their exploitation in terms financial and artistic and to bring working hours and conditions in line with professional standards. Charlotte may have been feeling the strength of union numbers as she became pickier about the roles she performed and more critical of the roles she had accepted.

Charlotte's reference to "harrowing difficulties" certainly applies to the mayhem of opening night, at the Winter Garden on July 24, 1913. "Just before the theater was due to open — the first nighters were already in the lobby — Wayburn ordered them held outside while he made drastic changes in the shape and form of the show," remembered Charlotte — not exactly circumstances guaranteed to put the cast at ease. "Wayburn cracked out his orders — cut this, cut that, eliminate this, change that entrance." Then his piercing eye landed on Charlotte. Wayburn abruptly announced to her that she was to follow up a ballet number, originally danced by ballerina Bessie Clayton, in which she would have to descend two-hundred steps meant to replicate the stairs of the Capitol building in Washington D.C., which stretched from the footlights up to where the flats hung above the stage.[1]

"Charlotte," Wayburn told the astonished young woman, "get up to the costume department and see if they have a ballet costume that is something like Bessie's. I want you to follow her number — the orchestra will repeat the music — and do a burlesque dance down the stairs."

"My heart sank," Charlotte recalled. "A dance without a single rehearsal before a wise New York audience and the critics. This was really something!"

All the costume department had was a wrinkled ballet tutu and a top that there was no time to iron. "I grabbed it and raced away."

> When I got [the costume] on and mounted to the top of the stairs I felt — and looked — like a drowned chicken. There was no fluff to the dress; it hung lumpily around my skinny legs; and those stairs looked interminable. Fortunately I am not subject to vertigo. I started down on the cue doing a makeshift burlesque ballet that met with immediate approval from the patrons. They thought it very funny; I didn't feel funny at all. I was perspiring so freely that the dead white liquid body makeup we used to use in those days was dripping from my fingertips as I gamboled down the [Capitol] steps.[2]

The ballet sequence and the disorganized nature of the Passing Show of 1913 proved to be one of the many ironies of Charlotte's career — a last minute addition which she was sure would fail, it proved one of her biggest successes. Yet she never had another chance to use it. And her unhappiness with the Passing Show — and perhaps with the tyrannical Wayburn — drove her finally to speak to the Shubert brothers. "[I] asked for my release," she wrote in her memoir notes. "Strange talk from a girl who had broken her neck, virtually, to get a foothold in New York. [J.J.] agreed, if I could find a better job." Herein lay another irony, because while the job Charlotte found was not a whole lot better than the one she was leaving, it was to bring her to the California coast and a role which was to alter her own professional destiny.

Just before the Passing Show closed, Charlotte was hired by California impresario Oliver Morosco to star in a musical version of L. Frank Baum's *The Tik-Tok Man of Oz*, as Queen Ann Soforth of the Oogaboos, the ambitious Amazon set on conquering the world. Though the show started off in St. Louis before progressing to the west coast, before it had been there very long Charlotte would leave it as she had left the Passing Show of 1913 to vanquish her own Emerald City: Los Angeles, the scene of many more of her stage triumphs than Broadway would ever be. And she would give birth to a character who in various permutations and costumes would keep her in business for the next quarter-century.

"I had been West before," Charlotte remembered in her memoirs, "but only as a small time vaudeville performer. This time, although I was not aware of it at first, I was to achieve greater success than I had ever known." Helping her do this was a somewhat eccentric but always imaginative producer with the vaguely magician-like name of Oliver Morosco.

Morosco was not Oliver's real name — that he took, as if an adopted son, from his "theatrical father," Walter Morosco, operator of a dance-hall theatre and circus in San Francisco in the last quarter of the nineteenth century. Born in Logan, Utah, in June 1875, Oliver Mitchell was the son of Esmah Badourah Montrose and one "Sir John Leslie Mitchell ... a titled Englishman ... a distinguished barrister and penman of Birmingham, England," a possibly fictional character whom his mother was said to have left suddenly one night, packing up her sons Leslie and Oliver and heading for California. How Esmah, the New England-born daughter of a Mr. Montrose and a member of the solidly yeoman Crockett family, met and married this titled Englishman, and what became of him after she left him, was clearly never of much interest to Morosco, because he passively declares that "[I] have been able to learn little about him." Perhaps this was because there was not much more to learn.

To complete the surreality of "Lady" Mitchell pulling up stakes overnight in Logan and embarking for points west, Esmah seems to have stopped in the featureless wastes of the Central Valley oil town of Bakersfield and purchased a hotel, which she then operated on her own before marrying a second time (as widow? divorcée?) to a man who Morosco describes in his memoirs as possibly worse than her first. It was with this husband, named (perhaps pseudonymously by Morosco) Joseph St. Mary, that Esmah and her growing family moved to San Francisco.

Thus was launched Oliver Morosco's own career, first in Walter Morosco's circus and many rungs up the show business ladder, progressing eventually to producer of some of the country's most successful shows and owner of some of its most successful theatres. A man of sweetly boyish features, Morosco had a tiger's instinct for the scent of fresh kill, in his case the spilled blood of audience interest in a particular fad or star, and he promoted and exploited his products and performers to the utmost.[3]

Morosco had first been interested in Baum's *Tik-Tok Man of Oz* through the music of Louis F. Gottschalk, which the composer played for him one day at Morosco's Burbank Theatre. The script itself came before the book — ample evidence, as if more were needed, of Baum's all-embracing fascination with the fantasy not just of words but of the stage, of film and a combination of all three. Born near Syracuse in 1856 to a wealthy oil family, Baum showed an early interest in the stage and acted in stock company productions in his teens under an assumed name; he also briefly took over the management of a chain of what were euphemistically called "opera houses" that his father owned. He also ran a printing press his father bought him, and later discovered bliss in the writing of plays. For one of these, a play with songs called *The Maid of Arran*, Baum wrote words and music, produced and directed and played the male lead. He was a handsome young man, tall and slender with a pleasant baritone singing voice. Always seeking, like Morosco, those greener pastures, Baum ended up a married man with children in the wastes of Kansas (Dorothy Gale territory, one must note), running a variety store and the local newspaper in Aberdeen; he later moved the family to Chicago, working there as a reporter and supporting his family through a variety of other oddball means, including peddling chinaware through the Midwest.

Only in the 1890s did Baum's genius as fantasy writer, borne out of the stories he told his sons, begin to come to fruition in ink and paper. The result was his several books about the Land of Oz, with its population of half a million and its capital, the Emerald City, with its nearly 10,000 buildings and complete lack of illness or despair. Only there did the animals talk, and were treated with all the respect of fellow human beings. For a free spirit like Baum, it should come as no surprise that in Oz, no police force was ever necessary.[4]

For Oliver Morosco, Gottschalk's music "carried me away to the mystical land of gnomes and fairies," and that was all it took for him to suspect it would do the same for children and their ticket-buying parents. "I signed a contract for the peerless child's extravaganza, *Tik-Tok of Oz*." Even at the time, he had in mind who he wanted to play Queen Ann Soforth: he had seen her performing with Sydney Grant at the Winter Garden in New York City. But Morosco the farseeing had even greater plans for Charlotte.

"The girl, Charlotte Greenwood, was exceptionally tall," recalled Morosco in his memoirs, "while her partner, Sidney Grant, was no more than five feet two inches in height. Mindful of the motto: 'In show business, make them laugh and you make money,' I reasoned that a good play built around that team would be a triumphant winner."[5] After signing Charlotte on, Morosco took *Tik-Tok* first to St. Louis, moving on to Los Angeles, where the show opened in 1913. Baum was involved in the production, having already had a success with a musical stage version of *The Wizard*, and with a cast composed not just of Charlotte but of James Morton as the copper-sided Tik-Tok and Frank Moore as the Shaggy Man, the show did well. It was, however, Baum's final successful turn on the stage, and he died six years later, long before the making of that Hollywood standard and MGM Technicolor goldmine, *The Wizard of Oz*.[6]

"California was in holiday garb" when Charlotte arrived, she remembered, "and with good reason. The state was entertaining two world fairs, the famous Panama-Pacific Exposition in San Francisco; and the San Diego World's Fair in that beautiful southern City."

There was no Hollywood, per se, in 1913; "it was Los Angeles in those days. Hollywood was merely a suburb, which was being turned steadily, relentlessly from an orange grove into a city of drama and dreams. The names of Cecil B. DeMille, Jesse Lasky, B.P. Schulberg, Mary and Doug, Charlie Chaplin, were becoming household words. To most of us in the theater, however, the movies were still something of a toy. Ours was the dignified profession." She was to change that opinion in just a few years, but for the moment the stage was truly where Charlotte's future lay, as she was also to discover shortly.[7]

The "good play" that Morosco envisioned to showcase the team of Greenwood and Grant was buried in an old script by Elmer Harris titled *Thy Neighbor's Wife*, the basic plot of which dealt with a brief experimental exchange of spouses between two couples. Morosco had produced the play at the Burbank a few years before, to some success, but as it called for a cast of only four actors, Morosco added, there was not much hope of taking the play to New York. (Here he is being especially disingenuous, since *Thy Neighbor's Wife*, produced by Daniel Frohman, *had* played the Lyceum Theatre on Broadway, though for a mere fifteen performances.) Now Morosco got to work and started augmenting the plot.

"I pictured Charlotte Greenwood ... and Sidney [sic] Grant ... as one of the couples, and May Boley, who played comedy parts at the Burbank and weighed about one hundred and eighty pounds, and Walter Catlett, a tall skinny comedian, as the other," wrote Morosco. Although Elmer Harris was doubtful that Morosco could make the play into the complex musical piece he envisioned, he confessed he had seen Charlotte in *Tik-Tok Man of Oz* at the Mason Opera House on South Broadway and found her delightful.

"The leading character in our musical book was named Letty," Morosco recalled, "and as Greenwood was the longest lady of our acquaintance, we decided to call the new venture *So Long Letty*."[8]

Here is where things get even more muddled, and the confusion has much to do with Morosco's proprietary nature. In fact, the musical play Charlotte was cast in after leaving

CHARLOTTE GREENWOOD
and
SIDNEY GRANT

Sydney Grant, pictured here with Charlotte on the cover of a song from *The Pretty Mrs. Smith* (ca. 1915), was the first of many short leading men to look up to Charlotte Greenwood.

Tik-Tok Man of Oz was *The Pretty Mrs. Smith*, as *Thy Neighbor's Wife* was retitled. She played a character named Letitia Proudfoot, "the fixer of the story ... it was my chore to try to untangle the life of Pretty Mrs. Smith who had a penchant for collecting husbands, all with the same name," Charlotte remembered. "By some accident, all of these Mister Smiths managed to assemble in one scene, and when I came loping onto the stage, I paused in my tracks and shrieked, 'My God, it's raining Smiths!'"

Kitty Gordon "of the classic back" (Charlotte's description) played Mrs. Smith; young comedian James Gleason played a waiter in blackface. Interestingly, Charlotte claims that part of what led to her character's spinoff from this play was a song Sydney Grant had written for her a year before, "Long, Lean, Lanky Letty" — "the success of the number was no doubt responsible for the revival of the name." But that was not the only reason. Charlotte was emerging as a distinctive character actor, with traits remembered by theatregoers from production to production. With her gangly legs and flailing arms, so out of place in the tailored female garb of the time, her irrepressible high spirits, her over-the-top ability to introduce chaos into the most refined of settings, her undaunted chasing of reluctant male quarry and above all, that astonishing "leg lift," Charlotte had created a character that would prove as durable as the name Letty for the next three decades.[9]

For reasons best known to himself, in his memoirs Morosco leaves out all mention of the Broadway production of *Pretty Mrs. Smith*, which opened at the Casino on September 21, 1914, and ran but 48 performances. (Charlotte describes it in her memoirs, with her own set of missing details, namely those dealing with Fritzi Scheff.) The glamourous Fritzi Scheff starred as Mrs. Smith. According to Gerald Bordman, Charlotte's upstaging of Miss Scheff virtually pulled the show out from under the star's petite feet.

The *New York Times* critic who covered the show on opening night made this point in no uncertain terms: "A more appropriate title would have been 'Funny Miss Greenwood.' ... it might be well to say that whatever fun or entertainment was furnished through the three rather dreary acts was due almost entirely to the limber-jointed ... Charlotte Greenwood."

Charlotte could even congratulate herself on having passed enunciatory muster with Ned Wayburn, as she was singled out from the entire cast for having made the lyrics understandable. Whenever Charlotte was on stage, "the star [Scheff] was completely eclipsed."[10]

It was after Charlotte's success in the role of Letty, Bordman insists, that Morosco had the idea of spinning off the character in a play of her own, titled *Long-legged Letty* (which became *So Long Letty*; Charlotte does not mention the earlier title). The show played the Shubert Theatre for almost one hundred performances between 1916 and 1917 — the first spinoff (so well known from television sitcoms of more than a half century later) in musical theatre history. Interestingly enough, when Fritzi Scheff made a silent film version of *Pretty Mrs. Smith*, the Letitia Proudfoot character was nowhere to be seen. If she called for the omission, one can hardly blame her, but the two women remained friends for years afterward.[11]

The confusion Morosco himself encouraged in his own mind and elsewhere about the genesis of the Letty character and the plays written or co-opted around her was to lead him to file a law suit against Charlotte years later, just as she was planning a world tour of what was to be her final and most successful Letty play, *Leaning on Letty*, in spring 1939. Charlotte claims that Harris and the young composer (later producer) Earl Carroll first got the idea that *Pretty Mrs. Smith* would make a good musical comedy. While she, actresses Blanche and Frances Ring (Charlotte's future sisters-in-law) and May Boley, Blanche's husband actor Charles Winninger and other actor friends went for a comical camping trip in the Adirondacks (Charlotte

Oliver Morosco, the theater impresario who helped usher the man-chasing, vase-spilling, wind-mill-armed character of Letty into the world, channeled through Charlotte Greenwood. This photograph of Morosco was the frontispiece of *The Oracle of Broadway*, 1944.

served breakfast on the porch and harangued the women into taking cold baths each morning), Harris, Carroll and Morosco worked out the nuts and bolts of the newly remodeled *So Long Letty*. The play opened in fall 1915 in Los Angeles to great acclaim, later moving to Broadway for the first of the many unaccountably short runs of Charlotte's plays that were otherwise immensely popular on the touring circuit.[12]

"I had achieved the distinction of absolute stardom," Charlotte noted in her memoirs, "and when we reached New York on October 23, 1916, the world was my onion." In fact, the short run of *So Long Letty* gave cause for tears to more than Charlotte, who with the optimism that made her such an audience draw insists in her memoirs that the Harris-Carroll *Letty* was up against a huge force of competition from what was admittedly one of Broadway's brightest seasons — Maud Adams and David Warfield were reviving *The Little Minister* and *The Music Master* respectively, and Minnie Maddern Fiske was lighting up the stage in *Erstwhile Susan*. It was also the season of John Barrymore's first serious role, in Galsworthy's drama *Justice*, part of which was set in a prison cell, a far cry from the frothy drawing room sets that had been Barrymore's stage home away from home since his career began. The Ziegfeld Follies were all the rage; a *Letty* cast member, Frances White, was so mesmerized by the Ziegfeld glamour that she left the play and joined the Follies. Ina Claire, Fannie Brice, Bert Williams, and W.C. Fields (who on meeting Charlotte offered to teach her how to juggle) were some of the names active during *Letty*'s short run.

But more than a plethora of successful shows was overshadowing the first of Charlotte's Letty plays, even as it was doing the same to those other shows. A war long foreseen and almost foreordained had broken out in Europe in August 1914. By spring 1917, despite a peace note sent the previous autumn to all combatants by the newly re-elected President Woodrow Wilson, the U.S. declared war on Germany, and thus entered that other theatre in which a whole generation of youth was mowed down like new grass.

"We had no thought of a world conflagration," Charlotte wrote, even after the United States was in the war. She was to know better when, some twenty years later, radios were crackling again with impending war, created by another mad German ruler with no thought of tomorrow.

10

Love and War

"ALL OF US PLUNGED at once into war work," Charlotte wrote. "[Broadway producer] Winthrop Ames invited me to make up a unit for overseas entertainment and I was eager to do it, but after some discussion the authorities felt I would be of more use at home. It was suggested that we continue with the eastern tour of *So Long Letty* and use whatever spare time we had for the entertainment of the boys and the sale of Liberty bonds." Ultimately, Elsie Janis, another high kicking comedienne, was made the organizer of the overseas unit.

Charlotte was proud to "adopt" the 45th Marines, and immediately drafted members of her cast into a small army of knitters. "I even got some of the men at work," she recalled, "but I must confess that it wasn't very satisfactory. As a matter of fact, the women's work wasn't any too good, but it was plentiful — helmets (knit caps), sweaters, socks and wristlets." If only they had consulted with the brass of the 45th, who gratefully accepted these knitted gifts but had to sheepishly admit that the men's helmets prevented them from wearing the caps under them; the sweaters had gotten wet in an accident en route and had shrunk to the size of children's garments; and had the young soldiers had any time while fighting for their lives in the morasse of the Argonne, they would have enjoyed trying on the socks for size. Only the wristlets turned out to have an immediate and welcome use: not for wrists but to keep rifle muzzles warm. Charlotte and her company took *Letty* to several Canadian hospitals and army camps, playing benefit performances for the soldiers.

"It was very difficult to be funny in the face of men torn, maimed and ruined by war," Charlotte recalled, "and for a long time I was haunted by the sights I had witnessed in the Canadian war hospitals."[1]

It seemed far easier to sell Liberty bonds, or so Charlotte thought:

In Boston I was assigned to a department store for a big bond sale. I found shortly that my persuasive powers as an auctioneer were limited. So long as I told jokes or sang songs, I had an audience; but when I attempted to jostle Back Bay out of money for Uncle Sam they were diffident. Finally, I decided to put it on a more personal basis. "If you'll buy a $50 bond," I clarioned, pointing a finger in the best Uncle Sam poster tradition and hoping it covered the entire assemblage, "I'll match the purchase." That did the trick.[2]

It was an expensive trick for Charlotte, but indicative not just of her patriotism but of the lengths to which she was willing to go to get an audience to eat from her hand — a characteristic blend of crossing-the-footlights energy and rousing enthusiasm which was to color nearly every role she played, not just on stage or screen but in life itself. Charlotte's matching purchases were also to form part of what would become her large future fortune — digging the bonds out of the basement a decade later, Charlotte handed them over to her banker, and walked away with enough money to buy her beloved house near Auburndale. ("Why didn't you get large denomination bonds, Miss Greenwood?" the banker asked her with a pained expression on his face. "Somehow," Charlotte recalled, "it didn't seem worth going into all that.")

As if the war were not spilling enough into the reassuring pattern of everyday American life, it could occasionally give rise to violence in the least expected places. One night, in a Philadelphia run of *Letty*, comic actor Percy Bronson was singing "Pass Around the Apples Once Again," and in overplaying his part started lobbing apples into the audience. One of them struck a sailor on leave, who became enraged and threw the fruit back at Bronson with an insult about the actor's poor aim. "Bronson, ordinarily the mildest mannered of men, lost his head and replied in kind," remembered Charlotte. "In a twinkling, the house was in an uproar. The stage manager came rushing to my dressing room."

> "There's hell popping out front, Miss Greenwood," he cried.
> Without pausing to get the details, I ran onto the stage in my dressing gown — I was engaged in making my costume change — and ordered Percy off stage.
> "Now I don't know the first thing about what happened," I called out in a voice that Wayburn would have found sufficient, "but I know that it must be based on a mistake. I know Mr. Bronson as a gentleman and a good citizen. Will someone kindly explain what is wrong?"
> In the audience, an elderly gentleman arose and gave me a brief sketch.
> "If the offended sailors will come back stage after the show," I said, "Mr. Bronson will certainly clear up any misunderstanding and apologize if necessary. Meantime the rest of you have paid to see the show — let's get on with it. Is there anything you'd like me to do?"
> "Yes," jeered a voice from the gallery, "sing the *Star Spangled Banner!*"
> "And don't you think I can't do it," I called back. "Play, maestro!"
> Frankly, I couldn't remember any more of the words than you can at the moment. I was in a cold sweat. Then the picture of the old Prince Street School flashed through my mind. I was no longer Charlotte Greenwood, the star of *So Long Letty*. I was that gawky kid in pigtails singing the national anthem by rote. And I went through all the verses without missing a word.

"As long as I live," Charlotte recalled, "I will remember the ovation I received; and after the show it was the sailors who apologized to Bronson.... I thanked God privately for the little red school house and its two-times-two-is-four method of memorizing."[3]

But it was another war-related incident that came out of this early *Letty* period that Charlotte described as closest to her heart, though it took place a world away from the stages she and her company danced and sang on during their tour.

"During my visit to Australia just before the start of World War II," she wrote, "I was presented with a copy of an old paper dating back to the period of World War I." One of the articles, in the *Sydney Morning Herald*, dated May 4, 1917, announced the torpedoing of the Ballerat, carrying forty-seven officers and 1,570 ranks of Australian reinforcements. The article read:

LOSS OF BALLERAT — AUSTRALIAN SPIRIT IN FACE OF DISASTER

> The troops who were on the Australian Transport Ballerat torpedoed and sunk in the Channel, came from all parts of the Commonwealth. They regard the sinking as a most trivial adventure and only see amusing features. They declare that a man who stammers, first saw the torpedo, which exploded before he could give warning.
> The Australian conception of discipline was not wanting in the crisis. The explosion woke up several who were asleep in the hatches. While standing at the boat stations, a humorist put up the Ballerat for auction; the first bid being threepence, Robert Lee became purchaser at 2/9, which indicates the spirit of the men in the face of the gravest danger....

The Australians had their first glimpses of the Navy's efficiency when destroyers dashed up from every direction and rescued boat loads of troops.... It was a wonderful sight to see the troops steaming onto the harbour, hours later under scores of searchlights from the land batteries.

As the article also mentioned, "Band Master Heydon, when departing, played on the cornet 'So Long Letty.'"

"Somehow it makes me very proud," Charlotte wrote, "to realize that 'my' song was the one so close to the hearts of those courageous Australians, that they were willing to face certain death with it on their lips." As if tailor-made for a looking-on-the-bright-side Charlotte Greenwood plot, the certain danger the men of the Ballerat faced was of short duration: just one man was actually dunked into the water before being rescued, and all aboard were taken off the sinking ship alive.[4]

For Charlotte, wartime brought not only occasional mid-performance mayhem from edgy servicemen and a lot of clicking of knitting needles backstage, but also an event that in her memoirs she drops from view as if it had never occurred: her quick (she accepted his proposal after knowing him for only three months) and troubled marriage, from 1915 to 1920, to the stage manager and character actor Cyril Ring.

Born in Boston in 1892 (thus two years Charlotte's junior) and an alumnus of Boston's prestigious Roxbury Latin School, Cyril Ring seems to have been a performer and a personality for whom good looks and family connections were his sole lifeline to the marginal stage and screen roles he played over the course of a thirty-something year career. One of his sisters, the beautiful Blanche Ring, was a great Broadway star; another, Frances Ring, was a charming actress of lesser magnitude and fame but always on the billboards of theatres in New York and the hinterlands; she was also a fair lyricist. The connections to fame spread out from there: Blanche was married to Charles Winninger, the well-known comedian and the first Cap'n Andy in *Showboat*, while Frances was married to stage and screen heart-throb Thomas Meighan. In future years, Cyril would have two well-known nephews: A. Edward Sutherland, the film director, and James Meighan, who played "The Falcon" on radio in the late 1940s.

Cyril's challenge, and one he never overcame, was that while his sisters were accomplished actresses, his own skills never extended beyond a few set expressions and physical stances — what Dorothy Parker wrote of Katharine Hepburn's early stage performance in *The Lake* ("She ran the whole gamut of emotions from A to B") would be far more appropriately bestowed upon handsome but limited Cyril Ring. The one film he is best known for is the Marx Brothers' madcap 1929 movie debut, *The Cocoanuts*, playing shyster Harvey Yates, and his performance is noted less for its skill than for the barrage of negative reviews that it summoned from critics. Ring delivers his lines, whether to Groucho Marx or Kay Francis, as if wanly pitching a squash ball to a wall; he can often be seen with hands in pockets, as if impatient to get the film over with. It's significant, as Hal Erickson points out, that the one film Cyril was in during which he actually had several lines to speak was the RKO mystery-comedy *Having a Wonderful Crime*, a co-star of which was his sister Blanche. His last film credit came in 1947, and when he died in 1967 he was virtually forgotten.

Exactly how Charlotte met Cyril remains open to conjecture. But one source[5] claims they met during the first run of *So Long Letty*, when Cyril was working on the production as company manager (and playing a bit part, "the Colonel"). As we have seen, Charlotte was also on friendly enough terms with Cyril's sisters Blanche and Frances to vacation with them in the Adirondacks, though Cyril's presence there was expunged from Charlotte's memoirs. In an interview in *The Morning Oregonian* from 1920, while she was on tour, Charlotte says that she and Cyril married in Los Angeles. There was very little of an engagement, and many people were surprised that a romance had been going on under everyone's noses and none the wiser. "I advise everyone to cut out the foolishness of being engaged," Charlotte quipped to a reporter for the *New York Times*, in flip words she would come to regret, "and get married right away instead." In what must have later seemed to Charlotte an ironic real-life rehearsal for her man-mad spinster roles for MGM, only her maid stood as witness to the civil marriage ceremony.[6] The marriage served a practical purpose, at least for the groom. When registering for the draft, Cyril Ring was able to claim enough dependencies (his mother and now Charlotte) to keep from being called up.

Cyril had last performed in *The Wall Street Girl* in 1912 (notably, the star was sister Blanche — there was even room in the "plot" for Will Rogers and his lariat), an experience which seems to have chastened him into staying backstage. Charlotte was a full-fledged star; but perhaps like her mother, who had always had a soft spot for life's strays, Charlotte's heart opened to this fellow actor who, despite being handed theatre connections on a platinum platter, was never able to rise to their requirements or use them fully to his advantage. His name appears in the *New York Times* as often for events unrelated to his acting as for it, as when he was named as being in Anita Stewart's car with Stewart's brother in law, director Ralph Ince, one night in early August 1923 when Ince beat up Stewart's brother, George, in the presence of Cyril's second wife. If she read about this, Charlotte must have breathed a sigh of relief that she was no longer part of Cyril Ring's life.

It is also clear that, particularly when she was performing on stage, Charlotte was extremely vulnerable — all the memories of childhood, of being laughed at, or seeing her mother's struggles, seemed to rise up to meet her when she stepped in front of the footlights, inspiring her to give her 150 percent best but also leaving her emotional doors and windows unbarred from intruders.

The experience of being married to Cyril Ring seems to have made Charlotte so much more miserable than any of the other miseries she had had to overcome in her younger years that she chose not to mention it at all, even at the expense of robbing future scholars of musical theatre of what may have been fascinating insights into the sadness behind the clowning of this happiest of performers:

> "Yes, it's all true," she admitted when asked if she were not suing Cyril Ring, whom she married in Los Angeles five years ago, for separation. "It doesn't bother me much because it's the best thing for both of us. I've gone along for so many years without scandal of any sort that I hate to see this sort of thing in the papers."
>
> Miss Greenwood [then] turned the conversation to other channels.[7]

To another reporter for the same newspaper, Charlotte was far more frank:

> You know, I am getting a divorce from my husband Cyril Ring, because he found another woman that he thought he liked better. At first I thought if I had been "dressed up" things might have been different, but that theory has been exploded because he claims to have discovered that he is madly in love with me now and is trying to patch up our differences — but I do not think this can be done, having done what he has once done he will do it again. I have no regrets and no inclination to change my mind, nor have I any bitter feelings toward Mr. Ring. It may all be for the best.[8]

In Charlotte's photo albums kept at the University of Southern California's Film and Television Library, many photos from the period of Charlotte's brief role as Mrs. Cyril Ring are torn from the pages, some leaving only one apparently inoffensive person visible. But where the photos were glued too securely to be removed one can see that on at least one trip to the Adirondacks, solemn Cyril Ring is there with Charlotte, along with his sisters Blanche and Francis and a host of other theatrical luminaries of Charlotte's circle. Most curious of all is a small card, such as is often attached to bouquets by a florist, pasted next to a clipping mentioning Cyril. On this card is written, in a hand that is not Charlotte's but seems delicately feminine, "Lonesome Cy — Hope you will accept this expression of something that is beautiful but cannot last without care." Is this a florist's card for a delivery Charlotte intercepted, or found by accident, precipitating the rupture in her marriage? Or is it a card for flowers she sent herself, returned to her by Cyril, or never sent? Cyril's next wife, Molly Green, was a Ziegfeld Follies dancer, than whom there could be nothing more different than Charlotte Greenwood — possibly she was the other woman who helped break up the marriage in 1920.

By the time Charlotte came to write her memoirs, beginning in the mid–1930s and continuing till the early 1940s, she was a happily married woman, and increasingly interested in the tenets of Christian Science, which at its simplest level adjured its followers to banish all negative thoughts, even if that meant banishing negative memory, lest these compromise health mental and physical. These factors seem to have played a part in erasing Cyril from every corner of her life and memories.

With stardom came wealth, and thanks to her alter ego Letty, Charlotte was able to purchase a three-story residence with broad porches shaded by old trees at Auburndale, Queens. The house came with farmland, which may have conjured for Charlotte the charm of those farms of Virginia where as a young girl she had regained her strength, learned how to play and appreciate the virtue of a hard day's work. Bayside was also a popular area with theatre stars happy to have a place of refuge from the manic pace of New York City and cross-country tours, yet close enough to the nerve center of the American theatre world. This house, along with marriage to Cyril seemed to set the seal of success on Charlotte's life — a busy career, a home she loved, and a handsome husband, who even had a chance to perform with his wife in her next Letty play, *Linger Longer Letty* (it opened at the Fulton Theatre on Broadway in November 1919, running its usual less than stellar number of performances in New York while breaking box office records on tour), his first return to the stage in four years. Dutifully, Charlotte added Cyril's surname to her own when autographing photos during these years.

Significantly, *Linger Longer*'s plot was a Cinderella-like story of the plain daughter who overcomes her physical drawbacks and wins the man of her dreams. Charlotte's performance was universally lauded, and she saved all the reviews for her scrapbook — as she points out in her memoirs, she even read the bad ones, refusing to hold critics in the scorn so many of her colleagues did. As a result, she made friends with many of them, which did nothing to harm her prospects in any show which said critics happened to be reviewing. (The modern day habit many critics subscribe to, that of remaining aloof from the subjects of their critiques, did not obtain as a rule during Charlotte's successes on the stage as much as it does now.)

Charlotte's glamourous image on the cover of this hit song from *Linger Longer Letty* belies the downtrodden Cinderella-like character she played in this 1919 Morosco production.

Miss Greenwood would probably be quite as funny as she is at present were she less of the skyscraper type of beauty. She has the real *vis comica*, not merely the force to shoot her left foot into the air while she carefully guides it to a halt with her left hand [*New York Sun*].

Her art is as definite and sometimes as delicate as Chaplin's. It is as smooth as slippery elm [Ashton Stevens, *Chicago Herald-American*].

Miss Greenwood can easily be remembered as the long, lean, limber creature, the human semaphore, the animated Beardsley drawing who burst upon us in *So Long Letty*—yet with all this grotesqueness, there is a certain charm. She is a true comedienne and not a low burlesquer [Charles Collins, *Chicago Tribune*].

Miss Greenwood, a long and humorous comedienne, is of course the principal comic spirit on display. As a joke-cracker, she is superior, having the knack of effective retort; and she dances as does no other dancer in the American drama ... [Percy Hammond, *Chicago Tribune*].

Charlotte Greenwood is a national institution — a sure cure for any sort of blues. To miss her is like missing the last train home [Edwin Schallert, *LA Times*].

Some day Miss Greenwood is going to get a real play and if she gets away from the junk she is doing now I, for one, will be glad to say "I told you so" [Patterson James, *The Billboard*].[8]

A glamour shot of Charlotte Greenwood, dating from the early 1920s. The beautiful eyes admired by Eva Tanguay when Charlotte was 15 were still very much in evidence. William Luce collection.

The day was still to come when persnickety Alexander Woollcott would publish his own paean to what the discerning could see were gifts far greater than were being put to use, for now *Letty* had all theatres it played wallowing in thick drifts of sales receipts. But the critics who lauded her performances in *Linger* were hardly low-grade stringers — Ashton Stevens, for example, was a celebrated reviewer who served as the model for the drama critic Jedediah Leland in Orson Welles' film *Citizen Kane*, while highly respected Percy Hammond has become best known for another connection with Welles: a few weeks after he blasted the director's "voodoo" *Macbeth*, he died a bit too suddenly for people not to raise eyebrows at the finding of "natural causes."

But however much it may have seemed to Charlotte that she had conquered all that her special niche of show business had to offer, there was still one territory remaining to be won — that of the film medium, which even then was still sometimes described using the quaint term "photoplay." In fact, a whole new career was to come knocking at Charlotte's gold-starred dressing room door before *Linger Longer Letty* was even a gleam in Oliver Morosco's hard blue eye.

11

Trotting Tintypes and
the Music Box Revue

CHARLOTTE WAS STILL IN THE middle of *So Long Letty*, in the popular touring company production, when a run of the play in Los Angeles brought her to the attention of the Famous Players-Lasky studios, that golden cradle of golden-curled star Mary Pickford.

Gold had been on Jesse L. Lasky's mind from his earliest youth, when he left his hometown of San Francisco, where he had been born in 1880, to seek his fortune in Alaska. A yen for the theatre, which he shared with his sister Blanche Lasky, moved both siblings to form an act, which they toured through the country. When Blanche married Samuel Goldfish (better known as the future Sam Goldwyn), Lasky joined with his brother-in-law in what was called the Jesse L. Lasky Feature Play Company (in 1913), a film outfit, for which Lasky and Goldfish hired as their first director the young Cecil B. DeMille. The new movie company started out in a barn located in the dusty burg called Hollywood. Paramount Pictures was Lasky's distributor — eventually this would become the name of Lasky's many-named company, though by that time Lasky had been forced by Depression-related money troubles to give up his position as head of production in 1932, after which he became a sometime independent producer.

By the time Lasky asked Charlotte to make a film for him, in 1918, the Lasky Feature Play Company had become Famous Players-Lasky, the biggest film concern in existence at that time. Charlotte protests in her memoirs that she was worried that film work might clash with her theatrical career.

"It was plain to see that the film industry was about to shake off its swaddling clothes and start on an important career," Charlotte remembered. "I was willing to have a part in this, so long as it did not interfere with my stage work."[1]

Screenwriter Frances Marion, who met Charlotte around this time, received a much different impression of the gangly young woman's opinion of the movies. She remembered Laurette Taylor, star of *Peg o' My Heart* and future star of Tennessee Williams' *The Glass Menagerie*, poo-pooing film work: "I shall never be lured into it, though they have trapped Madame Bernhardt, Lillie Langtry, and Minnie Maddern Fisk." The comedian James Gleason once cried, "Those trotting tintypes! I wouldn't be caught dead in 'em!" Yet when Frances asked Charlotte what she thought of the "trotting tintypes," she got a much different response.

> We glanced toward Charlotte Greenwood, a tall young comedienne with the long legs of a stork; she could balance on one and raise the other perpendicularly until you wouldn't have been surprised

74

to see a bird pop out of her pompadour and cuckoo "six o'clock." "Believe me, I'll go into the flicks if I ever have a chance."[2]

At a later date, when she met Charlotte with Oliver Morosco in tow, this enthusiasm for the "flicks" was reinforced. Morosco had congratulated the elegantly beautiful Marion, who besides being a screenwriter also assayed actress roles, on getting into what he described as "a booming racket," but declared with total lack of prescience that "I'll never let them be shown at my theatre, even the comedies I make with Charlotte."

"I don't care where they show the flicks so long as I'm in them!" Charlotte chirped. "What's more, I intend to stay in them until I'm so old they put me out to pasture!"—a remark that Marion, writing in 1972, found amusing, considering Charlotte's long movie career and the fact that several of her later films involved plenty of horses romping in plenty of pastures.[3]

To the press, however, Charlotte betrayed no such passion for film. "Pictures are no novelty in my young life," she told a reporter. "When I first became a star in *So Long Letty*, Mr. Morosco got me to appear in a photoplay called *Jane*"—quite a different attitude toward movies from what Morosco had shared with Frances Marion.

> I did *Jane* while appearing in *So Long Letty* and almost died. I'd no sooner close my pretty blue eyes than the alarm clock would call me to the movie studio. One thing at a time, if you please! That's going to be my motto.[4]

Charlotte Greenwood, captured in various scenes from her first silent film, *Jane* (1918). She is shown here in the premiere program with cast members (from left to right) Sydney Grant, Myrtle Steadman, Forrest Stanley, Howard Davies, Herbert Standing, Lydia Yeaman Titus and Syd de Grey.

At first, Charlotte liked *Jane*, at least on paper; she would also have as co-star her *Letty* sidekick, diminutive actor Sydney Grant. Adapted from the 1890 farce by English playwright William Lestocq, *Jane*'s plot revolved around the plight of young Charles Shackelton, played by a leering Forrest Stanley, who in order to please his wealthy uncle and show himself a proper heir to the avuncular fortune must prove to the old man that he has seen the error of his play-boy ways and has found a woman to marry.

Charlotte played Jane, Shackelton's maid, with Sydney Grant as the butler, Tipson. When Shackelton's uncle, who, pleased with the news that his nephew has married, has written him a large check, announces he is about to pay the young wastrel a visit, the frantic Shackelton offers Jane $500 to pretend to be his wife for the duration of the uncle's stay. The comedy and crassness of this scene is captured in a still used in the film's premiere program: an aproned Charlotte looks balefully at Stanley, who is pressing a check on her with an unpleasant smile, while beneath the photo are the words, "If you will be my wife for today, you get $500." There's a pungent hint of prostitution in the air.

To complicate matters, Jane is the secret wife of Tipson, to whom she avoids revealing the role she is playing with Shackelton. The mayhem increases when the uncle asks to see the baby that Shackelton and wife allegedly have produced, and Jane has to steal one from an unwitting laundrywoman, all the while enduring Tipson's jealous scenes. Of course, the wash-erwoman calls the police about her missing child, and the farce explodes when they discover the uncle dandling the stolen baby. In the end, Shackelton, who has managed to wring a "yes" from a real fiancée, tells his uncle the truth, and the plot rides off into the sunset, with Char-lotte sternly hanging on to the $500 and ignoring Tipson's importunate gaze.

"It would be pleasant to write that *Jane* marked a new epoch in the films," Charlotte recalled later, "but I am afraid it did nothing of the sort. If it had any value, aside from casual entertainment, it was to introduce Lloyd Bacon to the world as a director of promise"— and it would not be the last time Bacon directed a Greenwood film, she might have added.

As it happened, she didn't need to worry about her unhappy film debut, because Letty, her high-kicking, song-belting alter ego, was rattling her cage again, demanding to be let out in what became a series of plays either written or rewritten to showcase the zany character.

"It looks as though I will have to keep on being Letty until I retire from the stage," Char-lotte told a reporter around this time. Even so, she thought it amusing to contemplate doing a different Letty play every night of the week. At the rate she was going, she said, she would have enough and then some.[5]

Following *Linger Longer Letty* in 1919, Oliver Morosco decided that as Letty was his golden goose, he would cast Charlotte in a musical comedy called *Let 'Er Go, Letty*, which opened and closed in New Haven — "and even that was not quick enough," Charlotte quipped in her memoirs. Then Morosco adapted Charles Klein's play *Maggie Pepper*, which had starred Rose Stahl, for Charlotte, and he (not Charlotte, as Gerald Bordman claims) renamed it *Letty Pepper*. The plot was similar to *Linger Longer Letty*: Charlotte played a put upon girl, a depart-ment store clerk. When the manager fires her for seeking to better her position, Letty tells a friendly gentleman her sad story. The gentleman turns out to be the department store owner, who rehires and promotes her; they end up in love.

But if Morosco was hoping for a reprise of the hit that *So Long Letty* had been, he was mistaken: the musical comedy, with music by Werner Janssen, book by Morosco and George V. Hobart and lyrics by Leo Wood and Irving Bibo, ran a mere thirty-two performances at the Vanderbilt Theatre (from early April to early May 1922) before closing.

As Alexander Woollcott wrote in the *New York Times* on April 11, 1922:

> [*Letty Pepper*] was apparently designed as something in the vehicular line that should trundle the towering Charlotte Greenwood from town to town. Now as always she strongly resembles Laurette Taylor as Miss Taylor would look if caught in one of those mad mirrors at Coney Island. Now as always she comes to the rescue of a tottering scene by giving brief genial imitations of a clock at 6:15 or at a quarter of seven. Now as always, she goes clowning about the stage with just the flash of a suggestion now and then that she could be a thundering good actress if the occasion ever arose.[6]

Woollcott's oft-repeated belief in Charlotte's serious abilities as an actor were of little comfort in this polite announcement that *Letty Pepper* was a bomb. But there were not just bombs in Charlotte's theatrical life — her offstage world was coming to pieces as well.

According to Parish and Leonard's monumental book *The Funsters*, Charlotte and Cyril had a falling out in fall 1922, just as Charlotte was preparing for what would become another new chapter in her professional life, the second Irving Berlin Music Box Review (October 23, 1922). Parish and Leonard describe Charlotte fleeing her Bayside farm, and Cyril, and filing for divorce. Her interviews in *The Morning Oregonian* from 1920, however, indicate that she and Cyril were already separated.[7]

At the very least, few marriages between successful wife and obscure husband succeed, so it is perhaps a small miracle that Charlotte's and Cyril's marriage lasted as long as it did. The divorce did not sever Charlotte's connections with Blanche and Frances Ring and their

Boating with friends and colleagues in the Adirondacks, Charlotte's favorite place to relax. From left to right: Ed Wynn, Jr., William Gaxton, Thomas Meighan (Charlotte's ex-brother-in-law), Charlotte, and Ed Wynn, circa 1922.

husbands, who all remained lifelong friends, going on vacations together, working on projects together, remaining in touch till death parted them. (As late as her old age, in a small, memento-crowded apartment, Blanche Ring was still proud to tell a young visitor that Charlotte Greenwood had been her sister-in-law.)[8]

Much as "swaddling clothes" Hollywood had done a few years earlier, Irving Berlin's second Music Box Revue came knocking at Charlotte's dressing room door — literally, on this occasion. *Linger Longer Letty* was playing Philadelphia. Charlotte was making up for her next scene when a note was brought to her dressing room, straight from the redoubtable producer Sam Harris.

About fifty, slight of build and with an earthward nose that seemed bent on greeting his upper lip, like his new partner Irving Berlin, Harris was born and bred on the Lower East Side, and since his pre-teens had been living, at times literally, on the streets of New York. The son of a tailor, Harris soon grew fed up with helping his father in his shop and cast about for other ways not just to make a living but to make his mark. Entertainment of one sort (and quality) or another was where his heart was happiest — as promoter of featherweight boxing champion "Terrible" Terry McGovern, owner of race horses, and finally partnership with George M. Cohan in 1904. The latter deal was sealed even tighter when Harris married the sister of Cohan's second wife, ex-chorus girl Agnes Nolan. It took the actors' strike of 1919, in which Cohan stood firm with management against his fellow performers, to break up the winning team.[9]

Shortly afterward, however, Harris, who had bought a theatre of his own in prior years, met Irving Berlin and convinced him that he, too, should have his name across a house of entertainment. Berlin's suggestion was that a theatre be built specifically to showcase musical theatre — his own musicals, to be precise — and even had a name for it: the Music Box Theatre. By spring of 1920, Harris had purchased a lot on West 45th Street, then filled with old brownstones, and by the next year they had made way for a new theatre: a columned, Franco-Italian style building of Indiana limestone, as elegantly subdued inside as outside with its soft monochrome color scheme and amber-crystaled chandeliers. Charlotte's colleague Sam Bernard from *Nearly a Hero* was prompted to sneer, "It stinks from class," and in fact the project was enormously expensive, even for the beginning of the roaring Twenties — almost a million dollars — and would always waver on the brink of financial chaos. But the setting for Harris' and Berlin's plans for a series of eye-popping revues had been created.

The first of these, the Music Box Revue of 1921, was mounted under the guidance of British-born actor-director Hassard Short, who united a showman's sense of scale to an artist's intensely rich imagination. Born in Edington, England, on October 15, 1877, as Hubert Short, Short directed Irving Berlin's hit *As Thousands Cheer* (1933), Jerome Kern's *Roberta* (also 1933) and made a major hit out of *The Great Waltz* (1934) with its score adapted by opera composer and former child prodigy, Erich Wolfgang Korngold. On September 22, 1921, "Broadway saw for the first time a new, exquisitely beautiful theatre, the Music Box, and the initial edition of a new revue series.... The shows were [to be] opulent, but the smallness of the house did not demand broad clowning nor strong musical projection, and so allowed for some intellectualization of the sketches and a softer-toned immediacy between singer and audience.... As a result the *Music Box Revues* helped build a bridge between the open-handed lavishness of the *Follies*-type revue and the more thoughtful intimacy of the revues of the thirties." Short created scenes not seen even in the Follies: chorus girls costumed as the fare and place settings of a lavish dinner table; "The Legend of the Pearls" sung by Wilda Bennett as girls draped in $10,000 worth of borrowed pearls and many more of the fake variety pranced and danced against a black velvet backdrop.[10] In the future, Short would become not only a colleague of Charlotte's but a friend as well, in the U.S. and in Short's native England.

Before even meeting with Harris, Charlotte shared the glad news of his note with the cast of *Linger Longer Letty*. "The great Harris was to be in the audience that night," she told them, "and we must be up on our toes every minute. Naturally, we were all excited. When word reaches back stage that a great celebrity or a renowned critic or an important producer is in the audience, everything immediately take on an air of hurly-burly. Everyone is so anxious to put his best foot forward that nine chances out of ten the performance is terrible." This was, however, Charlotte's tenth chance, she remembered. "In all my years in the theater I do not believe I ever gave a superior performance."[11]

Disappointingly, however — and not just to her but to her colleagues, who were looking forward to meeting the producer — the word Charlotte expected Harris to send back to her never arrived. Never lacking in energy, Charlotte set her hat on straight and headed for Harris' hotel, where he had asked her to drop by to meet with him.

> I knocked at the door of his suite in some trepidation. I was arrayed in my best clothes, and frankly nervous. A voice bellowed "Come in!" and I entered to find a group of men lounging around the room. One of them was arrayed in pajamas and an elaborate dressing gown, with a perfectly huge cigar in his mouth.
> "Oh, it's you, Miss Greenwood," he said as he rose and came toward me with extended hand. "I've been taking it easy. Sit down."
> "Did you like the show?" I managed to gurgle after the formalities.
> "I didn't see it," he replied. "As a matter of fact I came to Philadelphia to see a prize fight, but I didn't see that either."
> "But I thought," I persisted, with my heart in my feet by this time, "that you wanted to see my work."
> "Lord, no," he chuckled. "I know what you can do; I don't have to see you do it. Now then, this is what we have in mind. I hope you're going to be with us."

Harris then began a lengthy disquisition on just what sort of revue he had conjured for the Music Box jewel-box, describing his friendship with Irving Berlin and making the proposition more attractive by the minute. "Before I was well aware of it," Charlotte recalled, "I had agreed to sign a contract and Harris was telling me about prize fights. Before I left the apartment I had agreed to go to the next important prize fight as Harris' guest. He felt that no one's knowledge of life was complete until he had inquired into the art of self defense." Growing up as Harris had done in the Bowery, this was advice well worth taken.[12]

The second Music Box Revue had many jewels in its crown, but two of the brighter ones were the comedy duo, mustached straight man Paul McCullough and impish, leering Bobby Clark, both born in Springfield, Ohio, four years apart and friends since boyhood. Before signing on to the Music Box Revue, the duo had made their legitimate debut on the London stage, and merely carried their act whole to New York. The cast was also enlivened by the Irish tenor heartthrob of the revues, John Steel, who sang in a sketch called "The House Tops" what has been described as an unforgettable rendition of "Lady of the Evening" with nothing behind him but the crags of rooftops washed in moonlight — proof that Hassard Short's sense of style extended as evocatively to the simple as to the ornate.

Grace LaRue was also on hand, in two numbers that must have made Charlotte relive the incident of the coral bead dress in *Nearly a Hero*. In "The Diamond Horseshoe," in which actors and actresses impersonated characters from operas of Richard Wagner, Jules Massenet, Giuseppe Verdi and others, LaRue, who was costumed as an exquisite Thaïs, wore a gown which carpeted most of the stage. Earlier in the show, as she sang "Crinoline Days," the stage elevator with which the Music Box was snazzily equipped lifted her high into the air, a giant bell of hoopskirt billowing out around her.[13]

Charlotte who was given what Gerald Bordman considers "the best comic bit of the evening." From playing "The Lady in Red" in a gangster sketch of the same name (with William Gaxton as a shady Chinese named Wong Lung and Bobby Clark emoting as "Mahomed Mahoney, an arch conspirator"), Charlotte re-emerged in the "Satan's Palace" sketch, during a duet of Berlin's snappy "Pack Up Your Sins and Go to the Devil," as performed by Margaret and Dorothy McCarthy. At the public dress rehearsal, while the McCarthy girls chirped out front, Charlotte suddenly appeared "thrown out of Heaven by either Gabriel or Michael into one of the mammoth pits that were a few feet below the stage." Amid steam and red glow, dressed in a red satin devil costume replete with pitchfork, she began to use the latter to heave impersonators of famed jazz musicians of the day into one of the chasms.

"I was duly consigned to the biggest and darkest pit of all;" Charlotte recalled, "dense smoke writhed and curled around me; the effect from the auditorium was wonderful, and got cheers. But it was the first time the smoke effect had been tried, and the producer had not thought what would happen to me. It was timed to have the curtain fall simultaneously with the top of the trap, so I could be released quickly. As luck would have it ... the trap door jammed and I was virtually suffocated before they could chop me out. Hassard Short ... decided that I was too valuable to lose in some stage accident. I was inclined to agree with him." Thereafter the song was given to a man, Robinson Newbold. (Confirming Charlotte's memory, the tour program from spring 1924 lists only the McCarthy sisters as performing this number.)[14]

Even had Charlotte's divorce from Cyril Ring been the lowest point in a life that had been challenged by one difficulty after another since birth, the fame she had won as Letty and the renown she was winning as queen of the revue, that quintessential giddy Jazz Age phenomenon (she even got to perform a little of her beloved opera, albeit as spoof, with William Gaxton and Leila Ricard), would have been enough to ease the hurt if not make her forget it for the time being.

All of this was topped off by an invitation to President Calvin Coolidge's White House, when Charlotte and a group of other performers, including John Drew, Al Jolson, and Raymond Hitchcock, were asked to a breakfast to support the President in his re-election campaign.

"Thirty-odd stars arrived at the White House not long before 9 o'clock," wrote a *New York Times* reporter on October 17, 1924, "after an all-night ride from New York, and sat down to an old-fashioned New England breakfast of sausages and hotcakes. The delegation came under the direction of the Coolidge Non-Partisan League, of which Colonel Rhinelander Waldo is President, to assure Mr. Coolidge of their support in the Presidential campaign."

"I have met you all across the footlights," Mrs. Coolidge said, "but it's not the same as greeting you here. Let's go into breakfast."

President Coolidge contented himself with leading one partner — Charlotte Greenwood — into the state dining room, where the breakfast was served.[15]

Later that month, the *New York Times* ran a photo of Charlotte, gowned in satin and pearls, descending a flight of stairs on the smiling President's arm. The smart and competitive Mrs. Coolidge got even by accepting not only Jolson's arm but that of Colonel Waldo as she entered the state dining room.

"We are all Republicans from now on," quipped Al Jolson to a reporter, singing a song on the White House lawn in the President's honor that wished the President "four more years!"[16]

Curiously, Charlotte makes no mention in the final version of her memoirs of what must have been a quite memorable day for her, but in an earlier version describes having had a fun time with both the President and First Lady.

> During what seemed to me a banquet instead of breakfast, the President was extremely gracious and interested in the theater and its people. When I confided to him that my position as America's long lanky Letty would never be the same after enjoying the generous hospitality of such a delicious menu [he joked], remarking that they were not in the habit of breakfasting with quite such a large family and that the cook was showing off a bit.

Charlotte later asked Mrs. Coolidge if she might run around the White House lawn and take a dive into an ornamental pool to work off all the food. "Run all you like," Grace Coolidge replied, "but don't go in that pool, the water hasn't been changed in years." [17]

One reason why Charlotte left out all details of this breakfast may perhaps be found in an article which came fast on the heels of the presidential photo spread. The Senate committee investigating presidential campaign funds heard testimony from Colonel Waldo and others on what was alleged to have been Waldo's effort to buy what would today be considered "ad spots" for Coolidge in the various theatrical guests' performance routines. Waldo defended himself by telling the senators his Non-Partisan Club paid the actors $1,332 "for fares and luncheon," hardly the sort of financial sweetener to make stars like John Drew or Al Jolson rewrite a scene in play or vaudeville to mention the unrhymable name "Coolidge."

Apparently it helped that after the presidential breakfast, Coolidge, Mrs. Coolidge and the stage stars went en masse to Walter Reed Hospital, where they entertained and cheered up the disabled soldiers — the allegations against Colonel Waldo were dropped. Possibly Charlotte's disinclination to point up her support of the Republican Coolidge had as much to do with the fact that at the time she was writing her memoirs, Franklin Roosevelt, of whom Charlotte was a staunch supporter, was in the White House, and it might seem she was stretching bipartisanship too far to bring Coolidge into her story.[18]

Thus there was much for Charlotte to be happy about in 1924 — there was her stardom (one sample of which came when the head butcher at the fabled Queensboro Public Market told a *New York Times* reporter that year that his market boasted such customers as "Charlotte Greenwood, standing right in front of the counter looking over the meats"— the only other customer that came to his mind was Enrico Caruso); the charmed attentions of the American President; and another new project on the horizon, one that would change her career and life in more ways than she then could discern. Not only would it involve a man she was coming to know very well — director Hassard Short — but another man who was then living in England, who at the time of Charlotte's obscure teenaged debut in 1905 in Wayburn's *The White Cat* was barely out of the cradle.

Forever after, her next show, Hassard Short's *Ritz Revue*, would be associated with meeting this man who, unlike Cyril Ring, seemed to offer exactly what Charlotte needed in a partner — stability and talent. The man would remain the only man in her life till death was songwriter, musical theatre composer and producer, Martin Broones.[19]

12

"My darling"

BROONES—WHOSE MIDDLE NAME, Joseph, he never used—was born in New York City on June 10, 1901 (this according to his death certificate; the 1920 census gives his age as 16, meaning birth in 1904, and still other sources would give the year as 1903). His parents were Dr. Joseph Broones, a Russian-born Polish osteopath, and his German wife Erma, née Schermann.

Martin was the youngest of the household, with brothers Arthur (who later became a successful Southern California businessman) and Otto (later a doctor specializing in psychological disorders), as well as sister Henrietta. Much later in life, Martin was to tell a friend that he had spent some time as a child in St. Petersburg, Russia. Given his father's Russian origins and his profession—the sort of therapeutic service performed in the great spas and watering places of the period—this is not impossible.

Martin also remembered with affection the old brownstone home of his boyhood. The family had at least one live-in servant, an Irishwoman named Lizzie. With a father who spoke Polish and a German-speaking mother, not to mention Lizzie's brogue, Martin grew up in a household full of widely varied languages and accents.[1]

By the time he was sixteen years old, Martin was a full-time music student, studying with the Hungarian-born and New York–based pianist and teacher Rafael Joseffy, who besides being one of the great musical pedagogues of the period was also a devout Christian Scientist, a faith that was to have a profound influence on Martin's future work.[2] However, it would appear that in this resolutely professional family, Martin's musical interests were not taken seriously. As Martin related in a lecture given at the First Church of Christ, Scientist in Boston in 1970, his father wanted him to be a doctor, and while willing and able to finance Martin's way through medical school, he frowned on his son's desire to go to Columbia University to study drama or journalism. If Martin wished to go into theatre or writing, he was told, he would have to pay his own way. This he did, and as he told his listeners in Boston, he had been working for what he wanted since late boyhood. Dr. Broones would not finance music lessons, either: Martin had to pay for them himself by working after school as pianist in a local movie theatre. Intriguingly, considering that Charlotte became a star there in 1912, only a few years before, Martin also served as rehearsal pianist at the Winter Garden Theatre.

Like Charlotte, Martin found his future at the Winter Garden. On occasions when a show needed what was called "interpolated music," a sort of improvisation of the show's tunes to fill up gaps in the score or the book, Martin would do so at the keyboard. Searching for a way to make the most of his musical experiences, Martin decided that if he could improvise to the director's satisfaction, he also had it in him to compose his own musical show. This he did (a show called the "Park Theatre Review"), and he took the completed score to various arrangers, hoping someone could orchestrate it for him. Several doors were closed in his hopeful adolescent face, until he found a genius of orchestration, African American composer, arranger, conductor and first black orchestrator for Hollywood films, William Henry Bennett Vodery. Born in 1884 in Philadelphia, Vodery had something else in common with Charlotte besides the same birthtown — his mother, too, had run a theatrical rooming house, where the young Vodery came to realize he wanted to be in theatre, too. From scoring songs for the black vaudeville team Williams & Walker, Vodery worked as score librarian for the Chicago Symphony Orchestra, and studied with the CSO's music director, the famed Dr. Frederick Stock; soon he was composing hit New York shows and had become a sought-after conductor and arranger. While working for Flo Ziegfeld (who employed him for two decades), Vodery hired a "slim, intense" young man named George Gershwin as rehearsal pianist — clearly, Vodery knew talent when he heard it. In 1918, Martin contributed songs to *The Blue Pearl*, a show that ran a mere 36 performances at the Longacre Theatre — but it was a start for a very young man.

By the time Martin brought his score to Vodery, the latter had returned from World War I, where he had served as director of the 807th U.S. Pioneer Infantry Band. Much as he had done for skinny George Gershwin (for whom he later also served as arranger), Vodery chatted with Martin as he looked over his work. To Martin's joy, Vodery offered to do the orchestration and to find a slot for the "Park Theatre Review," but whether or where it was ever performed is not known to this writer.

An early effort of Martin's, the 1920 ballad *Purple Dreams* (published by Stark and Cowan), for which Martin also provided a set of lyrics both romantic and goofy, shows how he was feeling his uncertain way stylistically, as well as exploiting the oriental theme then in vogue in music, art and fashion. Though a very youthful effort — Martin was 17 — it's still charming the way this boy, whose musical interests had been all but stamped on by his doctor father, tried to create an atmosphere of exoticism set in twilit deserts with caravans passing by, tying it all up with the roaming, unsettled feeling of being in love. (His 1922 song, *Some Little Someone*, set to lyrics by Alex Sullivan and published by Irving Berlin, is for all its lightness of style and subject a far more attractive and mature effort.)

Vodery had much to teach Martin about finding one's own unique sound. He was then leading his own band, called the Plantation Club Orchestra after the nightspot of that name, and had adopted a dance-band style ensemble, with brass and banjo interpolations, the tone and texture of which was to influence Martin's musical style and structure in the years ahead and lay the foundations for the floor-shows he produced in England.

According to Martin, the show Vodery orchestrated and placed on the boards for him not only helped pay his bills at Columbia but also allowed him to travel to London in the early 1920s, as a pupil of the eminent composer John Ireland. As with the saxophone and banjo riffs of Vodery's scores, some of the Elgaresque lyricism, largeness of vision and intensity of sentimentality of Ireland's *oeuvre* would fold into Martin's music in time to come. But in London, Martin would find his true specialty — the sort of light music-hall scores that his future friend and colleague Eric Coates (old enough to be Martin's father and thus well-versed in the Victorian music-hall traditions) had made uniquely his own. In the June 1924 issue of *The Illustrated Sporting and Dramatic News*, the newly opened Café de Paris was pictured,

Martin's youth and exuberence were on display in this shot of the young composer with Velma Deane and Winnie Collins, from his show at the new Café de Paris nightclub in London, summer 1924. This photograph was published in the June 1924 issue of *The Illustrated Sporting and Dramatic News.*

with Martin sleekly smiling at a grand piano on which several chorus girls lolled. The text described Martin as performer of the first show at what was to become a famous London nightspot, his songs heard on everyone's lips. Martin's songs were also catching the ears of the transcontinental theatre world, which is how Charlotte Greenwood became Mrs. Martin Broones.[3]

In the weeks leading up to the premiere of the Ritz Revue, Charlotte was in what can only be described as a "state."

"From the very first," she remembered, "things began to go wrong.... As is the custom with revues, the songs and sketches were contributed by a variety of writers and composers, but for some unaccountable reason I was still in need of song material.... In desperation I called on Billy Gaxton for aid."

Unlike Charlotte, who was already a star, in 1924 William Gaxton was not to make equal fame until his appearance as Martin in 1927's *A Connecticut Yankee*; but he was already a well-known figure from vaudeville, Charlotte's old stomping ground. Born in San Francisco in 1893 as Arturo Gaxiola, he did a stint at military academy and then the University of California before going on the stage as a song-and-patter man. Tall, spare and handsome in a regal way not unlike Charlotte herself, Gaxton was just as capable as she of entering from the wings like a king and ending up on the floor entangled with a maid and a tray of *hors d'oeuvres.*[4]

According to Charlotte, Gaxton knew everyone of any importance in New York show business, "and he had a facility for persuading people to do things for his friends." When she told him her desperation for some good songs for the Short revue, he assured her she had nothing to worry about. "Think nothing of it, Lottie!" said Gaxton. "Just go ahead with rehearsals; I'll have a couple of dandies for you without fail." Charlotte long remembered her sigh of relief: "With Gaxton on the job, my troubles were really over."

Or were they? "I lived in that fool's paradise for two days," she remembered, "and then one morning choked on a bit of toast as I read in the theatrical news of the *Times* a three-line item — Gaxton had gone romping off to England for a holiday." Charlotte immediately contacted Hassard Short to ask him what he knew. He knew nothing — not even a search through all the mail that had arrived at the theatre revealed any songs for Charlotte from Billy Gaxton. Charlotte went to Gaxton's apartment building and, like a scene from one of her own 1930s film comedies, convinced the manager to unlock his place for her, then ransacked the apartment looking for some sign that the absent miscreant had been good on his word to her. She found one equivocal bit of evidence: "a cryptic note on his desk calendar. It read: 'Lottie — songs — must do — doodle-oodle-d-o-o' and a series of musical notes."

Now more in a state than ever, Charlotte recalled, she completely forgot that Gaxton never let anyone down. No wonder: he was on an ocean liner even as she read his note. "What I needed was material," she fumed, "and there he was tossing about on the high seas, undoubtedly the life of the party."

What she only found out later was that Gaxton, of course, *had* been the life of the shipboard party, and that during all the merriment he had met Charlotte's old colleague Grace LaRue, the ex–Mrs. Byron Chandler and now wife of actor Hale Hamilton. Mentioning Charlotte's plight to these old friends of hers, Gaxton found out that they were acquainted with an expatriate American named Martin Broones, who for all his young years was already a composer, producer and man about London, with a successful revue in the West End's Vaudeville Theatre called *The Odd Spot*, starring the luminous Binnie Hale. Broones also had a reputation for having introduced the floor show to England — an exaggeration which, as it happened, made him all the more attractive to Charlotte.

American composers and lyricists came to London in legion in the years after World War I. "A war with Europe, a war in Europe, had cut Britain off from her great Victorian links to Germany and Austria, and American composers were quick to step into that breach," writes Sheridan Morley. "Some, in Europe for the first time as soldiers after the United States joined the war in 1917, simply stayed on in Paris or London to write music for the Jazz Age: others returned home to Broadway but continued to write with at least one eye on the West End, where much of the acting and singing talent was still centred."[5] (In fact, another star of *The Odd Spot* as well as lyricist was Dion Titharedge, who was to take what he had learned from London revues and bring it to Broadway in 1925's *Charlot's Revue*, which starred Jack Buchanan, Gertrude Lawrence and Beatrice Lillie and featured songs by Ivor Novello and Noël Coward, among other lights of lyrics of that time.)

With so much talent at his fingertips, to write for and learn from, Martin was particularly suited to carry his brand of light, quirky, tuneful and romantic songwriting to Broadway, a step ahead of everyone else. One of his *Odd Spot* hits, the song "Cocktail Time," could only have been written at the inception of the Jazz Age by an exuberant expat American. And perhaps with more prescience than he knew, one of Martin's biggest recent hits, displaying

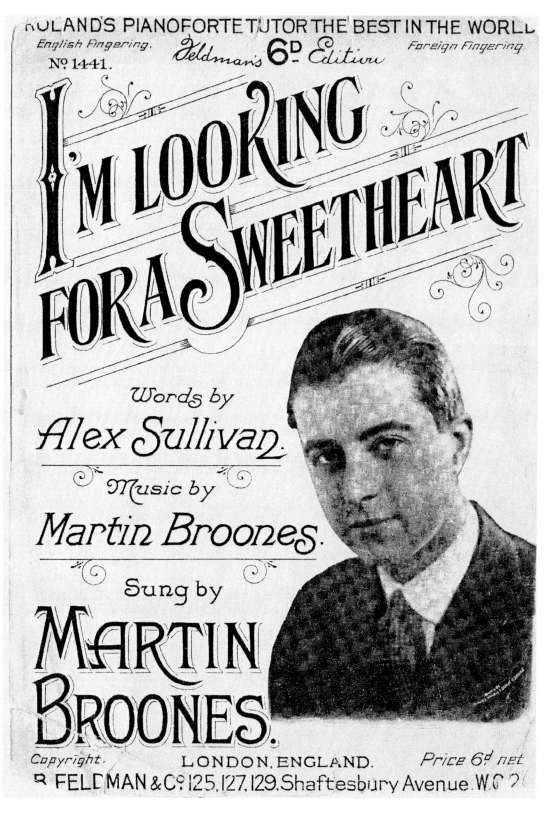

Twenty-something Martin Broones, pictured on the cover of his song "I'm Looking for a Sweetheart," in 1924, the year he found his sweetheart in Charlotte Greenwood.

his handsome face on the cover, was a soulful ballad for which he was also acclaimed as vocal soloist, "I'm Looking for a Sweetheart:"

> I've been nobody's baby ever since I was a child
> I don't know why girls pass me by, for me they don't go wild....[6]

Gaxton seems to have thought it would be easy to make this up-and-coming young man see that he was born to write songs for Charlotte Greenwood, established star. But he was mistaken. As Charlotte heard of the incident later on:

> They argued far into the dawn on every conceivable subject. They still do, and The Lambs [a famous private club for show business professionals] loses its habitual calm when both happen to be luncheon guests. The debate started over Broones' determination to reside in England. Gaxton liked England but he couldn't see the point of living there, unless of course you wanted to become an Englishman. As the days and nights went on the chit-chat became more bitter. Finally Gaxton expressed doubts of Broones' gifts as a composer and entrepreneur. All well and good to sell a song in England which was so backward it was just catching on to plumbing and hadn't yet mastered the first principles of central heating. New York was something else again. Gaxton seriously doubted if Broones could make the riffle there.
>
> If the hapless Broones had only been aware of it, he was being victimized by the crafty Gaxton, who was steadily leading him home.

Gaxton had already decided that Martin was the perfect man to write the songs Charlotte needed, "but he was too shrewd a poker player to show his hand," Charlotte recalled. As she heard later, the conversation went something like this:

> GAXTON (WITHOUT FURTHER ADO): "Ever hear of a girl named Charlotte Greenwood?"
> BROONES: "Never."
> GAXTON (IGNORING BROONES' NONCHALANCE): "Curious thing. Very clever, but can't get material. Nobody seems able to write songs for her."
> BROONES (RISING TO THE OCCASION): "That's ridiculous. Anybody can get material — anybody who is willing to pay for it. What's she like?"
> GAXTON DESCRIBED.
> BROONES: "I have two songs right here in my desk. They'd fit her like a glove. Here they are — 200 pounds apiece."

"Before they had finished," Charlotte wrote, "the pair had boarded the boat bound for America. Broones was returning home for the week-end to look this Greenwood over, sell her $1,000 worth of songs and then get back to England."[7]

Over dinner at Hassard Short's apartment, Charlotte met Martin Broones for the first time. "Frankly," she wrote, "I didn't like this Broones from the beginning. He was smug. He was superior. Of course, some people might argue that he was good-looking, and some might say that he had talent both as a musician and a singer. Nevertheless, he was smug. He even maintained a superior air as he played his songs."[8]

The Martin Broones Charlotte met that night at Short's was a far cry from Cyril Ring, both in looks and in ambition. Martin's was a boyish handsomeness set in a mild oval face, with black hair, large blue eyes, a fresh, open smile, all of which belied a healthy appetite for self-promotion and, in the very near future, a guard dog's interest in protecting and promoting Charlotte's career. Martin boasted height that compared well with Charlotte's own, and to her natural diffidence he opposed an entitled air combined of his upper middle class upbringing and his early successes in London. And his suave performance and voice at the piano seemed an aural extension of his sleek dark hair, flirtatious glance and dapper clothes.[9]

Though she claims they annoyed her on their first meeting, Martin's adopted British accent and clipped vocabulary clearly charmed Charlotte as much as they put her off. "I fell in love with him," she confessed, "despite his elegance." And, as she wrote later, she very much liked the songs he had brought for her — one was "Too Tall," with lyrics by May Tuller (which would later serve Charlotte in her first test recording) and one with a sample of Martin's characteristically lengthy song titles, "When You Come to the End of a Perfect Day, That's When the Wonderful Nights Begin."

Martin's songs did very well indeed for Charlotte, but it was another sketch altogether, without singing or dancing, that proved such a hit that Charlotte bought it from its writers and took it on the road, to even more success. When the Ritz Revue premiered on September 17, 1924, it is unlikely most in the audience expected, or desired, to see Charlotte Greenwood sitting naked in a bathtub. But since the Ritz Revue marketed itself as "A Sophisticated Revue for Sophisticated People," "lavish, smart, Rabelaisian...," perhaps no one should have been surprised when the curtains raised to reveal America's longest comedienne huddled in an oversize tub, hair twisted into a topknot, soap in one hand and back brush in the other.

In this sketch, Charlotte played an out-of-work girl trying to take her morning bath and prepare for a job interview, only to be prevented from completing her ablutions by a variety of interruptions: visiting friends, clothing store clerks, the gas meter reader, and the visitor who drew the most laughs — the iceman, who left a cake of ice which Charlotte, wearing only her towel, then had to somehow wedge into the icebox without losing her skimpy garment, all the while dancing around ice chunks on the floor. (A thief also made a brief appearance at the hapless bather's window just before curtain, yelling: "Hold 'em up!"[10]) No sooner would Charlotte sit back in her bath than she would have to rise again, re-wrapping the towel, to laughter which was, of course, tinged with titillated horror lest she should rise and leave the towel behind altogether.

"The business of making people laugh is one of the most complicated of trades," Charlotte wrote in her memoir notes. "The substance of humor underlying the scene is far more searching and lasting than the eyebrows you tilt, pucker, tangle, or wave." But sometimes, as in her best moments on stage and off, accident played its unexpected role.

"Ashton Stevens," remembered Charlotte, "the Chicago critic, once said that the proper place to see 'Her Morning Bath' was the top gallery. Many times the remark had been dropped: 'Oh boy — if you want to give us a big laugh — drop that towel.' The towel had to be handled teasingly and drop to a point, but never beyond." Charlotte made sure she never gave anyone the satisfaction of seeing her towel travel into the beyond. But on closing night of the Ritz Revue:

> ... when I came to the spot in the sketch where I tried to close the window to stop the breeze from blowing on me, after I had been called out of the tub for the third time to answer the phone, the window suddenly dropped, catching a corner of the towel and as I started to walk away from the window, the towel held firm and began to drop [too].
>
> Strange to say, instead of a laugh, a hush went over the entire house. Apparently it had been fun imagining what would happen if I dropped the towel, but the audience, faced with reality, didn't want to see me embarrassed.... Finally I managed to get back to the tub, sit down, and drop the towel.
>
> At this moment the musical director, knowing it was my last night, struck up 'The Star Spangled Banner.' ... Fortunately for me the curtain was released in time for me to get off the stage and into my dressing gown without being either unpatriotic or indecent.[11]

As with the second Music Box Revue, Charlotte was again in review heaven. The prominent Chicago critic Amy Leslie, a known aesthete who worshipped the boards Maude Adams

HASSARD SHORT'S
...RITZ REVUE...
with

Charlotte Greenwood

. . . . A . . . .

SOPHISTICATED

. . . . . REVUE . . . . .

. . . . . . FOR . . . .

SOPHISTICATED

. . . . PEOPLE . . . .

A Gay, Handsome Chorus   *An Amazing Cast of 100*

Shubert Detroit Opera House
DETROIT, MICH.
Commencing Sunday, MARCH 15
MATS. WED. AND SAT.

Charlotte Greenwood doing the kick (or what she called a "leg lift") that made her famous. From a *Hassard Short's Ritz Revue* program, 1924. William Luce collection.

walked on, wrote of Charlotte's performance in tones usually devoted to the work of Miss Adams: "Miss Greenwood has not enough to do; Miss Greenwood never has enough to do in any show." Leslie was seconded by Ashton Stevens, who wrote: "Miss Greenwood is a fine grave comic artist" — high praise for what was essentially a high burlesque act. One critic described Charlotte's bath sketch in terms better suited to a ballet performance: "Charlotte Greenwood's characterization of a woman walking on ice is among the most eloquent displays of pantomimic fidelity I can remember."

But the *pièce de résistance* was a review filed by Alexander Woollcott, drama critic of the *New York Times* and member of the famous round table at the Algonquin Hotel, who revealed himself a long-time admirer:

> But then there is Charlotte Greenwood, blowing through the show like a gale of fresh wind ... This opinion is recorded by one who has long cherished the conviction that the lanky comedienne is a first rate actress who would do herself proud in a genuine comedy which did not require her meditatively to stroke the ceiling with her toe.[12]

13

Mrs. Martin Broones

"It isn't true, as Billy Gaxton has contended so vociferously through the years ... that I married Martin Broones rather than pay his exorbitant fee for his songs," Charlotte wrote. "Martin, on the other hand, has always argued that I bought the songs for spite, because I never allowed material written for me to be published, and by being denied public sales he lost a fortune in royalties."

It is safe to assume that Martin felt he was getting something in Charlotte Greenwood far beyond a star who could keep him in the songwriting business. He and Charlotte were deeply in love. Judge Robert Kincaid of New Jersey, the man who married them, after their brief courtship at the theatre or in a restaurant called the Soho in Claremont Square, would leave an anecdote years later that proves that the affection that began over Hassard Short's dining table only grew stronger with time: "Never have I seen two people so content, so absorbed in each other," Judge Kincaid told a reporter in the 1940s. "It revives one's faith. Marriage is never a 'problem' with people like Charlotte and Martin."[1]

As the Ritz Revue approached closing in New York and starting on the road tour, and Martin's planned return to England seemed suddenly just around the corner, the couple decided over lunch, just before Christmas 1924, to get married as soon as possible. It was December 22, and a Saturday as well, and Charlotte knew that marriage license offices always closed at noon. Charlotte called on old friends of her mother's, the McOskers, who now lived in New Jersey and were related to a certain Judge Kincaid. The news was good. "If we could get there by three o'clock," Charlotte was told by her delighted friends, "not only a license but a judge would be forthcoming."

> That left us less than three hours and a good deal to do in the matter of transportation, trousseau and general arrangements. Martin gave evidence at once of his genius for organization. He began by calling his brother Otto, then an intern at Bellevue [Hospital], and commandeering him as chauffeur. Otto was willing — anything to get away from an afternoon of bedpans at the clinic! He arrived in time, outfitted with an automobile of ancient vintage and we started for the Jersey ferry.
>
> It was 2:30 and we were in the midst of a gala traffic jam. Martin was frantic; I was laughing myself into hysterics; Otto was trying desperately to maintain his medical calm. Finally he flagged down a passing traffic officer, and displayed a card identifying him with the staff of Bellevue. The policeman was moderately courteous and definitely disinterested. The boat was being filled with motor cars. It was obvious we were going to be on the wharf for an hour. The wedding was off. Then Otto had an inspiration.

"Never have I seen two people so content, so absorbed in each other" — Robert Kincaid, the New Jersey judge who married Charlotte Greenwood and Martin Broones on December 22, 1924. USC collection.

"Well," he sighed, with an air of resignation. "It's up to you. Personally I don't know what I'm going to do with those two!"

The officer peered into the tonneau and saw a glowering Martin, looking for all the world like a homicidal maniac; and a hysterical Greenwood whose convulsions might have passed for mild schizophrenia.

"Nuts?" the cop asked in growing alarm.

"What do you think?" parried Ott.

"Good God!" the cop yelled, and began to blow feverishly on his whistle. The boat traffic halted. There was a diligent rearrangement of machines ... one of the motor cars was backed off the ferry to make way for us.

At 3 o'clock we steamed up to the City Hall and by 3:15 we were man and wife.[2]

Martin was six months into being twenty-three (or twenty-one) years old, Charlotte five months past thirty-four. Whichever was Martin's true age, the age difference between himself and Charlotte was something which this otherwise most honest and self-effacing of performers would spend a lot of time and energy covering up for the rest of her long marriage.

As if to underscore the racy nature of their union, Martin paid homage to one of the world's most famed pair of legs by having a diamond ankle bracelet made for his bride. (Charlotte responded with a sapphire and platinum pinky ring from Cartier.) Charlotte wore the bracelet with her usual flair — in a photo op of the couple at a train station, Charlotte lifts her ankle for the inspection of the photographer, the way ordinary new brides show off a diamond wedding ring.[3]

There was no time for a proper honeymoon, but Mr. and Mrs. Martin Broones decided to make one of a short jaunt to Boston for the opening of the touring company of the *Ritz Revue*. While Charlotte held off reporters anxious to know the news about the sudden marriage, Martin made all the plans, as Charlotte and he, too, would come to regret shortly.

"My first shock came that evening," Charlotte remembered, "when I learned we were leaving at 7 A.M. on a train that took an unconscionable time to reach Boston and had no Pullman accommodations."

This was 1924 and the day of the swank streamliner with its parlor cars and private seats was a thing of the future. But Martin was not to be warded off his great plan. Even the news from the ticket agent that most of the hand luggage would have to be carried in the coach didn't dissuade him. He returned to the hotel aglow with enthusiasm and major plans. We would travel light. He would need practically nothing but his handsome English umbrella and a backgammon board, together with a change of linen. I could send all of my gear ahead in the trunks.

For seventeen years now [she wrote in 1941] we have been making similar resolutions and just as on that first trip we have invariably reached the station with a collection of luggage that appalls the porters. We arose at dawn and hustled to the station only to find that we should have been there hours before. Many other people had the same idea about this daylight trip. We were fortunate to find two seats to the rear of the car and our Lares and Penates were finally stored above our heads in a little rack with stray parcels packed around us on the seat. Martin's umbrella with its heavy hardwood handle occupied a position of honor on the pinnacle of the overhead pile. Then my beatific bridegroom settled back with an expansive smile.

It didn't last long. "Well, de-a-r," said Martin in his Anglophone accent, which Charlotte swore was more capable than anyone else's of putting two complete syllables in that single syllable endearment, "this is going to be fun!"

The conductor called all aboard, and the train lurched forward. "Down came the carefully piled luggage," recalled Charlotte, "in a shower of alligator hide, cardboard and an English umbrella. I wondered why Martin maintained that cherubic smile. When I took a second look I had the answer. The umbrella had landed smack dab on his head and the handle had stood its ground. He was out as cold as [Latin American boxing champ Luis] Firpo." Like that boxer, Martin also had a bruise on his forehead that was swelling by the minute.

"Yes," Charlotte echoed ironically, before ministering to her wounded husband, "fun!"

The rest of the trip was of a similar slapstick plotline. "Here I was," she remembered, "taking a daylight trip on an uncomfortable train through territory where I had played every water tank in some show or other for the last twenty years." Martin, meantime, was sleeping off his bruising, and thus missed Charlotte's adventure with a stocky woman passenger who decided to force open one of the windows, upon which "the ice blast from the Connecticut countryside virtually blew all of us out of our second growth," not to mention loose pages of a music score in Martin's lap. It took the combined forces of the loquacious peanut vendor and four other men to get the window shut again and the score retrieved. Then a porter decided to mop the entire length of the car, "a function that led directly to a nasty fall by a stoutish lady with a dialect." (In other words, she cursed a blue streak.) As the peanut vendor continued to sell his lemonade, ginger ale and other treats up and down the car, men rushed forward to help the injured and angry lady, during which a brakeman arrived carrying a telegram for a Mrs. Jones, and five different women of that name rushed forward to take it from him — a scene from *Pretty Mrs. Smith* brought to real life.

Just before they reached Boston, Martin himself slipped in the aisle and had to be revived with cold towels.

Once they got settled into their seat again, Martin turned to Charlotte and said, "You really should look at the scenery ... I've been told there is no better scenery in the world."

"You've been *told*," I repeated with some heat, "do you mean to tell me that you've never been on this trip before?"

"No, dee-ar," he smiled. "I've been all over Europe, but I've never been further north than 125th Street — I used to go up there to try out sketches...."

Had Martin not been so black and blue, Charlotte would have delivered a left hook then and there.

It looked as if she already had. "When we reached the theater next morning," Charlotte remembered, "Hassard Short came forward, hand extended for congratulations, and burst into a guffaw [at the sight of Martin's battered appearance]. I could hardly blame him. 'I have to hand it to you, Lottie,' he said when he recovered his poise. 'You certainly started off your married life with a clear understanding of who is to be boss....' I had only to flex my muscles before going on the stage to have stagehands and actors flee in mock terror."[4]

The *Ritz Revue* tour lasted until June 1925, covering the Eastern circuit to great success. When the show closed, Charlotte and Martin returned to New York, where they were invited to dinner at the home of vaudeville comedian Ed Wynn and his wife. Also attending were Frances Ring Meighan, Charlotte's ex-sister in law, and her husband Thomas, who were aflutter about their plans to take ship the next day for an extended sojourn in Ireland. (They were eventually to move there.)

Meighan had been cast in an English film called *Irish Luck*; and perhaps his enthusiasm for the work awaiting him across the ocean spurred Martin to bet on some Irish luck himself and get to work, too, on his musical adaptation of James Forbes' 1908 novel, *The Chorus Lady*, itself an adaptation of John. W. Harding's play of the same name. The subject seems to have obsessed Martin for some time, and no wonder. Described as a "slangy, sharp-tongued look at backstage life," the story peers into the life of a chorus girl named Patsy O'Brien, who risks losing her fiancé and her job to protect her naive sister Nora (also a chorus girl) when the latter gets mixed up with a roué. (Rose Stahl, who played the role at its premiere in 1906, later performed the lead in the same *Maggie Pepper* which was adapted for Charlotte and renamed *Letty Pepper* by Oliver Morosco.)

Like Alexander Woolcott but viewed through the eyes of a smitten husband, Martin's perspective on Charlotte was that there was more to meet the eye with her, even as there was more to Patsy O'Brien than that she was a chorus girl in loud, fashionable clothes — that Charlotte was a serious actress and a moral person under the figurative clown costume and risqué plots her vaudeville work thrust upon her. And though Charlotte never indicates one way or another, it is clear that Martin intended the lead role to go to her — the fact that he ploddingly worked on the score for years seems to point to plans for showcasing Charlotte as Patsy. Certainly, Charlotte knew all about the world that Patsy inhabited — the gossip and the backbiting in the chorus girls' dressing room, the concern of all too few about what the world thought of their way of life, just so the stage door johnnies showed up with flowers and maybe a modest jewel, to be displayed proudly, perhaps maliciously, to the other girls. Whether Charlotte had ever been tempted, as Patsy is in the novel, to leave her chosen career for love of a man is never mentioned or even considered in her memoirs; such a sacrifice was certainly not within her character, and would not have accomplished Martin's goal: of making his wife a respected actor at long last. Anyhow, it would be Martin who ultimately gave up his career for hers.

As for Martin, he was clearly moved by the lyric possibilities of some of Forbes' writing, which could turn a glance around electric-lit Edwardian Broadway into something more akin to perusing the display windows at Tiffany's: "The evening parure of New York is a splendid radiance of golden chrysolites, and white, liquid brilliants, with here and there the sanguine splash of a ruby, and here and there an emerald."[5] But the planned musical never went anywhere. Tellingly enough, its failure had the blessing of Forbes himself, who told Martin the play's plot, involving one sister's gallant protection of the other's reputation, was obsolete — it was a species of melodrama that had been going out of style even before World War I. (It should be noted that when this novel first appeared, Martin himself was only five years old.) It would remain for a later time for Martin to write a musical around his wife, and with much better results than the time worn *Chorus Lady* would have gained either of them.[6]

Their still-packed luggage in tow, Charlotte and Martin joined the Meighans on their ship next day, eager to see Ireland and Martin's old haunts in London. "I fell in love with England and the English people," Charlotte wrote. "I remember one of our sight-seeing trips took us down to Drury Lane and through the historic Theatre Royal where Nell Gwyn used to play and where Charles II had his celebrated stage box that led directly into the star dressing room." It was a theatre and a dressing room Charlotte would come to know very well in the early 1930s.

Having seen the city from which she had abducted her beloved Martin, Charlotte returned to America to start a vaudeville tour, featuring her in the "Her Morning Bath" sketch, which she had purchased; she toured the sketch for a month at a time in Chicago, San Francisco, Los Angeles and the glittering Palace Theatre in New York City, as well as in Philadelphia, Boston and other eastern circuit cities. Her earnings at the time, amounting to $3,000 per week, were, per her account, among the largest is the business. During this period,

Martin was offered a prime opportunity for so young a songwriter: to compose the score for a new revue, this one devised by Broadway producer Rufus LeMaire.

"It was a singular assignment," wrote Charlotte, "for up to that time Irving Berlin was about the only composer who had ever been entrusted with the writing of an entire revue score."[7]

"Rufus LeMaire had been the Shuberts' head man for casting and producing their successful revues for several years," recalled Sophie Tucker, who was the star of the revue's first cast. He had decided to mount his own show for a change. The new show even had a risqué name perfectly suited to the 1920s — *Rufus LeMaire's Affairs"* — and a cast as big and wild as a Park Avenue party in a household full of contraband gin.

While Charlotte tried to keep her towel on in theatres across the country, Martin worked on what came to be considered a score mediocre save for one song, with a characteristically lengthy Broones title, "I Can't Get Over a Girl Like You Loving a Boy Like Me," which was later a staple of sweet-voiced singers like Doris Day. *LeMaire's Affairs* presented bandleader and clarinetist Ted Lewis and Sophie Tucker, along with ex–Ziegfeld Follies Girl Peggy Fears, musical comedy performer John Price Jones and a cast of over eighty others in a series of sketches, dances, comedy routines, songs and the assorted other entertainments that typically made up a lavish revue of the day. The show opened in Chicago, where it ran for a successful 36 weeks. In this revue Tucker gave fame to a couple of songs, "The Turkish Towel," and especially Harry Woods' song "When the Red, Red Robin Comes Bob, Bob, Bobbin' Along." A minstrel scene with Ted Lewis and his band, singing Martin's regrettably titled "Bring Back Those Minstrel Days," was another hit of the show. "It wasn't only that the show was a success with the public," remembered Tucker. Everyone in the company got along famously during the entire five month run.[8]

After the Chicago run, LeMaire booked the show on the road and in New York City. And this is where the trouble started, because LeMaire also announced that some casting changes would be required before opening at the new Majestic Theatre in New York. Tucker advised LeMaire that as the show had been running for over eight months and doing excellent business, it was hardly wise to interfere with its manifest success. Listen to box office, she told him, not brokers. Unfortunately for Tucker and the show, it was her head that was on the block, as LeMaire told her to her shock: *she* was to be replaced with a performer who could act.

Her replacement was Charlotte Greenwood, LeMaire told her, with Peggy Fears cast in the singing lead. Disgusted, Tucker handed in her two weeks' notice, and before she left claims the show was such a success it pulled in $40,000 in Boston its first week there. "Then Charlotte Greenwood came in," Tucker sniffed. "The show was pulled all around, sketches changed, new costumes.... They played the second week with Charlotte Greenwood and the receipts took a terrific drop.... In six weeks the show folded!"[9]

Charlotte herself was not comfortable in *LeMaire's Affairs*, and at least some of her discomfort seems to have had to do with Tucker's abrupt sacking. "Although she had aided in the launching of the production and assisted materially in keeping it afloat in Chicago with her talent," Charlotte remembered, "she had other commitments that prevented her from going on to Broadway"— clearly, Charlotte either did not know the facts of the matter of Tucker's sudden disappearance, or did and chose, as with so many other topics which might be construed as negative, to gloss them over in her written recollections. She does offer evidence in a brief passage that she tried to make good toward Tucker in 1938 by suggesting her

THREE **INTERNATIONAL** **STARS**

TED LEWIS   SOPHIE TUCKER   LESTER ALLEN

IN

RUFUS

LeMAIRE'S AFFAIRS

CLEVEREST COSTLIEST REVUE EVER STAGED

MUSIC BY MARTIN BROONES   LYRICS BY BALLARD MACDONALD
BOOK BY ANDY RICE, BALLARD MACDONALD AND JACK LAIT
DANCES BY BOBBY CONNOLLY—DIALOGUE DIRECTED BY WILLIAM HALLIGAN
ENTIRE PRODUCTION STAGED UNDER THE PERSONAL SUPERVISION OF
RUFUS LeMAIRE

TED LEWIS' MERRY MUSICAL CLOWNS

More Brilliant Stars Than There Are In the Sky

An advertisement for *Rufus LeMaire's Affairs,* Martin's only Broadway show, before it came to Broadway. Its star, Sophie Tucker, was let go and Charlotte given her role. "They played the second week with Charlotte Greenwood and the receipts took a terrific drop," wrote Tucker. Charlotte wasn't happy with the role, either. William Luce collection.

for the lead in Vinton Freedley's and Cole Porter's *Leave It to Me*, a role Charlotte had been offered first. "She accepted, and the play was a hit," Charlotte wrote, though adding a bit frostily, "As for us, we were involved in plans for a world tour of *Leaning on Letty*."[10] Considering they moved in similar circles, had come up in show business in similar ways, and would both be stars of the London stage around the same time, Charlotte's name is as conspicuously scarce in Tucker's memoirs as Tucker's is in Charlotte's, so whatever sportsmanship they were capable of seems to have failed in this case.

Charlotte minces no words as to how she felt she fit into the newly remade production: "It wasn't a good replacement. I didn't fit into the Tucker assignment at all." Even so, she achieved another record, as the first "duplex" performer, appearing in both the first and the second halves of the bill. In a world from which vaudeville has vanished as thoroughly as the dodo bird, it is not clear just how unusual this duplex performance was. But from vaudeville's earliest days, where you appeared on the program was all-important — appearing first on the bill, as Charlotte and Eunice Burnham had done at the Victoria Theatre, was to be given what George Gottlieb called "the dumb act," comprised of dancers or animals performing tricks, so that latecomers would not feel they had missed anything special. The plum acts for a star were the fourth, or possibly the fifth (before intermission), and the eighth, when the show's real star appeared before a people-pleasing final number.

In *LeMaire's Affairs* Charlotte not only got the prime number in the middle, she also got the star turn at the evening's end. She also had a chance to perform with Martin, in the only instance the couple are known to have performed together on stage, in a sketch of songs with onstage piano.

14

Back to Hollywood

In the Majestic Theatre on 44th Street, on March 28, 1927, despite her misgivings Charlotte was critically successful in a burlesque (if such was possible with this over-the-top material) of Anita Loos' 1925 novel *Gentlemen Prefer Blondes*, playing Lorelei Lee, that quintessential Jazz Age flapper for whom diamonds were bosom friends. Perhaps falling back on what she had observed in her brief foray into Hollywood for *Jane* almost a decade before, she also played a movie star in a sketch called "Movieland"—a prescient bit of casting, given the film work which would again shortly come Charlotte's way.[1]

Rufus LeMaire's Affairs closed after only seven weeks (two fewer than the Chicago run with Sophie Tucker) and a plethora of tepid reviews, adding Martin's name to what Gerald Bordman calls "the growing list of writers with only a single [Broadway] score to their credit." He was in good company: Sigmund Romberg's *Cherry Blossoms* closed the very same night as *LeMaire's Affairs*, after a similar short-lived run (and a much less prepossessing show).[2]

Charlotte and Martin were in no mood to stay in New York after the show's closing, which is why, when Charlotte received a call from Metro-Goldwyn-Mayer to come to California to make a film — her first in nearly ten years — she and Martin both jumped at the opportunity. "Martin decided that he might get *The Chorus Lady* into shape if he went to California where ideas fell from trees onto deep thinkers reclining in the shade." As a result of this trip west he, too, would get something he had not bargained for.

David Selznick, the son of David O. Selznick and Irene Mayer, always remembered his maternal grandfather as a man with voice like "very dark maple syrup," and indeed Louis B. Mayer had his sweetly attractive qualities along with his stickily unattractive ones. Born Lazar Meir in a lumber-town in Ukraine in 1885 to Jacob Meir, a gifted ne'er-do-well and the hardworking Sarah Meltzer, the future head of one of Hollywood's greatest movie studios was brought by his needy family first to New York City and then to St. John, New Brunswick while still a child. He grew up watching his father peddle in the streets, and occasionally had to help him. As time passed, Jacob's luck turned for the better and he set up a scrap iron business; he also ran a dry goods store, which Sarah managed. Louis also worked for his father. In Boston in 1904, the nineteen-year-old Mayer married Margaret Shenberg, a rabbi's daughter. They moved to Brooklyn a year later, where Mayer started his own successful business selling scrap. By 1907, Mayer had acquired his first theater, a 600 seat mess officially monikered

The Gem but known to the locals as The Germ. With this purchase, Mayer was on his way into the high stakes and high drama world of show business.[3]

In 1927, the year Charlotte came to Hollywood to star in the film version of Margaret Mayo's play, *Baby Mine*, which had been adapted almost verbatim for the screen by Sylvia Thalberg (Irving's sister), Mayer was running a studio boasting the talents of directors Cecil B. DeMille (who joined MGM in 1928) and Edward Sutherland (Charlotte's nephew by her marriage to Cyril Ring and husband of actress Louise Brooks), leaving the artistic side of production to his "boy wonder," Irving Thalberg (Shearer's husband). Charlotte joined ranks with such stars as Greta Garbo and John Gilbert, Norma Shearer and Joan Crawford. In time, according to notes Charlotte did not include in her memoirs, she befriended the fascinating, fragmented Jeanne Eagels, showing her how to apply makeup as smoothly as she did, getting her dressed after one of her tantrums and helping her through the remaining two days of filming of *Man, Woman and Sin*, her final film with John Gilbert.

Besides overseeing MGM with his notorious eagle eye and exploding into regular fits of rage and tearful theatrics, Mayer was helping to found the Academy of Motion Picture Arts and Sciences that year, and doing what he could — which was much — to dissuade daughter Irene from marrying David O. Selznick, for whom Mayer had no great admiration and from whom he had much to fear. He was also hearing rumors of the approach of talking pictures, and like other film executives, writers, producers and especially actors, was worried about what this innovation might mean for future profits. Mayer could kick Selznick off the MGM lot, but he couldn't do anything to prevent the success of the second, and most influential, talking picture, *The Jazz Singer*, brought out by the canny Harry Warner in 1927, in which Charlotte's friend Al Jolson sang the now-legendary "Mammy!" in blackface. To make matters worse, Selznick joined the enemy by taking a job at Paramount Pictures.[4]

This was the busy scenario into which Charlotte stepped. "I arrived in Hollywood with appropriate fanfare," Charlotte recalled. "Notified to disembark at Pasadena, I found myself awaited by a delegation from the studio — press agents and camera men. There was a great flurry of excitement and no service was too great to perform for my comfort. This, I decided, was definitely the life."

Then the throng began to ask what to Charlotte seemed ridiculous questions. "No one seemed particularly interested in the things I had done," she complained; "they wanted to know about the celebrities I had met."[5]

The odd welcoming party over, Charlotte was just as suddenly left all by herself. She and Martin took up residence in a suite at the newly built Beverly Wilshire Hotel on North Rodeo Drive, in relatively newly built Beverly Hills. There, in her suite between that of producer Myron Selznick (brother of David) on one side and lyricist Buddy DeSylva (later executive producer at Paramount Studios) on the other, Charlotte proceeded to twiddle her lengthy thumbs. Just what sort of contract, if any, Charlotte had with MGM is not known. Clearly, though, the studio was not sure what to do with her; they just knew they had to hang on to her. "A week passed; then another week; then another. Each week brought a nice fat salary check, but I wanted to work," Charlotte complained. "In the theater no one ever thought of parting with money without value received."

She went golfing with friends, took riding lessons with Frances Ring under the piercing eye of a disenfranchised European nobleman whom Charlotte remembers as a Russian count, and tooled around Los Angeles in her speedy, expensive little Mercer roadster.[6] (This was possibly the same car stolen in a post-holdup getaway outside a Brooklyn theatre in 1922, reported by the *New York Times* as having outsped the pursuing police — something only a Mercer, with its 58-horsepower motor, could have done.) Martin made the most of the quiet time by conferring with writers Harold Atteridge (author of the hit song *By the Beautiful Sea*) and Paul Gerard Smith on *The Chorus Lady*—evidently feeling that more heads puzzling themselves over the troublesome musical's book and lyrics would speed up its sluggish progress.

Martin was also offered a job by Metro-Goldwyn-Mayer, as the studio's first music director following the advent and acceptance of talkies. He took it, and though he was not to remain long in the position, he turned out several solid scores, including music for one of the first deep-sea thrillers, the film version of Jules Verne's novel *The Mysterious Island* (1929). "Finally," Charlotte noted, pleased for the moment with the arrangement, "his vocation and his avocation got together, and the ghost of *The Chorus Lady* was laid for all time." Martin put the sketch aside and concentrated on his work at the studio, which put him in daily contact with Mayer, Thalberg and the other executives. At least, thought Charlotte, *one* of them was seeing the inside of Metro-Goldwyn-Mayer Studios.

After weeks spent in the confining splendors of the Beverly Wilshire, however, Charlotte got fed up with waiting and headed for MGM. The gateman recognized her, but could not admit her to the lot without a pass, which she was sent to obtain from another office. There she was confronted by a young man who not only didn't know who she was, but didn't seem to care much, either.

> "I am Charlotte Greenwood," I said with something of an air.
>
> "How ya spell it?"
>
> "It really doesn't matter," this with a trace of hauteur, "I work here. I'm an actress."
>
> He wasn't impressed, but he did condescend to look through an elaborate filing system, apparently containing the names of all bona fide employees. He seemed unable to find anything of importance under the G's, with the exception of Garbo.
>
> "Who'd ya wanta see?" he asked finally.
>
> "Well, no one in particular," I replied, getting smaller by the minute — embarrassment is a great antidote for height — "suppose you try Mr. Mayer or Mr. Thalberg, or Mr. Mannix, or Mr. Hyman. They could identify me."
>
> The boy became very suspicious. Apparently this was an old, familiar dodge. And then the matter was abruptly taken out of his hands. A door opened behind me and a strange man bounded out, paused, enveloped me in his arms and, implanting a resounding kiss, gushed "Charlotte darling! How nice to see you. Why haven't you been over? What's in the wind?"
>
> Before I could explain, the magic catch of the inner door was released by the boy and, arm-in-arm my effusive friend and I entered. An instant later, he dashed away with a hasty goodbye, and I was worse off than ever.... I was faced with a mystic maze of doors and hallways, and I hadn't the vaguest idea which way to turn when a familiar face and figure came into sight. It was Hedda Hopper, gracious, vivacious and friendly as ever.

Seeing that Charlotte was lost, Hedda went to her immediately, her hard, loud laugh and hard, loud theatrical voice echoing in the corridors. "She trotted gaily along," Charlotte recalled, "chattering like a magpie, and led me toward the hut where the press agents worked." Here Hedda spent as much time watching the press engine in action as she did working on the bit parts to which Hollywood consigned her before finally, and cruelly, tossing her out for good.[7]

The fourth wife of actor DeWolfe Hopper, Hedda, born Elda Furry to an Altoona, Pennsylvania butcher in 1885 (not on June 2, as widely reported, but a month earlier), shared much in common with Charlotte. Both were tall and gangly but wore good clothes with finesse; both changed their birth years to appear younger. Both had left school in junior high to pursue dreams of the stage, and in those dreams figured equally a passion for developing themselves as serious artists which, in Hedda's case, was never to come to fruition. Both had been insulted by Ned Wayburn (he took one look at Hedda in a chorus lineup and singled her out as "the awkwardest cow who ever tried kicking chorus").

One thing they did not share was Hedda's finely honed gift for spewing profanity that would have made a longshoreman blush. But banter they did, a sample of which can be heard on a segment of The Charlotte Greenwood Show, from 1944, on which Hedda was a guest — mild insults about age, for the most part, which both women well knew could have been even more insulting were their true ages revealed. It was Hedda's and Charlotte's little secret, among the many others we may suppose they shared over their frequent lunches in later years at Charlotte's house on North Rodeo Drive.

What Charlotte would most have admired about Hedda was what she admired about anyone who possessed it — bravery. When her acting career disappeared, Hedda worked at a variety of odd jobs, from selling real estate to modeling (at her age), in order to afford to put her son by DeWolfe Hopper through school. When it was her time to discover that she could write and that her writing would be read, Hedda seized on her newfound career with characteristic passion. But it was in the press hut in the 1920s, Charlotte insisted, that Hedda was unwittingly preparing herself for what she was really supposed to do — writing what would become one of the most feared and avidly read gossip columns, along with Louella Parsons', in newspaper history. Though Charlotte and Hedda had only been passing acquaintances before meeting again in an MGM corridor, they formed a sisterly friendship then and there that was to last until Hedda's death thirty-nine years later.[8]

15

"Life is just a circus"

B_{ABY} M_{INE} WAS, IN Charlotte's words, "a rough-and-tumble comedy, made in a haphazard sort of way and it took us the greater part of the winter to finish it." The Hollywood of the silents, Charlotte wrote, "wasn't obligated to turn out a given number of pictures on a definite schedule," therefore there was plenty of leeway for repeated takes, relaxation breaks, and script rewrites, which were often as not done while the cameras were cooling between scenes. Enlivening the cast, in which Charlotte played a supporting part, was the star duo of vaudeville, Karl Dane and George K. Arthur, along with pretty, petite and scrappy Louise Lorraine.

According to Charlotte, *Baby Mine* was the first stage play to be reproduced virtually intact for the screen; and in the filming of it Charlotte and Karl Dane performed a single comedy scene of 400–500 feet in length, a record in a time when the typical scene ran 15–300 feet total. (A typical film magazine holds only four to five minutes of film in thousand foot rolls, considered too long to hold on screen.) The original scene was not so long, but after conferring with director Robert Z. Leonard, Charlotte and Dane improvised as soon as the cameras started rolling, sustaining their antics till the action came to a natural stop. This scene was a kind of dry run for Charlotte's future impromptu onscreen wrestling matches with Bert Lahr, Eddie Cantor and Buster Keaton.

For the premiere, programs were handed out showing Charlotte costumed as an unhappy bride and Dane holding an unhappy baby, in a farcical plot involving that old standby from Charlotte's first film, *Jane*, the baby kidnapped to simulate parenthood in a childless marriage, much of which was handled in the unusual form of dream montages. The program promised the audiences of *Baby Mine* "a thousand and one roars," and indeed, Charlotte reports that the film did well, despite a starchily negative review by the *New York Times*' critic Mordaunt Hall:

> Horseplay, and not the play, is the thing in the screen version of Margaret Mayo's stage contribution, "Baby Mine." ... Charlotte Greenwood endeavors to whittle up the fun by gymnastic activities and queer grimaces, some of which probably suit the peculiar humor of this photoplay.[1]

Motion Picture Magazine (reviewing in April 1928) was more genial toward film and its star: "Charlotte Greenwood has come to the screen, and although it isn't enough for her, she and Karl Dane have put on the most uproarious love scene, if you can call it that, that has ever been performed.... [A]ll you have to bother about is the big scene with Charlotte Greenwood."

103

THE screen's greatest laugh team is here in a comedy riot, made from Margaret Mayo's sensational farce.

If you thought you learned about laughing from Dane and Arthur in "Rookies," just wait until you see this one! A thousand and one roars!

KARL DANE *and* GEORGE K. ARTHUR

in

BABY MINE

with CHARLOTTE GREENWOOD

Based upon the play by Margaret Mayo
Adapted by Sylvia Thalberg
Continuity by F. Hugh Herbert and Lew Lipton
Directed by Robert Z. Leonard

A Robert Z. Leonard production

A Metro-Goldwyn-Mayer PICTURE

Charlotte made filmed physical comedy history with Karl Dane in her second silent film, *Baby Mine* (1928). She is shown here in the premiere program with co-stars Karl Dane and George K. Arthur.

Baby Mine was impressive enough to move Warner Brothers, ever on the qui vive to outpace the other studios, to sign Charlotte up to make a film version of *So Long Letty*, in which Charlotte would play her original stage role. Though the plot of the stage version of *Letty* was changed considerably, one twist remained that for 1929 was more than a little risqué: the wife-and-husband swapping on which the plays' plot and comedy turns. There was also a cast change. Where Charlotte had played opposite diminutive Sydney Grant in the stage *Letty*, she now took on plump, wall-eyed tenor Bert Roach as Tommy, the husband who tires of being married to a playgirl, while Patsy Ruth Miller performed the role of Grace, May Boley's part, the domestic wife whose husband, played by tall, handsome but self-conscious Grant Withers (as Harold), wants a little more fun out of life. Consequently, the couples switch spouses for a trial period of a week.

In a subplot broadly sketched to show the high stakes of being married to just the right helpmeet, as well as to give a stark foil to Letty's mayhem-creating enthusiasm for life and all its entertaining possibilities, veteran character actor Claude Gillingwater plays Tommy's rich old Uncle Claude, who will leave his fortune to Tommy only if he has managed to marry a demure and domestic little woman, who will give the family an heir. When Uncle Claude mistakes Grace for Tommy's wife, everyone goes along with the sham, which explodes when Uncle Claude, annoyed with a loud party given next door by Letty and Harold, calls the police, discovers his nephew cavorting in Letty's den of iniquity, and ends up being hauled into court with everyone else. At the bench, Letty, Harold, Grace and Tommy have to confess that they have switched spouses, a revelation that while shocking to Uncle Claude doesn't quite floor him as much as the news that the little sweaters he had seen Grace knitting were not for a baby but for her dog.

A hoyden for the departing Jazz Age, unfazed by the Great Depression: Charlotte Greenwood as Letty in Warner's adaptation of the stage role that brought her fame, *So Long Letty* (1929). William Luce collection.

Letty, however, saves the day by telling Uncle Claude — whether truthfully is open to question — that she herself is expecting, and the film ends with everyone sitting happily around a table in a fancy restaurant, reconciled and pleased with themselves against a backdrop of dancing couples — the Jazz Age prosperity so soon to end.

For the first time, Charlotte received a positive response to her performance from the *New York Times'* Mordaunt Hall:

> The film is raucous and broad and the idea of an exchange of wives for a period of a week is not entirely new. But with the playful Miss Greenwood to carry it along its frivolous route it managed to turn up as a cheery photoplay, with many entertaining moments.[2]

So Long Letty is important for two reasons. Firstly, in this film many people unacquainted with more than still pictures or write-ups of Charlotte's stage performances were able to see her in full dynamic action — singing, dancing and playing; and this film is the only one from Charlotte's post-silents period in which she is not chasing a man and restraining her natural energies to fit into the mould of victim, but is instead a woman wholly self-possessed, interested in her own pleasure but also in vigorously giving pleasure to others.

In *What Made Pistachio Nuts?* Henry Jenkins sees the Letty character as moving from anarchy to acquiescence: "The film holds open the possibility of Letty's resistance (and the pleasures of her comic spectacle) to the very last second, then forcefully pulls her back into conformity with the demands of male authority and forces her to accept the domestic containment required for narrative closure," referring to the scene in which Letty confesses to Uncle Claude that she is pregnant.

One may, however, interpret Letty's disclosure to Uncle Claude as merely a more sophisticated tool for utilizing her capacity for anarchy, through means of a lie that will make him feel better and wrap up all the loose ends of his relationship with his nephew and with her. In fact, in the only close-up of Charlotte in the entire film, just before she confides her story to Uncle Claude, Letty clearly has a moment of revelation in which she sees that the way to do this is not through teasing and pulling at the old man, as she has done throughout the film, but to humor him in a manner he will understand. As a woman who paradoxically controls everyone around her with the slippery medium of chaos, Letty's place at the restaurant table at the film's end, presiding over a reunited Grace and Harold and a pleasant Uncle Claude, can be seen as her ultimate triumph over not just a bad situation but her own poor way of handling people. She's a wiser Letty at the end, not at all necessarily a more tamed one.

Unfortunately, in too few of her future films was Charlotte given a chance to continue developing this attractive, and positive, character trait. The days when Hollywood actors could take on a variety of roles without fear of being pigeonholed for the purposes of the box-office were going out with the waning Jazz Age.[3]

Charlotte's mother had remarried just before her daughter's career had begun to take off, and had moved out of New York City, but Charlotte made an effort to see her every time she

Left: Charlotte Greenwood, as captured by one of Hollywood's most revered still photographers and a favorite of Greta Garbo, MGM's Clarence Sinclair Bull, circa 1931. William Luce collection. *Right*: Charlotte Greenwood as glamour girl in white fox and pearls, circa 1929, an image of which she was fond: she displayed the Strauss-Peyton oversize photograph in her Beverly Hills home in an ornate silver frame.

was back east. During one vaudeville tour of "Her Morning Bath," when Charlotte was playing one of the more gorgeous movie palaces, the New Albee in Cleveland, Annabelle came to
see her.

> She searched and searched for an alley and finally in her own language said: "They have put this
> one where the actors can't find it." Her introduction to back stage was a scenario itself.
>
> She opened the stage door and looking inside saw red velvet drapes and carpet, shiny banisters,
> leading to a door-tender with brass buttons on his uniform, standing behind a locked gate. She took
> one step and apologized and turned to go. But the doorman recognizing her from my description,
> telling him to watch out for her, said — "Right this way, Mrs. Greenwood. Miss Greenwood is expect-
> ing you."
>
> When Mama was ushered into my dressing room its opulence overpowered her. She seemed to
> sink knee deep in the carpet and found herself unwittingly doing the Gibson Walk. [Manager] John
> Royal came in and urged us to come out to the lobby and see the paintings and the fine old rare
> tables, chairs and the most outstanding, magnificent, elaborate commodes that could ever be found —
> two of them.
>
> Mama blushed and was terribly flustered. "Oh, Mr. Royal," she protested, "not right out in the
> lobby!"[4]

A woman of simple ways but with a powerful faith in the great goodness that she was
sure was coming just around the corner, and a hard worker all of her life, Annabelle was very
much Charlotte's example of what it was to be a good person; she would serve Charlotte as
a model for the many strong women she played on the stage and on screen. By the time Charlotte was making *So Long Letty* in Hollywood, Annabelle's domestic situation seems to have
changed yet again, because she was living at Charlotte's house at Auburndale, caring for the
property, keeping the hearth warm for her daughter's return and sending her loving notes and
photos of missed Christmases and Easter dinners inscribed to "my darling Baby Girl." When
Charlotte received news that Annabelle was ill she hurried back to New York, where she found
her mother comfortable but clearly unwell. "The news at Flushing when I reached there was
not cheerful," Charlotte recalled. "Mama's case was critical but there was hope of improve-
ment. I stayed with her for a time and then had to return to Hollywood. It was August 1929,
the eve of the depression, and I had an offer for stage work." Charlotte was having to live her
own fondest precept: the show must go on.

Producer Henry Duffy, who in a few years was to play a role in introducing to the theatre
world a Charlotte Greenwood capable of more than high kicks and wise cracks, wanted her for
the play *She Couldn't Say No*, which opened at Charlotte's old stomping ground, Hollywood's
El Capitan Theatre. A comedy centered on the ambitions of a woman lawyer, Alice Hinsdale,
who is so dominated by her attorney fiancé that she serves him as secretary until able to prove
herself his superior in the courtroom, *She Couldn't Say No* gave Charlotte plenty of opportunities to upstage her blustering co-star, Kenneth Daigneau, much as Eve Arden would do to Roger
Pryor eleven years later in the 1941 film version of the play. (And as Katharine Hepburn would
do to Spencer Tracy in the ultimate remake of this film, 1949's *Adam's Rib*.) The play was a
hit — Henry Duffy had struck gold again — and the production moved on to San Francisco's
Alcazar, where Charlotte encountered a sobering slice of real-life drama.

> A few days after the opening I received a letter from a young woman who said that she had been
> reduced by circumstances to her last dollar, and having exhausted all the avenues she knew, had
> decided to commit suicide.
>
> As she was on her way to the ferry building, with a view to taking one of the boats for Oakland
> or Sausalito and jumping off midway, she happened to pass the theater and decided to see the mati-
> nee. As she put it, "I decided to at least go on my way with a laugh."

It so happened that I was using, instead of a curtain speech, a song that I liked called "The Clown," and it was this that appealed to her. She became impressed with the verses and decided to give life another whirl. I was enormously pleased.

Charlotte admitted her song (the lyrics of which she wrote) was not great poetry, but she believed it had enough philosophy in it to save a young woman's life:

> Life is just a circus
> While we caper for a while
> Learn to hide your troubles here
> Behind a pleasant smile
> When your limbs are tired and aching
> When sorrow spoils your fun
> Though your whole heart may be breaking
> Remember this, young one!
> The people out there expect a clown
> Every day to do his duty.

"Actually," Charlotte recalled, "I was trying diligently to keep these precepts in the front of my own mind." She had had more bad news from Auburndale. She took a fast train to New York and found that Annabelle had lost much ground. As luck, or its opposite, would have it, another professional commitment was looming: Charlotte had signed to do a pair of comedy shorts for Educational Films, *Love Your Neighbor* and *Girls Will Be Boys*, and needed to be on location in California. Charlotte wanted to back out of the contract to stay with her mother, but Annabelle, as she had always done, insisted she would be fine, practically pushing Charlotte out the door.

"The doctors told me that while the end was inevitable, there would be ample time for me to return to New York from California," Charlotte wrote. "The doctors erred." On the very first day of shooting for *Love Your Neighbor*, Charlotte received a telegram telling her that Annabelle had died (on August 9, 1930). "My first impulse, naturally, was to drop everything and rush back to New York. Then I reflected. If I followed by own desires, I would cause needless expense to Mr. Christy [of Education Films], but worse, I would throw people out of work. I remembered Mama's own Spartan courage, and decided to fight it through."

This short film, in which Charlotte plays a member of a women's group devoted to spreading kindness to everyone they meet only to end up ruining her life through too many good deeds per day, and shooting the woman who heads the group, is one of Charlotte's least sophisticated comedic efforts. Despite a few effective scenes — one of them, her struggle to get a block of ice into an icebox, is taken straight from "Her Morning Bath" — Charlotte's fractured emotional state is evident in her wandering attention and poor timing. It is obvious she has something else on her mind than comedy.

"No one knew that I had suffered a loss as we went through one farcical antic after another," she remembered; "no one knew [the night of Annabelle's death] as I sat as hostess to a dinner party for Louis B. Mayer and his wife that my heart was full. If my gaiety was a little forced, it was not evident to my guests. At last I was an actress. I had justified Mama's hopes for me."[5]

16

To London on the Santa Fe Express

THOUGH A DECIDEDLY EQUIVOCAL EFFORT, *Love Your Neighbor* doesn't seem to have worked against Charlotte's popularity among MGM's producers — they were to call her soon enough for another part. But she didn't wait to hear from them — she went right back to work, returning to the medium in which she felt most comfortable, the stage, in the 1917 farce by Charles Bell and Mack Swan, *Parlor, Bedroom and Bath*, which played a healthy run at the El Capitan Theatre. MGM's Lawrence Weingarten and director Edward Sedgwick happened to be passing by the theatre one day when they saw Charlotte's name on the marquee, and decided to go in for the show. "We saw it," Weingarten wrote later, "and it appeared to be the genesis of an idea. So we bought the play for $6,000, including Charlotte Greenwood's salary..."[1]

Weingarten's job was not to be envied — it was up to him to find vehicles for one of the greatest of silent film comedians, Buster Keaton, who was having a difficult time adjusting to the talkies. While his talking films had done well at the box office (the only standard the studio executives cared about or paid attention to), Keaton was mortified by the poor quality of the scripts and by having to speak in them, and his discomfort shows through even his most inspired performances.

Three years after the Depression, most of the big Hollywood studios were in dire financial shape; only MGM was still going strong, and for Keaton to have left the studio for one that would have allowed him greater artistic latitude would have been suicidal, particularly considering the expensive lifestyle his silent screen earnings had led him and his wife, Natalie Talmadge, to become accustomed to. He and Natalie had just returned from a trip to Europe when Weingarten asked him to look at the script of *Parlor, Bedroom and Bath*, with a view to filming it with Charlotte. (It had been filmed once before, in a silent 1920 version.) Keaton hated the script instantly, denigrating it as the sort of farce for which he had no special ability or regard. "Life is too serious to do farce comedy," pronounced the greatest deadpan artist of film history.[2]

It is not known whether Keaton also objected to working with Charlotte, who had worked at times exclusively in farce, but it is an interesting fact that both actors were frequently cast as very much their polar opposites — Keaton as a dopey playboy or a well-to-do idler, when he was in fact ill-spoken and uneducated in either the academic or society sense, while Charlotte was always cast as the raucous harridan who knocked things over in pursuit of some reluctant man, when she was in fact very much a proper lady, with good taste in clothes, furniture and friends and a secret passion for Brahms songs. If they compared notes or came to know each other well at all, we do not know; in her memoirs, Charlotte passes over the making of most of her films, devoting much more space and interest to her theatre work (except to note in one place that she was paid $5,000 per week for *Parlor, Bedroom and Bath*), while Keaton loathed the film and had no good memories of it to share.

In the script, Charlotte plays a Hollywood gossip columnist named Polly Hathaway, who gets entangled in the complicated affairs of an engaged couple played by clipped-toned Reginald Denny and sweet-faced Sally Eilers. The latter won't marry Reginald until her sister Angela, played by wisecracking glamour-girl Dorothy Christie, is also suitably married off. Yet Angela is only turned on by men who two-time with other women, making it difficult to find a man who can fulfill the schizophrenic profile necessary for Angela's happiness.

Enter Keaton as a mere sign tacker who, while plying his trade, is nearly killed by Reginald's roadster. He is brought into Angela's spacious Italian villa on a hill (in reality, Keaton's own Beverly Hills estate) and nursed by her after Reginald has fooled her into believing Keaton a dashing playboy of excitingly loose morals. The only way to get Angela to give Keaton her hand is to arrange for her to catch him *in flagrante delicto* with another woman. As the plot turns, Keaton is caught not merely with another woman but two others besides, one of whom is Charlotte, in a sequence in which she, in floppy hat and trailing silk dress, tries to teach the wooden Keaton in a hotel suite Reginald has reserved for them how to make love to a woman. This she does with escalating acrobatics and violence, including lifting him bodily, dropping him on the floor, and nearly pulling off his pajamas, all the while making him memorize a set phrase from antiquated melodrama: "Oh my *darling*! I love you *madly*! I *cannot* live without you! You must *never* leave me!" She teaches him too well, because he is soon chasing *her* all over the room, gets tied up in her arms and legs in passionate kisses, drags her over the furniture, and finally chases her off in a fright. From demanding Keaton's attentions with the memorable line, "I'm supposed to be the party of the second part in a regular orgy!" Charlotte flees the room, panting, "Mama no wanna play!"

Charlotte's and Buster's antics were not without injury. As she was to write a few years later:

> We did one of our scenes in such a realistic manner and it seemed to be going so well that nobody on the set was astonished when the director suddenly yelled out: "Cut!"
>   But after the cameras had stopped grinding we found out why. My lips were bleeding where they had come into contact with Keaton's teeth, and my always uncontrollable hands had made his eye into a sorry looking sight![3]

Both Keaton and Charlotte received warm reviews for this picture Keaton so evidently loathed making, particularly from Mordaunt Hall of the *New York Times*:

> [Keaton] has a turbulent time with Polly Hathaway, played by Charlotte Greenwood, who gives him an intensive training in the manner of approaching a proposal of marriage and a subsequent osculatory exhibition.... Like Mr. Keaton, Miss Greenwood displays marvelous energy and acrobatics.[4]

By her own admission, Charlotte had a much rosier time performing opposite Eddie Cantor in her next film, *Palmy Days*— an added bonus was that none other than *haute couturière* Coco Chanel had come over from Paris to design costumes for her. (Chanel returned to Paris soon after; other than *Palmy Days*, the only other Hollywood films she provided designs for at the height of her fame were Gloria Swanson's *Tonight or Never*, also from 1931, and 1932's *The Greeks Had a Word for Them*, written by Charlotte's friend Zoe Akins.) Charlotte had known Cantor in vaudeville days, and his eccentric comedic style not only meshed with her

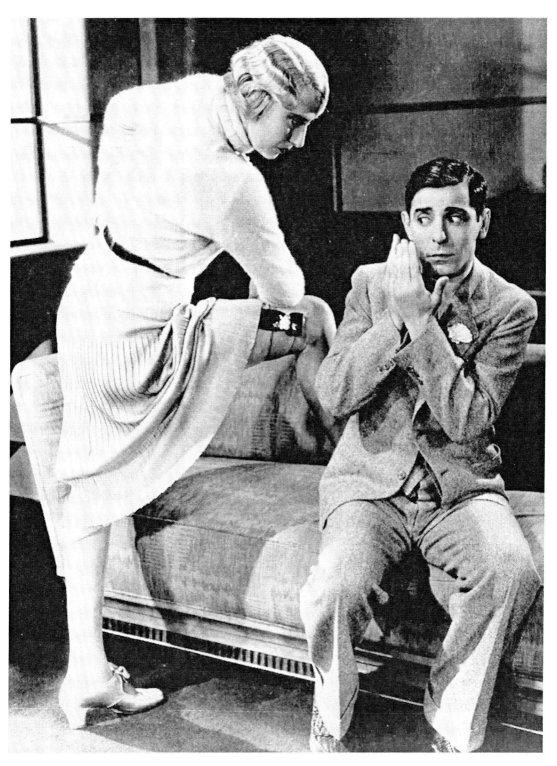

Charlotte tries out her Marlene Dietrich impersonation on a reluctant Eddie Cantor in this scene from their 1931 comedy *Palmy Days*. Coco Chanel and Alice O'Neill designed the costumes. William Luce collection.

own, but his diminutive height and banjo eyes brought back memories of Charlotte's work with Sydney Grant in *The Pretty Mrs. Smith*, *So Long Letty* and other plays. It is unfortunate that Charlotte's focus on her theatre work leaves so little room in her memoirs for details of her films. It's clear that *Palmy Days* seems to have been a happier experience for her than *Parlor, Bedroom and Bath*, not least because it would seem that Cantor, unlike Keaton or Lahr, was not threatened by Charlotte and happily invited her to become part of his family circle when filming was done. This was a personal touch Charlotte always had and always would warmly respond to.

Set in an Art Deco mega-bakery that seems to enjoy more than one design influence from the soaring sets of *Metropolis*, the film follows the adventures of a con artist's assistant, played by Cantor, who through a series of accidents bordering on the insane becomes the right hand man of the bakery's owner and a love interest for Charlotte, the bakery's feisty but love-lorn gym instructor. When the con artist, posing as a famous medium, catches up with Cantor, a mad chase is on for the cash contents of the bakery's safe, which Cantor has baked into a loaf of bread and must safeguard at all times. From wrestling with Charlotte on the floor of the bakery gym to joining her in wrestling with the con artist's thugs, Cantor emerges the unlikely hero by the film's end, as well as Charlotte's blushing bridegroom.

Charlotte had some strong singing opportunities in the film, including both Cantor's song "My Baby Said Yes Yes," and her own solo turn in the admonitory "Bend Down Sister," in which Charlotte warns the scantily clad young bakery girls that "ham and eggs should always be outside looking in," looking on as they gyrate and whirl through Busby Berkeley's kaleidoscopic choreography. (One of the chorus girls, incidentally, would come to play a major role in Charlotte's "second" film career ten years later — her name was Betty Grable.)

In her memoirs, Charlotte records one extended memory of working with Cantor on *Palmy Days*:

> There was a bathing pool scene. Eddie, in the disguise of a girl, was in the pool, although he cannot swim. It was my job to fetch him out. In the struggle in the water there was supposed to be an exchange of clothes; then he was to emerge in my clothes leaving me in the pool. For cutting purposes I was told by the director to stay under water for as long as I possibly could. The signal that it was all clear for me to come up would be a prod in the ribs with a stick.
> But in the excitement of the "shot" I was forgotten, and heroically determined not to spoil the picture I nearly drowned myself. Not until a few bubbles began to disturb the surface of the pool was it realized that all was not well with me![5]

Besides *Parlor, Bedroom and Bath* and *Palmy Days*, Charlotte made three other comedies in 1931: a film version of the hit Bert Lahr play, *Flying High*, with Charlotte again in hot pursuit of her man (in this case, Lahr), even in a preposterous flying machine that nearly ascends to the moon before falling earthward again; *Stepping Out* with Charlie Chaplin's director Chuck Reisner, in which Charlotte, a confirmed non-smoker, had to puff a cigar (and wore, she claims, a set of Greta Garbo's striped pajamas, lent to her by the tall Swede when the costume department failed to find any that would fit Charlotte); and as a cantankerous maid to Robert Montgomery's bailiff's man/butler in the naughty P.G. Wodehouse comedy *The Man in Possession*.

Like Keaton in *Parlor, Bedroom and Bath*, Lahr was not happy with the film *Flying High* (he also did not care to work with strong female comedians), and at times it shows, though

Charlotte doesn't accompany Bert Lahr in their 1931 comedy *Flying High*, but she does chase him around a piano and eventually out a window. Caricature from sheet music for song from the film, "We'll Dance Until the Dawn," by B.G. De Sylva, Lew Brown and Ray Henderson.

he, like Charlotte and co-stars Pat O'Brien, Hedda Hopper, and Charlotte's former brother-in-law Charles Winninger, pull out all the zany stops. The film includes several aeronautic-themed Busby Berkeley numbers that if hardly as sophisticated as they were once thought to be, are creative enough to impress even today. For whatever reason, Charlotte gives barely a mention to this film in her memoirs, even though she received good reviews for it. (As

In this scene with Cliff Edwards in the 1931 MGM film *Stepping Out*, Charlotte, a non-smoker by choice and by faith, holds a smoke with style.

Mordaunt Hall wrote, "Among those who contribute to the gaiety of this offering [is] Charlotte Greenwood, who delivers her usual riotous brand of fun.")

The Man in Possession rates only a sentence from Charlotte in her memoirs, though Robert Montgomery had starred the year before in a film for which Martin had written the music (and Charlotte at least one set of lyrics), *So This Is College*, and made an excellent foil for what the movie's publicity described as "the delightful, elongated comedienne, Charlotte Greenwood."[6] This movie was the penultimate one Charlotte would make in the U.S. until returning to Hollywood's sound stages in 1940.

If Charlotte was becoming restless in front of Hollywood's cameras, Martin was feeling the same behind them. In the January 1931 issue of *The Etude*, Martin was featured, as music director of MGM, with several other studio music directors, including RKO's Victor Baravalle, Fox Studios' Arthur Kay, United Artists' Alfred Newman and Universal's Heinz Roemheld, in what is believed to be the first article ever written about the process and the personalities behind the creation of music for films. The author, Verna Arvey, was the future wife of black American composer William Grant Still, and a fine musician in her own right. She was also extremely curious about the special problems inherent in creating and shaping music for film, and asked intelligent questions of all the music directors who found time to answer them.

Most were enthused about the brave new sound world they had entered — "I try to give

In *The Man in Possession*, Charlotte played the maid to an improvident socialite whose home is being held hostage by a bailiff's man, Robert Montgomery, who then plays the socialite's butler to impress the parents of her well-heeled admirer (and gets the socialite in the end). This 1931 film was the next to last Charlotte would make before returning to Hollywood in 1940.

the audience the feeling that it is hearing what it sees" said Paramount's Nat Finston — though Arvey is careful to quote ex–Fox Studios' music director Charles Wakefield Cadman, who wrote bitterly in 1930: "The musical taste of most of the studios is very low, and it has not improved one whit since music for sound pictures came in." Cadman added that the music used to accompany the silents (frequently a mishmash of excerpts from the symphonic and operatic canons) was far better than what was being created following the advent of sound.

Arvey points out that several of the studio music directors had been concert pianists, including Martin in this group (unaccountably, as it is not clear how much time the very young man would have had to organize a concert career before turning his energies to the composing in England for which he became known by age 21). But Martin is singled out from the herd by a single statement, which to the others may have sounded somewhat traitorous. "Martin Broones avers that, although he is head of the *music* department at M.G.M. studios, he is primarily interested in pictures," wrote Arvey. "The picture comes first, the music second." On the other hand, Martin told her — in full face of the trend well known to everyone in the business in 1931— that in his opinion musicals were not falling out of fashion but as strong as ever.[7]

In fact, by late 1931, Martin and Charlotte both seem to have decided they were finished with Hollywood and what Charlotte regarded as its "indifferent bosses." Charlotte writes that as soon as her latest film was completed, she made plans to return east, where her Auburndale house was being cared for by Eunice Burnham, and where her beloved world of the stage — a world that held the theatre, as she did, in higher esteem than mere "flickers" — stood waiting for her with open arms. Martin was chafing to travel further east than that. "He was eager to get back to England, where he had business interests," wrote Charlotte. Unmoved when a "delegation from the studio" came calling at their hotel suite, "urging us to reconsider," Charlotte and Martin packed up and got on the train for New York.

"As we left the station on the Santa Fe Chief," Charlotte recalled, "Martin sent a wire to Eunice ... announcing our arrival. By the time we reached Albuquerque, we had a long and troubled telegram from Eunice. She hadn't expected us for several weeks at least and would we mind putting up in New York for a week or so in order that the painters and decorators could finish their job. She had planned a surprise for us and we were spoiling it." While the train clacked eastward and the couple thought about how to rearrange matters once they got to New York City, another cable came, this one from Hassard Short, who was in England, and wanted Charlotte and Martin very much to join him for the opening of Derby season.

> Somehow it seemed a good idea. We booked passage by wire and sent a cheerful note to Eunice telling her to let the decorators have their way. We would see her and the new house when we returned.
> As it happened, it was to be years before we actually got there.[8]

As it also happened, Charlotte had started on a journey, via the Santa Fe express, that would take her not just out of Hollywood and into the London theatre scene, but also into an entirely new professional world — that of dramatic actor.

PART TWO

There is something a little pathetic in the efforts of the
ugly duckling to become a swan. I never had any such high-blown
aspirations. I simply wanted to be an ugly duckling who had fun.
— Charlotte Greenwood

17

Wild Violets

"IT WAS 1932," CHARLOTTE wrote in her memoir notes, and "the world was gradually beginning to right itself ... life was gay for all of us."

At least it was gay for wealthy American travelers like the Brooneses, who decided to skip Southampton, where a worried Hassard Short waited for them fruitlessly on the chilly docks, and instead head for what had become the *sine qua non* destination of the worldly wealthy, the south of France. Their goal was the beaches of Antibes.

Once the stage for the antics, inspired or bibulous, of Gerald and Sarah Murphy and Scott and Zelda Fitzgerald, by the early 1930s Antibes and Cannes had become what one writer describes as "a millionaire's playground" — in other words, Bohemians were no longer welcome. The Murphys had decamped to Paris, having found the avant-garde now devant-garde and far too bourgeois for their taste. "[A] new, more social crowd had come to La Garoupe, people who were less interested in painting and poetry and more interested in parties." This included people like Harpo Marx and members of the Algonquin round table — Robert Benchley and Alexander Woollcott, Charlotte's long-time admirer — and film studio moguls, among others, who would not have been entirely welcome there in the halcyon days of the 1920s.

Antibes was Martin's decision: "[He] had an idea that the South of France would be the ideal place to rest and he knew just the proper spot at Antibes," Charlotte recalled. "It was near the home of W. Somerset Maugham, of which he wrote in his interesting series of war articles some years later."[1]

But the Brooneses were not to enjoy the pebble beaches for long. Hassard Short tracked them down via telephone from London, annoyed that he had waited in vain for them at the Southampton docks. He insisted they cross the Channel immediately, not just for the Derby but for closing night of his success, *Waltzes from Vienna*, with its sparkling score arranged by former musical *Wunderkind* and successful opera composer Erich Wolfgang Korngold from the music of Johann Strauss and his son. The show had run at the Alhambra Theatre in the West End for 607 performances. (As if to thank her for showing up on such short notice, and adding to her growing collection of theatrical mementos, Short later gave Charlotte an engraved sterling silver charger presented to him by the thankful chorus of the show on closing night.)

Charlotte and Martin had planned only to stay in London the one day and night it would take to see the show and congratulate its producer, their old friend Louis Dreyfus, head of

London's Chappells Music. "It was apparent directly after we reached London that both Dreyfus and Short had a fish to fry," Charlotte remembered, "though neither Martin nor I could
decide just what it was."[2]

When Martin pointed out that he and Charlotte intended to return to France immediately to resume their vacation, Dreyfus said he couldn't be happier, but that he wanted them
to go quite a bit eastward of France — namely, to Germany — and with him as traveling com-
panion. He could visit his relatives in Wiesbaden, and Charlotte could see a country she had
not yet visited. "Before we had a chance to say yes or no, the plans were fulminating, and
almost before we were aware of it in mid–Channel — Louis and Jeanne Dreyfus, Hassard Short,
Martin and myself [were en route to Germany]." The Dreyfuses and Short took one car, while
Martin and Charlotte hired their own car and driver.[3]

"Motoring through Germany, per se, was a decided disappointment," Charlotte recorded
later. There was a regimentation, of things as of people, that astonished and disconcerted her.
Everything seemed to have been put to "compulsory production." The birthplace of her ances-
tor Jean Paul Jaquet, Dutch Governor of Delaware, Germany had survived many vicissitudes
since Jaquet's seventeenth century advent but none like the one it was about to endure under
its new leader, the Austrian corporal, Adolf Hitler.

By 1932, the summer before Charlotte and Martin motored through Germany, the
Republic's restrictions on Hitler's S.A. and public demonstrations had been lifted, with predictable violence in the streets. For the Brooneses and especially for the Jewish Louis Dreyfus to be traveling through Germany at such a time showed how little the outside world
understood or knew of what was unfolding there. In fact, the day the party arrived in Frankfurt, the ancient imperial city of Habsburg coronations and of the poetry of its native son,
Goethe, they came close to colliding with the brawling power trip that was Nazism when they
had to put on the brakes for a passing parade of *Hitlerjugend*, which filled the streets with
brown shirts and the red, black and white swastika flags.

As Charlotte found out, she and Martin had been brought to Frankfurt for what, against
the troubles brewing there, seemed in retrospect the silliest possible reason: to see a comic
operetta by Robert Stolz called *Wenn die kleinen Veil'chen blühen*, which Dreyfus insisted had
a part in it that would make Charlotte a star in London. (Another Stolz adaptation, *White
Horse Inn*, had had a good run at the London Coliseum in 1931.)

"I'll always remember Frankfort [*sic*], not so much for the city or the play," Charlotte
recalled, "as for the sight of [all the young men marching through the streets].... [W]e were
informed by the police to drive slowly as the youth of Germany was parading for the first
time in tribute to Adolf Hitler, and we were under no consideration to use our cameras!"[4]

This was Martin's cue to flirt with disaster by pulling out his handheld camera and shooting footage of the Hitler Youth rally from the windows of the slowly moving car — an act of
disobedience to the regime which could easily have got him thrown in jail. "He got
some amazing pictures of youngsters from 10 to 12 — most of them I suppose are long since
victims of World War II — on the march," Charlotte wrote in her memoirs. By the time
the curtain rose on the Stolz operetta that night, it was easy to forget what they had just
seen, and even easier when Dreyfus spilled all the beans: he had taken out an option on the
property, with Charlotte in mind, and intended to produce it at Drury Lane, the famous theatre Charlotte had first toured with Martin shortly after their marriage. Hassard Short would
direct.

Charlotte was at first remarkably flippant about the offer, considering the honor of starring at Drury Lane, but she was also dodging continued offers from Hollywood to return to make various films, and cables from Broadway offering her roles in various plays.

"Somehow I was not impressed with the importance of returning to work," Charlotte confessed. "I was slowly succumbing to the spell of the Continent and was quite content to ramble along aimlessly, seeing new places, meeting new types of people, enjoying life." In all fairness, Charlotte had been working steadily, and harder than most people who worked ordinary jobs, since the age of 15: if she wanted an open-ended vacation, nobody could blame her.[5]

But Dreyfus pulled her up short. Charlotte and Martin were staying at the Eden Hotel in Berlin when Dreyfus told them they had loafed enough and that it was time to go back to work. Charlotte wasn't to regret giving up her planned vacation in the south of France — London would soon be at her famously large feet.

18

Toast of the West End

WENN DIE KLEINEN VEIL'CHEN BLÜHEN, retitled *Wild Violets*, was in the sturdy lineage of operettas dealing with how its cast of characters handles misunderstandings, misconceptions and cross purposes, in this case against the unlikely dignified settings of a finishing school and a university.

Stolz set the operetta in the fairytale half-timbered Rhine town of Bacharach, which Short moved to the Swiss Alps, as being far more familiar to most who would attend the show at Drury Lane. Charlotte's role was that of Augusta, a middle-aged woman who, with her husband, runs a mountain inn called The Stone Jug. A trio of young men — Paul, Otto and Erik — arrives at the inn en route to a reunion of old schoolmates, and the scene flashes back to earlier in the century, when Augusta, formerly a housemaid at a local school for girls, remembers the romantic entanglements the young men had with three young women from the school, a connection the headmistress, Paul's aunt, discouraged. In order to gain entrance to the academy, Paul arrived in the disguise of the new staff music teacher (echoing the well known disguise scene in Rossini's *The Barber of Seville*), only to have the real Dr. Franck show up, resulting in Paul's ejection (despite the best efforts of Augusta, the other girl students, and Augusta's sidekick, Hans, played at Drury Lane by Jerry Verno). Yet Paul and his sweetheart, Mary, meet at last outside the school's walls and elope. The scene then returns to the present, the past reviewed by Augusta and Hans before the roaring fire at The Stone Jug, and lessons reviewed that were never taught in school.

For Charlotte's arrival, Hassard Short had thought of everything, even to having white carnations — Charlotte's favorite flower — placed to overflowing in her suite at the Berkeley Hotel. "As we approached the opening night of 'Wild Violets,'" recalled Charlotte, "we discovered that Short had a terrifically heavy scenic production and that it would be quite impossible to take the show on a break-in tour, so Dreyfus decided to shatter another London tradition. We would open 'cold' in the West End, preparing ourselves for the ordeal by doing a series of semi-public dress rehearsals." It was October 1932, and the cold outside crept into the old theatre.

> The cathedral quality of Drury Lane, the time-hallowed traditions, the court rules that obtained — for the theater was under Royal Grant — and the natural excitement of an opening of a new play in a new type of role, had all of us on our toes. I was at once excited and eager to make an impression on my London debut but, curiously, more eager to give a good performance for the sake of the show.
>
> Up to now I had been little more than a song-and-dance girl. True, I had played short comedy and dramatic scenes in revues and I had put in considerable time working with vocal and dramatic coaches, but I had yet to be assigned a part that required me to sustain dramatic action.[1]

Charlotte need not have worried; she was an instant hit. "On the first night, the audience called on me for a speech. It was a wonderful moment. As simply as I could I said how very much I appreciated and how grateful I was for the kindly reception of my efforts — when a voice from the gallery interrupted me and yelled: 'You deserve it!'"[2]

Not only was Charlotte the first American comedienne to star at the Theatre Royal, but was the first actress to ever perform before four reigning kings and two queens at a single performance. "The occasion was a royal birthday," she remembered, "and since Europe was not then threatened by war, the royal [families] assembled from the four corners. My audience in 'Wild Violets' ... included on that evening the Swedish King and Queen [Gustav V; his Queen, Viktoria of Baden, had died in 1930; possibly the king was in company with his daughter-in-law Crown Princess Louise, née Mounbatten] and their entourage; the King and Queen of England [George VI and Queen Elizabeth], their hosts; the King and Queen of Norway [Haakon VII and his wife, the former Princess Maud of Great Britain] and the King of Iraq [Faisal I of the Hashemite dynasty and Lawrence of Arabia fame], who passed away shortly afterward [in 1933]. When royalty appears at any public place in England it is the custom for all to curtsy, but not in the direction of the monarch. Actors, as a result, do not look toward the royal box but make their obeisances toward the audience. I couldn't help but think as I performed the rite how far I had traveled since Philadelphia ... I who couldn't do a simply curtsy at school without landing on my nose, managed as pretty a dip as you'd want to see."

As she had already lifted her legs and her skirt a few dozen times during the evening — doing the splits on a china hutch while carrying saucepans in either hand, propping open an ice chest with her left leg in her well-known icebox routine, balancing the right one on Jerry Verno's shoulder in the presence of the stiff-necked Madame Hoffman (played by Jean Cadell), and showing plenty of shapely calf in a scene with the three young men in which she sang her biggest hit of the evening, "When I do love, I do love," Charlotte had managed several pretty dips before curtseying to the several crowned heads that night.[3]

Charlotte, who was disposed to make friend of critics, was warned that she was on different territory now from Broadway and American regional theatre, and should especially watch out for the dastardly James Agate. "He doesn't like anything," she was told, "least of all musical shows!" Yet when it came time for Agate to review Somerset Maugham's play *For Services Rendered*, running at the same time as *Wild Violets*, Agate paid Charlotte what for him was the supreme compliment of stating that, in contradistinction to Maugham's play, "'When I love, I do love' is Drury Lane's chief contribution to the season's gaiety." That was Charlotte's song.

Charlotte was also given to understand that *Daily Herald* critic Hannen Swaffer was another man who wrote his reviews with the blood of crucified performers — he was first banned from a theater at age 18 for his acerbic reportage — but her friends were proved wrong again. Swaffer began "one of his pontifical Sunday reviews with the unequivocal: 'I beg to inform my American colleagues, that I have discovered Charlotte Greenwood — the actress.'" Coming from a critic who for criticizing the Americanization of the English stage had been publicly slapped by an American actress, these words were as conciliatory as they were perceptive.[4]

Writer Ian Fox had even greater plaudits to share with his reading public, though he did so with the tongue-in-cheek style of a British journalist loathe to show too much of his hand, or his heart, right away. After reading Fox's piece, which was titled "The Actress with the

Top and opposite: Charlotte romping across the stage of the Theatre Royal, Drury Lane, London, in 1933, with her co-star Jerry Verno in a shot from the *Wild Violets* program. "I beg to inform my American colleagues, that I have discovered Charlotte Greenwood — the actress," wrote Hannen Swaffer, theater critic for the *Daily Herald,* London.

Laughable Legs," and reproduced a shot of Charlotte showing them off in her Bert Lahr comedy, *Flying High*, Charlotte "decided ... that Fox was not so much a humorist as a research scientist." Throughout the article, Fox referred to Charlotte's height, which grew at least a foot for every paragraph; by the end, "I said goodbye and she knelt down and shook hands. Stop Press: Charlotte Greenwood is fifteen feet in height."[5]

Perhaps inspired by this article and its elongated Modigliani-like image of Charlotte, the London society portraitist Flora Lion, who had painted everyone from poet and playwright Lady Gregory to composer Sir Alexander MacKenzie (uncle to writer Dame Rebecca West) to Queen Mary, asked Charlotte if she might commit her image to canvas. Delighted, Charlotte agreed; and the resulting portrait, in which Charlotte is shown reclining against white furs wearing a filmy red dress, one hand on her hip and her head held high as any movie goddess', hung for years on the landing of her house at 806 North Rodeo Drive in Beverly Hills. Beneath it, like the talisman it still was for her, she hung a framed piece of paper bag bearing Max Hoffman's scrawl and a fading stamp: "Engaged"—the endorsement that got her into the chorus of *The White Cat* in 1905.

Miss Lion successfully requested that Charlotte's portrait be exhibited in the central salon of the Royal Academy, and it was among the 1,750 works chosen from a total of 11,327.

"I am fully aware that it was the artistry of Miss Lion and not the classic beauty of Miss Greenwood that attracted the attention of the gallery directors," Charlotte wrote later. "Yet the fact remained that Greenwood was there hanging 'on the line,' just as she used to be hanging on the fence at Norfolk, trying to whistle through her teeth."

The painting was also used on the cover of the British magazine *Woman's Home Journal* and in the program for Charlotte's next turn at Drury Lane, Kern and Hammerstein's *Three Sisters*, ensuring far wider publicity than peering down from the walls of the Royal Academy.[6]

19

"Charlotte Greenwood, the actress"

*W*ILD *VIOLETS* RAN IN THE West End for a solid year. (Martin also had successful musical show at the London Hippodrome: *Give Me a Ring*, with lyrics by Graham John, book by Guy Bolton and music by Martin, opened in June 1933 and ran for 239 performances.) During this time Charlotte and Martin made such friends as the Rev. Victor Albert Baillie, Dean of St. Georges Chapel at Windsor Castle and Chaplain-in-Ordinary to King George V, who found Charlotte's performance "refreshing" and showed his warmth of character and his interest in theatre folk by inviting Charlotte and Martin to lunch with him at the Deanery,[1] as well as with the so-called Gallery Girls, groups of young women who clubbed together to attend performances, sitting in the cheapest seats in the house.

Against the regulations of the Theatre Royal, Charlotte asked for and got massive amounts of hot tea brewed backstage and distributed to the young women waiting in the cold outside the theatre. For years afterward, she continued to correspond with several of them, and was heartened during the Blitz to hear that they were still "queuing up for their favorite shows just as if Hitler were still an obscure paper hanger and not the bogey man of the civilized world."

Charlotte and Martin also became acquainted with the future King Edward VIII, then Prince of Wales, through the medium of recorded rather than live music. One night when the Berkeley Hotel orchestra had closed up shop, the playboy prince expressed his desire to dance one more round. Per a note for her memoirs now in the Film and Television Library at USC, Charlotte described how the Prince, having heard that she and Martin had a portable Victrola in their suite, asked to borrow it. The Brooneses sent the Victrola forthwith, "including our disc of 'Begin the Beguine,'" Charlotte noted, and back it eventually came with a kind note of thanks. Charlotte added that she and Martin treasured the little Victrola for years, and when they met the Duke and Duchess of Windsor in 1950 at the opening night party for *Out of This World*, they all had a laugh about the incident from not just another time but from another world entirely.[2]

During the run of *Wild Violets* Charlotte became better acquainted with James Forbes, author of *The Chorus Lady*, who years earlier had advised Martin against rewriting the story as a musical comedy. "He wanted us to see a current hit, 'The Late Christopher Bean,' which was a great success in New York with Pauline Lord and in London with [later Dame] Edith Evans. While we were chatting [at intermission]," Charlotte recalled, "Forbes said: 'Charlotte,

A sardonic Charlotte Greenwood, photographed on New Bond Street, London, in the early 1930s, with an inscription that says it all: "Come hither," her trademark smiley face beside. William Luce collection.

that's the sort of role you should do!'"[3] The role Forbes referred to was that of Abby, the maid of all work in Sidney Howard's play, around whom most of the plot revolves, including its surprise ending.

"It seemed a little fantastic," wrote Charlotte. "True, I had ambitions for drama and had spent much of my spare time studying" (she was to even tell a London reporter that she harbored ambitions to sing Brahms songs in a public concert, as good an example of Charlotte's brave derring-do as any that can be found) "but the role of Abby in 'The Late Christopher Bean' seemed a good deal beyond my scope. I thanked Jimmy for his vote of confidence."[4]

James Forbes was not the only man of parts to urge Charlotte to leave light comedy behind for higher ground. At the closing night party at the Savoy Hotel for *Wild Violets*, in fall 1933, Charlotte met up with composer Jerome Kern. Louis Dreyfus had been after Kern for some years to write a work for Drury Lane, but Kern had always countered with the complaint that he had nothing or no one to inspire him to do so. "Now he was in a different mood," recorded Charlotte.

"This is the first time I've seen you, Charlotte," he said.

"Oh, come now, Jerry," Dreyfus said, "surely you've seen Charlotte before."

"Of course I've seen her," Kern said, "and yet I've never *seen* her. Until tonight I took her for granted as an entertainer unique in her chosen field. It has never occurred to me that she has potentialities that have not been plumbed."

Naturally, I was thrilled with all this, and when the party moved down to the Dreyfus home at Wimbledon and Kern agreed to do a show especially for me with Oscar Hammerstein II, it seemed too good to be true![5]

Pleasures long postponed, however, had to be attended to first. After taking in the matches at Wimbledon, Charlotte, Martin and the Dreyfuses picked up where they had left off the year before and made plans to return to Antibes, first heading for the social season in Venice. Charlotte had never been there and was enchanted by the lagoon city. She and Martin booked rooms at the famous Excelsior Hotel, and were assigned one of the blue and white striped cabanas along the stretch of beach, known as the Lido, below.

Our cabana was situated about fourth from the center path leading down to the sea. On either side were rows of similar cottages, all decorated according to the different tastes of their occupants. We set about arranging ours to suit our needs and wondered who our nearest neighbors might be. We didn't have to wait long. Directly after lunch a beautiful young woman came swinging along the path. Her face lit up with a smile as she caught sight of me and she came over with:

"Why hello, Charlotte Greenwood, how nice to see you here. I've seen you so often on the stage, I feel I know you. We're giving a party tonight, won't you join us?"

Then, seeing that I did not recognize her, she smiled again and said: "Perhaps I'd better introduce myself. I'm Barbara Hutton M'Divani."[6]

Billed the richest girl in the world, with the better part of the Woolworth five and dime store fortune, estimated at $28 million, waiting for her to spend as soon as she reached her majority, Hutton had just married a faux Georgian "prince" named Alexis M'Divani. Given the rate at which her fellow heiresses and Hollywood movie stars were collecting titled husbands, there was no current fashion with which pearl-hung Barbara Hutton could not keep up.

The first of her seven husbands, M'Divani was followed by several others, of titles real and surreal, as well as a genuine Hollywood prince in the form of actor Cary Grant, while Hutton continued to destroy her body with pills, alcohol and the self-abuse that comes from not having anything constructive to do in life. She also destroyed her fortune, leaving a few thousand dollars in the bank at her death in 1979 and a mountain of debts for her caretakers to chip away at by selling off what goods and chattels were left.

At the time Charlotte met her, however, Hutton was a radiant twenty-one years old, and happy with her phony prince, who had not yet started throwing all the temper tantrums that were to help end the marriage a few years later.

No sooner had the barber's daughter from Philadelphia met the richest girl on earth than a stir made everyone turn around, and "our neighbor on the right arrived ... the powerful voice and commanding figure of the oncoming dowager filled my ear and eye." Charlotte had been asking Martin for her dictionary, as she was preparing to write letters to friends back home, when the dowager erupted with: "Why don't you use the words you know?" Charlotte made a wisecrack about needing to rely on Mr. Webster when it was necessary to know how to spell more than "yes" and "no."

"What word do you want to know about?" demanded the old lady.

"Is there one 's' or two in occasional?" Charlotte asked her.

"Oh just write it fast and run it all together," the old lady ordered (she clearly did not know how to spell the word either). "No one cares so long as they hear from you."[7]

The dowager in question, who became fast friends with Charlotte on the spot, was none other than Venetian socialite and social arbiter Princess Jane di San Faustino, born in Orange, New Jersey, not far from Charlotte's own birthplace and that of her immediate forebears, and widow of Prince Carlo di San Faustino. A fanatic for backgammon (like Martin and, in time, Charlotte), bossy Princess Jane, then in her 70s, had just made Barbara Hutton's acquaintance. She had also made an impression on the young woman which Hutton later recorded in her diaries: "She would sit in her cabana and play backgammon for hours on end, sipping Amaretto and cream, talking a mile a minute about any subject that popped into her mind, interrupting herself to screech at servants and complain that the Italians were the slowest, dumbest, laziest people on earth.... She loved unsavory details, loved dirt."[8]

"So Martin and I perched in our cabin," Charlotte wrote, "with the world's richest girl on one side and the leader of social Rome on the other, thoroughly at peace with the world."[9]

The party that night, held at the Grand Hotel, to which one hundred couples were ferried in gondolas, was a whirl of satin and gems — Charlotte danced with the tall, dark and handsome Aimone, Duke of Spoleto, who later was advanced by Benito Mussolini's Fascist government as the puppet King Tomislav II of Croatia, in 1941. (He abdicated when Italy surrendered in 1943.)[10] Charlotte was in seventh heaven: "It made me wish that for just that dance, I could have been Irene Castle instead of Charlotte Greenwood." The favors alone for this party cost Hutton $20,000.[11]

After partying in Venice, the Brooneses took their Rolls-Royce (nicknamed "Bertha") and driver Harris of the waxed handlebar mustache (and his "impeccable manners and his attitude of disdain for all foreigners"), and drove to Lake Como, which they only reached after what Charlotte describes as "the earmarks of 'Tait's Motoring,' an old and successful vaudeville act with which I had appeared on many occasions." Twenty miles outside Como, the Rolls burst a tire and lurched off the Autostrata. Capable Harris parked as neatly as was possible along the highway, then set about repairing the tire, "greatly embarrassed that we should have this annoyance."

> He was engrossed in his work when a small Italian child with nine years and enormous curiosity emerged from a ditch determined to help. To the horror of Harris, the youngster immediately set about taking everything apart and moving all the tools. Since he had no English, and Harris would have died rather than foul his tongue with Italian, "or any other forrin lingo," an impasse was reached ... Martin came into the affair with a dash of Spanish twisted, so he believed, into passable Italian. All he wanted to say was "Stop," but if he did get the order out, the child ignored it. For a time it looked as if he would get the car dismantled before Harris could assemble it.[12]

Harris eventually tried to dissuade this future Italian mechanic to get his nose out of the Rolls' engine by tossing him an old tire, but nothing worked: "What he wanted most was to wrench off something, even a good tire," Charlotte recalled with amusement. "We rewarded our little one-man destruction gang with a few lira and proceeded on our way."

This was not the only comic scene in which Bertha was to play a part. Martin loved to tell the story, among friends and in Christian Science lectures, of the Sunday he and Charlotte were driven down to the Thames near Maidenhead for a little restorative relaxation, only to be harassed from behind by a driver who wanted to pass the slowly moving car. (Martin himself always drove very slowly and probably instructed his chauffeur to do the same.) Given the size of a Rolls-Royce of that day and the diminutive nature of most English roads, the wonder is that Bertha wasn't holding up more than just one driver. Now furious, the man behind the Rolls found his way alongside, shouting at the chauffeur, and screeched to a halt in front of its gleaming grille. Out burst the driver to berate Martin and Charlotte's chauffeur, an intimidating experience even for the usually scrappy Martin, who happened to be sitting in the open driver's area of the car to catch some rare English sun.

The chauffeur stared straight ahead throughout the scene, and only when the man in the road had stopped screaming for lack of energy and wind did the driver turn and respond quietly: "*Piffle! Piffle!*" In relating this experience to his Christian Science listeners years later, Martin found in it the substance of Mary Baker Eddy's teachings: not to meet personal attacks with anger or resentment. "A match cannot strike unless you present a rough surface," Martin would add as a finish. Charlotte got her own kind of use out of the incident, however, quite apart from anything related to faith. All Martin had to do was agitate himself over something, in the way he had done since she had first known him (challenged by producers' inability to see a hit when it was right before their noses, or infuriated by perceived inefficiency in waiters), and Charlotte would smilingly set him straight with a "*Piffle!*"[13]

There was no reason why, given the fact they were in Italy, something akin to

Italian farce shouldn't continue to follow Martin and Charlotte even after Harris fixed Bertha's tire. They reached Lake Como and their hotel, late for dinner. Charlotte asked the manager if evening dress was necessary for the dining room, and was assured that indeed it was. Perhaps Martin's Italo-Spanish should have been brought into play again, or perhaps it was at fault, because when he and Charlotte, who was gowned in a sumptuous Molineux gown, appeared at the door, having dressed in considerable hurry, "not a soul in the restaurant, with the exception of the waiters, was in evening attire. Some were in slacks, some in plus fours, there was a bishop in gaiters and a group of Americans in Hollywood sports shirts."

They didn't stay in Como long enough to embarrass themselves further but motored directly to Antibes, without further incident from Bertha. What they found at their rented summer home there instead of the relaxation they were hoping for, however, was an armful of telegrams from Henry Duffy in California.

"He was stewing in his own fat far away on the Pacific coast, raging because we had not done him the courtesy of answering his messages," Charlotte remembered. "To assuage him, Martin took to the long distance telephone and explained that the messages simply hadn't caught up with us." Duffy, she added, with his flaming red hair, was not so easily appeased.

"If you're telling the truth," he screamed across a couple of continents and an ocean, "you'll get to San Francisco at once. I need you desperately to open a play that has to start in eleven days. You can make it by plane from New York!"

I was listening, second hand, by this time, too.

"Ask him what the play is," I whispered to Martin.

"Yes, yes, yes," Martin kept saying on the phone. "Yes, I think so!"

"Ask him what the play is," I repeated.

Martin covered the transmitter with his hand and turned to me with a very baleful eye:

"He wants you to do 'The Late Christopher Bean.'"[14]

"My knees," Charlotte remembered later, "turned to jelly."

20

The Late Christopher Bean

Bᴏʀɴ ɪɴ Rᴏᴜᴇɴ ɪɴ 1882, playwright René Fauchois started his career early, writing a play in 1906 on what one would not have thought the most stage-friendly subject, composer Ludwig van Beethoven (the title role of which Fauchois himself was to play in revivals in the 1920s and late 1930s).

Fauchois was affiliated with a living composer in the person of Gabriel Fauré, for whose "musical poem" *Penelope* (1913) Fauchois wrote the libretto. Though not considered particularly valuable as literary works, his plays' plots were always popular and his notions of farce and comedy competent and even inspired at times. At least one of them, *Boudo sauvé des eaux*, served as the basis for a movie made over a century after his birth (*Down and Out in Beverly Hills* from 1986).

But the best known of Fauchois' plays, *Prenez garde à la peinture!*, is the 1932 adaptation American playwright and screenwriter Sidney Howard developed from it, which he titled *The Late Christopher Bean*. At first titled *Muse of All Work*, Howard's adaptation featured the homespun charms of Abby, maid of all work to a down-at-heels New England doctor's family living outside Boston early in the twentieth century. The play opens as Abby prepares to serve her last day in the Haggett household, having been called to her brother's home by the death of his wife. While the Haggett daughters mourn Abby's leave-taking and social-climbing Mrs. Haggett complains that she'll never find another "girl" to work so cheaply as Abby did for fifteen years, Dr. Haggett has received a telegram from an art expert, asking for a visit in connection with a boarder of past years, an alcoholic artist named Christopher Bean.

Before his early death, Bean had left numerous paintings in the Haggetts' care, where they were hidden in the barn or used to patch holes in the roof. Only Abby treasured Bean's work, in form of a portrait of her working in the Haggetts' kitchen. When the visiting art expert tries to buy the family's collection of Bean paintings, which since Bean's death have become extremely valuable, the Haggetts are devastated to realize that the only painting in saleable shape is the one Bean gave to Abby. They then scheme to take it from her, with the risible claim that because the picture was painted of her during her working hours, as their employers the Haggetts have a right to claim the portrait as their own. Abby refuses to part with the picture, and then reveals not only that she saved several of Bean's canvases from the Haggetts' incinerator but that when he asked her to marry him, she couldn't refuse the sick man, and so is in fact his widow, and all the pictures hers by right.

ALCAZAR THEATRE

O'Farrell Street, near Powell   Telephone KEarny 3170

NOW PLAYING

HENRY DUFFY

presents

DIRECT FROM HER LONDON TRIUMPHS

CHARLOTTE GREENWOOD

IN THE INTERNATIONAL COMEDY HIT

"THE LATE CHRISTOPHER BEAN"

WITH A BRILLIANT SUPPORTING CAST OF PLAYERS

Bargain Matinees: Sun., Wed. and Sat., 25c, 50c, 75c
Every Evening: 25c, 50c, 75c, $1, $1.25, $1.50 (plus tax)

NOTE:_____

MISS GREENWOOD CAME DIRECT TO SAN FRANCISCO
FROM LONDON, ENGLAND, WHERE SHE STARRED FOR
ONE SOLID YEAR AT THE DRURY LANE THEATRE IN A
MUSICAL EXTRAVAGANZA ENTITLED "WILD VIOLETS."

Novelist John Forbes told Charlotte that she was made to play the role of Abby the maid in Sidney Howard's play *The Late Christopher Bean*. She took the challenge and surprised the critics with moving performances in San Francisco and Los Angeles in 1933.

A multi-faceted parable on the fashion tides of art appreciation and the sharks that swim in those shallows, as well as on the beauty of simplicity in life as well as in art, *The Late Christopher Bean* had been played to great acclaim by actress Pauline Lord, and would serve as the ill Marie Dressler's last film (in 1933, with Lionel Barrymore as Dr. Haggett) before her death shortly afterward.

The play gave Charlotte some priceless lines, written as if specially tailored to her drily sarcastic delivery — e.g., "I should think when a baby comes that quick after a wedding you'd pretty near have to brush the rice off it."[1]

First, however, she had to learn the part, and she had less than eleven days in which to do so, as Martin had to fly out that night to London to pick up a copy of the play and to make arrangements for the journey home. Louis Dreyfus also assisted, while wife Jeanne helped Charlotte pack.

"At Cherbourg we caught the *Majestic*," Charlotte recalled in her memoirs, "and I settled down for three days of intensive study. When we reached New York I had the lines of the role pretty well in hand and I was letter perfect when rehearsals started in Hollywood."

Unfortunately, the press had caught up with the Charlotte whirlwind, thanks to Henry Duffy's quick announcement (and *The New York Times*' habit of publishing the names of

celebrated passengers arriving in port). Commentators who thought they already had Charlotte's number received the news "with uplifted eyebrows. The critics and commentators were
frankly dubious. There were sly remarks that America's foremost woman clown had suc-
cumbed to a Pagliacci complex and New York's Ward Morehouse had reduced the advance
opinion to a single devastating phrase.... 'Henry Duffy is producing *The Christopher Bean* in
San Francisco with Charlotte Greenwood, of all things, in the Pauline Lord role.'"

> And the question of my ability to cope with Abby wasn't limited to the professional playgoers. In
> her Berkeley home, across the Bay from San Francisco, Mrs. Duncan McDuffie [for whose husband,
> real estate developer and Sierra mountaineer, Mt. McDuffie was named], sister of Sidney Howard
> ... was definitely troubled. Fortunately, I wasn't aware of this furor. I was too busy with the play and
> my part in it to give more than a passing glance at the front pages of the newspapers, and I wasn't
> even aware of the existence of Mrs. McDuffie.
>   Nevertheless I was deeply moved when, after the first matinee performance of the play at the
> Alcazar Theater, she was announced, identified herself, and said:
>   "I feel I owe you an apology, Miss Greenwood. When I heard that you had been cast in the role
> of Abby by Mr. Duffy, I was outraged. I had enjoyed your work in the theater but I felt that Mr.
> Duffy was offering Sidney an unnecessary affront by casting a musical comedy actress in a serious
> role. I wondered why Sidney permitted it.
>   "Now, I see that I was wrong. You have not only given a magnificent performance but, my dear,
> I really feel that you are precisely the type of woman that my brother intended for the role. He might
> well have been writing the play with you in mind. I hope you'll forgive me for my early doubts."

Charlotte did more than forgive Mrs. McDuffie for her understandable reservations — she
was only echoing what the press, in far more public fashion, had been muttering ever since the
news of Charlotte's casting as Abby had become known. Charlotte wrapped her arms around
Sidney Howard's sister and kissed her in thanks, smearing both with her tear-drenched makeup.[2]

The notoriously hard to please San Francisco critics were also to give Charlotte reason
to hug them — "They expressed astonishment that I had obviously been preparing myself for
just such an adventure, between my musical comedy engagements, and heaped critical praise
on my work." For herself, she could confess that the experience was worth leaving the south
of France for foggy summer San Francisco.[3]

✷ ✷ ✷

Christopher Bean could have run indefinitely, as seemed to be the case from its sold out
performances in Los Angeles, but Charlotte had to close the show in January 1934, when she
received word from Jerome Kern that he had finished the Drury Lane musical comedy he had
promised her the year before. (She had already had to turn down Lee Shubert's repeated offers
of a starring role in a new Broadway play, *Swing Your Lady*.) The libretto of *Three Sisters* arrived
and Charlotte had it in hand when she and Martin booked a cabin on the "A" deck of the
liner *Bremen*, for what both hoped would be a quiet and productive journey across the Atlantic
to London.

"[We] reckoned without Father Neptune," Charlotte recalled.

> In all my crossings I have never experience such a trip. It was the first time in the annals of modern
> shipping, so I was told, that a passenger liner had to heave-to in mid-ocean. Heaving-to as I
> understood it was simply giving up the struggle to forge ahead and letting the Old Gentleman have
> his fun. For three days he had the dandiest time. All the furniture in the salon, with the exception
> of one chair bolted to the floor, was smashed. It was impossible to stay in the stateroom unless
> you felt able to cope with acrobatics as trunks, luggage and furniture came sliding your way at a
> terrific pace.

Of course, I was in my element in this department. Martin took to his bed and proceeded to defy the storm by having a nice long sleep. I spent most of the first day doing long-legged hurdles over trunks as they slithered my way.

Eventually, Charlotte commandeered a steward, who found her a deck chair which he had bolted securely to the promenade deck and the cabin wall. During the day, Charlotte would struggle out of the cabin, *Three Sisters* under one arm, and using the guy rope stretched down the center of the deck would pull her way to the chair, to which the steward then tied her, "bundled up like an Arctic explorer. Most of the day," she recorded, "I spent on this improvised throne studying 'Three Sisters' and trying to create for myself the light and airy spring song atmosphere of the play, which was a charming, fragrant, light-hearted fable with lilting tunes."[4]

According to Hugh Fordin, Oscar Hammerstein's biographer, *Three Sisters* was inspired by Hammerstein's visit to the Derby, where he and Kern found people-watching far more

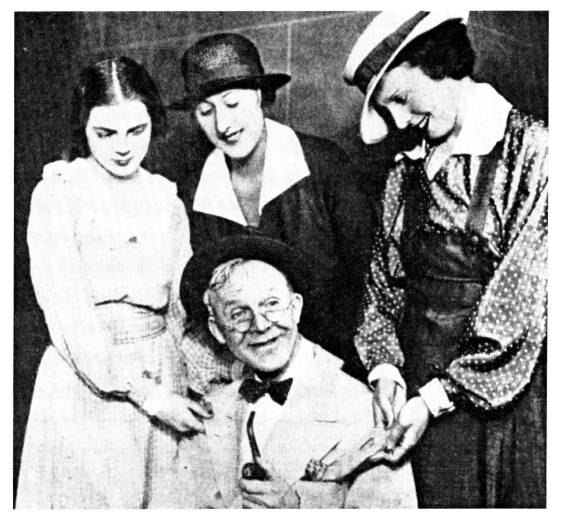

In her role as Tiny Barbour in Kern and Hammerstein's *Three Sisters*, Charlotte was taller than either Victoria Hopper (on her left) or Adele Dixon (to her right). Eliot Makeham played the father of all three. From *Three Sisters* program.

interesting than horse-betting. The carnival people and gypsies who congregated at the racing event, hawking their wares and telling fortunes on the back steps of caravans, seemed the perfect backdrop to a light romantic comedy.[5]

In the by then hoary tradition of *verismo* theatre, Kern and Hammerstein decided to write an operetta based on the hither and yon lives of these people, specifically focusing on Barbour, a traveling photographer, and his three daughters, one of whom loves a police constable, another who fancies a nobleman, and the third — Charlotte's character, a great galumphing girl named Tiny — who can't live without the love of a Gypsy lad. There was a certain amount of politics behind the Kern-Hammerstein choice of subject. Of late, British critics had been decrying what appeared to be Louis Dreyfus' obsession with producing foreign plays starring non–British performers at Drury Lane. The way back into those cold hearts seemed to be laid out on a silver platter in this quintessentially English "fable."[6]

Having survived her storm-tossed journey on the *Bremen*, Charlotte stepped on English soil knowing her part perfectly, and met her two "sisters" at rehearsals — sweet-faced Victoria Hopper and life-of-the-party Adele Dixon. (The latter had performed with Charlotte in *Wild Violets*.) Eliot Makeham played their bespectacled and pipe-puffing father. The operetta's premiere in February 1934 marked the first time a comedienne (Charlotte) had ever starred for two consecutive years at Drury Lane; and though Charlotte seems to have thought its four month run evidence of success, *Three Sisters'* charms, of which we can now hear an abundance, were not generally appreciated by the critics of the time, with predictable effect at the box office. Hammerstein's familiarity with the ways of the English proletariat he was aiming to describe and give song to was understandably weak, while some of Kern's efforts to Anglicize his trademark sound world did not go over any better.

"[Just] one critic," writes Hugh Fordin, "noted that the 'let's-be-British' regime at the Drury Lane had started with an American author, and American composer and an American leading lady (Charlotte Greenwood), but found the show satisfactorily British in flavor." He was a lone voice in the West End wilderness.[7] Kern's response was to return to Hollywood.

21

Gay Deceivers

Unfortunately, when Decca recorded excerpts from the operetta, including a medley of its major melodies, only Charlotte was missing from among the original cast members. Charlotte sheds no light on why this should be, but by the time *Three Sisters* was ready to wrap up in summer 1934 (and having made in the meantime a film farce with James Gleason and Cyril Maude called *Orders Is Orders*, which did not receive good reviews) she was already thinking of another show — again, an adaptation of a foreign play that had a role that seemed cut to fit all her dimensions. On a weekend visit to Paris, Charlotte and Martin had attended a performance of the Moïse Simons comedy, *Toi C'est Moi*, in which the fragile loveliness of Simone Simon was on display as the young love interest.

The Simons plot, set on a sugarcane plantation (originally in one of the French island colonies but transferred to a Spanish colonial locale for the English version), turns on the Parisian adventures of playboy Bob Guibert, who has angered his wealthy aunt Isabel — to be played by Charlotte — whose sole heir Bob is, with his expenditures and high-living, aided and abetted by his friend Patrice. To teach Bob something of the harshness of real life, Isabel sends him to one of her colonial estates, bearing a letter to her foreman there that Bob is to be "worked like a slave."

Of course, en route to the islands Bob opens the letter and is horrified. His amiable sidekick Patrice agrees to stand in for him, while Bob pretends to be Patrice's private physician. While Pat slaves away, Bob makes merry with the estate manager's daughter, Maricousa, and a French relation of his named Viviane, who has been living with her Governor father in the islands. Finally, Pat gives in and telegrams the aunt in Paris, who takes ship for her estate and, upon arriving, sets matters straight, cutting some undeserved slack to Bob and his tropical love affairs, which are blamed on the magic of hot jungle nights.

Reginald Arkell wrote the adaptation of Simons' play, which was re-titled *Gay Deceivers*, with a score by Martin, and starring besides Charlotte and American actress Claire Luce, as Maricousa, daughter of Aunt Isabel's estate manager, a mostly English cast. (Clifford Mollison played Pat, Bob's friend; Clifford's brother, William Mollison, was the show's producer.) Charlotte was given three big songs, including a rhumba number, "Serenade," with scampering lyrics by Graham John, that was later sung at the Hollywood Bowl by Grace Moore and remained a favorite among Martin's songs for many years.

This and another hit song from the show, *It Happened in the Moonlight* (though sung in the London production by Claire Luce), were produced by His Master's Voice in 1936, as the first recording Charlotte ever made of songs from one of her stage performances. Another first: *Gay Deceivers* provided Charlotte the first and only time she ever entered a stage via parachute (as she did in the gardens of Barrington, the Governor of the island, he being the object of her spinsterishly intense affections).

Gay Deceivers opened at the Gaiety Theatre in late 1935, a house well known to Martin as he had had shows there in the 1920s and was involved in its management, and proved an instant hit. "David Hutcheson as Bob Ferris and Clifford Mollison as Pat Russell as the gay deceivers certainly leave nothing to be desired in the matter of gaiety," wrote the critic for the July 1935 *Play Pictorial*, "nor for that matter does Charlotte Greenwood as Aunt Isabel; whether as the result of liberally helping herself to 'jumping beans' or of meeting the Governor by moonlight, her antics are equally mirth-provoking."

The Martin connection would become something of a problem, however. Almost before he had finished the music for *Gay Deceivers*, Martin had been working on the score for a musical comedy starring Leslie Henson and Louise Brown, with book by playwright Guy Bolton and screenwriter Fred Thompson and lyrics by Martin's tried and true collaborator, Graham John.

This show, called *Seeing Stars*, was set in a hotel in Antibes at which gathered the sort of blue- and red-blooded crowds to be found in any such high-class French establishment, ranging from an Archduchess Helen and daughter Princess Valerie to Leslie Henson's insouciant hotel owner, Jimmy Swing, several ex-officers and a reporter named Miss Watson, in several subsidiary and evocative settings: "Outside Kyra's Sanctum," "Poldi's Villa, 'Le Chateau Gris," and the bedroom of the "Archduke Rollo."

The plot revolves around the antics of Swing and fellow Englishman and business partner, Ken Carraway. Their hotel is in financial straits and they are both looking for a way to find a lot of cash in a very short time. Enterprising Jimmy persuades Ken to don drag and pose as an expensive but famously effective fortuneteller, "Kyra." Soon an ex-monarch named Cyril relies on Kyra to tell him when it is time to sell the crown jewels he managed to abscond from his former kingdom, the proceeds from which will pay the dowry for his daughter, Princess Valerie. But Valerie doesn't want her father to sell the jewels at all, since she wants to marry not the royal her father has in mind but Ken Carraway (who, we will recall, also happens to be "Kyra"). But before Ken can attend to this he has to find out what has happened both to Jimmy, who has disappeared, and the crown jewels, which have also gone missing. In short, Martin's show is love, West End Gaiety-style.

Unfortunately for Charlotte and *her* show, Martin's needed to open at the Gaiety — evidently *Gay Deceivers* was not believed to be a long-lived production, or Martin's *Seeing Stars* was finished faster than planned.[1] Whatever the reason, among Charlotte's many firsts that she does not list in her memoirs is that in which a wife and her hit show are ousted from a theatre by her own husband, to make room for *his* new hit show — surely something of a rarity in the annals of theatre, but perhaps not one of which she cared to remind herself or others.

Opposite: **Another crabby spinster transported on the wings of love, Charlotte is seen here as Aunt Isabel in *Gay Deceivers* (1935), her solicitor (Ivor Barnard) beside her. According to Charlotte, American actress Claire Luce, by skipping out during the run, caused the comedy to fold its tent early in London's West End. From *Gay Deceivers* program.**

In notes for her memoirs that were not used in the final typescript, Charlotte seems to vent more than a little resentment over this predicament:

> [*Gay Deceivers*] would have had a longer run had it not been for Martin who had finished the writing of a musical called "Seeing Stars" and had a prior right to the Gaiety. You'd think a husband wouldn't want to edge his wife out of a run, but not Martin. Business was business; they had engaged the theater and they proposed to use it. We moved "Gay Deceivers" to the Coliseum.
>
> Of course, it would be interesting to point this moral up by reporting that "Seeing Stars" proved an abject failure while "Gay Deceivers" went on to bigger and better things. Interesting, but not at all true. "Seeing Stars" was a terrific hit; and while "Gay Deceivers" survived the move to the Coliseum, a perfectly huge theater, it didn't survive a whim of Miss Luce.

"In America," she added in her unused notes, "if Miss Luce had suddenly decided she needed a holiday in the midst of a run, there would have been serious trouble. In England the management felt that whenever an artist needed a rest, there should be no debate." One can almost hear Charlotte's sarcasm embedded in the word "artist." As the sweet and pretty love interest who really was pretty and appeared to be sweet, Claire Luce was, beside Charlotte, one of the big audience draws for the musical — not only did she sing and act, but she performed with specialty dancer Robert Lindon. Somewhat cattily, as befitted a woman playing the owner of the estate on which Claire's character's father is manager, Charlotte graciously describes her as "one of the loveliest things I have ever seen," but she was not to feel that way for long.

Claire seems not to have been too concerned about what would happen to *Gay Deceivers* when she asked for and received permission to drop out in the middle of the run in order to travel to Moscow to study the famous Art Players. Gina Malo took over Claire's role. "But the play fell apart," Charlotte wrote, "and soon its West End engagement was over." *Gay Deceivers* had run almost five months (123 performances). Charlotte was clearly of the opinion it could have run longer, and was also clearly bitter about the fact that it was not allowed to do so, thanks to an unprofessional young actress's "whim."[2]

Fueled in part by her frustration to continue working, and by a more personal motive — for love of an old friend — Charlotte threw herself into another project before the dust of *Gay Deceivers* had even cleared. "I made my debut as a radio producer," she recalled, "as a result of a chance remark by John Royal, vice president of NBC — the same Johnny Royal who had shocked Mama with his [talk of] his fancy commodes. He had come to England to arrange the broadcast of the King George V Jubilee program. Noel Coward, Gertrude Lawrence and I were selected to head the bill. I was very proud to represent America. Next morning, Royal called me at the Berkeley [Hotel] to offer congratulations. It seems that my voice had registered very well — that 'nice voice' of my childhood."

Charlotte had not known that the broadcast was to be trans-oceanic. She told Royal that had she been aware of this, she would have included greetings to her former brother-in-law, Thomas Meighan, who was seriously ill with cancer in New York City (he died surrounded by family in July 1936). Royal had an idea: "Why don't you assemble some of his cronies and do a special broadcast for him?"

Royal had some idea of Charlotte's enthusiasm as a performer, but her swift work off stage must have flabbergasted not only him but his NBC associates. Within a week, Charlotte had gathered together a small galaxy of stars, all friends of Meighan's from years back. With Martin's Gaiety associate Debroy Somers and his band providing the music, a cast including superstar Irish tenor John McCormack (who had recently made a broadcast recording of Martin's song, "Love's Roses," with lyrics by Meighan's wife Frances Ring); Sir Seymour Hicks (actor and playwright famed for such one-liners as: "A man does not buy his wife a fur coat to keep her warm, but to keep her pleasant"); American actor Joseph Coyne, the famed Danilo of the 1907 London premiere of *The Merry Widow*; Texas-born film star Bessie Love; and Jimmy Walker, ex-governor of New York City and now an expat living in London. Charlotte herself completed the roster. Charlotte conceived and wrote the program, which may come as a surprise though not to those who knew her. Few people today know that she regularly wrote lyrics for songs set by Martin — some of the songs in Martin's early MGM talkie, the studio's first, *So This Is College*, were written by Charlotte, as was a fox-trot she and Martin released on the Blue Bird label in 1938, titled "When I Walk with You in the Cool of the Evening."

With her radio program Charlotte achieved something of a diplomatic coup. Not only did the broadcast bring happiness to the ailing Meighan, reminding him of friendships that stretched to all corners of the globe, "but it brought to an end the feud between Jimmy Walker and his estranged friend, Franklin D. Roosevelt," Charlotte recalled. "Midway in the program a messenger arrived with two radiograms, one for Walker, one for me."

Visibly moved, Walker read his to Charlotte: "It's from the little White Father in Washington — congratulations." It was the first friendly overture between the two men in years.[3]

The other radiogram was of a very different nature, but by now Charlotte almost knew already that such a sudden communication could only be from one person — Henry Duffy in California. Once again, Duffy had discovered what he described to Charlotte as "the ideal play" for her. It was *Post Road*, a comedy-drama by short story writer Wilbur Daniel Steele and actress-playwright Norma Mitchell (the latter had written Charlotte's successful sketch, *Her Morning Bath*).

Charlotte writes that in its 1934 run on Broadway, *Post Road* "had had moderate success," but not many of the plays and musicals she was in were hitting Steele and Mitchell's 212 performance run. Duffy saw Charlotte in the role played by Lucile Watson, that of Emily Madison, whose quiet Connecticut boarding house is turned upside down when she has to solve a kidnapping mystery and bring the criminals to justice.

Duffy wanted to cash in on the name recognition of past Lettys and did so not only by re-casting Emily in Letty's name and image but also by re-titling the play *Leaning on Letty*. Charlotte liked the play and the idea enough to agree to a run of one week in San Francisco and another in Hollywood — staying, as usual, away from New York. "And as casually as that," she wrote, "I embarked on a project that was to occupy me for some years to come."[4]

22

Letty's Last Dance

Leaning on Letty OPENED IN San Francisco the week before Christmas 1935. "[To] the astonishment of everyone but Duffy," Charlotte recalled, "who had always had absolute and unshakeable confidence in his selection, we found we had a hit."[1]

Moving on to Hollywood, the play then ran for thirteen weeks before returning to San Francisco's Alcazar Theatre, a Duffy house. It was in the alley outside the theatre after a performance that Charlotte met her old friend and patron of Broadway days, Lee Shubert, and while she was glad to see him he was obviously not feeling the same.

"He had seen the show and enjoyed it," she remembered, "but he had been informed by Duffy that I was planning to return to London. It seemed to Lee that I might do better by my country to remain here instead of galloping back to the aid of Britannica." He suggested she try a run in Chicago — specifically, at one of the Shubert theatres there. What were Charlotte's London social duties compared to opening in The Loop in a new play that trailed success like a parade confetti? [2]

Anxious to get back to England — very likely an anxiety more reflected from Martin than originating with her own needs — Charlotte was tempted to laugh Shubert off. Chicago's theatre world had been in a slump roughly approximating that of the country's Depression, and had shown few signs of ever emerging from it. "Ever since the Depression, no star or show had been able to sustain a run in Chicago," Charlotte wrote in notes for her memoirs. "No one could understand it."

The Loop was widely believed to be jinxed, and for Shubert to suggest that Charlotte Greenwood, the toast of London, who happened to be enjoying a brief success in California before returning to the city on the Thames, should risk money and reputation by walking into that known quagmire seemed to Charlotte foolhardy, if not insane. On the other hand, "I had been the recipient of many kindnesses from the Shubert office," she recalled. "I felt I owed [Lee] and his brother a debt of gratitude that had been long standing. It was through their courtesy in releasing me from 'The Passing Show of 1913' that I had been able to branch out as a solo star."[3]

Though his meeting with Charlotte in the Alcazar's dark alley and his pressing on her an obligation dating back many years has about it something not quite kosher, Lee Shubert's instincts for a Chicago run of *Leaning on Letty* proved to be worth his own weight in ticket receipts. The play opened on Thanksgiving eve of 1935, "and helped materially to rout the jinx from The Loop. I went in and did twenty-one record-breaking weeks, and since that time Chicago has been a haven for long runs."

> It was during that engagement, by the way, that I introduced what was accepted as a new form of entertainment. Instead of the usual set curtain speech after the show, I elected to try an after-piece, a full song and dance turn. It was received with acclaim by the theatergoers, but, frankly, it wasn't new. The originator of that amusing device was a lad named Shakespeare, who used to stage a dance — the Morris dances — after each of his performances.

This after-curtain turn also included music from Charlotte's earlier Letty plays and a medley of Martin's songs. He had even agreed to the cannibalizing of Charlotte's hit song from *Gay Deceivers*, "Moon Melody," for use in *Leaning on Letty*—when the song was released by Schirmer, it bore Charlotte's photograph and the somewhat dishonest descrip-

A glamour shot of Charlotte Greenwood as Letty Madison in her last Letty stage turn, *Leaning on Letty*, 1936.

tion, "As introduced by Charlotte Greenwood in her new comedy hit, 'Leaning on Letty.'" So much for London!

In her memoir notes Charlotte added that she had discovered that Shakespeare had been paid only the equivalent of 5 pounds for his immortal *Hamlet*—while some news wag had estimated that Charlotte's two legs had earned her almost $5 million over the course of her then-thirty year career. Given Charlotte's increasing knowledge of the history of her art and her intention of being recognized as a serious performer, this sobering fact was not lost on her.[4]

Reviews were uniformly positive. In the *Chicago Journal of Commerce*, hard-to-please critic Claudia Cassidy wrote, "Miss Greenwood remains as endearing a comedienne as the theater knows." Ashton Stevens of the *Chicago American* called the play "a farce with thrills," and went on to write: "Miss Greenwood can act. I mean really act; without overdoing either the levity or the gravity. She has an unfussed power over words that I have never suspected."

Only one other Chicago show did as well as *Leaning on Letty—You Can't Take It with You*—starring Charlotte's friend, the ex-vaudevillian Eddie Conrad, and produced by her old colleague Sam Harris. (In Burns Mantle's *The Ten Best Plays of 1936–37*, Charlotte's show received the honors for having the longest run of the period; after *Letty* moved on, Conrad's remained to set a new record.)

At first there was some contumely between the two shows, which were playing side by side. *Letty* did a greater matinee business than Harris' show, which meant that chairs had to be borrowed by Charlotte's theatre to provide places for the surplus audience to sit. "Sometimes our boys were rather ruthless about the chairs," remembered Charlotte, "and took them without regard to the convenience of the other players."

One afternoon, Eddie Conrad came "roaring" into Charlotte's dressing room, where he "spluttered with his particular kind of comic rage ... 'What have I got to do — stand up to

HENRY DUFFY

presents

America's Incomparable Comedienne

CHARLOTTE
GREENWOOD

IN

The New Non-Stop Laugh Hit

"LEANING ON LETTY"

From "POST ROAD" by
WILBUR DANIEL STEELE and NORMA MITCHELL

Charlotte had reason to celebrate when her final Letty play, *Leaning on Letty*, drew rave reviews at Chicago's Selwyn Theatre in 1936 and 1937.

make up!'" Charlotte eventually got the situation sorted out for him. Later on, when both Conrad and Charlotte were working exclusively in Hollywood, whenever the comedian met her "he would make a sweeping bow and with mock gravity read John Drew's old line from 'Trelawny of the Wells,' the roar of the Irish squire: 'What, have we no cheers?'"[5]

During the run of *Leaning on Letty*, Charlotte and Martin lived in the Mary Garden Suite at the Congress Hotel, and right beneath them was the pianist Myra Hess (later Dame Myra), who was performing a recital in Chicago that week. The morning of her recital, Hess began practicing and did not let up for most of the day, entrancing the Brooneses, who stayed put the whole time to hear the great musician going through her manual calisthenics. "We were amazed at her nonchalance," Charlotte recalled. Though the auditorium where Hess would be performing was next door to the Congress, as her time to go on stage — 8:30 — drew nigh, "the woman seemed to have no intention of stopping."

> Apparently oblivious to time, Miss Hess continued. The clock moved to 8:10, 8:15, 8:20 — I was in a dither. Should I phone her apartment and warn her? Had she forgotten about the recital? What to do?
>
> At 8:27, to the second, the music stopped as abruptly as it had started. Three minutes later Miss Hess was bowing to her audience that filled the spacious auditorium to the very rafters and was starting on a two hour recital as fresh as a daisy. [In] my agitation about the likelihood of Miss Hess missing her show, I very nearly missed my own. Fortunately my curtain rose later and I, too, was on time, thanks to a diligent and fearless taxi driver....

It was an object lesson in Charlotte's own oft-repeated admonition that a performer be focused and, above all, be on time.[6]

As distracted as she and Martin had been by the British Miss Hess, they were even more diverted by the doings in England leading up to the coronation — not of King Edward VIII but of his brother, George, erstwhile Duke of York. In spring 1937, Charlotte closed the Chicago run of *Letty* and went on a brief tour of the Midwest, terminating in Kansas City. "Two days later," she recorded, "we were aboard the *Queen Mary* bound for London and the coronation of George VI," laughing at a passing newspaper headline as they went up the gangplank:

CORONATION ATTENDED BY NOBILITY AND NOBODIES!

Perhaps by Buckingham Palace standards Charlotte counted among the latter, but the friends who greeted her and Martin on their return to London were nothing if not part of the warp and woof of London society, whether of social station or of talent. Martin's frequent collaborator Graham John met the couple, who had had the thrill of being on a ship so fast it had overtaken both the *Berengaria* and the *Bremen*. They were delighted by the pennants and parades of London's approaching gala as John escorted them to their quarters at Whitehall Court.

"We were particularly fortunate in this connection," wrote Charlotte in her memoirs. "For weeks before the end of the tour [of *Leaning on Letty*] we had been in communication with various London hotels and it began to look as if we would have to camp in the Mall. Quarters were simply not available. It wasn't until the eve of departure that a cable arrived from Whitehall Court, saying that an Indian maharajah had given up his reservation and we could be accommodated."

Charlotte and Martin could not have found a better ringside seat for the coronation procession: from their balcony, they could see not only Westminster Abbey, where the post-ceremonial procession began, but also Big Ben and the Thames, bright with merry-making boaters. They looked out on a city filled with a joy that was, in part, a form of visible relief after a year of suspense and frustration regarding the fate of the previous king — and of the empire he was to rule — the short-reigned Edward VIII.

The coronation itself was set for May 13, 1937. As Charlotte later described, "London itself was a blaze of color — red, white, and blue, with gold trimmings everywhere. On each light post a gold crown perched; reviewing stands were everywhere, even on top of buildings, and all decorated in the same colors." The post-coronation procession from Westminster Abbey was nearly two miles long.[7]

As *The Illustrated London News* reported on May 8, "Bands will be stationed along the route and others, including a Canadian Service band, will be in the procession.... [T]he King and Queen will wear their Crowns and the King will hold the Sceptre with the Cross and the Orb, while the Queen will hold her Sceptre and Ivory Rod." On that same day, all across the empire, from Victoria, British Columbia to Auckland, New Zealand to remote outposts in India and even in parts of the United States, local dignitaries supplied with acorns from Windsor Great Park (or mango and coconut seedlings for tropical climates) planted them and placed identifying plaques in honor of their new king and queen.[8]

"We invited a number of friends to join us," Charlotte recorded, "and at five o'clock on the morning of the Coronation they began to arrive." The Brooneses had been told by the district police that as the entire parade route would be locked down by 6 A.M., any guests would have to arrive before then. One of these was dark-eyed Humbert Wolfe, the Italian-born, Oxford-educated poet and dramatist, then serving day-job time as under secretary of the Ministry of Labour, whom Charlotte found "peacefully sleeping on the divan in our living room when we arose." If for no other reason, Wolfe would have endeared himself to both Charlotte and Martin with a canto from his just-released spoof on Byron's *Don Juan*, titled *Don J. Ewan*, in which the omniscient narrator travels the world over, not leaving Hollywood and its peculiar culture of ex–Bowery men turned arbiters of cinematic art off his itinerary.[9]

It was Wolfe who had given a name to a little creature that had entered Charlotte and Martin's life shortly before the Coronation and would remain a part of it almost till the end of Charlotte's career. This beloved being was a white Pekingese, which Charlotte had once taken with her to the Ritz Hotel's dining room for a repast with Wolfe and Martin. When a waiter gave Wolfe trouble over an order, Charlotte recalled, the dog barked and lunged at the man, as if to protect the poet. In gratitude, "Humbert formally knighted the little dog," remembered Charlotte, giving him the moniker "Sir George Winkie, Bart." (A name combining that of the newly crowned king, that of the dog's aristocratic English grandsire, Winkle of Parkfield, and the title of baronet, least of all available hereditary titular honors in the U.K., being just the right size for the animal's tiny frame.)

Known as Winkie thereafter, the Pekingese not only went everywhere Charlotte and Martin did, but was frequently photographed with them or with Charlotte. While being driven to the south of France in their Rolls-Royce (in which he rode wrapped "like a fur piece" around Charlotte's neck), they had stopped for lunch at Versailles and allowed Winkie to ramble over the royal lawns, rushing back to sip water from a silver cup given him specially by Lady Willert, wife of Sir Arthur Willert, the London *Times* correspondent in Washington D.C. In many ways, as friends of the Brooneses still point out, Winkie was the child they never had. Even after death,

Charlotte's striking personal elegance and her love for her dog Winkie are on display in this formal portrait by Lucas & Pritchard (1936). Sir George was knighted, per Charlotte, by her friend the poet Humbert Wolfe in the restaurant of the London Ritz.

yellowed evidence of his "accidents" would be left untouched on the antique Chinese silk rugs in Charlotte's Rodeo Drive house, cherished, as one friend put it, like relics of a deceased saint. After he died, in 1948, Charlotte wrote a moving tribute that was published in *The Tailwagger Magazine* and sums up the relationship this small animal had with his tall owner: "We dwelt together in deepest understanding, devotion and shared laughter."[10]

Once the Whitehall Court flat was filled with the Broones' friends, they, Charlotte, Martin and Winkie all settled in for the morning's events.

> So we had our breakfast listening to the start of the Coronation services on the radio; and then the procession itself. It was a memorable occasion. The voices of the people cheering their monarchs sounded like the roar of the surf; waving handkerchiefs became like so many white birds flying in tribute. And then it rained. The multitude merely unfolded their raincoats, opened their umbrellas, and never missed a cheer.[11]

But when the procession ended, the bobbies below politely herding similarly polite throngs in single file out of the area, Charlotte and Martin's day had only just begun. The circles Charlotte and Martin moved in in London were emblematic of the split that the Edward VIII/Mrs. Simpson situation had opened throughout the city and its society. They knew writer Hector Bolitho, who turned against Edward, and the Duke of Kent, who supported him; they attended a ball in honor of George VI, at which the Duke of Kent danced, but in Chelsea, where the less straight-laced atmosphere allowed more smudging of lines that in other circles must not be crossed. And they had been charmed by Edward, as Prince of Wales, at the Berkeley Hotel in the early 1930s. Such was London town in May 1937.

> That night we attended a colorful Coronation Ball [at the Albert Hall], a costume affair, chiefly of the Shakespearean period. I have never seen such jewels on display, nor, for that matter, had such an opportunity to rub shoulders with royalty. Our hostess was Mrs. Dennis Cohen, who looked positively regal herself in a brocaded French Empire gown with white feathers flying high in her hair. She provided a landmark for us until the approach of dawn, when her plumage began to droop.... There was a pageant of Shakespeare's plays and characters ... the Scotch Highlanders set the high mark for the evening with their bagpipes. Their arrival was the cue for breaking down of all class barriers. The dancers ... formed in groups behind the pipes and then broke up into smaller groups for impromptu folk dances. It was all very spontaneous and democratic.

Among the royals present were George Duke of Kent, brother of the new king, and his wife, the former Princess Marina of Greece, who had been married in a lavish ceremony the year before. And Crown Princess Louise of Sweden (born a Mountbatten; Charlotte erroneously describes her as Queen) was there, wearing a gown with such a long train that during the folk dances extra steps had to be added to avoid treading on it. At the party's end, remembered Charlotte, "they released from the dome of the building what seemed to be thousands of balloons — all colors and sizes — with spotlights following them down."[12]

Charlotte and Martin reached home in broad daylight, rested briefly, and then prepared to go out again, this time to Covent Garden to hear the London debut of their friend, the bass-baritone Lawrence Tibbett, in the role of Scarpia in Puccini's *Tosca*. It was at a party shortly afterward, given in Charlotte and Martin's honor by Baroness Ravensdale, daughter of Lord Curzon, Viceroy of India, that Baroness Ravensdale insisted that Charlotte's talents must derive from some extraordinary background, to which Charlotte replied she did indeed come of an extraordinarily long line — of Philadelphia barbers. (She might have added her saloonkeeper grandfather to the pedigree, but anything to do with alcohol was far beyond the pale of Charlotte and Martin's Christian Science lifestyle.)

To add to the exhaustive schedule, the couple went to see Martin's hit show, *Swing Along*, a farcical tale of a man who, having lost everything at Monte Carlo, feels free to mingle with underground political sects as a saboteur. The obligatory love interest, between a disguised member of one sect and the dashing female leader of another, made up the subplot. This was thin material, but with its scene set on the famous Blue Train, *Swing Along* did very well indeed, running nine months at the Gaiety Theatre. Martin had not yet seen the show and did so in company with Charlotte and Lawrence Tibbett and his wife.

When it came time to leave for some relaxation at Antibes, it was all Charlotte and Martin could do to drag themselves on the boat. But once there, even on the beach, Charlotte got no rest. "There, sure enough, strolling along the sands was Lee Shubert...," she remembered. "We talked of America and England and finally *Leaning on Letty*. This time he was pursuing different tactics. 'Chicago was grand,' he was saying, 'I wonder how the show would do on the Eastern circuit — I suppose not, plays have to be pretty sophisticated to play the East. We'd better not risk it.' Of course, that got Martin's dander up, as Lee suspected it would."

"Before we parted, it was decided that I would return immediately after a holiday and start anew on 'Leaning on Letty.' It was a junket that was to take us to the Antipodes and into the films again."[13]

23

"To the Antipodes and back"

"THE FINAL TOUR OF 'Leaning on Letty' started in Philadelphia," recalled Charlotte, "and our first problem was one of booking."

The Shuberts' booking executive, Jules Murry, was of the opinion that a two week run of *Letty* at Philadelphia's Chestnut Street Opera House would be plenty long enough, believing as he did that unless one were Katherine Cornell or Helen Hayes, a longer run was implausible. "Martin wasn't impressed by the logic," Charlotte wrote dismissively, "and proceeded to plan his campaign on the basis of a four week engagement."[1] Incidentally, this is the first firm indication in Charlotte's memoirs that Martin's energies had turned from composing and promoting his own work to managing Charlotte's career.

Despite the bad weather of that fall, a massive illuminated parade had been planned and it happened to fall on the opening night of *Leaning on Letty*, a circumstance that caused alarm in the Shubert offices and in Charlotte's hotel when they read that the line of march would take the bands right in front of the theatre. "It is quite enough to play to comparative quiet," Charlotte quipped, "but to offer vocal competition to a series of brass bands is an uninviting prospect," even to the singer who had trained under Ned Wayburn.

The Shuberts' general manager, however, was not to be conquered. He worked out a deal with all the bands to go tacit or quiet when marching in front of the Chestnut Street venue, save for the drums, which had to beat to give the ensembles their rhythm. "As a consequence, we played 'Leaning on Letty' to a background of rolls and rat-tat-tats and boom-booms until I thought we'd all go mad," remembered Charlotte. "Not until the final scene of the play, when we had machine-gun effects on the stage, did the passing bands actually prove useful." Nonetheless, the play was a hit and when it ran a full four weeks, Jules Murry had to cheerfully eat his hat.[2]

They moved on to Pittsburgh, which to Charlotte was "a lovely old city, much maligned by those who like to dwell on its smoke and forget its hospitality, and it has a theatrical landmark in the old Nixon Theater, with its hallowed atmosphere and its slanting stage. In some respect, the Nixon traced my own curious history in the theater. My progress from the chorus to stardom can be counted in the flights of stairs leading from the top tiers of dressing rooms to the stage level."[3]

Years earlier, when she was in the chorus, Charlotte had had to get into costume and makeup in a closet-sized room three flights above the stage. As she was given a few lines to deliver, she descended to the second flight; and once she became a featured player, she moved to the first. "Now I found myself on the stage level, surrounded by pictures of stars on the back stage walls and in the dressing rooms, entering with a proprietary air the very dressing room whose door I had looked upon with ambitious desire."

The Nixon stage has a quiet and dignity that comes only with the mellowing years and with constant association with great stars, each of whom has left in some indelible way his mark upon the theater. There, for instance, is that strip of worn red velvet carpet encircling the back of the stage for artists to walk upon. If it could only speak, I am sure it would say: "I am the carpet that Harry Brown brought in great haste so that Fritzi Scheff could walk from her carriage to the stage door without coming in actual contact with the soil. I have softened the footfalls of John Drew, E.H. Sothern, Otis Skinner, Walker Whiteside and the Barrymores. My nap has been lightly ruffled by the feathery footsteps of Maude Adams as Peter Pan, or Marilyn Miller as Sunny, of Anna Pavlova. I marked the way for Ethel Barrymore and Guy Bates, for Katherine Cornell and Brian Aherne, for Helen Hayes and Maurice Evans. My warp and woof is the warp and woof of glamour!"[4]

In her memoirs, Charlotte reproduces a diary entry[5] she made while playing the Nixon, late in 1937, in which she looks back on what was already a long career, little thinking of how much more lay ahead, thankful for all the lucky breaks and the people from whom she had learned, both the hard way and the sweet way:

It is Wednesday afternoon. The matinee is over and as usual I am remaining in the dressing room waiting for the evening performance. A very pleasant waitress has just brought in my dinner from the restaurant with: "It has been a pleasure to serve you, ma'am. I had the honor of serving Miss Cornell when she played here."

In this room at the Nixon where I sit are portraits of Fritzi Scheff, with whom I appeared in New York in "Pretty Mrs. Smith," Nazimova who sat next to me recently at a studio preview of "Blood and Sand," in which she did a fine piece of work as the troubled mother of the hero, and Mitzi Hazos — little Mitzi who was for so many years the gold mine in the Henry W. Savage office. There are pictures, too, of Lillian Gish, Lenore Uric, Fred and Adele Astaire and Dorothy Stone — I recall what a sensation there was when Fred allowed his little girl to appear with him and they danced together.

There is an echo on the stage of the Nixon today. Somehow I do not remember it, and somehow I do not mind it. It echoes the language of the theater, the real theater [that] was built up by the greatness of great artists, who worked and studied to determine what Shakespeare meant by some of his obscure phrases.

I like the modern architecture and smartly severe interiors of the new theaters, but when you go out front and sit in one of those red velvet chairs and look on those warm draperies, so luxurious in comfort and plush, you feel happy to have been a part of that era when they flourished, and secretly wish that this new generation could share in the rich warm glow that you felt as a child sitting there and weeping over such performances as Virginia Harned's "Anna Karenina" or Sarah Bernhardt's "Camille."[6]

(The Nixon would be demolished in 1950 to make way for the ALCOA Building.)

Letty moved on to St. Louis, and though Charlotte had not been seen there for eighteen years, Paul Beisman, the manager of the American Theater there, burst into Charlotte's dressing room and before kissing her hand, said breathlessly: "Madame, St. Louis has made you important people. I have been forced to open the top gallery to take care of the crowd. We haven't had that heavenly retreat open since Cornell did 'The Barretts.'" [7]

The show toured for five months, closing finally in Boston in January 1938. For the first time in years, Charlotte and Martin had a chance to return to their house at Auburndale, which Eunice Burnham had had redecorated for them long before. But they were not satisfied — home didn't feel like home any more.

"It was winter in Auburndale," Charlotte recalled, "and I'm not mincing words. To begin with the house looked awfully small. I had the feeling that if I lifted my head too suddenly, it would poke through the ceiling. Years in London with the vaulted domes had done something to my sense of proportion."[8]

Under an image of a laughing Charlotte recumbent on the parlor stair rails of the *Leaning on Letty* set, Charlotte told *Collier's* writer Kyle Crichton that same wintry month all about her life, both on stage and off, starting with her birth and background in Philadelphia, Boston and Tidewater Virginia. (Though, as she had done for years, she takes two years off her age.)

Crichton touches on an issue far more sensitive than Ian Fox's obsession with Charlotte's long legs when he notes that "Charlotte Greenwood always gives up the chance of big money just at the moment of her greatest popularity. Why is she going to give up the little gold machine known as *Leaning on Letty*? The truth is that the lady is ambitious." Charlotte told Crichton she had been studying drama and singing for years[9], and that she had no desire to be remembered "for a pair of long stems." Leaving no mystery on that point, "SHE'LL BE AN ACTRESS — OR ELSE" blared one of the paragraph headings.[10]

Charlotte's ambition was bursting the walls of the Auburndale house, and for all her talk about missing the place, she and Martin did not remain there long. "We wandered around the house like a couple of lost souls for days that seemed like years," she wrote later, "when a letter arrived from Nicholas and Pansy Schenck. They were in their Miami Beach home and wanted to know if we wouldn't like to drop down some time."

Throwing caution to the winds, the Brooneses packed up again and headed south. In the six weeks they stayed there, discussion clearly took place about the pros and cons of taking *Leaning on Letty* on a world tour, which both Charlotte and Martin had been thinking about for the past year. "Hoping to visit countries we had missed in our previous travels [and] aiming to meet at least some of the theater-goers who had supported me in pictures and had listened to Martin's music and applauded his plays." Contrary to Kyle Crichton's impression, at least in this respect, Charlotte was obviously not giving up the little gold mine of *Leaning on Letty* just yet.

Martin threw himself into plans for the tour with all the energy he brought to assembling one of his London shows, casting the show, sending telegrams and making $300 long-distance phone calls, dealing with embassies over performers' passports or lack thereof, arranging for scenery. Australia was to be the first port of call, and everyone assembled in Hollywood awaiting the final go-ahead. Then a ghost from Charlotte's past emerged to almost ruin it all.

Since his successes with Charlotte in the 1900s and 1920s, Oliver Morosco had had troubles, both business-wise and in his personal life. Married to a woman who, to go by his memoirs, coupled being a termagant with some form of mental illness, Morosco had begun an affair with a younger woman who was to become his second wife and happier helpmeet. But this couldn't fill his coffers to the brimful levels he had formerly been accustomed to, and when he heard that Charlotte was to take her newest Letty play on a world tour, he called his lawyers and discussed bringing suit against her and the production for infringement of his ownership of the Letty name and concept.

Charlotte is silent on this score in the final version of her memoirs (as is Morosco in his), but in her notes she records the shock of reaching the point of departure on her newest professional adventure, with theatres booked throughout the South Pacific, South Africa and India, only to find that her erstwhile colleague had threatened to stop the whole show. Citing a prior ownership of the "Letty" character, as derived from his involvement in adapting and producing the early series of Letty plays, Morosco not only wanted the tour stopped but demanded a share of the proceeds from the play to date — a sizeable chunk of change by anyone's standards. According to the *Los Angeles Evening Herald Express* of March 3, 1939, Morosco "contended that Miss Greenwood was seeking to deceive the public by appearing in a 'Letty' role."

Charlotte — and, more importantly, Martin, who could outdo Sir George Winkie when it came to snapping at the unfriendly and the unwanted — countered the claim by pointing out that when *Leaning on Letty* was produced in Hollywood five years earlier and was such a success that Morosco could hardly have been unaware of it, he had pressed no such claim to the name or the profits.

Charlotte's lawyer, George Acret, also contended that Morosco had abandoned any claim to the name years earlier when he ceased to produce any further plays dealing with the name or the character (by now so identified with Charlotte that she was often called "Letty" by fans on the streets of New York and London). "As a further defense," the article went on, "it was declared Morosco had gone through bankruptcy and if he ever had any rights to the name 'Letty,' they were not owned by the trustee in bankruptcy."

Morosco dealt with, there remained the matter of securing the comfort of Winkie, who could not accompany his parents on this long journey. "We did take time out for a laugh by impressing on one stolid official that Sir George was really a British subject, having been born on English soil and never having taken out American citizenship papers. We left him puzzling over this situation and left Winkie with friends in Beverly Hills."

Charlotte also had one more professional appointment to see to before leaving — a lunch meeting with Nat Goldstone, the producer and talent scout, whose interest in Charlotte would pay off in ways perhaps neither of them anticipated on the eve of the *Letty* tour. Over luncheon, young Goldstone "impressed me no end," Charlotte recalled. "I didn't know much about him, except that he was a representative for artists in the motion picture industry," an industry and a world which had been far from Charlotte's thoughts since fleeing Hollywood with Martin in 1932.

> He was enthusiastic about my returning to Hollywood to make pictures — reminded me that I had left Hollywood eight years before, not with a failure but with a huge success, *Palmy Days*. He gushed on, "You could be the greatest thing on the screen..." He had just seen me do the old spinster [Letty Madison] who said she didn't care about babies, but who actually would have given up her life for one particular baby in *Leaning on Letty*. He went on, "Not that you are anything like them [spinsters], physically or otherwise," but felt I had the same homely, natural appeal that Marie Dressler and Will Rogers had. He started to say, "Look, they were great, great performers on the screen, yet they weren't young or beautiful, had no glamour — were more or less physical misfits — but had a quality that transcended all physical limitations..." and he stopped abruptly. He probably thought he had gone too far and was hurting my feelings. But I quickly assured him that if I had relied on my beauty, well ... it was too long a story to go into then!
>
> However, I did appreciate his enthusiasm and his visions about me, but explained that we were just embarking on a world tour which would probably take two to three years. I thanked him for his wonderful encouragement and hoped someday to return to Hollywood.[11]

Everything was set — the company (consisting of Russell Fillmore, Isabel Withers, Romaine Callender, Wendy Atkin and Charles Martin) was ready to board the *S.S. Monterey*. The only thing left, and this somewhat against Charlotte's practical frame of mind, was to give in to a friend's argument that she should have a permanent her last day in Hollywood. Having been suspicious of these coifs since her friend, the dancer Bessie Clayton, had had her hair reduced to wire springs by a permanent gone bad in 1912 (Charlotte's borrowed jeweled Juliet cap had been heavy enough to suppress the curls during the dance but gave Bessie a splitting headache afterward), Charlotte had stayed away from the process, "the gadgets and the olive oil and the mysterious heat."

Those days of potential disaster were over, stated Charlotte's beauty operator in the up-to-date hair care era of 1939. "Now the mechanics of permanent waving had reached such a high degree of excellence that nothing ever went wrong. And how I would enjoy the freedom that the permanent wave would give me! Day after day I could give my head a toss and go out on deck the perfectly coiffed traveler." The result, however, was ominous —"[my] hair was set in a series of tight ringlets that were actually stiffening into cardboard texture." Thinking nothing of having pasteboard hair, which at least would stay put in the stiff ocean breeze, Charlotte got on the ship, which set sail that night.

"In the morning," she recalled, "I sat up in bed, looked out of the lanai window to see the blue ocean well below me, reached for a comb and began leisurely combing my hair from forehead to nape. I had made a pass or two when Martin strolled in, gasped, and yelled: 'What in heaven's name are you doing?'" He held up a mirror. Charlotte beheld herself and nearly yelled, too: "I was as bald as an American eagle in two spots where the comb had taken off ringlets and all."

Martin contacted the shipboard beauty shop (Elizabeth Arden) and got an attendant to their stateroom at the double-quick. For the next week, Charlotte had to lie with half her head in a bucket of oil, have the stiffness gradually worked out so as to save the rest of her hair and, not unimportantly, the tour of *Leaning on Letty.*

"I was left," Charlotte quipped, "with about three inches of sound hair, which made me look like a suitable candidate for the role of Maria in 'For Whom the Bell Tolls.'" She had to make do with a blonde switch she found at the bottom of her luggage, which had been given to her years earlier by her friend the opera star (and fellow tall blonde) Maria Jeritza.[12]

It was an inauspicious beginning for a world tour that was supposed to move from Australia to South Africa, the Dutch East Indies and New Guinea, Borneo, Batavia, Java, Bali, Singapore, and ending in India. As it happened, they circumnavigated very little of the world. In planning their newest *Letty*'s adventures, Charlotte and Martin had reckoned without the "little paperhanger" they had heard of in Frankfurt back in 1932.

24

Battle Drums

THE NEW YEAR OF 1939 offered a great deal more to be worried about for those paying attention to political undercurrents than a lawsuit from a bankrupt producer or a poorly done permanent wave, but for Charlotte and Martin, and most people in the world, things were looking up — for a brief while.

Hitler's *Anschluss* in late 1938 had ruffled the Austrians, but not too many other international feathers were set out of order. Part of the problem, of course, was that Hitler knew better than to force Germany into a war with the world when his military machine was not in shape to do so, nor his generals all in favor of such a scheme. He knew, as all mad geniuses know their opponents' greatest weaknesses, that appeasement was the order of the day, both from the British and the French — the former demonstrated in spectacular fashion in Munich and with Neville Chamberlain, who managed to lull an unsuspecting world that "peace in our time" could be a soothing rather than alarming turn of phrase, that allowing Hitler to occupy the Sudetenland in Czechoslovakia was as far as his hunger would take him.

Unfortunately, many foreign governments were stocked with minds that saw nothing much wrong with Hitler's professed need to turn the lands east of the German frontiers into farming and living space for Germany's burgeoning populations. Germany's Jews, most of whom were just as German, if not more so, than so-called Aryan Germans themselves, already knew how Hitler really felt about certain issues, namely their existence within his Reich: from initial thuggish attacks on Jewish businesses and people perceived to be Jews in the streets of Germany's cities, the Reich's gun muzzles and its legislators pointed directly at the nation's Jewish population, with boycotts of Jewish businesses, banning of Jews from the arts (including destruction of works of art created by Jews, even safely converted ones like composer Felix Mendelssohn), along with art considered by the Nazis to be "corrupt" and therefore deserving of condemnation in a "moral" way never before or since applied to tangible expressions of the human imagination. Jews were stripped of German citizenship by the 1935 Nuremberg Laws, and by the following year they were not allowed to participate in elections. With the advent of 1938, the restrictions were such that those Jews who could or would get out of Germany were doing so.

The pot that simmered throughout July, August and September came to a boil when, in late October, a Paris-dwelling Jew named Herschel Grynszpan protested the relocation of German Jews of Polish origin across the border to Poland (where they were no more wanted than in Germany) by shooting and killing a German Embassy official. Hitler's propaganda chief, Goebbels, found this a convenient *raison d'être* for a pogrom, the like of which had not been seen since the halcyon days of Imperial Russian bigotry — the two days in November known as "Kristallnacht," named after all the windows broken in Jewish-owned shops and homes across Germany, and the Jewish heads broken with them. Synagogues were burned, cemeteries desecrated, and thousands of Jews were arrested and sent off to the first of the concentration camps. It was, in a very real way, the beginning of the Holocaust.[1] And Hitler's clear intention of not remaining within the gossamer cage into which Chamberlain and other not-in-our-timers felt sure they had placed him would have far greater consequences for the world than the grabbing of more sovereign land — it would make obvious the sham of the Munich agreement, and make a fool of Neville Chamberlain, who when annoyed was not very appeasing at all.

As the *Leaning on Letty* production was preparing for Melbourne in April 1939, the first silent shot in the loud second World War was fired in what was perhaps as much a moment of piqued *amour propre* as solid political judgment, when Neville Chamberlain turned about face and pledged Britain's support for Poland against German aggression. France joined in; and with the special perspective afforded hindsight, Winston Churchill would write of this fateful chess-move: "[Now] at last the two Western democracies declared themselves ready to stake their lives upon the territorial integrity of Poland. History, which, we are told, is mainly the record of the crimes, follies, and miseries of mankind, may be scoured and ransacked to find a parallel to this sudden and complete reversal of five or six years' policy of easy-going placatory appeasement, and its transformation almost overnight into a readiness to accept an obviously imminent war on far worse conditions and on the greatest scale...."[2]

When Hitler decided he was good and ready (though neither he nor his forces were either) to make his move into Poland in September, Britain and France were half–Nelsoned into making good on their offer, and the real matches were held to the real powder kegs of a second world war.

✯ ✯ ✯

In the mean time, Charlotte fell utterly in love with Britain's former penal colony on the South Seas.

> I loved what I saw of Australia.... My introduction to it was ideal. Our final day at sea found the ocean calm and a gentle breeze blowing. There was a feeling of spring in the air although it was the beginning of Australia's winter.
> There [were] wide stretches of beach, huge combers crashing along the shore line and the South Head, on the day of our arrival, as wreathed in a halo of fog.... We proceeded slowly through the channel, following a line of buoys that marked the deep water.
> Once in the channel you are apparently walled in by rocks. It is as if you were inside the house of Australia, having entered her front door and proceeded down her long reception hall.
> Australian hospitality was soon in evidence. We were ... hustled off to the Hotel Australia through an army of photographers, interviewers, customs officers and autograph seekers.

The production company of *Leaning on Letty* had reached its first port of call, Sydney, Australia. From there, they took the train to Melbourne, where the company put up in the Menzies Hotel. The play opened at the King's Theatre on May 27, 1939.[3]

Shortly before curtain, Charlotte had been shown the yellowed newspaper clipping announcing the torpedoing of the troop transport Ballarat in the English Channel during World War I, and the troops' singing of "So Long Letty" as they were being rescued by British destroyers. With war in the air yet again, and Charlotte so enraptured over Australia and its hardy, handsome men, she stepped onto the creaky raked stage of the King's Theatre with tears in her eyes, passing the cage within which the euphoniously named Mr. Nightingale served the purpose of stage manager and prompter, and spoke her first lines as Letty Madison, spinster crime-solver. Mr. Nightingale would have a chance in those first few minutes to see just what a professional Charlotte was.

> It was, for me, a very important occasion, marking my first visit to Australia, and I was particularly anxious to have everything proceed like clockwork. I reckoned without one of the members of my company, a charming lad who had little or no conception of time. It was his chore in the first act to set the whole plot in operation. As a chauffeur, he was to come stealthily into the living room with a dog basket in which, subsequently, we would discover a kidnapped baby. He was to enter while I, as chatelaine of the house, was on a quick trip to the kitchen, and I was to come bustling in to catch him. So I bustled out on cue and bustled back on a time elapsed cue and found to my horror that I was occupying the stage alone. The young actor had missed his entrance cue.

Not only had he missed it on Charlotte's first tour of duty, he missed it when she went to a window and loudly mused on chauffeurs and town cars and then fell to improvising — something Charlotte did fluently with her body but not with lines, which once learned were, for her, graven in stone. "The audience, meantime, was laughing gaily at my antics," Charlotte recorded unhappily in notes she did not use. "I didn't feel gay." Finally, after Charlotte had left the stage and bustled in a third time, the young man appeared, at full run from his dressing room. The act then proceeded as planned.

"When the curtain fell, so did my heart," Charlotte recalled. "The balcony and gallery began to stamp their feet in unison."

> In America, this has ominous connotations as any baseball pitcher knows, and I was heartsick until Mr. Nightingale came bouncing out of his cage to embrace me before he ordered the curtain raised for my bow. When Australia stamps its feet, he confided exultantly, it is a stamp of approval and he, Mr. Nightingale, had never experienced the like, in volume and intensity, since Nellie Melba sang.
> Dame Nellie probably contained herself and her emotions. I let loose with a kiss that Mr. Nightingale will remember for some time to come. It was that loose, noisy kind that Mama had warned me about so many years ago.[4]

Some of the emergencies inherent in any touring show were very real indeed, like the incidents that followed the company's arrival in Brisbane. After a lengthy trip on the "Kyogle" train line from Melbourne, with hardly anything to eat except what Charlotte and the rest of the cast could quickly scrounge during the infrequent stops, they arrived at the theatre, only to find the place deserted.

"No one was in evidence but a property man," remembered Charlotte. "Martin asked if our scenery had reached the theater. He discovered somewhat to his horror that it hadn't even reached Brisbane. I had heard old actors tell of the good old days when troupers were not only willing but able to rustle scenery, make up props and post bills, but had never experienced the need. Nor had my players, but they caught on very quickly."

Rummaging through the theatre's attics, Martin and the other men in the company dug out scenery that had probably seen a good many touring Gilbert and Sullivan shows and found where they could borrow furniture from the good citizens of Brisbane, while Charlotte and the women washed, ironed and mended costumes. "By dinner time we had assembled enough costumery, props and scenery to give a performance and we dashed across the street for a bite to eat."

On their return to their elegant hotel, still covered with the cobwebs of the theatre's attic, they were "confronted by a perfectly elegant gentleman in tails with his assistant in ditto and that assistant's assistant also in ditto.... 'Ah, Miss Greenwood,' he said, with a deep bow, 'so happy to meet you. I do hope you found everything ship-shape.'" It turned out that this was the theatre manager, who had decided to take a day off despite the fact that the *Letty* company were coming into town and expecting to rehearse. He was no more helpful when it came to complaints from the cast about a persistent draft that washed across the stage without warning, chilling the actors in mid-phrase. "Ah, that!" he told them. "Very annoying — beastly awkward, isn't it?" It seemed there was a hole above the stage door that had been long thought troublesome, but which the manager had never found anyone to mend.

"The draft proved more than troublesome," Charlotte recalled, "when the steel curtain was lifted just before the performance, the stage curtain billowed out toward the audience in a great wave. Five stage hands leaped to it and finally hauled it back into place." The audience, however, well knew the issue of the drafty stage: "There they sat, bundled in fur coats with blankets around their knees as we related the story of Letty Madison and how she dealt with the villains who invaded her peaceful home on the Boston Post Road," teeth chattering all the while. Yet the enthused response was enough to warm everyone through.[5]

They had made it to Sydney and were just about to finish a successful run there and continue on the rest of the planned world tour when sobering news from Europe reached

"Now all I have to do is justify 'Charlotte Greenwood' by winning on Academy Award for high stepping or something" — Charlotte Greenwood on Charlotte Greenwood, the Australian filly named for her that won the Maiden Handicap at Melbourne Cup Day, Feb. 8, 1941.

Australian shores. "The war clouds had continued to gather in Europe, and were now emitting bolts of lightning," Charlotte wrote in her memoirs. "There was a series of conferences, some with friendly government officials, and it was decided that our best interests lay in an immediate return home." All passports had been cancelled, leaving the company little recourse to do anything else.

To say that Charlotte and Martin, who had planned the entire tour, were devastated by both the cancellation and the advent of yet more war would be putting it lightly. "We were all depressed because we had traveled a month by water and faced another month to return, and yet had been able to play only a few weeks in Australia and to visit only three cities.... However, Man proposes and Dictators dispose."[6]

The homeward journey took place not a moment too soon — while they were en route, Hitler invaded Poland, on September 1st, and two days later England and France perforce declared war on Germany. "We were in the middle of the Pacific," recalled Charlotte, "when the news came through [on September 3rd] that the *Athenia* had been torpedoed and sunk off the Hebrides. If we hadn't realized it fully before, we now knew in no uncertain terms that this was war. Wild rumors were flying all over the boat — rumor of German raiders in the South Pacific during the last war and how they operated. Yet here we were, bold as life, sailing in these very waters. The *Monterey* and the *Mariposa* were painted pure white from stem to stern. An easy target on even a dark, foggy night." Ironically, the *S.S. Bremen*, which had braved a storm to steam Charlotte to London a few years earlier for *Three Sisters* at Drury Lane and given her so many good memories, had been outfitted as a transport ship in Germany, to be used to convey troops for what Hitler believed would be his great invasion of Great Britain. (Like the Nazis, the *Bremen* never made it and was scrapped in 1946.)

What worried Charlotte the most, however, was not her own situation but that of the Australians on board, who had no idea now just when or if they would be able to return home. "We got very little sleep," she recorded, "until we reached California waters and safety and home."[7]

As it turned out, California was to be, for the peripatetic team Charlotte and Martin had been for most of their marriage, very much a home base for the rest of their lives together. While still on board the *Mariposa*, Charlotte received a radiogram from her admirer, Nat Goldstone, asking when she would be arriving home. The man who guided the careers of Robert Taylor, Robert Young, Alice Faye and other stars of the era would soon be of assistance in guiding Charlotte back from her cancelled world tour into the safe harbor of Hollywood.

It was a comfortable safety that, for both Charlotte and Martin, would come at a price.

25

Zanuck and Stardust

"Except for activists like Myrna Loy, Melvyn and Helen Gahagan Douglas, Edward G. Robinson, and the sensitive ones, like Greta Garbo," writes Roy Hoopes in *When the Stars Went to War*, "most members of movieland had not paid much attention to the storm gathering in Europe since Adolf Hitler had become Germany's chancellor [in 1932]."

Some actors gained their information through experiences with Nazi Germany that could leave no illusions as to where the Hitlerian ship of state was cruising. In Hamburg in 1933 (the year after Charlotte and Martin stumbled into the *Hitlerjugend* parade in Frankfurt), Harpo Marx would be stunned to see storefronts plastered with the damning Star of David and Jewish storekeepers staring with anxiety within, attempting to go through the motions of everyday life. Thanks to Hitler's boycott, few customers came into Jewish shops, heightening the surreal atmosphere of political uncertainty with a large dash of the reality of looming bankruptcy. Marlene Dietrich, a Berliner by birth, also had special experience of Hitler, in form of an offer from the Führer to enjoy the purported delights of his bedchamber (from which at least one woman, Hitler's niece Geli Raubel, had fled via suicide).

Dietrich refused to have anything to do with Hitler carnally or politically, and her outspoken loathing for the Nazi government and sympathy for the Jewish victims of it earned her the Führer's undying fury. One of the great patriots of the American war, Dietrich would return to Hollywood's flim-flam afterward with a hatred for the place and its shallow values almost as burning as her sentiments toward Hitler — she was particularly disgusted when home-coming American servicemen were asked to don ties before being allowed into the same tony restaurants where, during the war, they had been idolized in their plain uniforms.[1]

What makes 1939 an even more intriguing year in Hollywood history, however, is the several immortal, and several more demi-immortal, films made during that single year — seventeen in all, ranging from *Gone with the Wind* to *Wuthering Heights*, *The Wizard of Oz*, *The Women*, *Dark Victory*, *Stagecoach*, *Ninotchka*. It was as if the dream factory in the Los Angeles Basin, like the luxury liner *Normandie*, were delivering up its last and most glittering goods before being refitted for wartime work. Unlike the ship, however, Hollywood would remain very much afloat throughout and beyond the conflict. It was the United States' abrupt awakening from its isolationist daydream, on December 7, 1941, that would not only start the factory churning out hundreds of war-related films, many not to be distinguished from propaganda, but would give actors wondering what point there was to their lives in such critical times a job to do and a reason to feel proud of their work.

As the vaudeville dancer Hal Leroy once pointed out, "It takes twenty years to learn how to walk on with class, and twenty years to learn how to talk with class, and twenty years to learn how to walk off with class."[2]

Charlotte had certainly won her wings in less than the prescribed six decades. And she was lucky (and not always so lucky) in the timing of her comeback. More than ever, Hollywood had become more adroit at exploiting certain character types and had been presented by fate with wartime conditions combining stereotyping opportunities with those not far removed from military propaganda. From 1940 onward, studios would make use of Charlotte's signature brand of sunny optimism in the face of opposition and derring-do in pursuit of love and affection, those qualities which had come off almost frantic in her younger years but now had settled easily into her matronly but lanky frame, combining both sophisticated timing with maternal warmth.

Significantly enough, it was one of Hollywood's most vocal and partisan studio executives, Darryl Zanuck, who brought Charlotte back into the movies, just when she was about to rummage through the several stage offers awaiting her on her return from Australia and return to the comforting embrace of the theatre. One of these stage offers was for the lead in the London success *Under Your Hat*, produced by Lee Ephraim, who had produced *Gay Deceivers* a few years earlier, while another was for the lead in a play by John Golden. Though she seriously considered the part, Charlotte remembered Martin's abortive *The Chorus Lady*— Golden's play was in need of revision — and decided against the property. Before she could make a decision on Ephraim's offer Zanuck had sent Lou Schreiber, Charlotte's old friend from vaudeville days, and now casting director at Twentieth Century Fox studios, to meet her over lunch.

"Schreiber told me that Darryl F. Zanuck had decided to use me in *Star Dust*, if I were available," Charlotte recorded in her memoirs. "It was an interesting proposition because I had previously worked for Mr. Zanuck at Warner Brothers Studios and had great respect for his methods."

Despite the fact that Charlotte had made the extremely successful *Palmy Days* with Eddie Cantor and had lucrative film offers raining down on her blonde head, it was disgust with the ways of film moguls and producers that, according to Charlotte, had set her and Martin both in flight to the London theatre world in the early 1930s. In a passage stricken from a draft of her memoirs, with the note that she did "not like the feeling of any of this!," Charlotte wrote with some bitterness: "I had virtually dismissed the screen from my life. Somehow I didn't seem to fit into the new order of things in Hollywood, and while for a time I had entertained ambitions for films, I had abandoned them entirely. As a matter of fact [I had dismissed] the agent who had been representing me in Hollywood without much success, and I had severed our business relations before I left for Australia."[3]

Zanuck was different: he would give not only Charlotte but many others in Hollywood's notoriously opinionated atmosphere plenty to admire when, well before the United States entered the war, he backed up his belief that the U.S. should intervene in the European conflict by entering the Army Reserve in January 1941; soon afterward, he began preparations in Hollywood for some of the first Army training films. Mayer, however, was a staunch non-interventionist, fearing to make enemies anywhere lest box office receipts suffer the consequences — a position with which Charlotte would have had absolutely no sympathy.[4]

No wonder, then, that she wrote in her memoirs of Zanuck as "an amazing person. He has the flair and showmanship of a Ziegfeld and an uncanny faculty for anticipating entertainment trends," rather like some of the big-time vaudeville producers Charlotte had known and admired in her youth. She even went so far as to use the g-word: "There is a much abused word bandied about in Hollywood — genius — but if it can be applied to anyone with reason, it can to Darryl Zanuck, whose personal story is far more exciting and thrilling than any of the glorified biographies he has prepared for the screen."[5]

Zanuck was certainly unlike most of Hollywood's movie executives of the Golden Age in that he was American-born, a native of Wahoo, Nebraska, and had actually been involved with the production side of movie-making—first as a child extra and later, in the 1920s, as a respected screenwriter and production chief. (As a man who had worked at everything from bantam-weight boxing to clerking in a shoe store, he also had experience of everyday life and everyday people that gave him a keen perspective on public tastes for consumption of goods and entertainment.)

As Charlotte and Martin had left MGM in the early 30s, Zanuck had left Warner Brothers in 1933 to start his own company, merging with William Fox's company to become Twentieth Century Fox, with Joseph Schenck as his partner. Not all his stable of stars liked him — Shirley Temple, whose curls and dimples Zanuck's studio exploited till Temple left in 1941, frankly loathed him, but this was as much due to her controlling mother's negative attitude about Zanuck as her own opinion.

Mrs. Temple had gone the rounds with Zanuck over his relentless typecasting of her daughter, who was still being trotted out as a living Shirley Temple doll past the age when a girl normally played with one (Temple admits in her memoirs that she never cared much for dolls, preferring the boy-like hobbies of collecting bugs and pretending to be a police chief). Mrs. Temple seems to have transferred to Shirley her belief that to Zanuck "[w]omen to him were mostly tramps, a sexy, bitchy, unscrupulous lot who got what they deserved. Of children, his record was blank." She quotes a critic who declared that "Never has [Zanuck] demonstrated any liking for women stars," and was even more at a loss with a child star (like Shirley Temple).

Of course, Zanuck could and did point out that artistic discussions about character development aside, Shirley's typecasting films were making a bundle of money in difficult economic times — in 1936, profits topped close to $8 million, and Shirley's films *Dimples* and *The Stowaway* brought in over $1 million in America alone. "Each of my other films," wrote Temple later, "was expected to return five times its cost in profits." Besides this proof that anyone who changed a hair of Shirley's curly head would be throwing away the golden egg-laying goose, Zanuck insisted that his job was to mine out all the riches presented by an identifiable film personality by making the most possible of their unique characteristics, a mission he took quite seriously.[6]

For all his interest in Charlotte and her respect for him — in a 1950 interview with Boston Post drama critic Elliott Norton, she and Martin both lauded Zanuck for having "believed in Charlotte as a dramatic actress" — Zanuck was to visit this theory and method on her with a vengeance for the next several years.

"My first step in this return to Hollywood," wrote Charlotte, "was a conference with Walter Lang, who had been assigned the direction of *Star Dust*, which was to introduce, in her first really important part, a very interesting newcomer, the lovely Linda Darnell."[7] In the script, written by Robert Ellis and Helen Logan, Charlotte played a dramatic coach named

Lola Langdon (an ex–Mack Sennett silent screen comedienne), opposite Roland Young's talent scout Thomas Brooke (an ex-star of stage and silent screen), both of whom work for Dane Wharton (William Gargan), head of "Amalgamated Pictures," in what was a clear hint at Zanuck and Twentieth Century Fox itself.

"As a documentary film of the trials and tribulations of Hollywood neophytes," wrote *New York Times* film critic Theodore Strauss, when the film premiered in spring 1940, "'Star Dust' is unlikely to stem the westward migration of youngsters with hallucinations of swimming pools and a six-figure apotheosis to stardom."[8]

Hollywood hopefuls Arkansas soda jerk Carolyn Sayres (Linda Darnell), throaty Texas contralto Mary Andrews (Mary Healy), and handsome Bud Borden (John Payne, aptly playing a would-be football star) are Brooke's discoveries. A tragic subplot turns on Darnell's deceased actress mother having once been involved with Brooke before he left her to pursue his film career. Carolyn's resemblance to the lady torments Brooke in a way that gave Roland Young's perpetually pained expression a *raison d'être* unappreciated by critic Strauss, and leads him to abandon the girl as he had done her mother.

Unlike her mother, Carolyn proves herself a regular Arkansas Eve Harrington, forging a letter from Brooke to Amalgamated Studios recommending her for a screen test. When it becomes clear to both Lola and Brooke that they have star material on their hands, Brooke ceases to be annoyed at Carolyn's chutzpah and he and Lola stop at nothing to get the screen test in front of Wharton. The latter, meanwhile, is distracted by the wiles of another of his scouts, the weasly Sam Wellman (Donald Meek), who tries to sabotage Carolyn's powerful screen test by having it destroyed. Langdon outwits everyone by arranging for the screen test to be inserted into a newsreel at a gala Grauman's Chinese Theatre premiere, with Wharton and Wellman in the audience. Wharton is so won over by Carolyn's manifest beauty and ability that he fires Wellman on the spot and makes Carolyn a star.

The film ends with Carolyn putting her footprints in wet cement outside Grauman's, with the real Sid Grauman at her side in a brief cameo, while Langdon turns to Brooke with bedroom eyes and makes it apparent that success with Darnell's career isn't the only mark chalked up on her scoreboard.

Star Dust is a fascinating comeback for Charlotte, in that it presents her in virtually documentary fashion as the personality she was offstage — gregarious, a little pushy in the process, but loving and warm — and yet also as the personality she had always aspired to be: an expert on the art of serious acting. (It is also significant that Charlotte's character, Lola, had started out in Mack Sennett farces, even as Charlotte had started in stage and silent farce.)

Unlike the films that Zanuck offered her afterward, *Star Dust* allows Charlotte plenty of latitude to develop the character of Lola as well as to use a few — but not too many — of her old vaudeville tricks, excluding the fan kicks and the Camel Walk. She has only one musical number but it's a good one, a rousing version of Hoagy Carmichael's song "Don't Let It Get You Down," which lugubrious Mary Healy had been dragging her heels through a moment before. "Watch grandma!" Charlotte peals joyfully as she launches into an up-tempo performance in what is arguably the film's brightest scene.

But there is also a tense scene of Lola angrily shouting at the production staff, who surround and confuse Carolyn during her screen test, which fully justifies Theodore Strauss' description of Charlotte as "the hard-boiled dramatic coach with the heart of gold." In this scene's few moments, the fluffy myth that Charlotte Greenwood was unable to play anything but "lean, long, lanky Letty," that she was dizzy queen of the mindless physical comedy sketch,

is chipped down to a hard edge of reality. When a cameraman keeps criticizing Darnell's position, as if the camera were more important than the actress, Charlotte explodes with a memorable line: "Say, listen, Rembrandt — what's the use of my slaving for days to make a scene natural if you're going to queer it with that galloping Kodak?" — a complaint most film actors would echo even now. She then turns to Darnell and with a sincere but never gushing tenderness guides her through the remainder of the test.

Charlotte is ready to burst into song — Hoagy Charmichael's "Don't Let It Get You Down" — as studio drama coach Lola Langdon in *Star Dust*, her first film for Twentieth Century Fox after her return to Hollywood (1940).

We get hints of the real Charlotte Greenwood in other parts of *Star Dust* — when Brooke dismisses Darnell as a "stage-struck kid," Charlotte glares at him with genuine disgust: she, too, had started out a stage-struck kid, and had she listened to people like him who knew where *she*'d be? And one must wonder: Is Lola's temper a hint of Annabelle Greenwood, on one hand the eternal fixer of other people's problems, a refuge in time of storm, on the other "equal to all of the Sabine women with some of the Amazons thrown in for good measure" when her outrage was inflamed by the merest hint of anyone giving trouble to the ones she loved? It is quite likely her mother's persona played some significant part in Charlotte's characterization, even as she did in the composition of Charlotte's own personality.

Of the entire cast, only Darnell and Charlotte got the nod of approbation from Strauss, with Darnell coming off "not only well behaved but [as] one of the more comely starlets," while Charlotte "amusingly posts about on her long gangling legs to save the day for Miss Darnell, but for the picture, not quite."[9]

Zanuck, with his eye on the creation of iconic character types, had made the most of Charlotte's pratfalls with Donald Meek and her hilarious spinster's passion for Roland Young, and the ticket sales that could be produced from exploiting them. Yet Charlotte's performance was strong enough for him to offer her not only another picture — one that turned out to be Shirley Temple's final bow at the studio — but a long-term contract with Fox. With Charlotte firmly corralled by the studio, its chief executive could have the leisure to think about and look for just the vehicle to exploit her dramatic gifts. This vehicle, hitched to a prize trotting horse, would not be long in coming.

26

Down Argentine Way

CHARLOTTE'S NEXT FOX FILM, *Young People,* was directed by Charlotte's old friend Allan Dwan, and with score and lyrics by Mack Gordon and Harry Warren, was her first musical for the studio. Zanuck was capitalizing on Charlotte's vaudeville background with this film. He paired her with fellow vaudevillian Jack Oakie as Kit and Joe Ballantine, a husband and wife act whose song and dance show is fading out with vaudeville itself. They become parents by default of infant Wendy (Shirley Temple), orphaned daughter of actor friends, who has been left in a basket at the Ballantines' theatre.

Kit and Joe raise the girl as their own; and when she shows talent for show business, she becomes part of their act. In an effort to give Wendy something of a normal childhood experience, the Ballantines retire from the stage and move to a farm in New Hampshire that had been left to Shirley by her parents.

Amid the white spires of Congregationalist churches and the no less forbidding white spires of neat picket fences, the ex-show folk try valiantly to blend in with the town's upright and uptight denizens (rather the way Charlotte's character does in her radio show of several years later). Only when the Ballantines and Wendy, on their way out of the unfriendly town, save a group of stranded children during a hurricane are they finally accepted for who they are by the townspeople — even the old village biddy, played like a dreadnought in flowered hat by Kathleen Howard, befriends the grateful trio. The film ends with a song and dance number in which Charlotte shows off not only high kicks but the splits and the Camel Walk, all while dressed in an elegant black and white gown.

Per her own admission, Temple was not thrilled to work on the film. Compared to her recent film work, she wrote in her memoirs, *Young People* was something of a comedown, in both budget and in what she calls "general cast quality," noting that the film's "obvious simplicity" allowed her the relief of its early completion. That it was not every young actor's fate to have the chance to perform with two veteran theatre and film stars like Charlotte Greenwood and Jack Oakie seems not to have occurred to Temple even when writing her recollections as an adult.

New York Times critic Bosley Crowther described *Young People* as "one of the more charming of the miracle child's films," noting that if it really was her final picture, "it is not a bad exit at all for little Shirley, the superannuated sunbeam." However much Temple hated the film, she made good impressions on both Crowther and Charlotte, because according to the latter, Temple was a "gracious, talented darling ... whose picture, which is on my Steinway, is autographed by her, 'To my Friend.'"[1]

Charlotte adored working with Jack Oakie, who had just played Mussolini in Charlie Chaplin's Hitler spoof, *The Great Dictator*, at the gala 1940 premiere of which Charlotte was sketched by *Fortune* Magazine's caricaturist Alan Reeve alongside Somerset Maugham, Harry Warner and Ethel Barrymore. "His ready wit, his enormous vitality and his basic sense of humor brought back vivid memories of all the real comedians and vaudevillians I had known — the Catletts, the Skellys, the Errols, the Bernards and the Hitchcocks.... I'm looking forward to more important work with him," she added. As critic Crowther aptly pointed out in his review, "Mr. Oakie and Miss Greenwood make a couple of amusing hoofers," and anyone watching the film today can feel the electricity between the two. Well should Charlotte have hoped to do more work with Oakie. However, as with many of the performers with whom Charlotte had formed memorable teams in films past, further film partnering was not to be in the cards.[2]

If *Young People* established the farm as one of the perennial settings for Charlotte's Twentieth Century Fox films, *Down Argentine Way* brought race horses into her professional film life, where they were to stay till her retirement over fifteen years later.

A flagrant vehicle for fresh-faced Betty Grable, *Down Argentine Way* was directed by Irving Cummings in the saturated Technicolor that made it also an ideal U.S. debut for Carmen Miranda. "The story is a silly trifle about an American lass, Miss Grable," wrote Charlotte's and Martin's friend, critic Bosley Crowther, "falling in love with that old gaucho, Don Ameche, and hanging around the night clubs, horse farms and race tracks of Argentina until everyone has had a chance to perform in a song and dance or two."[3]

Charlotte plays Grable's worldly wise aunt, Binnie Crawford, a woman of wealth who tries to guide her niece in a hot-and-cold romance with Ameche while falling head over heels for a gigolo named Tito Acuna, played by tall Russian character actor Leonid Kinskey. In Binnie, Zanuck gave Charlotte a role to play which steps quite a bit outside her hapless manchasing roles of the past — she's something of an older, wiser Letty, a rich woman of a certain age, gowned in supermodel style (by costume designer Travis Banton), who can buy anything and anyone she wants. She's the sort of woman who can hang out the window of a Rolls Royce and shout raucous greetings across the boulevard and somehow come off charming instead of mortifying. (Charlotte had known plenty of theatre stars who did worse.) And when she gets what she wants, she lets the world know it. After their first meeting in a nightclub doorway, during which Charlotte sizes Kinskey up like a prize racehorse, she carries him through the film like a piece of new jewelry, flaunting him in everyone's face while showing him who's boss every step of the way.

In keeping with maintaining the money-making image he had so carefully crafted, however, Zanuck also gave Charlotte her famously familiar routine of kicks and assorted mugging opportunities before the film's end, including a tango with Kinskey. That this rigorous routine is carried off with ease is something of a triumph all its own — the fact that the fifty-year-old Charlotte stands her ground and then some against much younger performers — including a big song and dance number ("Sing to Your Senorita") among a fiesta crowd — says much for her still-powerful physical energy.

Bosley Crowther thought rather more of Charlotte's final film of 1940, a musical

Powdering her nose in a fancy New York nightclub, Charlotte took the role of rich and man-hungry older woman to new heights as Binnie Crawford in the immensely successful Fox musical *Down Argentine Way* (1940). (Charlotte is seen here with Robert Conway). William Luce collection.

comedy with a gangster plot called *Tall, Dark and Handsome*, which co-starred Cesar Romero and Milton Berle. (Even though Crowther does not mention Charlotte in the review.) As the hard-boiled Chicago nightclub singer Winnie who agrees to pose as Romero's housekeeper for Christmas, Charlotte had fun working with Romero, who played Shep Morrison, a Chicago gangster so loathe to kill he locks up his murderous rivals in the basement, yet nevertheless has to maintain his reputation by pretending to be a party to real gangsters' crimes. To impress love interest Judy Miller, played by Virginia Gilmore, Shep tries to appear respectable by engaging a reluctant Winnie to serve as housekeeper of his mansion and Stanley Clements, mouthy young son of a gangster, as his child. The truth, of course, comes out when the gangsters in the basement break out, but in the end Shep gets his girl.

Romero was, Charlotte remembered in her memoirs, "a tall boy ... who had taken advantage of every inch of his height and has made it pay handsomely" — traits she admired and encouraged in tall actors. Romero's grace and graciousness made one forget he was taller than Charlotte almost by a head, and affirmed her belief that there was nothing to keep a tall actor from holding the attention of his or her audience with more than just their height. The script, which was nominated for an Oscar, is full of sparkling one-liners for Charlotte, and gave her a music and dance number at the top of the film. While singing Ralph Rainger's "Alive and Kicking" she does her trademark leg lifts and splits, along with a trick twirling on her derriere that she uses in no other movie. (Those who have seen this scene know why.) She also has one of the best deadpan lines in the film. At the Christmas tree Virginia Gilmore confides her life story to Charlotte, then notices her wandering gaze. "Am I boring you?" she asks. Charlotte straightens up and says, "A little. But you have a sweet voice — go on."

With *Tall, Dark and Handsome* wrapped, and *Down Argentine Way* setting records at the box office not seen since *Gone with the Wind*, Zanuck was prepared to offer Charlotte a new contract; and it was at this point that the Brooneses decided they were safe to purchase a house to live in. Having put the Auburndale house on the market, they found at 806 North Rodeo Drive the place which was to be their home for the rest of their lives together — a sprawling two story white shingled villa, with green shutters and a second-floor balcony running the entire façade of the building, located at Rodeo and Lomita, the two oldest streets in Beverly Hills.

Behind the house were extensive grounds that included a swimming pool both Martin and Charlotte used religiously. (Martin would have a perennial tan from this time forward.) Though Charlotte professed to play a bad game of tennis, there was a court on the grounds that she, Martin and guests made frequent use of. In front of the house, where a pair of tall Himalayan cedars guarded it from Rodeo Drive, a broad, roofless porch led to an inconspicuous entrance door. Here one rang and spoke through an intercom, usually to Charlotte herself, whose booming voice is still remembered by friends who came to call.

In many ways, the Rodeo Drive house was the perfect substitute for Charlotte's beloved farmhouse on Long Island. Previously the residence of stars Maurice Chevalier and Fred Astaire as well as writer Edgar Rice Burroughs, the house had the atmosphere of both a sophisticated mansion and a charming country retreat; its simple interiors were given color by the elegant furnishings, paintings, rugs and the loads of books and souvenirs Charlotte and Martin had collected over the years. Living there, the Brooneses were surrounded by other members of the Hollywood film and music communities, including Jackie Cooper, George Murphy and pianist Amparo Iturbi, among others.

Charlotte's pride in the house is evident in an interview-tour she gave one reporter, accompanied by photos of Charlotte sitting at the great Chinese Chippendale desk (actually Martin's) in the living room, pretending to write in her date book with a quill pen dipped in a silver inkwell. Behind her is a shelf of mixed knick-knacks and *objets d'art* collected from around the world and shelves of books warmly inscribed to her and Martin by scores of friends from the worlds of literature, show business and high society: social-worker Irene Baroness

Ravensdale, writer Louis Bromfield, actress Billie Burke (Glinda the Good in *The Wizard of Oz*), pianist and raconteur Oscar Levant, director/producer/screenwriter Paul Bern (who inscribed John Vassos' darkly-illustrated 1928 edition of *The Ballad of Reading Gaol* to Martin a little over a year before his mysterious death), and of course, poet Humbert Wolfe, who had knighted Charlotte's Pekingese with a Ritz Hotel butter knife.

Charlotte was particularly proud of the Sir Jacob Epstein watercolors she and Martin had collected while in London in the 1930s, when Epstein was exhibiting his abstract floral series at the Bond Street gallery of Arthur Tooth and Sons. Charlotte's eclectic sense of style was obvious from the inclusion of these abstract works with reproduction Louis XIV armchairs, antique Chinese rugs, porcelains and bronzes (she even had an early nineteenth century silk and gold-embroidered dragon robe hanging on one wall), and warmly upholstered sofas comfortable enough to stand duty in a hotel lobby.

Martin's more soberly decorated wood-paneled music room opened out on the pool area and was the place where his Steinway grand piano stood littered with music, manuscript paper, and framed photos. This room was understandably but a bit poignantly lined with more proofs of Charlotte's career than his — framed souvenir programs and billing notices, along with thickly textured oil paintings by Danish-born Philip Kran Paval, the Hollywood artist and drinking friend of actor John Barrymore and journalist Gene Fowler. And the wide white staircase, which ran up to a landing that branched off into two smaller staircases leading to the rooms above, served as the perfect proscenium for the showy portrait of Charlotte by Flora Lion. Everyone entering the house first saw Charlotte's red-draped figure from 1932, reclining against white furs, peering down at guests with the lanky golden-haired languor of a showgirl and the cool appraising hauteur of a duchess.

The house also had the history Charlotte loved, to the degree history was possible in still wet-behind-the-ears Beverly Hills. Charlotte was delighted to find that the remains of an old bridle path (perhaps dating to Spanish times, when the local watering spot for one's horses was the "Rodeo de las Aguas" — "Gathering of the Waters" — where the Beverly Hills Hotel now stands) ran right through the property and under her study window, in a garden now cluttered with huge old banana trees. Charlotte couldn't know it at the time, but this bridle path was just one of many connections to horses that was to characterize much of her future work with her new studio, Twentieth Century Fox.[4]

Settling into domesticity again also seems to have moved Charlotte to get serious about writing her memoirs. She had been writing for years — mostly song lyrics for Martin, and before that, during the run of *Linger Longer Letty*, she was rumored to have completed a book of theatrical epigrams titled *Epi-drama-grams* for the Boston publisher Little, Brown (no trace of which exists). She had also dabbled in some form of her life story since the early 1930s, even to writing a long article she called "American Days" while starring at Drury Lane in London which described her early childhood illnesses, her indomitable mother, her ambition to go on the stage and that fateful first meeting with Eva Tanguay in the lobby of the Royal Arms Hotel in Times Square. Neither Charlotte's papers given to William Luce nor those at the University of Southern California show evidence of this article having been published anywhere. The papers she gave Luce show that even while on the aborted *Leaning on Letty* tour in Australia in the late 1930s, Charlotte was still adding to her life story. A newspaper account from July 1940, saved in her scrapbooks, mentions that Fox studios was interested in making a biographical film about Charlotte's eventful life — this, despite Darryl Zanuck's response, through his secretary, to a draft of Charlotte's memoirs sent to him for perusal: why did Charlotte, "still in the flower of your youth," want to write an autobiography, something that only old people did? This was in August 1941, shortly after Charlotte had finished what she considered to be the final draft of her memoirs (and the only draft I have found with the dedication: "To Martin") dated to July.

That she was plugging away at the book that summer is evident from a note appearing late in the manuscript, news heard "last night," that Jenny Dolly of the famous Dolly Sisters, whom Charlotte had known well in her vaudeville days, had committed suicide: this dates Charlotte's work on the book to early June 1941. Had Fox encouraged Charlotte to sign on with the studio using this offer of a biopic (like that of *Star Dust* for young Linda Darnell) as a sweetener, then decided the project was not financially feasible? Whatever happened, Charlotte mentions nothing about it in her memoir notes, perhaps for the same reason Cyril Ring is expunged: it was a failure that did not merit close examination.

In fact, the only part of Charlotte's memoirs to reach print was an excerpt from early in her autobiography, concerned her first glimpse of New York City, hurrying to her mother's hotel and tripping in front of gracious Eva Tanguay. These two pages from the manuscript were printed first in *Variety* magazine's annual issue in 1950, and were later issued by Henry Holt in 1952 as part of a collection of *Variety* articles titled *Spice of Variety*. This is all that made it to paper and ink. For reasons that seem strange today, when any teenaged rock star or hotel heiress can scribble a few words on a page and get an instant contract with Simon & Schuster, Charlotte's richly funny and highly detailed memoirs of a life stretching from the flowering and death of vaudeville to the rise of Hollywood were not deemed suitable for publication by several publishers whose rejection letters (from 1941 to 1950) are scattered among her papers at USC and the papers she gave to William Luce. Among those houses that rejected *Never Too Tall* were Brandt & Brandt, Random House, Harper & Brothers, and Prentice-Hall. Biographer Donald Day, whose opinion of *Never Too Tall* had been sought by Martin, recommended that the book be rewritten as a third person biography, and further suggested that Rosemary Taylor, author of the 1943 memoir *Chicken Every Sunday*, be enlisted to perform this job. Nothing came of what could have been the key to break what to Charlotte was an unfamiliar run of failure in the publishing realm.[5]

While Martin argued the book's merits with publishers, agents and writers, Charlotte did what she could to perfect it (even sending a draft to Joseph Fields, son of Lew Fields of Weber & Fields, to confirm her recollection of certain song lyrics from the mid–1900s) and publicize it, though these efforts were sometimes mangled by her PR office. One statement issued to the press claimed Charlotte had written her memoirs "between scenes of *Moon Over Miami*," which is not true — she had been writing about her life, as we've seen, since the early 1930s, and was making lengthy notes (now in the Luce collection) well before she signed with Fox in 1940.[6]

Ten years after the book's completion, and knowing the value of an interview with Hearst gossip columnist Louella Parsons, Charlotte told Louella in June 1951 that "I *am* going to write my book — but with a different title than *Never Too Tall*. I want it to apply to everyone who feels that he or she is a freak," something Charlotte must have felt herself to be among the reluctant publishing executives of the day. The next month, information was released to *Time* Magazine listing *Never Too Tall* as among autobiographies which had "reached the working stage," including Princess Ileana of Romania's *I Live Again* and Agnes de Mille's *Dance to the Piper*. Both of these were published in 1952, but not Charlotte's book.

By the time Charlotte retired from films in 1956, she had had such a full and fascinating life there was no reason why she should not have settled down again to fill in the rest of her memoirs and again try to get them published, and no reason why a publisher should not have recognized the importance of a performer's life that spanned the better part of what was the most eventful century of show business. But Charlotte's papers at USC show no evidence of any further serious memoir writing after 1941, and it is obvious she decided to stop trying. It would appear that the last effort Charlotte made to make something of her life story was at age 87, when she gave William Luce the lion's share of her memoir materials after seeing his one-woman play, *The Belle of Amherst*, hoping he could translate them into a work for the stage. It was as if, having failed at all other methods, she turned again to the one that had never failed her, the theatre. She did not live long enough to see what he might have made of the materials, but giving them to Luce, author of a classic biographical stage piece famed around the world in a dozen languages, must have brought Charlotte some measure of comfort.

Returning to film work brought Charlotte a whirlwind of activity as great as anything she had known when a touring young theatre star. But now she wasn't being challenged to footraces in Midwestern towns (as had been done back in 1912) but asked to give broadcasts in New York City and Washington, D.C., and invited to dine at the White House not as part of a cast (as in the Coolidge administration) but as an individual star. This activity would only increase after the United States entered the war, culminating in Charlotte's participation in the Hollywood Victory Caravan of 1942.

By way of showing what she had to do and how capable she was of doing it, in her memoirs Charlotte provided a sample of her schedule for the last two weeks of January 1941, when she traveled to New York and then Washington, D.C. for the birthday celebrations of President Roosevelt, in tandem with George Raft, Wallace Beery, Deanna Durbin, Kitty Carlisle, Robert Young, Sterling Hayden and others. Charlotte's characteristic clipped and witty style makes no bones about her opinions of just about everything she saw, heard or did:

My Trip East, or What You Can Do in Two Weeks
Left January 19 from Pasadena at twelve o'clock on the Chief. Arrived in Chicago at 1:30 Tuesday and by Wednesday, the 22nd with the help of the 20th Century — the engine not the studio — landed in New York at 8 o'clock. Then the fun began.
1. Met by Mr. Kahn; Lunch at the Biltmore. Dinner at Pierre's. Rehearsal for the broadcast which had to be called off until 10 A.M. the following day because everyone was unhealthy. a. Miss Hathaway who writes the scripts — ill in bed. b. Mr. Welch who puts on the show — also ill in bed; but the show had to go on, Mr. Welch arose to put it on, at least re-write script.
2. At 7 P.M. on Friday we received a corrected script — the show had to go on in an hour. (The costume for the occasion was a Nettie Rosenstein model, with chartreuse drape in front with coral neck piece — nice no?) On the air at 8. Four hours later — same thing. On the air.
3. On Saturday, January 25, a new day dawns. Matinee Ethel Barrymore "The Corn is Green" a really wonderful characterization and Miss Barrymore was never better. I saw her when I was a little girl in "Captain Jinks of the Horse Marines." Saturday night — "Panama Hattie " [by Cole Porter, starring Ethel Merman] — great show and very fine entertainment.
4. All of Sunday was mine until noon. Carl Engle (President of Schirmer Music Publishing House) for lunch at Passy's (28 East Street — for future reference, because they had fine French food). Dinner Sunday night with Mr. and Mrs. Louis Dreyfus. He owns Chappell's in London.
5. Had the morning free again to comb my hair and get ready for lunch with Mr. Leo Friedman, he is Mr. Nicholas Schenck's friend and lawyer. Dinner Monday night with Mrs. Nicholas Schenck, also went to the theater to see "Pal Joey." No like! Joey was the kind of man that nice people don't know exists and most people who do know try to forget.

6. "Pal Joey" and the fact that he wasted a whole evening of mine is still rather annoying but today is relative day. My Aunt Laura [not related to Charlotte by blood but a friend of her mother's] baked and sent me over her usual package of fresh doughnuts and a huge jar of cole slaw, which means the basis of a good lunch in anybody's language. So with Margaret, Helen and Peggy Omara (Mrs. Omara is Aunt Laura's daughter and married to Senator Omara of Jersey City...) we feasted. This is still Tuesday in case you have lost track. Tuesday evening to the Fulton Theater to see "Arsenic and Old Lace," Boris Karloff's play. Lots of excitement, lots of laughter but none of it very probable. A strange coincidence — they have dead men come out of the cellar to take a bow. Reminded me of "Tall, Dark and Handsome." [Charlotte is referring here to her film with Cesar Romero, in which the latter claims to have murdered a crew of mobsters out to collect an old debt from him, but instead keeps them imprisoned in his cellar.]

7. Wednesday. Still don't know what day it is maybe because today is cleanup day. Hair washed, teeth cleaned and aboard the Congressional Limited for Washington and at 5:30 P.M. in Washington. Time to get clean again and change clothes for a broadcast at the station at 10 P.M. I refuse to keep track of the broadcasting stations anymore.

8. Mr. Muto called for us at 11 A.M. on Thursday. We were taken to Commissioner Hazen's office and given the keys to the city, introduced to a chap named [Red] Skelton [emcee for the Willard Hotel birthday ball] and we each did a broadcast, then off to the White House for luncheon with Mrs. Roosevelt and the President. Luncheon was over at a quarter of three which proves it was not like visiting royalty in England. Here you actually see the food and eat it instead of watching it go by. Hair dressed to prepare for dinner at the Willard Hotel. Costume for the occasion — beige dress with black lace, diamonds and aquamarines. At banquet table I sat next to Wallace Beery. I collected about $10 in autographs at a dime apiece (Beery insisted on having his dinner without interruptions...) Introduced by Clifton Fadiman whose brilliance and knowledge of each artist was astounding but then I guess that it why he is one of the brain children of Information Please. In introducing me, Mr. Fadiman said: "A lady who has an original and unique talent and then two other talents — two long legs. Will you show them what I mean, Miss Greenwood?" So I kicked over Wallace Beery's head, first with my left leg and then with my right. Mr. Beery managed to survive it beautifully. Most people sit down after dinner but we were different and started on a series of broadcasts and public appearances, finishing with the Earle and the Capitol theaters, and then back to the Carlton Hotel for the Gold Plate breakfast which they tell me consisted of bacon and eggs and coffee. I wouldn't know because at that point I was introduced and it happened to be 4 A.M. that I was making my last public appearance just about six hours after my normal bedtime.

9. Friday lunch and tea with friends. 5:45 P.M. off to Chicago. P.S. This is the 31st. Arrived at the Blackstone Hotel, due for another clean up. Visited Mrs. Snyder's candy shop then saw picture called "Night Train [to Munich, starring Rex Harrison]" [Good]. 7:15 on the Super Chief.

10. Arrived in Pasadena at 8:50 A.M. Monday. Came home and the pool looked so inviting that I just jumped in clothes and all.

PS: Did I have fun? PPS: You bet I did.[7]

27

The Stars at War

THE HOLLYWOOD VICTORY CARAVAN was organized by the Army-Navy Relief Fund as a means of using big name stars to raise money for the families of servicemen killed in action — a kind of Hollywood Canteen (where Charlotte also loyally served, earning her a certificate signed by Canteen president Bette Davis) on rolling stock.

Stars such as Joan Bennett and Joan Blondell, Olivia de Havilland and Claudette Colbert, James Cagney and Bing Crosby, Stan Laurel and Oliver Hardy and even Metropolitan Opera star Risë Stevens were lined up to board a seventeen-car train that would start in Hollywood, cross the country in three weeks, making entertainment stops along the way, and end up finally in Washington, D.C., where everyone would meet President Franklin D. Roosevelt at the White House and put on another show. "If that train had wrecked," claimed Desi Arnaz, one of the lesser lights on board (Lucille Ball, to her fury, was not invited), "Hollywood would have been out of business."[1]

Several of Charlotte's former colleagues were among those invited to take part, including Bert Lahr and Pat O'Brien, her co-stars from 1931's *Flying High*. Bob Hope, for whose radio show Charlotte would prove a successful pinch-hitter in the next few years, was also on board, and recorded his impressions in a memoir of his wartime entertaining, *Don't Shoot, It's Only Me*, by describing how annoying Arnaz and his bongo drums were, earning a not entirely unserious threat from Pat O'Brien of re-enacting the Spanish-American War, and Groucho Marx's response when the train pulled up at Union Station in Washington, D.C. amid a sea of cheering fans: "If this is the American public, we ought to surrender now."[2] Carey Grant also came along. An old friend of Charlotte's from her London days, Charlotte noted how he once strolled onto a lot at Fox and asked for his "favorite glamour girl." Who was that, asked the crew — Carole Landis? Alice Faye? Betty Grable? No: he wanted Charlotte Greenwood.[3]

John Lahr's biography of his father includes some insights into what it was like traveling on a train with the largest collection of stars ever assembled in one place outside the Oscars. When the Caravaners first came to a town they went to their hotel to freshen up and rest. Then "[a] parade through the streets in the afternoon was a usual part of the ceremony," wrote Lahr, "and the show in the evening — a three-hour extravaganza — ended with the stars and starlets going out into the audience to ask for donations."

Bert Lahr remembered an on-board doctor dispensing Benzedrine by the handful — few of the actors had a chance to get much sleep, which with the uppers would account for some

The cast of the 1942 Hollywood Victory Caravan, from left to right: producer-director Mark Sandrich, Claudette Colbert, Hollywood Victory Committee chairman Kenneth Thomson, Frank McHugh, Eleanor Powell, Charlotte Greenwood, Groucho Marx, Elyse Knox, writer Allan Scott, Joan Blondell, Cary Grant, and opera singer Risë Stevens.

of the hysterical goings on both on the train and off. According to Lahr, who was hanging out with Groucho Marx and high-voiced Frank McHugh, when the trio got into the car of the well-meaning lady from the American Women's Voluntary Service, thrilled to be taking three Hollywood luminaries about her town, the lady asked charmingly, "Where would you gentlemen like to go?" and Groucho responded without flitting an eyelash, "Is there a cathouse in the area?"[4]

When the Caravan reached Washington, the passengers cleaned up their clothes and their behavior and were greeted by Eleanor Roosevelt, who stood as hostess in her husband's absence. Groucho was as usual distinctly on his own terms where behavior was concerned. From asking Mrs. Roosevelt, in the midst of the receiving line, whether they were late for dinner, to telling a passing general, who asked where the First Lady might be, "She's upstairs filing her teeth," Marx brought a touch of real Caravan anarchy into the solemn precincts of the President's official home.

And he wasn't the only one. Dressed to the hilt in satin and pearls, Charlotte greeted Mrs. Roosevelt with one of her leg lifts (some accounts claim she whirled a leg right over the seated First Lady's head), and Marx leaned confidentially toward Mrs. Roosevelt, murmuring, "You could do that if you put your mind to it."[5] After being photographed with Mrs. Roosevelt on the White House lawn (Charlotte sitting on the grass in her pearls, opening her mouth to say something just as the flash went off), the stars rehearsed all night long for their fundraising show that would open the next evening at the Capitol Theater. Afterward, the grueling trip back home, through fourteen cities, lay ahead. Though the two Joans, Blondell and Bennett, chose to continue the risqué hilarity of the trip by sending telegrams after it was over to everyone who took part, saying simply, "ARE YOU GETTING MUCH?," Bert Lahr was moved to tears by the sense of camaraderie he had enjoyed with his fellow performers, calling it "a caravan of love." Oliver Hardy felt the same way, weepily telling Lahr and the others not to let the good feelings disappear by losing touch with each other.

The Caravan certainly fulfilled Charlotte's privately expressed belief of how to survive war. "As long as hate and greed are believed true," she jotted, "we will believe it necessary to use combatant methods. The armaments of peace are what we need to put on — LOVE, INTELLIGENCE, TRUTH, FREEDOM and HONOR." The Victory Caravan had done that and then some.[6]

From the gangster antics of *Tall, Dark and Handsome*, Charlotte was next paired with the catty Jack Haley in her second Betty Grable film, *Moon Over Miami*, a remake of Stephen Powys' 1938 play *Three Blind Mice*. Playing Susan Latimer, the short order cook aunt of waitresses Grable and her sister, played by Carole Landis, Charlotte opens the film in a cook's hat and spends most of the rest of the time dressed as a maid (for the first time since her role as Abby in the 1933 play *The Late Christopher Bean*). But even so drably dressed — and with Grable as stiff competition — she manages to become the bright spot of the film.

Moon Over Miami skids by on the age-old masquerade by which an ambitious young woman of no fortune uses a small inheritance to buy her way into the sort of moneyed milieu where she's sure to find herself a rich husband and live happy ever after, with a series of subplots to temporarily subvert her plans.

Grable plays the young gold-digger who heads for the bachelor wealth of Miami, with Landis masquerading as her secretary and Charlotte as a cantankerous maidservant who never quite answers the door with professional panache but manages to snag the affections of hotel major domo Haley. Fate steps in when the Miami millionaire Grable falls in love with — affable Don Ameche — turns out to be the scion of a ruined family, a man who now has to work for his living. Rebounding from this disappointment, Grable then nearly marries a really rich man whom she doesn't love, played by a perpetually grinning Robert Cummings, with all the comic pitfalls such subterfuge entails. But as audiences could have guessed, she ends up with Ameche, Landis with the rich boy, and Charlotte with Haley, in her second movie scene wearing a bathing suit (after *Palmy Days* of over ten years before), as she stands atop her love interest's shoulders in a water-skiing sequence. This is also Charlotte's first and last instance of being engaged in that particular sporting activity on film, though not her last exposure in that particular sporting garb.

Reviews of *Moon Over Miami* were mostly good, but Charlotte's old nemesis at the *New York Times*, Theodore Strauss, chose to fruitlessly seek serious intentions in a film that makes no secret of being silly fluff: "Jack Haley and Charlotte Greenwood, as a waiter and a maid, frolic through some comedy grotesqueries which are never quite funny enough," he sniffed.[7] (In fact, most critics would agree today that the best musical number — and perhaps the best realized scene — in the entire film is Charlotte's with Jack Haley, when they have their comic love duet in "Is That Good?" by the great Ralph Rainger.)

During filming, which had been set back by Charlotte's trip to Washington, D.C., for

Charlotte and Jack Haley making the most of an egg as the put-upon help in the 1941 Betty Grable musical *Moon Over Miami*.

President Roosevelt's birthday celebration, some comedy infiltrated the set in tandem with the tourists who had somehow got in that afternoon to watch the proceedings. "I had my back to the camera," Charlotte recalled, "[when] the false tooth-cap that I wear over a receded tooth for close up shots decided to come loose from its moorings.... They were shooting over my shoulder for a close up of Betty Grable. She had most of the lines and I was diligently trying to push the wayward tooth back into place with the tip of my tongue. Presently Betty saw what was happening and burst into a gale of laughter. Walter Lang, the director, was astonished because Betty is always sure fire and rarely if ever blows up in a scene. 'What's the matter?' he asked. 'I can't go on,' Betty shrieked, doubled up with mirth, 'Charlotte's losing her teeth.'"

> With that the entire troupe burst into laughter because in films you have no secrets from your colleagues. Eventually I got my floating canine back in position and we prepared to go on with the scene. Just then in a stage whisper from the visitors' side of the stage came:
> "Of course, I knew she was old, but I didn't think she was disintegrating."
> Again we were in convulsions.
> Finally the visitors left and we made the sequence. That concluded my work for the afternoon and as I walked toward my dressing room, I happened to pass the tourists again. This time I dropped my manuscript and stooped to pick it up. Again I heard a side remark:
> "Well her teeth may be falling out but I wish I could bend as gracefully as she does."[8]

Charlotte's next two films for Fox cast her as a society lady laboring under comical difficulties created entirely by herself, and as a prim secretary whose tipsy episode in a resort restaurant gave the script writers a perfect opportunity to run her through all her high kicking high jinks from vaudeville days.

In *The Perfect Snob*, made and released in 1941, Charlotte played the social-climbing Martha Mason, who tries to force her daughter, played by Lynn Bari, into marriage with a millionaire while on vacation in Hawaii. Charlotte's husband, played by Charlie Ruggles, wants his daughter to marry for love, and tries to foil Martha's attempts to marry her off. Bari responds by falling in love with Cornel Wilde, an apparently penniless young islander, who at the end of the film emerges as the heir to a sugar plantation, ensuring Martha's happiness as well as her husband's. While not the kind of role most people associated with Charlotte Greenwood, snobbish Martha Mason came off successfully, showing that Charlotte could play a heavy as well as she usually played the sympathetic comedy relief.

Springtime in the Rockies, set at the Chateau Lake Louise overlooking that watery jewel of the Canadian Rockies, paired Charlotte with her male counterpart and one-time vaudeville partner, lean and lanky Edward Everett Horton, both as rather unconvincing if no less amusing servants. (Horton, whose real surname was Hale, shared a similar Revolutionary War background with Charlotte, being a descendant of a nephew of the martyr-spy, Nathan Hale.)

Charlotte is cast as a sort of companion-duenna to Betty Grable (she patiently lifts a shoe to the dressing table each time Grable needs to strike a match), a nightclub performer so unhappy with her partner and some-time boyfriend (played by John Payne) she has taken on another partner to spite him, played by suave Cesar Romero.

Horton plays a butler who, though heir to a fortune, has taken on the job of serving as John Payne's valet in order to learn something about real life. Given the fact that Carmen Miranda begins pursuing him in her relentless fashion soon after the film's start, he learns a few things soon enough, not to mention the fact that it's Charlotte who really wants him and is willing to take on Miranda's considerable arsenal of charms to get him. *Springtime in the Rockies* is one of the few Twentieth Century Fox films in which Charlotte's eccentric dance routine is actually worked into the plot with something approaching plausibility — left alone at a table in the Chateau Lake Louise's nightclub, she drinks too much and stumbles onto the dance floor to do her full dance

Charlotte Greenwood snoooting it up for all she was worth as the social-climbing Martha Mason in *The Perfect Snob* (Fox, 1941).

Edward Everett Horton hides behind Charlotte Greenwood as erstwhile admirer Carmen Miranda glares from her spot beside Cesar Romero in this scene from Charlotte's 1942 Fox musical, *Springtime in the Rockies*, set at the Chateau Lake Louise in Alberta, Canada.

routine, including splits and Camel Walk, before realizing she's being watched by everyone in the restaurant. She flees in embarrassment that is just as funny as the dance routine.

Far more successful and better rounded was Charlotte's performance as showgirl-turned-Westchester investor's wife in the 1943 musical extravaganza (and camp classic), *The Gang's All Here*—which, incidentally, is also Charlotte's first war-themed film. As Mrs. Peyton Potter—the former showgirl Blossom Murphy, who set 1920s Paris ablaze with her apache dance—Charlotte was paired with Edward Everett Horton as uptight Mr. Potter, who is persuaded to host a bash at their country estate to celebrate returning war hero Andy Mason (played by James Ellison) and, of course, to sell war bonds.

To the estate comes the entire crew of a swanky New York nightclub, which includes everyone from Blossom's former Parisian dance partner, band leader Phil Baker (as himself), to Carmen Miranda (wearing a different and more outlandish costume for each scene and, as in *Springtime in the Rockies*, pursuing Horton with a vengeance), torch-singer Alice Faye as the on-again off-again love interest of Sergeant Mason, and Benny Goodman and his band, as well as a host of lesser lights, to put on a vast show in the Potters' fountained and statued back yard.

Charlotte confers with co-star Phil Baker in the 1943 Busby Berkeley extravaganza *The Gang's All Here,* Twentieth Century Fox's most over the top wartime musical and a classic of the genre. William Luce collection.

The thin plot, involving assumed identity and assumed affection and all manner of cross-purposes, breaks down by the final scenes of the back yard extravaganza into a fever dream of quirky Busby Berkeley numbers (Berkeley was choreographer as well as director), succeeding one another in mad silliness until the last scene, in which Alice Faye, thrilled to finally catch her man, turns into a giant blue polka dot then metamorphosizes into an increasingly complex kaleidoscope scene before joining the heads of the primary cast members floating in a clear blue sky to sing Harry Warren's "A Journey to a Star."

Given the fact that this is also a film made infamous by Carmen Miranda's "The Lady in the Tutti Frutti Hat" number, in which chorus girls frolic with gigantic phallic bananas, nothing that happens anywhere in the script should come as a surprise. However, amid all the mayhem Charlotte gives one of her strongest comic characterizations since Binnie Crawford in *Down Argentine Way.* Slim and elegant in her Yvonne Wood gowns and sporting a crown of upswept blonde hair, her Mrs. Potter moves through her scenes as one to the manner born until tripped up by the urge to dance when her prim husband isn't looking or when annoyed by the omnipresent mantrap Miranda. Her jitterbug with one of her daughter's young friends (played by twenty-year-old Johnny Duncan) shows again just how much energy this fifty-three-year-old woman still had to burn, while her bull's-eye wisecracking throughout the film shows how superb she could have been in the sort of rapid-fire comedies usually given to Rosalind Russell or Eve Arden.

And Charlotte was still a magnificent athlete. A scene that was cut out of the already very long film, in which Charlotte impersonates Whistler's mother during a game of charades by first sliding backwards down a banister, ending up flat on her back at Phil Baker's feet only

Charlotte mugging as Martha in the 1944 farce *Up in Mabel's Room.*

to leap into a rocking chair and freeze within an empty gold frame, shows both nimbleness and perfect comedic timing.[9]

Not that the *New York Times'* Theodore Strauss appreciated much of her or anyone else's performances. "Despite the almost stupefying prettiness of its Technicolor trappings, 'The Gang's All Here,' now playing at the Roxy, makes a mighty dull Yuletide offering," he wrote. Nor did the anatomical implications of Berkeley's banana sequence go over Strauss' head: "One or two of his dance spectacles seem to stem straight from Freud...."[10]

The mystery, of course, is why Charlotte was not cast in more such clever roles, instead of always someone's supporting maid, secretary or elder aunt tossed the occasional bone of a good scene. But perhaps the answer is that Darryl Zanuck had finally seen the light. From exploiting Charlotte's colorful clowning, he had come to realize — through Martin's badgering or on his own — her abilities as a serious actor. Though he would cast or lend her for two more frivolous films, the poorly received *Dixie Dugan* (based on the comic strip of the same name; Charlotte took on the substanceless role of Dixie's mother), and the rather more popular and rather more clever farce *Up in Mabel's Room* (in which Charlotte hilariously goes from sweeping through rooms in an evening gown to donning hunting gear and a rifle to chase an imagined burglar from her property), Zanuck had plans to divest Charlotte of her gowns, silly blonde hairdos and high kicks. He would give her a chance, wearing gingham and an apron, to perform her first filmed dramatic part: as Aunt Penny in 1944's *Home in Indiana*, a role she would profess to be her favorite one prior to the making of *Oklahoma!*

Hedda Hopper, in a column from February 17, 1942, addressed the issue of Charlotte's wasted abilities with her customary pointedness: "Why is it that on the screen we see Charlotte Greenwood only in short comedy roles, playing second fiddle to newcomers who aren't nearly as good? ... Charlotte is an actress."

It had been over a decade since the stage had already accepted and lauded Charlotte as a dramatic actor. As Penny, Charlotte would demonstrate that she only improved with age. To assist her she had developed some theories about her craft that, read today, are still valid, for comedians and serious thespians alike, upon which she enlarged in her memoir notes:

> The definition of a good actor is one who *knows*— knows why, what, how, when and where to be at the right time, and who has that resource to do what the audience thinks he should be doing at any given period in the play ... the actor must [also] know just how far to go [and] where to stop.

This discipline, earned through years of learning from actors she admired and from mining her own greatest dramatic resource —*knowing* herself— was to stand Charlotte in good stead for the serious roles to come.[11]

28

Home in Indiana

SINCE SIGNING HER CONTRACT WITH Zanuck in 1940, Charlotte had only made one horse film for Twentieth Century Fox, the immensely successful musical spectacle *Down Argentine Way*. The horses seen in that film were the racing kind grazing in expensively kept pastures glimpsed from Charlotte's Rolls-Royce. But when Darryl Zanuck got his hands on George Agnew Chamberlain's novel *The Phantom Filly*, he knew he had a horse vehicle for Charlotte that would offer spectacle of another kind — a real-life part far removed from the society grande dames, nightclub hoofers and spinster secretaries that had been Charlotte's lot up to now.

Chamberlain had written a novel about harness racing in Indiana which developed and exploited several strands of the human experience most needed during the war: the optimism of youth, and its ability to inspire those without hope to renew their faith; the always popular subject of an animal's rise to fame; and the even more popular subject of young love beating the odds. The novel was considered so restorative, in fact, that it went into more than one Armed Services Edition reissue in 1945, published in a size and shape to enable it to be carried in the pocket of American G.I.s.

The story begins when a young man from Connecticut, Sparke Thornton, who has had a troubled boyhood and has just lost his guardian, an elderly aunt, is brought to Roundhouse Farm, the home of his Aunt Penny and Uncle "Thunder" Bolt, to be taken into their care. Roundhouse had once been a successful trotting horse breeding stable. But after a single failed race the losing horse had been shot by her co-owner, Godaw Boole, Thunder's partner, causing a fight between the two that broke up the partnership. Boole set out to ruin Roundhouse Farm, which fell into disrepair, mirrored in Thunder's own hopelessness and a drinking habit that arose every spring when he could hear the sound of Boole's trotting horses getting their workout on the course next door.

Thunder's wife, Penny, a strong-minded farmwoman, has spent the years since Thunder's failure alternately covering for his weaknesses and serving as his support. When Sparke says, his first time at the Bolt dinner table, "I take to horses!," Penny groans, "Oh, Lord," and watches Thunder as he excitedly talks with the boy about the history of harness racing: it is as if an ex-drug addict were giving a disquisition on the pleasures of opium. Penny knows the racing circuit is no better than a drug, and that Thunder's bad luck in the game has caused his financial and personal ruin. But she also knows that without racing, Thunder is a lost man, wandering blindly in a wilderness. And she loves him too much to let him wander alone.

"[Darryl Zanuck] was one of the first — one of the few — who have had faith in my ability to act a dramatic role." Charlotte Greenwood in her breakthrough role of Aunt Penny in *Home in Indiana* (here with Lon McAllister), 26 years after entering films. William Luce collection.

In her finest scene in the film, and the first big dramatic scene she had ever been given in any film (not to mention, at 3 minutes 35 seconds, one of her longest filmed dramatic sequences), Charlotte is discovered by Sparke as she admonishes the drunken Thunder, who has donned his wrinkled racing silks and is brandishing a worn-out whip. This plainly dressed woman, lacking makeup and with her hair drawn back in a severe bun, who commands the stumbling Thunder to go upstairs and pray on his knees for salvation, is a far cry from the fashionably gowned clown of the musicals of just the year before.

The dramatic technique Charlotte displays in this scene and the one that follows, in which she tells Sparke the sad tale of Roundhouse Farm, layering anger at Thunder, at fate, at horses, with a thirst for love and a desire to see Thunder happy again, proves that critics like Alexander Woollcott and James Agate were right when they stated that if given good enough material, Charlotte Greenwood would make a splendid dramatic actor. (Writer Winston Miller, who had distinguished himself assisting David O. Selznick with the screenplay for *Gone with the Wind*, and is at least as much responsible for Charlotte's triumph in the role of Penny as director Henry Hathaway, also had a Letty connection: his sister, Patsy Ruth Miller, played the other wife, Grace, in Charlotte's first talkie, *So Long Letty*.)

Charlotte had demonstrated her ability on the stage; now she showed what she could do on film. Her growing distinction as an actor is nowhere more evident than in the scene she has with Sparke at the kitchen table, where they've had a mournful supper while Thunder sleeps off his alcohol upstairs. Hunched over the table, her simple pans and cups and English transfer-ware dishes gleaming behind her, Charlotte explains how "Some menfolk quarrel over women ... with Thunder, it was a mare...," and her eyes are those of a woman who has ceased to wonder whether, if it came to it, Thunder would save her or his favorite horse first from a burning building — she already knows the painful answer. Yet there is still hope — ironic hope — in her voice and in the proud set of her shoulders that she can somehow prove as worthy to her husband as his best trotter — that she can see him through to the success that has always eluded him. It is a scene the viewer goes on thinking about throughout the film, the dark heart of the several tragedies that unfold around a man who is obsessed with a dream, and forgets to take notice of the world, and those who love him, all around him. In an interview at this time with *Los Angeles Times* film critic Edwin Schallert, Charlotte related Henry Hathaway's astonishment that the scene was shot at one take after one rehearsal: "Charlotte, you could not have done that except for your experience as a comedienne." In comedy, after all, as in drama, timing is everything.[1]

Home in Indiana boasted not just this splendid dramatic performance by an actor who to most movie-going people was no more than a high kicking eccentric, but also solid characterizations from Walter Brennan and three young actors who made their credited debuts in this film: Lon McAllister (as Sparke), June Haver, as Godaw Boole's daughter, and Jeanne Crain, the horse trainer's daughter whose secret love for Sparke creates as much dramatic tension throughout the film as Penny's painful adoration of Thunder.

Not only did the film gain an Oscar nomination for its rich cinematography by Edward Cronjager (already nominated five times), which includes some tracking shots of the races that still bring the viewer to the edge of the seat. Henry Hathaway's sensitivity to emphasizing Charlotte's dramatic gifts, and correctly identifying her character as the warm, heroic heart of the story, is also a part of what makes *Home in Indiana* such a satisfying film — Charlotte was not to have such careful guidance again until Fred Zinnemann's direction in *Oklahoma!* over a decade later. The movie should have received another nomination for Hugo Friedhofer's beautiful score, which with its swelling main theme is as good as anything screen composer Max Steiner put to paper. (Friedhofer, in fact, served as orchestrator for Steiner's *Gone with the Wind* score.)

While the *New York Times'* Bosley Crowther cannot be blamed for stating that "Neither [Crain nor Haver] is a Duse," his description of Charlotte as a cast member who filled a "minor [role] in a thoroughly competent fashion" seems to show that he was not paying close attention to the new corner she had turned with the role of Penny — that of a performer who was not just a superb actor, as capable of drama as of comedy, but of a performer who brought to her roles an energy and determination that proved to be inspirational for audiences, and would soon became identified with any character Charlotte played. Zanuck had realized that at her age, Charlotte's opportunities to make a go of the physical comedy which had been her stock in trade for years were becoming few, and that with her years came a dignity that was as much worth exploiting as her leg lifts and Camel Walk.

This was the period when Charlotte became, almost overnight, America's favorite "aunt" — a woman old enough to have seen it all and wise enough to guide others who hadn't — as exemplified in the part of Penny Bolt as well as a role Charlotte played for two years not on screen but radio, in the two series of programs that came to be called "The Charlotte Greenwood Show."

✷ ✷ ✷

Starting in June 1944, Charlotte took on the formidable job of replacing Bob Hope, the perennial Pepsodent spokesman, who due to his wartime USO show tours was unable to keep his contractual commitment to his NBC radio show. After the first few shows, critic John K. Hutchens of the *New York Times* gave Charlotte some backhanded compliments. Citing news for "the nostalgia department," Hutchens announced Charlotte's role as Bob Hope's stand-in. "What the Hope public, especially the younger members thereof, think of Miss Greenwood's show it would be interesting to know," he wrote, referring to Charlotte's "gentle comedy" and describing her comic contribution as "pretty tame" by comparison to Hope's.

Hutchens has a point, on two levels, when he describes The Charlotte Greenwood Show as relying on Charlotte's long-time arsenal of comic tricks and quips and on plots that were "little," "mild," "ingratiating."[2] To begin with, casting the elegant Charlotte Greenwood as a star who has adopted three children in a small town somewhere in the Midwest, the picket fences and front porches of which she yearns for even when she's on the set with the cameras rolling, is stretching the imagination too far even for the fantasy world of radio.

Charlotte had played a make-it-all right "fixer," as she does in her radio show, almost since her first significant roles on stage, and had played somebody's aunt numerous times — it's not hard to see her mothering these three orphaned children, who so sweetly call her "Aunt Charlotte" and ask whether she'll ever be in a "real cowboy picture." But it was too much against her true character — that of a city-living, hard-driving, super-disciplined, always smashingly dressed star — to pretend that she really wanted to be back home in the village with her adopted kids, leaky pipes and power outages. A publicity photo from this period, probably meant to emphasize the simpler virtues of Aunt Charlotte's life in fictional Lakeview, says it all. As Bobby Larson, the boy actor who played the youngest Barton, hands her a neat little bouquet, Charlotte sits in full movie star costume on a poolside chaise lounge behind her big Rodeo Drive house, Winkie at her side and a copy of the trades in her hand. Whatever the publicists intended, this certainly isn't the Aunt Charlotte who pines for the pines of Lakeview.

Only when Charlotte entertains guests like Hedda Hopper or Lionel Barrymore is her wisecracking fire unleashed, and you realize what a pleasure the show could have been without the kids or the small town or the hollow image of Charlotte as really just a homebody at heart. Hutchens is right, too, about the tame humor, using as a sample an exchange Charlotte has with a lady friend: "What's that on your head?" "My new chapeau." "I knew it wasn't a hat." Her mildly barbed exchange with Hopper ("I knew you were here, I saw your broom in the driveway") wouldn't pop a soap bubble.

Yet what Hutchens couldn't see so early in the show's run was that the motherliness Charlotte projected, the sense that all would be fine when she came home, that beyond glamour and wealth and fame there were small things that really mattered, sleeping in their beds in a tiny town, worked entirely in the show's favor. Far from just replacing Bob Hope for the summer, The Charlotte Greenwood Show was taken up by Hallmark Cards for a second season. With its constant commercials for the cards that helped Americans best express, as the jingle ran, "your perfect taste, your thoughtfulness," and sugary harp glissandi between scenes, the show proved just the antidote for wartime and post-wartime anxieties. If the simple things of life were sufficient to seduce a star like Charlotte Greenwood, the show's message seems to say, shouldn't everyone examine his or her life to see what it is that really matters, and cherish it? Something in all of these qualities clearly impressed the body who decide whose star to place on Hollywood Boulevard, because Charlotte was to receive a star there (located at 1601 Vine Street and Hollywood, right in front of Molly's Coney Island Hot Dogs) not for film but, ironically, for radio.

On *The Charlotte Greenwood Show* (1942–1944), Charlotte played a movie star in charge of three young orphans in a small town. Here Bobby Larson, youngest of the children, presents Charlotte with a nosegay beside her swimming pool at 806 North Rodeo Drive. Photograph ca. 1942.

This view of Charlotte's house is one she and Martin and their friends often saw from the swimming pool. One of the two old Himalayan cedars guarding the entrance can be seen over the rooftop. Photograph ca. 1942. USC collection.

"We dwelt together in deepest understanding, devotion and shared laughter"— Charlotte Greenwood on life with Martin and Winkie. This is from a Christmas card Charlotte sent to friends in the mid–1950s. William Luce collection.

Throughout this period Charlotte's screen personality glowed with this same wholesome quality, both funny and inspirational. The bristly but affectionate chemistry between her and Walter Brennan was strong enough in *Home in Indiana* to gain them another film together, the strange but solidly written *Driftwood* (1947), which would also introduce child star Natalie Wood.

Before that film came the strange and not so solid drama, *Wake Up and Dream* (1946). Based on Robert Nathan's novel, *The Enchanted Voyage*, the film stretches its simple plot around two examples of blind faith: an elderly ship-builder who has constructed a small yacht in his landlady's backyard, far from any plausible water source, the presence of which has all the tongues of the small Maine town wagging, and a little girl whose brother has been reported missing after a U.S.–Japanese skirmish in the Pacific and believes him safe and sound on an ideal white sand island, a fantasy which none of the adults has the courage to deny her. The girl, Nella (played with disturbing intensity by Connie Marshall), is also sure the elderly ship-builder can guide her on his boat to the island where her brother is.

Charlotte plays Sara March, the landlady, who has a secret hankering for her landlocked ship-builder, Henry Peckett, played to the hilt by wizened Clem Bevans. But she also wants his boat (which, though named for her, *is* her competition) out of her yard. For the romantic subplot, waitress Jenny (June Haver) is in love with Nella's outgoing serviceman brother, Jeff (John Payne), who leaves his sister with a cousin till his return home from war. Nella, however, runs away from the cousin and hides out in Peckett's boat; when Jenny tries to take Nella in with her, her landlord objects to the girl's dog and kicks them both out. They both end up with Peckett, whose boat has been sold out from under him by Sara; to make things worse, news comes that Jeff has gone missing.

Now enter a storm, which blows the boat, set up on a wheeled trailer, out of town and on an adventure which Nella, with steely determination that verges on brattiness, insists will end when they find the island her Marine brother is stranded on. Through plot twists that do not surprise, since the film makes no secret from the start that it is a fairy tale in modern dress (even to quoting, in the score, from "We're Off to See the Wizard" from *The Wizard of Oz*), Nella and Jenny are reunited with the man they love, and Sara gets her man, too, if Charlotte's sneaking looks at Clem Bevans at the movie's end are any indication of what happens next.

Offering a more likely man, and a far greater range for her as an actor, is *Driftwood*, which again starred Charlotte opposite Walter Brennan, this time not as a husband but as a long-time suitor. *Driftwood* still has about it much of the fairytale flavor of *Wake Up and Dream* and many other Hollywood wartime films but is kept firmly to the ground by a uniformly strong cast, including silent screen star H. B. Warner in a cameo role, the one exception being Ruth Warrick, as the romantic interest, who stubbornly chews scenery from first scene to last. (Among the cast was the superb character actor Margaret Hamilton, as counter-girl Essie Keenan, whose presence in this film signals Charlotte's performances over the years with a good portion of the cast of *The Wizard of Oz*: Bert Lahr, Jack Haley and now Hamilton, a wicked witch for the ages.)

Driftwood follows the story of a little girl named Jenny Hollingsworth, played by Natalie Wood, who is left an orphan in a Nevada ghost town at the death of her preacher grandfather (H.B. Warner). While trekking across hills to the nearest town, Jenny encounters a wounded collie, the lone survivor from the crash of a secret research plane. Jenny and the dog are picked up by local doctor, Steve Webster, played by Dean Jagger, who ends up caring for her in the home he shares with his adoptive father, Murph, town pharmacist and confirmed bachelor, played by Walter Brennan.

Besides speaking in the Biblical precepts of her isolated upbringing, Jenny also can't help speaking her mind, and soon has townsfolk either charmed or outraged — the former represented by Steve's on-again, off-again love interest, Susan, played by Warrick, the latter by Susan's prickly elderly maiden aunt, Mathilda, played by Charlotte. The plot turns less on Jenny's blunt childhood honesty than it does on Steve's research into eradicating spotted red fever from the town, which is complicated when the collie, named Hollingsworth by Jenny, is taken away from her by force by the mayor, an opponent of Steve's research, in the process upsetting trays of infected ticks in Steve's porch laboratory. When Jenny comes down with the disease, everyone despairs until it is discovered that Hollingsworth is an experimental lab animal which has successfully been rendered immune to spotted red fever. With the help of the doctor involved in the experimentation, Jenny is injected with the dog's serum and recovers.

In the role of Aunt Mathilda, Charlotte is at her most cantankerous and her most loving. From distrusting Steve for making her niece wait for a marriage that might not even occur, she softens enough to reveal to him in a porch-side chat that she herself had been frustrated by a man who wouldn't make up his mind (who, it is implied, is Steve's foster father, Murph). Mathilda has no intention of seeing the same fate await Susan, hence her not infrequent hostility — one of her best lines: "When a girl gets to be my age she appreciates a compliment or two, even if it is from hunger." Through Steve's tender care for Jenny, she gradually understands that he's the best man her niece could have for husband. And in Jenny, though at first annoyed by her, Mathilda sees a female as outspoken as herself, and as innocent as she once was, and through the child's illness comes to love her. It's a transformation subtle and moving.

Though Charlotte banters with Walter Brennan — an actor born to play opposite her — it's clear he was the man that got away from her years before, and that under her façade of prim hats and gloves and unsmiling demeanor she still cares about him more than anyone else in the world. By the film's end, as with the final scene of *Wake Up and Dream*, subtle glances from Brennan to Greenwood show that he feels

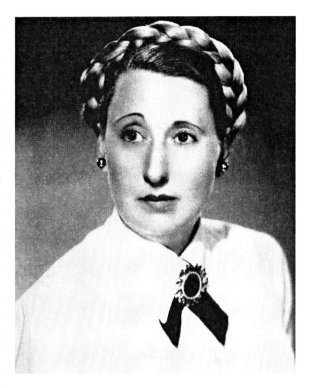

Charlotte Greenwood as Aunt Mathilda, a cold woman warmed through love of a child. The child was a young Natalie Wood in her 1947 debut film *Driftwood*. William Luce collection.

the same, and that the two will find happiness in the sunset of their lives.

From hard-faced spinster at the movie's beginning to woman glowing with renewed love and faith in Jenny's sickroom, Charlotte's Mathilda takes the viewer on a journey through a heart awakening not just to love but to renewed religious inspiration, as evinced in her intense prayer on the steps leading up to where Jenny lies ill. In fact, at this time in Charlotte's own life, religion — as directed through the precepts of Christian Science — was intensifying its hold on her and on Martin. It would ultimately prove as important to her as her hard-fought career. Perhaps, in the end, it was even more important than that.

29

Mrs. Eddy

Where Charlotte first heard of Christian Science and when she first adopted it as her personal faith is not known. We do know that Martin, through his New York piano teacher, Rafael Joseffy, had opportunity to be exposed to Mary Baker Eddy's beliefs and writings (perhaps all the more attractive to him as the son of a man who worked in a medical field, and brother to another who became a doctor). In a 1970 lecture given at the Mother Church in Boston, Martin also pointed to an earlier exposure: a young friend of his in New York City, who took the eight-year-old Martin along to a Christian Science Sunday School, where Martin learned Mary Baker Eddy's children's prayer, "New Year Gift to the Little Children." (Incidentally, it was here he also volunteered to play for services when the church's pianist stood up the congregation, an early blending of music and religion that would remain a theme till the end of Martin's creative life.)

The fact that in the mid–1950s, Martin went on to become a Christian Science practitioner (by definition a person who, according to Mrs. Eddy's system, may professionally practice healing through prayer after three substantiated healings) — a role erroneously ascribed to Charlotte at the same time — seems to indicate that Christian Science was a faith he had been following not just as one of the devout, but as someone who intended to become a healer himself. The Church was happy enough to welcome him into their roster of professionals. As one of Martin's close friends would later comment, "Officials at the Boston church began to realize just how useful Martin was to the organization, with all of his show business connections. His participation and his connections were greatly encouraged. Charlotte's enthusiasm for Christian Science was a part of Martin's rise in the organization, as well as her desire to support him in all he did."

It is significant that in her memoirs Charlotte does seem to be adhering to Christian Science precepts forbidding alcohol, without pointing out that they derive from her religious faith, when she reports that even at London society parties in the mid–1930s, amid all the flowing champagne, she and Martin stuck to "grape juice," the literal kind. Prior to that, in her filmmaking days in the early '30s, Charlotte describes herself approaching a scene requiring her to smoke a cigar as if she had been ordered to walk a gangplank at gunpoint — one wonders if she ever knew about the fact that her photo was printed on a tobacco silk in 1932 by the German cigarette maker Lande.

Along with material medicine, Christian Science unequivocally forbade either of these two stimulants. As these remarks seem to crop up most frequently after her marriage to Martin, it would appear that Charlotte's Christian Science devotion came through him. (Admittedly Charlotte also had professional reservations about cigarettes and drinks being used as props: "Smoking cigarettes and drinking are not essential to poise," she noted in an early version of her memoirs. "You may look at ease, sister, but you smell like nobody's business.") During the 1920s, Martin was photographed with cigars and cigarettes in his hand, but never after that — another way of gauging just when Christian Science took firm hold.

There was much in Mrs. Eddy's story to attract a hard-working perfectionist like Charlotte Greenwood (not just Mrs. Eddy's advice to "Never record ages"), even without Martin's influence. Because Eddy had, not quite single handed but with an immense amount of willpower and charisma, and her canny ability to manipulate the unseen, created from nothing her own highly effective reality — a feat a veteran theatre actor like Charlotte could only admire.

Mrs. Eddy's scientific approach to the Judeo-Christian scriptures was already nearly thirty years old at Charlotte's birth in 1890, and Mrs. Eddy herself such a legend that she was forced to insert into her Manual adjournments against what would now be called "fans" loitering about her Concord, New Hampshire driveway when she took her famous daily carriage rides. Born in 1821 of old New Hampshire stock, Mary Morse Baker was brought up in the Congregationalist church, the paradigm-shifting structure of which probably went farther toward influencing her own revolutionary ideas than she knew or was willing to own up to. A Protestant movement from the 1500s, Congregationalism rejected all presbytery oversight in favor of direct management by members of the congregation. Their white-spired churches had free reign to determine their own form of worship, an intellectual, self-determined approach that should not make it surprising that the founders of preeminent universities like Harvard and Yale also belonged to the sect.

Sickly in her youth, Mary had ample time and, as the future would show, ample reason to study the Bible for its many references to healing through faith. Her first husband, and her third, showed a marked sickliness as well: her first, George Washington Glover, died a year after their 1843 marriage, while Asa Gilbert Eddy, who suffered from a weak heart, died after a marriage of three years. (Mary divorced husband No. 2, a dentist named Dr. Daniel Patterson, on grounds of adultery, possibly giving her an even worse opinion of medical men than she had had before.)

Thus through her attempts to change her poor health, which she suspected as having a mental rather than physical cause, Mrs. Eddy's forensic interest in healing practices in Biblical times grew stronger through having been a patient of Phineas Parkhurst Quimby, the New Hampshire–born, Maine-bred faith healer some twenty years her senior. Son of a poor blacksmith, Quimby was able to attain only the rudiments of an education, but considerable intelligence and charm made up for this lack. His own son, who was what Mrs. Eddy would have termed "classically educated," once pointed out that had he and his father been invited to the White House to meet the president and a host of guest intellectuals, his father would have held center stage while he, the college-educated son, would have hugged the walls, a blushing wallflower.[1]

A part of this charm came from Quimby's gift for seizing on the thought of particularly suggestive persons and bending it to his own will, and part came from his own highly suggestible nature, which had led him to mental healing in the first place. A sickly boy who had been apprenticed to a clockmaker (he continued to make clocks for many years, even after his faith healing fame began to spread), Quimby believed he had healed his own tubercular lungs despite the fact that a medical doctor had told him there was no hope of recovery. Thus, in his early 30s, Quimby was ripe to begin investigating Mesmerism, via the Transcendalist-influenced varieties growing rife in New England, and specifically through attending the lectures of self-proclaimed doctors who claimed the ability to heal the body using nothing but the unharnessed powers of the mind (using the vaguely scientific test of administering sugar-pill placebos in place of genuine medicine).

"[T]he trouble is in the mind," jotted down Quimby's students in what was to become his several volumes of *Complete Writings*, "for the body is only the house for the mind to dwell in...." Illness was mere belief, Quimby asserted, allowed in by the faithless or imposed upon the unwitting by an "invisible enemy," and like even the most firmly rooted malefic beliefs, willpower and treatments at the hands of Quimby could unseat the enemy and bring back health to the patient who truly wanted it.

Not till 1859, just seven years before his death from cancer (which he blamed on overwork and not being sufficiently on the *qui vive* in fending off "the enemy"), did Quimby open his own practice in Portland, Maine. But the patients and students who flocked to him made up for lost time. Among the latter were Julius and Annetta Dresser, who assisted in getting the semi-literate Quimby's thoughts down on paper, and a combination student-patient named Mary Morse Baker Glover Patterson, who by her own admission was of a mind that what Quimby's teaching needed most was a strong dose of Christianity (to dissolve the taint of Mesmerism, a perceived evil Mary Baker Eddy was to combat throughout her career) and Mrs. Patterson's overconfident but eager competency for the written word. In later years, Mrs. Eddy (as she became via her final marriage to the short-lived Asa Gilbert Eddy) held fast to her manuscript copies of Quimby's writings, gradually adding to them her own take on his theories and finally subsuming much of what made up the basic fabric of his Mesmeric healing methodology in a shroud of Christian holiness, and herself with it.

For years, the founder of Christian Science suffered very real pains for her beliefs. With family members tired of taking her in, and running out of friends and followers whose homes she would overtake in a cloud of good will and depart from, often with her luggage thrown after her, in storms of misunderstanding, Mrs. Eddy kept working at her book, the future *Science and Health with Key to the Scriptures*. As her luck or talent in healing patients became better known, through her own efforts and those of her growing coterie of students, she was able to finally solidify her church of the mind with an organization of the three-dimensional variety, The Church of Christ, Scientist, in Boston in 1879. This was thirteen years after Quimby's death. Perhaps not without an adroit sense of timing, the founding also came thirteen years after her own allegedly disastrous fall on an icy sidewalk in Lynn, Massachusetts, in February 1866, from which the comatose sufferer rose from her bed convinced that she had healed herself by prayer and could help others do the same.

Science and Health went through some 84 revisions, and it's easy to see why: with her preferred literary device of less than water-tight syllogisms, Mrs. Eddy ran into some difficult issues of logic and consistency which continue to plague her book to this day (even after the educated and good-humored John Wiggin was brought in to clean up her tortured spelling, punctuation and syntax). It is her initial and admittedly inspiring claim that Divine Science triumphs over materialism that loosed her into the thorn briars of etymological hairsplitting, always dangerous for the long-term survival of a religious sect. By definition and usage, science relies on a materialistic world — a comparison of this to that, experimentation of one nature against another — and if it all took place in mind and not in laboratories, it would not be science but something like conjecture and, therefore, closer to Spiritualism than Mrs. Eddy was ever willing to admit. Silent prayer is useful, but is secret Science plausible? Mrs. Eddy never addressed that question or most of the others raised by the frequent mismatches between her idealistic creed and her very human way of living (and making a highly lucrative living) in the everyday world, consumed as she was by unnamable fears she tried to combat with the aid of "watchers," students who bent all their mental energies against the forces of bad weather and the bad thoughts codified as "malicious animal magnetism."

It was the official Mrs. Eddy — the white-haired, benevolent, courageous "Mother" of The Mother Church in Boston — that Charlotte Greenwood clearly revered, and she certainly emulated Mrs. Eddy's brand of selective memory in choosing for her memoirs just those events of her life to memorialize on paper and which to leave out. The irony of Charlotte's memoirs, however, with their absence of any mention of her sad first marriage to Cyril Ring, is that they also display a conspicuous absence of anything to do with Christian Science. So marked is this absence that a Christian Science friend of Charlotte's who helped her arrange her notes for the book, remarked in a letter to her and Martin that perhaps Charlotte's account of her life could do with some Christian Science references and testimonies.[2]

Despite *Science and Health*'s relentlessly stirring tone of sacred tablets brought down from the New Hampshire hills, and its often tedious denials of the flesh, many parts of Mrs. Eddy's *opus* read less like religious text and more like the affirmations beloved of the American 1970s and '80s. There was a literalness, combined with charismatic spirituality, that might have made Charlotte, with her powerful self-will and belief in the efficacy of faith, feel right at home. "To develop the full might of this Science," wrote Mrs. Eddy, "the discords of corporeal sense must yield to the harmony of spiritual sense, even as the science of music corrects false tones and gives sweet concord to sound"— a musical simile which must have struck a sympathetic chord in Charlotte.[3]

Another factor to which Charlotte surely found herself attracted was Mrs. Eddy's feminism, an element of her personal crusade every bit as fiery as her fight against the error of thought and motive. Woman, thundered the elderly lady known as "Mother," had every right and then some to her own wages, to own property in her own right and dispense with it at her pleasure, and to do with her children whatever she saw fit, without a husband or his family butting in — words that could only have resonated with Charlotte and her cherished memories of her own hard-working mother.[4]

It's not clear why she left out of her life story the religious faith that meant so much to her and Martin, but the chronology of Charlotte's memoirs may be a clue. The latest of her manuscripts is dated July 1941, almost a year after her return to Hollywood from the aborted *Letty* tour. The nation in general and Hollywood in particular were in a state of extreme uncertainty over the outbreak of war in Europe. Would the United States have to enter the war, and how long could intervention be held off? If America did not intervene, would Hitler fulfill his self-professed destiny of conquering the world for the good of the Nazi order? And from the movie moguls' standpoint, what affect would all these re-drawings of political lines in wartime have on ticket sales? Before the war even reached American territory, it was dividing people into camps: those who favored pacifism, those who favored involvement; those whose German origins tainted them in an increasingly politicized atmosphere, those whose British origins put the pressure on them to leave the U.S. and jump into the fray at home.

Charlotte was nothing if not patriotic, and had proven the lengths to which she would

go to help out during the first World War. If that war had sobered her burlesque efferves-
cence and made her see with the eyes of the wounded men she attempted to entertain in over-
crowded hospitals, the Second World War seems to have done something else: to manifest
and strengthen a powerful religious faith which had always been latent in Charlotte's character, but now had a prime opportunity for fulfillment in the serious roles she was given to play
and the Christian Science in which Martin was now beginning to work as a practitioner.

30

Doris Day

Some biographical references to Charlotte mention that she was a Reader in the Christian Science Church — a position of great importance within a specific church, entailing Sunday readings of selected texts from *Science and Health*[1] — but neither this nor the various accounts of Charlotte serving as professional practitioner are correct.[2] She certainly acted in a counseling capacity for actress Doris Day, who in the middle of what was eventually found to be a spate of panic attacks seized on Christian Science as the only way out of her ills; but it was Martin, by then a full-fledged practitioner, who guided Day through this particular dark valley. In recent years, he had been doing the same for various Hollywood stars who had turned to Christian Science, including actress Joan Crawford, meeting with them over the vast Chinese Chippendale desk at 806 North Rodeo Drive and putting in regular appearances at his and Charlotte's congregation at the big, beautiful church in Beverly Hills.[3]

Urged to explore CS by her husband, the producer Marty Melcher, who became a zealous convert to Mrs. Eddy's system, Doris Day had at first tried to control her heart palpitations, shallow breathing and generalized anxiety by reading from *Science and Health*. When Mrs. Eddy's prescription to meet physical disease with "mental negation" did not work for her, Day called on Martin.[4] "He was a warm, sensible, compassionate man," Day recalled, and though he had not encountered a client with Day's particular problem, he gave the case his level best, reading to her from particular precepts in *Science and Health*. Her husband would awaken in the middle of the night to administer what CS treatments he was capable of, but all efforts were useless. What Day was going through was a walking nervous breakdown, compounded of overwork and untreated anxiety. It took a 2 A.M. summons to Martin, who arrived without delay, and Day fainting in his presence, to convince Martin and Day's husband to obey one of Mrs. Eddy's lesser known printed precepts: that medical assistance could be drawn upon when all Christian Science efforts have signally failed to obtain relief. In Mrs. Eddy's words: "If from an injury or from any cause, a Christian Scientist were seized with a pain so violent that he could not treat himself mentally, — and the Scientists had failed to relieve him — the sufferer could call a surgeon, who would give him a hypodermic injection, then, when the belief of pain was lulled, he could handle his own case mentally." (Mrs. Eddy availed herself of her doctor's hypodermic often enough herself.)[5]

Martin proved more useful for Day in advising her on her career, even on a subject which he himself had handled differently with Charlotte from the way in which he advised Day to do. During her recuperation from the nervous breakdown, Day made regular visits to Martin at 806 North Rodeo Drive, and complained to him about what she regarded as the inferior quality of scripts coming her way from Warner Brothers Studios. She had in mind risking suspension by dropping out of the latest film, *Lucky Me*, which despite a cast including herself, Robert Cummings, Phil Silvers, Nancy Walker and Eddie Foy Jr., seemed to her just another piece of cinematic garbage. Martin asked her if she was under contract, which she confessed she was for a seven year term, and that the contract's stipulation was that Day do whatever pictures were given to her in return for her weekly salary. "Then that is the only right thing to do," Martin told her, "honor your word and your commitment" — quite a change from his and Charlotte's own treatment of Hollywood studios in the early 1930s, when they ignored the pleadings of studio executives and left to pursue the London theatre.

Yet his advice was, in a way, reflective of what he himself had done in his career. If one did one's work, he told Day, with the abiding thought that one was "about one's Father's business," one could not go wrong. Leaving behind his flagging career as musical theatre composer and impresario to manage Charlotte's still vigorous career as film and theatre star, Martin had listened to the same voice which, years before, had told Charlotte in front of a vaudeville dressing room mirror that her destiny was not to be a "sinker of sat sonks" but a clown — in Martin's case, he was to help Charlotte shed that clown image and don that of serious actor.[6]

Day remained a good friend of the Brooneses for several years. She looked up to both Martin and Charlotte as parental figures; continued to sit down with Martin to sort out her troubles via the precepts of Christian Science, and enjoyed the presence of Charlotte on the sets of her films, where between scenes Charlotte dispensed advice while knitting away in a corner when Day was on camera. "Always remember, Emma," Charlotte once said to Day, using the nickname she had given her (Day had a similarly dowdy nickname for Charlotte), "your strength is in your simplicity," advice Day took strongly to heart and for which she was clearly grateful.[7] When Day was in Marrakesh during location shooting for Alfred Hitchcock's *The Man Who Knew Too Much*, she had a sumptuous brass charger made in Cairo especially for the Brooneses, engraved with poetry in Arab dialect and pyramids with camels as well as set with their names in silver in English and Arabic. She and Melcher purchased a house on North Crescent Drive, two streets away from Rodeo; their friendship with Martin and Charlotte was featured in a short article with photographs of the two couples together in the September 1952 issue of *Motion Picture Magazine*.

Then something happened that completely changed the close relationship. It began while Day was working on her last picture for Warner Brothers, *With Six You Get Egg Roll*. Melcher had been experiencing fatigue and told Day he felt he was catching a cold. Based on what she describes next, it would seem that Melcher had been sick for some time, but had been able to conceal the symptoms from Day — an act of paramount importance to so strong a proponent of Christian Science as Marty Melcher was. Melcher was close-lipped to his wife about how he felt, but soon had to give in to appearances, and was bedridden for three months with chronic diarrhea. Day was frantic; she studied *Science and Health* with Melcher and called Martin, who was then on an extensive lecture tour and was only able to provide assistance over the phone.

Day sensed that her husband was mortally ill, and at one point, shortly before his death, she telephoned Martin and begged him to break his tour and come back to Beverly Hills, so he could help Melcher in person. Given his commitments, Martin was unable to oblige.[8]

Melcher died in the hospital of what Day says his doctors told her was a heart condition, and she acknowledged in her memoirs that his death "was the one thing that happened in my life that I really handled badly." In the years that followed, she gave up Christian Science, friends — including Charlotte and Martin — and even the God she had been so sure was on her side. Time would change her views on this. Part of what caused her to handle Melcher's death badly was the additional shock of discovering that his business practices had left her bankrupt. But she was able to work out a philosophy for his death thanks to this knowledge: knowing that things were in such a mess, Melcher had basically let himself die, instead of seeking treatment that might have allowed him to live, effectively committing suicide. Whatever her philosophy for developing this personal saga or shutting the Brooneses out of her life, she never shared it with them or explained her motives. The pain never quite went away. What could be considered a signal failure of Christian Science apparently did as little to shake Charlotte's ironclad faith as it did much to weaken Martin's, as he would tell a close friend shortly thereafter.[9]

31

Out of This World

In early December 1950, Charlotte sat down with *Boston Post* theatre critic Elliott Norton in the living room of 806 North Rodeo Drive and talked about a new musical she was preparing to star in — her first Broadway turn since the flop of *Rufus LeMaire's Affairs* in 1926. "Charlotte Greenwood was living contentedly in Southern California, which, so they say, is out of this world," bubbled Norton, "when along came Cole Porter and invited her into 'Out of This World,' to personate the goddess Juno."[1]

Porter's new project was a musical version of the Jean Giraudoux play *Amphitryon 38*, which had received its English adaptation at the hands of S. N. Berhman and its Broadway premiere by Alfred Lunt and Lynne Fontanne in 1938. Based in turn on a myth related by the Roman author Plautus, concerning Jove's desire for a mortal woman and his assumption of disguise as the woman's husband to gain access to her, the play was a success in both Europe and America, but seemed to depend — for obvious reasons — on stars being cast as Jove and Juno.

Five years earlier, Charlotte had had to turn down a starring role in a musical that altered the face of the genre for time to come, Rodgers and Hammerstein's *Oklahoma!* In the middle of her commitments to Fox, Charlotte had received a letter from Oscar Hammerstein, suggesting that in his and Rodgers' adaptation of Lynn Riggs' *Green Grow the Lilacs* there was a role they had in mind for her. That Charlotte knew the play very well, and that she knew what part Hammerstein wanted her for is made humorously clear in her reply: "If you're talking abot thet thar Aunt Eller, 'f it had to be me I'll lose more'n a leg (page 85 *Green Grow the Lilacs*). But oh, Oscar, it's a purty kind a thought." (Referring to Aunt Eller's remark to Ado Annie in Scene Six, when the latter croons about being married and Eller tries to dissuade her from any such thought: "Time you're as old as me, you'll be settin' around, jist the way *I* am, 'th a wooden leg and a bald head, and a-rippin' up old floursacks to make yerself a pair of drawers out of.")[2]

The loss Charlotte refers to would be her good relationship with Zanuck, should she break her contract to play Eller on stage. As it happened, Betty Garde created Eller for what would become one of the greatest theatrical hits of its time — created her, at least, for the time being, because Hammerstein was not finished coaxing Charlotte to play the part he had her in mind for all along.

Charlotte's contract with Fox ended with *Oh You Beautiful Doll* in 1949, in the part of Fred Fisher's wife, Anna, a role which George Jessel told Charlotte she had been born to play

Charlotte clowning with Charles Coburn and his monocle between scenes on the set of *Peggy* (1950). William Luce collection.

but which is her most subdued on film. Her next film, made for Universal, was a fluffy romantic comedy called *Peggy*, co-starring starlets Diana Lynn and Barbara Lawrence (later to play Gertie in *Oklahoma!*), with a hunky bit-part played by Rock Hudson as Charlotte's football-playing son. Built around a slim romantic comedy set before and during Pasadena's famed Rose Parade, *Peggy* starred Charlotte as what *New York Times* critic Howard Thompson described in his review as "the aggressive widow next door," opposite a monocled Charles Coburn. A letter to Charlotte from Universal Pictures director Fred de Cordova, dated March 1950, seems to have been prompted by her need of reassurance: "I feel more than confident," writes de Cordova, "that 'Peggy' will meet with distinct public favor, and your efforts will be greatly responsible." Such they apparently were, because she received good notices ("Charlotte Greenwood ... the brightest thing in the picture"[3]) and the film did well. Best of all, with *Peggy* released, Charlotte could concentrate on Porter's *Out of This World*, her first foray on Broadway since the late 1920s.

As she told Elliott Norton, on returning home to Rodeo Drive from Cole Porter's house, after singing and reading for him from the nascent score, Charlotte announced to Martin, "I think I am going East to play in a musical."

At first, Charlotte was doubtful about going back to the stage in a role that called on all the abilities she had last displayed there in the late 1920s: singing, dancing, and all the other components that went into the creation of a Greenwood characterization. Porter really wanted her, she told Norton, because he sweetened the role of Juno by telling Charlotte he'd written a song especially for her, the raucous, "Men, Men, Men." "That really won me over," she explained. "[I]t's a swell song."[4] Charlotte had, however, not been Porter's first choice. Clearly seeking a woman younger and with more box office pizzazz, Porter had first gone after Carol Channing, who refused in order to do *Gentlemen Prefer Blondes*, followed by Judy Holliday, fresh from the success of *Born Yesterday*. It was only after *she* turned the role down that Charlotte was approached — perhaps explaining Porter's tasty carrot of the song written especially for her. (Even though the show had snagged a star of Charlotte's reputation, however, she had to agree to have her name follow not precede the title, a major break with tradition and one that went against most of her own history on Broadway and elsewhere.)

Charlotte knew that by agreeing to perform in *Out of This World* she was taking a number of risks. She was almost 60, and had not been on Broadway for over two decades. And as she confessed to Norton, she had pretty much given up the sort of "low comedy and high kicking for which she won a reputation." The serious roles she had taken for Zanuck had led her to her first serious stage part since her return to film, that of Mama in the road production of John Van Druten's play *I Remember Mama*. Based on Kathryn Forbes' book *Mama's Bank Account*, a series of vignettes of life in an immigrant Norwegian family living in San Francisco built around the character of the indomitable, wise and down-to-earth *materfamilias*, *I Remember Mama* had played Broadway's Music Box Theatre for almost two years with Vienna-born Mady Christians in the lead (and the youthful Marlon Brando as son Nels). Rodgers and Hammerstein were the producers of that hit run of 713 performances, between 1944 and 1946. The play served as basis for the 1948 film starring Irene Dunne. Rodgers and Hammerstein even considered, ten years later, turning the play into a musical for Charlotte and Shirley Jones, a project that had to wait till a lyrical but ineffective effort from an ailing Rodgers and miscast star Liv Ullman in 1979.)[5]

For the road show, Russell Lewis and Howard Young took over, and as Charlotte related to Elliott Norton, their choice of Charlotte was considered "daring." Charlotte understood why American audiences, with her Fox extravaganzas still fresh in their minds, would have a hard time imagining Charlotte Greenwood in an apron and sturdy shoes, dispensing household wisdom to her brood without a pratfall to fall back on. "Charlotte fooled everyone," wrote Norton. "She didn't so much as turn a cartwheel." Charlotte, in fact, won the San Francisco Drama Critics Award for her performance. And Irene Dunne, who had created

At age 60, playing the wife of a Jupiter young enough to be her son, Charlotte exemplified the perks of being a goddess in Cole Porter's 1950 musical *Out of This World*. Emmett Brennan collection.

the role of Mama on screen, sent her a warm note: "From one 'Mama' to another — congratulations!"[6]

"That I loved," she told Norton wistfully, "playing Mama. But few people have ever believed I could do it."[7]

Few people, she and Martin both added — for Martin, now serving as Charlotte's manager, was present at the Norton interview — except for Oscar Hammerstein II and Darryl Zanuck.

Charlotte cited Hammerstein's and Kern's London musical, *Three Sisters*, as early proof that Hammerstein believed in her solid acting abilities, adding to her dramatic scene each day. Hammerstein, Charlotte told Norton, was one of the few people in the business who had had faith in her as a serious actor. Martin added that Zanuck was another who had had faith in his wife, noting dismissively, "The movie people have generally failed to accept her as anything but a comedienne."[8]

Porter's well-known charm had evidently overcome any qualms Charlotte or Martin may have had about her return to Broadway in something as rollicking as his new musical. And as Charlotte told Hedda Hopper, "When Cole Porter asks you that's a request from the top."[9] But he and his producers, Saint Subber and Lew Ayers, knew they needed a big name to attract

Top: A role Charlotte loved, and was loved in — that of Mama in the touring production of *I Remember Mama*, 1949. She is shown here with Raymond Roe as Nels, Mary Joan Bradley as Dagmar, and Little Liza (the cat). *Opposite*: Charlotte was proud of the several shelves of autographed books in her library. Novelist Kathryn Forbes, author of *Mama's Bank Account*, source for the play and film *I Remember Mama*, signed a copy of her novel for Charlotte's collection.

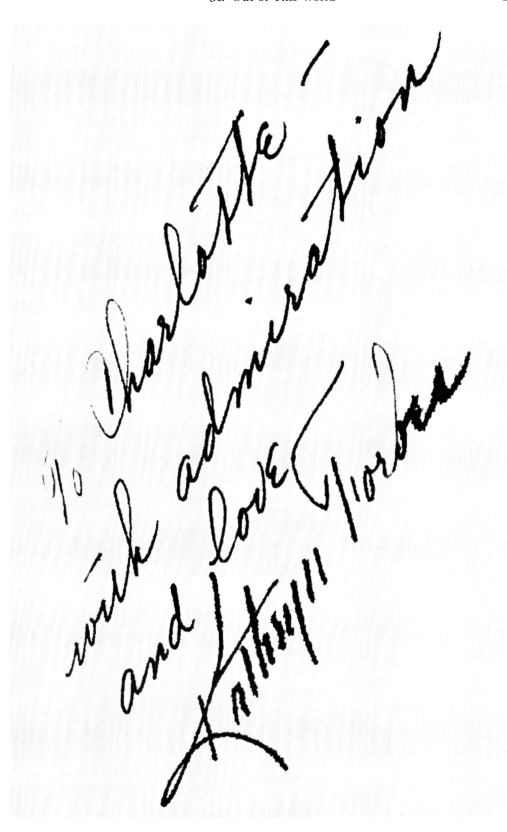

To Charlotte —
with admiration
and love Gioretta

Kathryn

audiences for a new musical following so fast on the heels of the phenomenally successful *Kiss Me Kate*, which was still running after two years and put Porter in the ironic position of hoping that his new musical could compete with his earlier one.

But well before the show got on, Porter already had his doubts about *World's* ability to match up. When first working on the show, he had written to his mother that the Amphitryon legend made for one of the most hilarious plots in theatre. In most ways that mattered, the plot was perfect for theatrical success, as Lunt and Fontanne had proven a dozen years earlier. In Behrman's adaptation, Jupiter falls in love with a married American woman named Helen, using his son Mercury as the go-between. Helen is lured to an inn in modern day Athens, where Jupiter (by this time pursued by his jealous wife, Juno), means to seduce her in the guise of her husband. Helen discovers Jupiter's trick in time and is reconciled with her husband. Cue for all the cast to sing a song of eternal love and understanding.

There was no problem raising money. Investors who had made a killing on *Kiss Me Kate* were not about to miss out on raking it in from what promised to be a bigger, shinier new show. The problem was turning out a book that satisfied everyone concerned, and from the beginning that was the sticking point. Dwight Taylor, son of actress Laurette Taylor, had written the first book, which so little impressed Porter that Betty Comden and Adolph Green were brought in to doctor it. When they were unable to smooth out the knots in the plot,

Charlotte Greenwood as Juno and George Gaynes as Jupiter rise to Olympus on a cloud while William Redfield, as Mercury, looks on in this scene from Cole Porter's Greek-themed 1950 musical *Out of This World*. William Luce collection.

Reginald Lawrence was hired to doctor their doctoring. The result was a score simply laid over a book, with all the troubles, hidden and obvious, that that implies.[10]

Porter was also having problems negotiating the roller coaster of his life. His wife, Linda, a serial smoker whose severe lung problems required frequent hospitalization, was ill again, and Porter himself had never been the same, physically or emotionally, since shattering a leg in a riding accident over a decade before. There was much to hope for from the director, choreographer Agnes de Mille, who had helped revolutionize American musical theatre with her work on *Oklahoma!* (and now was the first woman director of a Broadway musical) but troubles began when friction emerged between her and the show's official choreographer, Hanya Holm, whom de Mille alleged was "jealous" of her. De Mille also had disagreements with Ayers about how the show should look and be staged, which Subber's agreement did not help.[11]

The cast, once Charlotte was placed as Juno, was filled with several talented performers: George Jongeyans (who later changed his name to George Gaynes), a New York City Opera baritone who was the son of Porter's friend, Russian émigré Lady Abdy, and was just then starring in *Wonderful Town*, was chosen as Jupiter — that he was young enough to be Charlotte's son does not seem to have posed a problem on or off the stage. Rotund comedian David Burns (later part of the original *Hello Dolly!*) was cast as the Greek gangster, Niki Skolianos, whom Juno mistakes for her husband and engages in a dueling duet in a taverna; he was the prankish *enfant terrible* of the production. Silvery-voiced Priscilla Gillette sang Helen to William Eythe's Art O'Malley. Ballerina Janet Collins danced the symbolic figure, Night, pirouetting against vast stage curtains, golden and dark blue, representing day and evening, while Gisella Svetlik, just as scantily clad, danced the role of Venus. The sets were certainly breathtaking, as remembered by actress Peggy Rea, who played the role of Vulcania, whom she describes as "Charlotte's idiot daughter."

"There were two proscenium curtains that went across the stage, both chiffon," she recalls. "One was Night and the other was Day. Janet Collins ... just floated across the stage, and pulled these curtains. The one went from a clear ivory to deep orange-red — that was Day — with the signs of the zodiac in bugle-beads on them. I tell you, it was just fabulous! The other one went from pale, pale lavender-blue to a deep navy blue, the same thing with the zodiac images." Rea notes that Charlotte's and George Gaynes' age difference was noticeable — "He was supposed to be her *husband*. That was all off-kilter." But Charlotte's presence, at the age of 60, was outstanding. "She was absolutely *full* of energy and joy," remembers Rea, "and did her high kicks just as she had done years before. That's what kept us running! People couldn't believe it."[12]

Perhaps because of his European background and what he describes as his "fresh off the boat" politeness, George Gaynes was less sensitive to the difference in ages. "Maybe she was 60," he laughs, "but she could still kick a high leg, though. Her leg went absolutely perpendicular to her head and body. Extraordinary. And I would confirm," he adds, "that Greenwood kept that show going. Four months' run. It might have closed after one week without her."

She also lent a certain elegance to the risqué proceedings, even in the spiky-diademed pseudo–Olympian draperies that made up her costumes for the role. Charlotte, Gaynes felt, had an unconscious "aristocratic air," a poise and graciousness made all the more attractive by her clownish onstage antics, which was not likely to have impressed a scion of Russian aristocrats had it been the sort of act put on by many aging movie stars. "She could do this incredible act and still look like the lady," he recalls. As Charlotte told a reporter thirty years earlier, during the tour of *Linger Longer Letty*, "[Some] people are surprised to find that I talk like a human being. If I came into a room and slapped my host on the back and said, 'How are yuh!' this individual would think, 'My goodness, she's awful!'" And here she was again, lanky Letty to the audience and refined Miss Greenwood to her colleagues.

The show did contain a great deal of exposed flesh, Gaynes notes, which, with Porterian irony, meant that the men were wearing less than the women, and ensured an audience for that portion of the show if not for the show itself. (In support of this, images of Lew Ayers' set designs show that the giant Greek-style statues of male figures standing above the scantily-clad cast were a great deal more suggestive and, indeed, sexier than the female ones.) The naughtiness was helped along by the antics of David Burns, who one back stage observer recalled on at least one occasion exposing himself behind the bar of the taverna, in full view of a giggling male chorus, during his dueling duet with Charlotte. "I was not witness to such proceedings," remembers Gaynes. "He was a naughty boy, but terribly funny."[13]

Charlotte seems to have sailed through all the near-nudity and sexy lyrics unscathed — she had plenty of the latter to sing herself, as when Porter wrote one of the best songs ever composed for her, "Nobody's Chasing Me," a song which Charlotte apparently told friends she believed to be the theme song of the entire show, and which, ironically, were to be ordered stricken from the script by the censor at the Boston tryout. As Charlotte's own copy of the show's book would demonstrate, however, with its many penciled out and rewritten lines, these were not the only changes exacted of her, and before long she would refuse to make any changes at all.[14]

The show was slated to open at the New Century Theater in New York City on December 21, 1950, whether or not its patchwork book was ready. Its first tryout was scheduled for November 4 in Philadelphia, Charlotte's hometown; but there was a kind of dress rehearsal for the first tryout the night before, at the Shubert Theatre, when the company put on a benefit performance for the United Service Club of Philadelphia, the oldest enlisted men's club in the nation. A sparkling souvenir program filled with images of G.I.s and Navy men was distributed; the one cast member whose picture was printed within was Charlotte's.

It was in Philadelphia that problems with the book began to raise their heads. Without consulting de Mille, who was still technically the director, George Abbott was brought in as directorial doctor, with F. Hugh Herbert as the last of the script wizards to work on the show. Incensed, de Mille was sure that Porter, whom she thought a "coward," was responsible, despite the producers Subber and Ayers taking the heat for the decision.[15]

Confirming Porter's fears, critics immediately pounced on what was described almost universally as a "bogged down" script, which, as always, remained uppermost in the company's minds as they performed, even though the show was doing well at the ticket office. De Mille was angry; the cast was destabilized. When the show was perceived by the producers to be failing, they started removing songs, like ballast from a sinking balloon, to the point where Porter was at wits end. "I have never seen anyone suffer the way Cole did with that show," said one close associate. "He was destroyed."[16]

George Abbott probably committed the worst mistake of all the many cooks stirring this broth to death by demanding that the number "From This Moment on," which went on to become the one hit of the score, be cut from the show. (In fairness to Abbott, consensus among the cast and Porter's entourage pointed to William Eythe's inability to sing the number as the real reason it was dropped.)[17] A blue-nosed female critic in Boston came down hard on the show's risqué lyrics and fleshpot dancers. Charlotte was clearly disgusted with all the trouble, which it would appear she blamed on the new "director," Abbott and his writer. Porter's biographer George Eells tells of Charlotte's mental block toward all the new lines she had to learn (compounded by her habitual inability, known from other sources, to unlearn lines once she had committed them to memory), and was not on speaking terms with either Abbott or Herbert.[18] Perhaps to assuage her frustration, a suffering Porter rose to the occasion and in Boston wrote another song for Charlotte, "I Sleep Easier Now." (Porter's third new song for her.)

Nobody was sleeping easy by the time the show made it to the New Century on Broadway, but with advance sales of some half a million dollars, and a sparkling first night audience every bit as glamourous as that for *Kiss Me Kate*, the show went on. As had been the case in Philadelphia and Boston, Charlotte was the biggest hit of the evening, though critics savaged the show: "The male dancing chorus is almost as unhampered by godlike raiments as the customers in a steam bath"; "*Out of This World* [is] a modern Amphitryon story with thread unraveled from golden G strings." Brooks Atkinson of the *New York Times* considered the whole show old-fashioned (especially about sex) and, like several other critics, believed Charlotte, along with George Gaynes' singing, the best thing about *Out of This World*. Playing a "humorously ungodlike Juno," Charlotte lent what was good about the old days to a show that Atkinson thought rife with too much of what no longer worked on the stage. "[I]n the happiest moment of the show, she swings those long legs in a cartwheel motion that delighted New Yorkers after the first World War, and delights New Yorkers of today." Dance critics, on the other hand, wrote favorably of Hanya Holm's work; Walter Terry described Charlotte, Janet Collins and Holm as "an incredible tango." *Times* dance critic John Martin waxed similarly affectionate over Charlotte's performance, asking that his readers not "overlook a kind of Olympian square dance in which the irresistible Charlotte Greenwood is pretty well snatched off her feet by her succession of heavenly partners," listing Charlotte's vaudeville kicks and splits and Camel Walk beside ballerina Janet Collins' "long and sustained [physical] phrase."[19]

Audiences certainly loved the show — and Charlotte — and before the New Year sheet music featuring numbers from *World* was selling at a pace to compare with any of Porter's biggest hits. Yet there was no saving the sinking ship. After 157 performances, *Out of This World* closed on May 19, 1951. Before it faded away, however, the show would be recorded (on 45 rpm discs), and as such is Charlotte's only Broadway performance to be archived for posterity. And caricaturist Al Hirschfeld, as if taking a leaf from Ian Fox and his 1932 interview of the incredibly growing Charlotte Greenwood, drew an image of her in her Greek robes and tiara, one sandaled foot in stage right, another in stage left, while a miniature Janet Collins twirls like a sprite in between.

Despite the fact that "I was finally on Broadway, and it was a big musical, and a total flop," Peggy Rea remembered having the time of her life, and she also recalls what a tower of strength Charlotte was for her. During the Boston tryouts, Rea had had a terrifying experience. On returning to her hotel room before the evening performance, she was attacked by a man who, it was later found, had broken in and concealed himself there in wait for her.

"He could have been the Boston Strangler for all I knew," she says. "But I had a few pounds on him so I survived, and I went on that night." The experience disturbed her so deeply she went into therapy, something that was new for a woman brought up in Christian Science. Rea knew Charlotte was a devout Scientist, but she had herself pulled away from the church. During therapy following the attack, it emerged that Charlotte had assumed in Rea's mind the same stalwart, iron-clad figure as Rea's Christian Scientist father, not as a maternal force but as a "father-figure ... that's what she was to me," she explains, "even though I never spoke to her of the incident in the hotel room. She served that purpose of strength and fortitude for me. She helped me through," even as she high-kicked Porter's troubled musical far past its natural life span. That strength, amazing to people who did not know Charlotte was 60 instead of her official "58" (she denied her real age even in her candid interview with Elliott Norton), seemed to gather in force with age. If it took an entire lifetime's experience to burnish Charlotte's abilities as an actor, it was worth waiting for the end result: Aunt Eller Murphy in Rodgers and Hammerstein's *Oklahoma!*[20]

32

Oklahoma!

IN THEIR INTERVIEW ABOUT *Out of This World*, Charlotte told Elliott Norton about the time several years before when Oscar Hammerstein called her to tell her that he had written a new show — namely, the future *Oklahoma!*— that had a part in it only Charlotte could play. Charlotte didn't let on which part it was, but anyone reading Norton's interview must have had an inkling that Aunt Eller was the character Hammerstein had had in mind for her. Charlotte's comment to Norton — "I wanted badly to take that" — speaks volumes for her passion for the part and also her principles when it came to an agreement: with twenty weeks to go on her Fox contract, she could not in good conscience break it. She had to say no. So late in her career, Charlotte was still doing things the hard way, "the Greenwood way."[1]

First born of scribbles in, of all places, Paris' Deux Magots café in 1928, Lynn Riggs' *Green Grow the Lilacs* is a tale of rustic chivalry and rustic justice little different from Mascagni's *Cavalleria rusticana* except for being set in the Oklahoma territory. It is full of music: the uncut script contains eleven folk songs, some of them obscure but all proper for their place, in its six scenes. Before Richard Rodgers and Oscar Hammerstein ever touched it, Rigg's play was already something of a "musical," requiring actors who could sing or were, at the very least, musical enough to lend lyricism to the songs that helped paint their characters and set the scenic and emotional mood. The script's pivotal song "Green Grow the Lilacs," a lover's lament over his lost sweetheart and his hope of forgetting his sorrows by joining the Army, is itself a miniature opera on themes of Civil War loss keenly appreciated by many in the post–World War I world of the play's 1929 premiere.

But *Green Grow the Lilacs* is not just a parable on frontier drama, any more than it is, as one wag put it, just a tale of who's to take Laurey to the social. In all his plays but especially in this one, Riggs mined his own family history for material. Born near Claremore, Indian Territory in 1899, Riggs was the son of William Grant Riggs, a cattleman who later became a banker, and his wife, Rose Ella, who was one-eighth Cherokee.

Thus from birth Riggs already derived his identity from two opposing worlds, that of the Plains Indian and of the white capitalist whose manifest destiny marked the end of the old native ways. Rose Ella died when Riggs was a year old, and the woman brought into the household with his father's remarriage was uncongenial to all the Riggs children, particularly Lynn, the youngest. Thus he came to stay more and more often with his aunt Mary Riggs Thompson, a strong, plain spoken and plain-faced woman who gave him the mothering he

"She knew what she had and she knew who she was"— Shirley Jones on Charlotte Greenwood, seen here in a still shot by Schuyler Crail between scenes during the filming of *Oklahoma!* She inscribed this photograph to the late Rod Steiger, who played Jud Fry: "Thank you Judd [sic] sez Aunt Eller."

needed. Riggs was to repay her with the creation of Aunt Eller Murphy, the wise widowed aunt who serves as mother, fixer, judge and humorist in *Green Grow the Lilacs*, the warm, shining sun around which the play's characters revolve.

The land and the experiences of it that shaped personalities like Mary Riggs Brice and Aunt Eller was named by the indigenous Choctaw Indians after their words for "people"— *okla*—and "red"—*humma*, but it was also called the "beautiful land" for reasons obvious to the first non–Native settlers. As William Howard Harper wrote in *Harper's Weekly* in May 1889, a month after the first great land rush: "The whole expanse of space from zenith to horizon was spotless in its blue purity. The clear spring air, through which the rolling green billows of the promised land could be seen with unusual distinctness for many miles, was as sweet and fresh as the balmy atmosphere of June among New Hampshire's hills." That the promised land was not quite as sweet as the hills back home became apparent to many, however, as more people converged on the area than even its expanses could hold. "Unlike Rome," wrote Howard, "the city of Guthrie was built in a day."

To be strictly accurate in the matter, it might be said that it was built in an afternoon. At twelve o'clock on Monday, April 22d, the resident population of Guthrie was nothing; before sundown it was at least ten thousand. In that time streets had been laid out, town lots staked off, and steps taken toward the formation of a municipal government. At twilight the campfires of ten thousand people gleamed on the grassy slopes of the Cimarron Valley, where, the night before, the coyote, the gray wolf, and the deer had roamed undisturbed.[2]

Problems arose quickly: the United States marshals sent into the territory ahead of the settlers to lay down a semblance if not a fact of law and order often staked out claims well in advance of the legal date for doing so, usually selecting the best parcels with the most abundant pasturage and water sources they could find; and with thousands of people wandering an unknown landscape looking for water when they were thirsty, it soon became clear that Indian Territory's beauty was merely skin-deep. They dug for water and encountered sand, beautiful but heartlessly dry sand: "Believing that all of the Oklahoma country consisted of this red, white and gray sand, thousands of home-seekers took the earliest trains back into Kansas, more than ever contented with the fertile soil of the homes that they had left in the first rush...."

In fact, it was typically those men with means who prospered best in the territory, rather than the real and would-be farmers who came with a wife and six children and a dollar between all of them and starvation, waiting till the crops came in — if they did. These men of means "came to take up the claims of those whom drought and mortgages and hard times had driven to the wall." The rivalry between farmer and "cowman" that spices Lynn Riggs' Oklahoma family history probably got its start in the comparative ease with which cattlemen found the territory less devastatingly expensive to get a grip on than the farmer, with his dependence on weather and seeds and the backbreaking work that went into maintaining a paying farmstead. "The ultimate success of Oklahoma as an agricultural region depends as much upon rainfall as upon the fertility of the soil," observed Howard, back at his big city desk; "and those who plough the land in hope will have to wait in faith for the rains to come."

With this hardscrabble existence came violence, almost as a matter of course. Lynn Riggs' own family, despite a financial situation more fortunate than most, was a case in point, to such a degree he was able to fill several books and plays with its dramas and tragedies. His first cousin, Raymond Riggs, was murdered in April 1928 by his wife Bessie in a crime of passion made the worse by the fact that Bessie killed her husband on Easter Sunday. Claiming self-defense and temporary insanity (she tried to shoot herself, succeeding in inflicting only flesh wounds, when her sister-in-law, owner of the boarding house where the shooting occurred, walked into the room and saw her brother dying on the floor), Bessie was let off a mere month later. Riggs would use this account as the basis for his unfinished novel, *The Affair at Easter*.

Research has shown that the leitmotif of fire than runs through *Green Grow the Lilacs* may have had its origin in a mysterious blaze at Christmas 1920 in the farmhouse of Riggs' Aunt Mary Riggs Thompson — Riggs' cousin Willie Thompson, the inspiration for Ado Annie, was also in the house at the time. And the malevolent farmhand Jeeter Fry — renamed Jud by Oscar Hammerstein for purposes of scansion — was based on a hired hand named Jeeter Davis whom Howard McNeil, son of the woman on whom Laurey's character was based, remembered as a violent, drunken individual "who pulled a knife on a family member ... one of these guys who would get drunk on Saturday and thought he was a whiz with the women...."[3]

Riggs had a knack for painting these people with a brush as theatrical as it was accurate:

> Gamblers, traders, vagabonds, adventurers, daredevils, fools. Men with a sickness, men with a distemper. Men disdainful of the settled, the admired, the regular ways of life. Men on the move. Men fleeing from a critical world and their own eyes.[4]

On the other hand, Riggs also used the positive images and personalities he remembered from his childhood in the plains of Oklahoma, which in turn had as much influence on Rodgers and Hammerstein as any of the song material with which *Lilacs* is loaded. The play opens, wrote Riggs, on "...a radiant summer morning," in which the landscape and everything on it — cattle, farmers, freshly growing corn, streams running down meadows — seemed so new and strange it was as if they had never existed before this hour.[5]

It is in the middle of all this radiant summer glow that Aunt Eller is first spied at the beginning of both the play and the film, churning butter under a tree, much as the musical itself first took shape under a spreading oak at Rodgers' country place in Fairfield, Connecticut. What became *Oklahoma!*, a masterpiece of musical theatre that set standards and broke records for everything that came after, was also the inaugural project for a team that would make theatrical history. Though Richard Rodgers and his lyricist Larry Hart had been a byword of success for years, Hart's alcoholism, depression and self-destructive behaviors were causing problems that showed no sign of abating. Rodgers made every concession to the gifted Hart's human failings, but by 1941 it was clear that the duo would have to break up. It was at this juncture that Hammerstein came on the scene, with an idea for a musical that perfectly suited his gifts as lyricist — Lynn Riggs' *Green Grow the Lilacs.*

The project was planted in soil as arid and unpromising as that found by many of the first settlers in Oklahoma. While war raged in Europe and the Pacific, producer Teresa Helburn and Theatre Guild founding member Lawrence Langner were engaged in a losing battle to save the Guild, which was fading like an unwatered cornfield. Active for a quarter century, the Guild was also suffering from unsuccessful productions and decreasing funding (as a result of the failures) for future ones. It was in the middle of this darkness that Helburn, somewhat to Langner's horror, proposed mounting a new production. "To Terry goes the full credit," wrote Langner, "for having conceived the idea of producing *Oklahoma!* and for bringing together [Rodgers and Hammerstein] to create the work."[6]

Clear hindsight vision aside, these were at the time not the magnificent ingredients they seem to us now. "*What* team?" marveled Ethan Mordden. Rodgers had had a long established career writing tunes to the witty lyrics of Lorenz Hart, while Hammerstein "had spent the same years mainly in operetta and its derivations, where waltz mattered more than wit and the *poète* roamed, not the *flâneur.*"[7]

Helburn herself came at the project in the beginning with a good deal of negative baggage where any type of musical theatre was concerned. "When I was very young and opinionated," she explained in her memoirs, "I regarded musical comedy as a kind of intellectual slumming. It is ironical now to know that what reputation I leave behind me will rest chiefly on my contribution to a field I so long looked upon without respect." Yet it was at this very time of political, social and economic uncertainty — the Depression was still in effect for many Americans and had created the direful byproduct in Germany of helping to bring Adolf Hitler, now setting Europe aflame, to power — that Helburn felt "the moment had come for the fulfillment of my dream, the production of a totally new kind of play with music, not a musical comedy in the familiar sense but a play in which music and dancing would be aids to and adjuncts of the plot itself in telling the story."[8]

Those measly $30,000 held in the bank by the ailing Theatre Guild, while they were to be added to by a variety of investors, played their own role in the look and character of the embryonic *Oklahoma!* The work would resemble no other musical theatre production in one other important respect: the simplicity of its sets and costumes, lacking in the accustomed Broadway pizzazz and substituting for elaborate stage furnishings a sort of painting-like one-dimensional arrangement of primary colors, bold calicos and horizons painted to outdo even the red-streaked sunsets of Oklahoma itself. What resulted was a basic love story with a cheerful exterior around the dark kernel of Jud Fry's malevolence, not unlike the canvases of Thomas Hart Benton, where countrified humor and whimsy (a nude young woman sleeping under a tree) occupy visual and sensual space alongside the ugly and the disturbing (a prurient old farmer peering at her from above), or where a jealous lover stands over his slashed girlfriend, bloodied knife in hand, while a man fiddles amiably over a game of cards nearby.

Agnes de Mille was wowed by the new duo from the start. "The impression on first meeting them," she recalled, "was that here at last were the aristocrats of the business." Physically and personality-wise they were an odd couple. Short and swarthy, with strong arms and hands and a way of looking, per de Mille, like "a primitive ... eyes ... as opaque as an Aztec's" when in the midst of creation, Rodgers was intense, precise, razor-sharp in his pronouncements and gifted with what de Mille asserted was a quality that belonged to both him and Hammerstein: "professional watchfulness."

That was one of Hammerstein's few resemblances to his partner, however. Tall, gangly, he seemed to de Mille "too neighborly, too understanding, too philosophic for our gypsy and disreputable trade." Unlike Rodgers, whose smoking led to cancer of the mouth, Hammerstein lit up seldom, hardly drank, got exercise (he had a special standing desk at which to do his work at home). Yet it was Hammerstein who reached for the daring in form and fashion, in contrast to Rodgers' more classic style. De Mille claimed neither had much of a sense for color, but she was referring to the business more properly the bailiwick of the production designer. In their words and music, color took on a meaning it had never had before in musical theatre, and would change what the entire genre was supposed to be about after their first project together.[9]

"[I]f the Rodgers and Hammerstein coupling hadn't existed," asserts Ethan Mordden, "Broadway would have had to invent it." What they did do, at the heart of all their endeavors, he points out, was offer the opposite of what had become so decrepit and junky, the old-fashioned Aarons-Freedley show that Charlotte and plenty of her fellow theatre stars had played in for at least a quarter century: "start with a solid story, then let all the showman's arts follow that story."[10]

"The weeks of rehearsal were frenzied," wrote Helburn. The theatre was crowded to capacity and then some, she remembered, with Rouben Mamoulian, Agnes de Mille, chorus and principals and dancers all working at once. Helburn made an almost fatal mistake by interrupting de Mille in mid-rehearsal, which resulted in the hotheaded choreographer throwing objects at Helburn and having to be dragged off the set by dancer Marc Platt, who held her head under a faucet to cool her off. Then de Mille caused another kind of angst for all concerned when she came down with German measles and gave them to members of the ballet. Helburn remembered everyone having to be dosed with extra greasepaint to conceal their spots.

One commentator sneered that the show would not last a week. But *Oklahoma!* ran for a total of five years and nine weeks in New York (22,248 performances) and has been performed around the world. In 1944 it won a special Pulitzer Prize for drama. It also saved the Theatre Guild, not least due to the fact, as Helburn points out, that even those investors who grudgingly put down their $1,500 (rather like the reluctant bidders at Aunt Eller's lunch basket auction in the play) ended up with a return on their investment of some $50,000—not bad money for war time.[11]

33

"She knew what she had and she knew who she was"

Iт wʌs тнɪs рненомеnʌl success on the stage that pricked up the ears of Hollywood producers, who in 1943 began angling for the rights to film *Oklahoma!* For obvious reasons, Rodgers and Hammerstein wanted the production to run as long as possible and held out as far as 1951, when they purchased sole rights to the musical from the Theatre Guild and the original investors for close to a million dollars. Even then, they continued to be just two boys who couldn't say yes to increasingly tempting Hollywood offers. Yet for these men who supposedly had no sense of color, per de Mille, it took a radical new cinematic process, known as Todd-AO, to bring them to the bargaining table.[1]

Developed by impresario extraordinaire Mike Todd, Todd-AO was bigger and better than anything that had been used before in film. There had been many efforts to deepen and expand the visual and aural experience of cinema for several years — Cinemascope and VistaVision were among the biggest of these experiments — but Todd-AO went one better. Besides a bigger, specially curving screen and stereo sound of the highest possible quality for the time (six-track orthosonic), the system also used a film speed not seen before, enhancing the quality of the image.

Since the advent of talking film the universal speed was 24 frames per second. Todd ran his film — 70 millimeter positive — at 30 frames per second, creating what film critic Roger Ebert describes as "film that would look amazingly brighter, cleaner and more brilliant [with] an additional illusion of depth."[2] Cinerama used three cameras; Todd-AO's required just one. If Todd-AO had to be shown on a special curved screen, boasting a 128-degree scope, few theatre owners would disagree that converting to the new setup was a bad investment. From the comfort of their seats, audiences could sit awash not just in a kind of surround-sound but in what was also a kind of surround-scene — precisely the drama and color Rodgers and Hammerstein wanted for the spectacle of *Oklahoma!*

The choice of director Fred Zinnemann further ensured quality. Born in Austria in 1907, Zinnemann came from a family of doctors, and wanted originally to be a musician. He claimed to have lacked any talent for music, but his cinematic eye recalled many things from a childhood spent in the aftermath of the great war, from which Germany and Austria emerged shattered: lack of food and warmth, the relief brought by Herbert Hoover's ARA, the elderly Emperor Franz Josef parading prior to the war and the weird limbo of life in Vienna after Armistice Day, 1918.[3]

Prior to being tapped for *Oklahoma!*, Zinnemann had directed a string of masterpieces, each one of which contained elements important to his crafting of Rodgers' and Hammerstein's magnum opus: *From Here to Eternity*, *A Member of the Wedding*, *High Noon*. He had never before directed a musical. Mike Todd and producer Arthur Hornblow Jr. suggested his services to R&H. "I was eager to accept," recalled Zinnemann. "The idea of exploring new avenues of movie making was most exciting." He also happened to love *Oklahoma!* the musical and its "radiant optimism and joy of life," so at variance with a world torn and soured by war. He even took a salary cut to work on the film. "[Rodgers and Hammerstein's] choice of Zinnemann," notes Hammerstein biographer Hugh Fordin, "reflected their desire not to make yet another 'Hollywood version' of a Broadway show."[4]

As with Zinnemann, Charlotte's role in the film also called on something of everything she had done before — indeed, Aunt Eller was a role that drew more heavily on that virtually unknown quantity, Charlotte's dramatic stage roles, than on any of her film work. Next to her luminous Aunt Eller her last stage part, as Juno in the underappreciated *Out of This World*, was a throwback to the shallow old days of "Greenwood the clown."

Other Greenwood films open with Charlotte very much at the top of the show and the focus of attention — in *So Long Letty* she bounds onto the set like a manic gazelle; in *Palmy Days*, she towers literally and figuratively over all the tap-shoed Busby Berkeley chorus girls and the film's star, Eddie Cantor; in *Star Dust*, it's Charlotte we see before anyone else, sweeping out of Grauman's Chinese Theatre in her black velvet and diamonds.

Oklahoma! was different in several respects, not least the fact that when the camera discovers her, Charlotte is silent and serene, sitting under a tree churning butter and looking off into the imagined morning distances of the Oklahoma plains. Zinnemann knew how to capture this quality — without Charlotte lifting a finger, his camera turns her into a scene-stealer of the first rank. Here we have a glimpse of Charlotte as she played the elderly Augusta in *Wild Violets* nearly thirty years before at Drury Lane, reminiscing on past adventures beside the hearth at The Stone Jug, or as Abby the maid in *The Late Christopher Bean*, remembering how she was once loved by a dying artist. Not that her comic gifts go wasted. In her leap from shock to worldly amusement at seeing the "French pictures" Will Parker brings back from Kansas City, we see a reprise of Charlotte's many sallies as respectable matron turned harum-scarum hoyden in such roles as Blossom Murphy in *The Gang's All Here*. The over-the-top (and over the sofa) scramblings and occasional weapon-wielding of her early physical comedies are behind her casual firing of a gun to break up a fight at the box social and her matter of fact manner of directing its muzzle into the faces of startled cowboys and farmers, commanding them to "Sing! *Sing!*"

But in her best scene, in which she consoles the distraught Laurey after Curly is taken to jail for the death of Jud Fry, we see what brought Charlotte such critical and audience acclaim in domestic dramas like *The Late Christopher Bean* and *I Remember Mama*. She pauses in her work and sits beside Shirley Jones, and in a voice as soothing as if she were singing a lullaby, puts the young woman's world back together again. As Aunt Eller says in Riggs' play, "Oh, lots of things happens to a womern. Sickness, being pore and hungry even, bein' left alone in yer old age, bein' afraid to die. And you c'n stand it. They's one way. You got to be hearty. You *got* to be."[5] Charlotte put not only the experience of a woman like Aunt Eller but that of women she had known, and mostly that of herself, into this glowing scene.

As dancer/actor James Mitchell, who played the "Dream Curly" in the film, recalled of

Charlotte, "She was a trouper through a lot of thicks and thins,"[6] and in this brief scene that experience and courage flash bright and hard as diamond.

Shirley Jones still remembers the maternal warmth and total professionalism of this "trouper," who had begun her career fifty years earlier. "I needed all the help and pats on the back and taking care of that I could get," Jones recalls, "during those nine months in Nogales, Arizona. We were working fifteen hour days, seven days a week, in extreme heat, rain and everything else. It was not an easy task for a little girl from Smithton, Pennsylvania." Jones, after all, had never acted in a film before, and had the additional responsibility of being Rodgers and Hammerstein's sole protégée. Had it not been for Charlotte, Jones says, she would have had no one to talk to among the cast. The only other woman actor on the set was Gloria Grahame, who Jones remembers was not particularly drawn to her. Charlotte was open and friendly from the start. But Jones' connection with Charlotte went deeper than mere chitchat. "She was my mother, my sister, the person I could talk to about anything," she remembers. "We always had breakfast together, and when she noticed that I was being hounded by the director and others on the set about my diet — so young and from a small town, what did I know about dieting?— she'd say, 'You know, instead of putting sugar on your oatmeal, why not try some fruit?' She handled it beautifully." Jones was also inspired by Charlotte's continued enthusiasm for her work. "She'd been in the business so long, and yet she still *loved* it. She knew what she had and she knew who she was. Sometimes people with careers as long as hers get disillusioned. Not her. She was absolutely like a kid — she thought show business was the greatest thing that ever happened."

"As an actor she was so *honest*," says Jones. "That was the thing that amazed me. Yes, in her kicking scenes she was far out and all that. But in the sensitive scenes we had together in Laurey's bedroom, she was so very, very honest," adding: "Talking to her was like talking to my own mom."[7]

Where Charlotte was concerned, something in the "kid" also needed to be a mother.

Lots of things had happened to Charlotte Greenwood to make her who she was, as woman and actor, some of them not so much because of life or fate but because, as she herself confessed, she could only do things "the hard way, the Greenwood way." And yet a lot of things had not happened as she had wished them. Her girlhood dreams of taking the stage like Bernhardt, or of pitching her contralto voice to the back of the Metropolitan Opera House in grand opera, had taken numerous beatings and, finally, bribings by the success of her comedy work to retreat to the world of ideals put to pasture.

A photograph of Charlotte taken during location shooting speaks the proverbial thousand words about the power and charisma she brought to the role of Aunt Eller — and how much she had developed as an artist since her giddy Fox musicals of a decade before.

This image, taken by Schuyler Crail, the production's still photographer, almost has the immediacy of a candid shot, though everything about it points to careful staging. Charlotte sits on a stump, wearing the blue and white checked gingham dress, apron and crocheted black shawl in which she is discovered in her first scene in the film. Behind her is the barn, split rail fence, some stray cattle, and the high bright sky. Anyone who has seen faded photographs of real frontier women will recognize many striking similarities. There are the same eyes squinted from too many hot summer suns, hands made gnarled and dark from the ceaseless labors of raising a family in a sod-house, planting and harvesting crops, milking cows in the snow. There is also the upright dignity of the lone windswept tree, or a bare but handsome mountain, raising itself as enduring proof against the passing ages.

Lynn Riggs' Aunt Eller was a small, round woman whose blank expression before the photographer belied a strong sense of humor and a kindly charity toward the weak and defenseless. Charlotte and Crail capture that strength magnificently. But something else glows, like a clear flame flickering in a battered old lantern. Charlotte gazes off across the plains, a light of hopefulness in a face set in lines of enduring what life threw at her, come what may. Everything that happens in *Oklahoma!* turns on this woman's wise guidance, yet even she is pushed to the limits of her powers in assuring her niece the greatest possible happiness — behind which is a certain desperation to enjoy, vicariously, happiness she had never known.

All this can be seen in Crail's photo, which Charlotte seems to have admired enough herself to give out to members of the cast. One such print ended up in the hands of her co-star Rod Steiger. Steiger's Jud is no mere criminal living under the guise of a farmhand but a man who, for all his anger and danger, is at the same time a tortured soul, twisted by a perpetually unmet hunger for love. With her sympathy for the underdog, Charlotte inscribed Steiger's photo with the words: "*Thank you Judd sez Aunt Eller*" — a little gesture of understanding which Charlotte, though she could not extend it on screen, made sure she offered him in real life.

"What has gone before is merely the groundwork," Charlotte wrote during the war years, when starting her film career all over again. "Now I should begin to go places, in the phrase of the day, to do something. What I have done in the theatre and on the screen is little more than preparatory work for what is to come." For a group of Philadelphia drama students, she had this advice to share: "Once you start carrying the torch, you must carry it through failures as well as successes; you must be prepared to sacrifice all of your personal interests to your ideal.... We can't wait to be discovered — we go ahead unprepared, and life invariably catches up with us."[8]

To her memoirs she confided:

> [The word discovery] always amuses me. I have been discovered three times — Broadway discovered I could dance, but didn't discover that I had been diligently practicing in secret; California discovered that I could sing, and didn't bother to inquire into the countless scales that had preceded my first stage ballad; London discovered that I could act without musical trimmings, and no one so much as asked if I had been studying drama throughout my musical comedy career.[9]

What caught up with Charlotte, in the role of Aunt Eller, was who she had wanted to be, and prepared to be, all along. Not just herself — the woman of strength, will-power and self-sufficiency, with plenty of energy left over to help with the lives of others. But also the actor of subtle, deep, arresting dramatic gifts, who could give people in silence just as much as she ever gave them in the clowning of her earlier stage and screen work.

New York Times film critic Bosley Crowther certainly sat up and noticed. "Charlotte Greenwood's rangy Aunt Eller is an unmitigated joy," he wrote in October 1955 after *Oklahoma!*'s premiere. "She has added a rare quality of real compassion to the robust rusticity of the role." In fact, few in the film received anything less than rave reviews, and its first showing, at Hollywood Boulevard's Egyptian Theatre (site of the first recorded movie premiere in 1922) was a gala event the old Egyptian had not seen for decades.

Shirley Jones and Gordon McRae arrived in a fringe-topped surrey, and following close behind were such stars as Lucille Ball, Marlene Dietrich, Jeff Chandler and Grace Kelly. Like

Lola Langdon, the glamorous drama coach from Charlotte's first film for Twentieth Century Fox, Charlotte swept on to the sidewalk in gold lamé, jewels and white fox, her age-defying golden hair drawn back in a sleek chignon. When handed her corsage for the evening — a clump of corn on the cob — despite her elegant gown and furs, she threw back her head and whooped. Aunt Eller had come to Hollywood Boulevard.

Oklahoma! is often thought to have been Charlotte Greenwood's final film, and insofar as it was her finest, it was the film by which she would and should be remembered. But like the trouper she was, through those thicks and thins, she could not remain still. As the film broke records and the cast album was selling almost as fast as the hip-jiggling croonings of Elvis Presley, Charlotte was learning another part — that of Agnes Tilbee in RKO's vehicle for grown-up Margaret O'Brien, *Glory*. The last but one of Charlotte's several on-screen co-habitations with horses, *Glory*'s plot, assured the studio, was "a romantic comedy about race horse people, not race horses." Yet from its first scene the film cheerfully reels off equine facts and figures like an earnest Pathé newsreel of an earlier era.

Partly filmed in Lexington, Kentucky, the movie casts Charlotte as O'Brien's grandmother, Agnes Tilby, widow of a horse breeder gone bust. Fallen on hard times, Agnes and her granddaughter Clarabel, played by a pert O'Brien, live in a trailer, boarding their few remaining horses at a stable. A filly is born, much to Agnes' disgust but to Clarabel's joy, and she names the filly Glory. Convincing her hard-bitten grandmother that Glory will live up to her name on the racetrack, Clarabel's obsession with a horse that never wins races turns into bankruptcy for Agnes. When money is tight, and Glory isn't winning any races, Agnes enters her in a claiming race, where she is promptly won by Chad Chadburn (John Lupton), handsome and wealthy young stable-owner and romantic interest of Clarabel. Because Clarabel is distraught at having lost the filly, Chad pulls strings to make it possible for Agnes to

Charlotte's gigantic signature, which sometimes took up the entire width of a page.

win her back in a rigged game of poker. She returns the horse to Clarabel, who enters her in the Kentucky Derby, which she wins; and of course, Clarabel also wins Chad into the bargain.

Adding additional spice to the plot is Charlotte's final screen pairing with Walter Brennan, with whom she plays up what for most who watched the film expected to be a prickly relationship turned eventually to the good. As the rough-hewn Agnes, claims the film's press book, Charlotte is given "rare opportunities to run the emotional gamut and she doesn't miss. She turns on the tears, the laughs and the temper, clucks with tender sympathy, and calls on the resources of a vocabulary well peppered with vinegar and mustard." Vinegar and mustard indeed — that Charlotte and Brennan didn't actually take swings at each other is surprising, since they spend most of the film shouting in each other's faces when not narrowly missing each other's noses with slammed doors. As with all of Charlotte's pairings with Brennan, what comes across like a warm up for a prize fight ends with a beguiling moment when it's clear that behind the raillery and insults are two hearts more than a little fond of each other. But with its predictable plot, broad gestures and dragging length, *Glory* is a come down for the woman who created Aunt Eller on screen the year before. Yet Charlotte's least useful casting was still to come: her thankless role as Lucy in a musical version of Clare Boothe Luce's 1939 script, *The Women*.

Renamed *The Opposite Sex*, with lyrics by Nicholas Brodszky and music by Sammy Cahn, the film has suffered from comparisons to *The Women*, and as with most comparisons, there is an element of unfairness in the judgments passed. *New York Times* critic A. H. Weiler decries much of Joan Collins' cheesecakery in the role of the chorus girl turned husband-snatcher, Crystal, but in truth she is at least as wickedly saucy as Joan Crawford in the same role, and far more kittenishly attractive. June Alyson makes a clever, good-hearted Kay (she whose husband gets snatched by Crystal), her creamy alto singing voice audible proof of her character's goodness. As Sylvia, society dame and gossip par excellence, Dolores Gray wears bitchery as redolent as Chanel No. 5, while plump, long-lashed Joan Blondell (veteran, with Charlotte, of the Hollywood Victory Caravan) sensuously promotes the joys of motherhood like a domesticated Venus. And few would quibble with Agnes Moorehead's campy sendup of the much-divorced Countess Lavaliere, in her loud greens and purples, furs and pearls.

Charlotte's own role was just as campy — that of Lucy, proprietress of a dude ranch in Nevada for divorcées-to-be. She doesn't appear until the film's second half, she has no songs to sing, but her gangly figure, dressed in jeans, boots, bandanna and cowboy hat, is memorable, as is the resounding thwack she places with a large flat hand on Moorehead's rear-end, just as the Countess prepares to sail grandly into the ranch house. (A gesture perhaps given in retaliatory fun for all the times Moorehead, playing Charlotte's crabby secretary on *The Charlotte Greenwood Show*, complained of her employer's too-democratic behavior.) Over many years Charlotte had become experienced at making silk purses out of sow's ears. Watching her make the best of so little, in her last turn before a film camera, it's easy to revisit discerning critics' laments of her wasted talents expressed three decades before. It was the same old story: with a few exceptions, such as Allan Dwan, Walter Lang, Henry Hathaway and Fred Zinnemann, neither directors nor editors seemed to know how to capture or package the phenomenon that was Charlotte Greenwood. With her last two screen roles so quickly forgotten, it's also easy to see why many think that Aunt Eller was Charlotte's last part before retiring. It's just as well they think so. The ugly duckling had had her fun playing a swan.

34

Farewell Performance

Cʜᴀʀʟᴏᴛᴛᴇ's ʀᴇᴛɪʀᴇᴍᴇɴᴛ ʙʀᴏᴜɢʜᴛ ᴡɪᴛʜ ɪᴛ not a renewed effort at completing and publishing her memoirs, which were heaped with all accompanying notes into a cardboard box, but an even greater immersion in Christian Science. Not even Oscar Hammerstein's offer of the part of the Mother Superior in the film version of *The Sound of Music* could entice Charlotte out of her comfortable domestic routine.[1]

It was two years later that a future playwright was to meet Charlotte and Martin at the organ console of the Christian Science church in Westwood Village.

By that time, remembers William Luce (author of *The Belle of Amherst* and other renowned one-person plays), the couple were very much entrenched in the Church, with Martin working full-time as a practitioner and Charlotte doing her own kind of practicing of Mary Baker Eddy's credo for a few close friends. (Contrary to what is sometimes written about Charlotte, she was never a formal practitioner, though Luce remembers she was registered as a practitioner after Martin's death.)

Martin, in fact, was probably already tiring of the Church — he would reveal as much to Luce in later years — but Charlotte seemed to grow ever stronger in her faith and belief in Mrs. Eddy's system. These were the years when Charlotte, Martin and Doris Day were close; Day and husband Marty Melcher, in fact, were present when the Broones couple met Luce after the service that Sunday. Mary Dean, the church's soloist, suggested that Luce, a published poet since boyhood, could write lyrics for Martin's sacred songs. Luce soon became not just Martin's lyricist but also something of the son he and Charlotte never had.

That the couple, though past middle age, were still in love with each other came as a delightful surprise to Luce. "They were very close and solicitous of one another," he recalls. "I noticed that they were playful, in that they enjoyed humor and banter — he especially."

Martin, he recalls, often called Charlotte by the rough-and-tumble nickname "Butch," while to her, Martin was always "my darling." (According to Martin's inscription in a book of poems given to Charlotte, he apparently enjoyed the nickname "Barkis," after the Dickens cart driver who was so willing to marry Clara the maid in *David Copperfield*— another hint at the playfulness, and shared literary tastes, of the Broones marriage.)

Till the end of her life, Charlotte would turn any and all conversations to this favorite topic of "my darling."

Luce began to pay visits to the Rodeo Drive house to work with Martin on songs, and

Mr. and Mrs. Martin Broones, photographed outside the doors of First Church of Christ, Scientist, Beverly Hills, California, circa 1969. William Luce collection.

found the rambling old villa somewhat unkempt. Charlotte and Martin still used the pool, beside which Martin was often to be found, roasted to a golden brown. Luce was convinced that Martin's piano-black hair was not quite due to nature, and noted that Charlotte maintained her own blonde locks, peroxided for her regularly by Martin himself. Because they had been in cahoots to conceal Charlotte's true age since the start of their marriage (even to telling the census taker, in 1930, that Charlotte was the same age as her younger husband), there was no way they could stop now, when she really was on the brink of being an old lady — according, at least, to her well-hidden Philadelphia birth certificate.

Luce also noticed that the couple never dined in their silk-carpeted dining room, with its Grecian-inspired china and Bohemian cut glass goblets, but instead heated Stouffer's boxed dinners in the big kitchen or got take-out from Nate 'N' Al's Deli not far from their house and sat there eating it at the kitchen table. The Brooneses went to Chasen's for the occasional grand appearance and the famous chili, Charlotte in her sealskin cape and Martin as dapper as if he had never left London's fashionable squares.

Even with its frayed edges and chipped paint, 806 North Rodeo Drive was an experience Luce never failed to appreciate. On his arrival at the front door, he would push the doorbell, activating the intercom. Charlotte, he recalls, almost always answered, because the speaker was near her desk in her office upstairs. "Hello?" the big voice would boom through the tiny speaker. "It's Bill, Charlotte," Luce would announce. "Hello, Bill!" the big voice continued. Without covering the speaker, Charlotte would then lean back in her chair and call out to Martin: *"Darling! Your boyfriend's here!"* — a reference that amused Luce at the time and later became endearing. Martin would answer the door and show Luce into the foyer, where Charlotte's glamorous Flora Lion portrait gazed down from the stair landing, then usher him into his office and seat him at the big Chinese Chippendale desk, or into the room where the piano and the walls of Charlotte's memorabilia were, and they would set to work. Luce and Martin ultimately wrote over a dozen songs together, some of them recorded by Doris Day and Gordon McRae.

Martin once looked up from some of Luce's verses and told him, "You should be writing for theatre." It was a kind of premonition, though he would not live to see it fulfilled.

Whether because he felt a need to counteract his doubts about his Church work with frantic busyness, or to keep pace with Charlotte's enthusiasm, Martin maintained a heavy schedule as a lecturer and practitioner, traveling around the country and ignoring the challenges brought on by increasing age.

In the mid–1960s Luce visited him at Rodeo Drive after one of these grueling trips. "He had had a rough lecture tour," Luce recalls, "during which time he'd fallen and hurt his leg or hip. He wasn't free from pain after that time." Luce, who felt concerned that Martin would not see a physician for his ailment, had seen him struggling to walk home from an errand along Sunset Boulevard and to Martin's manifest relief gave him a lift to the house. It was during this visit, perhaps egged on by the nagging physical pain in his body, that Martin touched on other troubles — namely, his doubts about the Church organization.

By this time, Luce had moved on from playing organ for the Church and was soon to leave the organization altogether, slowly feeling his way to a writing career. This circumstance clearly did not trouble Martin — if anything, he seemed relieved. He said, "'Bill, I'm glad you're still young enough to move away from the church and go into a creative field,'" Luce remembers. "He told me he was too old and too long away from the entertainment industry to 'catch up.'" (Luce remembers hearing that Day had, rightly if mercilessly, commented that Martin's music was "old hat" — what catching up Martin would have had to do would probably have taken more time and energy than the sick and aging man had left.)

Martin hinted to Luce that he was having strange sensations in his heart, physical symptoms "that he didn't like." He admitted that he knew whereof he spoke because he had studied pre-med at Columbia University, a revelation that took Luce, used to Martin the anti-medical Christian Science lecturer and healer, by surprise. Martin had smoked in the 1920s, but was not a drinker. With Charlotte, who had picked up her share of bad eating habits on the road, Martin was a hearty and unwise eater. He was in his late sixties and overweight, a fact of which he must have been aware though it appears he did nothing to address the problem. The fast-paced days of managing Charlotte's career, of travel and rehearsals and dashing from place to place, of thrilling excitement before premieres, had been taken up since the 1950s with the increasingly sedentary work of being a practitioner, meeting with clients sitting across from him at his Chippendale desk, or conveying treatments via telephone. Even the lecture trips and other Church business were no match for the exhilaration of his busy days and nights in show business. This inactive life, with the ordinary effects of aging and lack of all medical oversight of his health, would soon take their toll.

For whatever reason — Luce's separation from the church and pursuit of a creative career is as good as any — in his last conversation with Luce, Martin made it clear in serious tones that his involvement with the Church was little more than a matter of going through the motions. He had lost his faith in the organization, he admitted, and had also clearly feared for what it and its demands would do to his young friend. Watching Luce's development as a writer was a bright spot in Martin's last year of life. In August 1971, Luce was in Las Vegas. He was about to leave his hotel room when Martin called him from Beverly Hills. Luce remembers, "Always solicitous for my happiness and health, he reiterated what he had said many times — how much I meant to him. He again said how at peace he felt about my moving into a new life and out of the Church organization. 'You're safe now,' he said. As he signed off, he laughingly told me to put a nickel in a slot machine for him. It wasn't till I was back home in California a week later that I learned he had died."

On arriving home, Luce found a letter from Charlotte, asking him to call her. "She said she wanted to tell me herself and not have me read it somewhere," he recalls, "or hear it from someone other than herself." As it turned out, Martin had died of a heart attack in the early hours of morning, after making his evening call to Luce's hotel room. He was seventy years old.

Perhaps this was what Charlotte, in girding herself in Christian Science and its uncompromising unacceptance of death as the final curtain, had been preparing for — but Martin's sudden loss shook her as nothing else in her long life had done. From perspectives personal and professional, he had been everything to her. His music had brought her success in New York and London; later, he had given up his own career as composer and impresario to manage hers as theatre and movie star. And as their friend Judge Robert Kincaid noted in the 1940s, "Never have I seen two people so content, so absorbed in each other." They had truly had one of those rare marriages of equal affinities, the breaking up of which is not so much the separation of one of a pair from the other as the splitting of a single personality.

"I'm just old fashioned enough to look on marriage as something more important than a perpetual horse show or Easter Parade or grand march," Charlotte jotted in notes she did not use in her memoirs. "[I]t is a serious business and must be founded on compatibility and community of interests. A man may be just the right height, but if he likes music and you like bridge — there's trouble ahead."

Charlotte and Cyril Ring had been from opposite poles, of interests, of ambition, of worlds. Martin had meshed with her perfectly on all levels. When Luce went to see Charlotte, he remembers how even with him she put on her armor of faith and optimism. "My darling is here, right now," she told him vigorously. "He has not gone anywhere. *He is with us.*" Some of this was Christian Science creed, but for the most part it was powered by the ironclad conviction Charlotte had had since her sickly, accident-filled, yearning childhood — that if she believed in something long and hard enough, it would become reality. Inspiration had served her this long; there was no reason for her to doubt or abandon it now, any more than Martin had ever let her down at any time in their many years of marriage.

But Martin's death was troubling in other ways, at least to Luce and to the Christian Science practitioner who had tried to help him in his last hours.

"Charlotte told me about the night he started failing," Luce remembers. "Martin was in bed with the phone to his ear, very weak and failing fast, listening to a Christian Science friend and practitioner in San Francisco. She was delivering a rousing but ineffective verbal prayer-treatment of CS platitudes. Charlotte couldn't understand why this pillar of the Church couldn't heal 'her darling.' 'He just slipped away,' she told me. Later, the friend in San Francisco told me that she couldn't seem to reach Martin — that she had failed him. She was distraught that the healing power had not availed itself in this case." Luce wanted to tell her, "Well, Charlotte should've called the medics."

Whether medical help at what was (per his death certificate) the late stage of advanced heart disease could have done anything to help Martin is questionable. But Luce — and possibly Charlotte — was haunted for years by the might-have-beens.

Epilogue

THE NEXT SIX YEARS of Charlotte Greenwood's life were a gradual winding down and a catalog of increasing health problems, all of which she denied with the same forcefulness with which she affirmed that Martin was still with her, impervious to death.[1]

Well before Martin's passing, many of Charlotte's friends and colleagues from the old days had died: Hedda Hopper in 1966 (Charlotte read Mrs. Eddy's words at her service, which was conducted in secrecy to — ironically — keep the press away) and Buster Keaton the same year. Eddie Cantor died two years before that, and Edward Everett Horton had died the year before Martin. Carmen Miranda, who had first shot to stardom in Charlotte's 1943 film *Down Argentine Way*, died of a sudden heart attack in 1955 the night after shooting a television program.

Oscar Hammerstein II, the great believer in Charlotte's ability as a serious actor, had died in 1960, and though Richard Rodgers was still going strong on his own, his poor health physically and emotionally made life a continued challenge. Charlotte's ex-sister in law, Blanche Ring, long faded from her former stardom and from most people's memories, had died in 1961; Cyril Ring died six years later.

Younger actors from Charlotte's Twentieth Century Fox days were still around but were in retirement or doing something else: Shirley Temple (now Mrs. Black) had run for Congress on the Republican ticket, had worked for the United Nations, and would become U.S. ambassador to Ghana; Betty Grable had gone from possessing legs insured by Lloyd's of London for $1 million in the 1940s to taking jobs in commercials and in nightclubs in the 60s (she died of cancer in 1973).

Like her circle of Golden Age film and stage colleagues, Charlotte's household was reduced — just herself and her secretary-companion, Lillian Stransky, a fellow Christian Scientist who managed all her affairs and who would be her co-executor after death. Life in the rambling Rodeo Drive house eventually became problematic for the eighty-one-year-old Charlotte, who was suffering from debilitating arthritis in her legs. Years of fan kicks, impromptu splits, Camel Walks, pratfalls and non-stop dancing since her early teens had finally caught up with her. She couldn't get up the stairs and had to move to the ground floor.

Even as Martin had let his own health condition grow out of control because he would not seek medical intervention, Charlotte refused to receive medical treatment or relief from the pain of her disabling arthritis. She would go even further than that — to deny that such a thing as arthritis even existed.

One concession was made to Charlotte's health situation, and one that must have cost her dear: to leave Beverly Hills and enter Broadview, a Christian Science rest home in Pasadena. Here she could have access to CS practitioners as she needed them, to help her through her bouts of pain and the depression from barely being able to walk. The treatments seem to have done her too much good, from the point of view of Broadview's staff. Luce remembers coming to visit Charlotte at the rest home, and before he had even seen her, hearing her stentorian voice rolling down the hallway as she gave a Christian Science affirmation to a captive listener in a wheelchair: "*There is no Mind in matter,*" she intoned, "*and no matter in Mind....*"

According to Luce, Charlotte's vigorous and uncontrollable habit of giving impromptu treatments to her fellow Broadview residents was a problem for the management, and perhaps Broadview itself took some getting used to for Charlotte, with its sudden reduction of her living space from a Beverly Hills mansion to a single room. (Charlotte did generously remember the institution in her will.)[2]

Luce also believes Charlotte's need to be an actor even here was partly the reason for her interference in the other residents' lives. "She had to be on," he notes. "She had to be performing. It was ingrained in her. There was no stopping this big, tall creature roaming the halls in her chenille bathrobe, 'preaching the gospel to every creature.'"

Stransky soon found another home for Charlotte, an apartment in Westwood, at the corner of Wilshire Boulevard and Comstock. By this time, in 1976, Luce had written *The Belle of Amherst* for Julie Harris. She took the one-woman play, based on the life and works of poet Emily Dickinson, to Broadway, where it became a classic success and a classic of its genre, winning Harris her fifth Tony Award. Luce kept Charlotte apprised of his and the play's progress, and remembers her "pride and joy," like that of a mother for her child. She also told him that Martin had often predicted all this for him. "'My darling knew all this would happen,'" Luce recalls her telling him. When Harris recorded the play (winning a Grammy Award), Luce sent Charlotte a copy of the LP set and received a loving note in return: "I know you are happy with your progress, and so [am I]."

When *The Belle* reached Los Angeles, Luce invited Charlotte to the first performance at the Huntington Hartford Theatre. By this time, walking at all was a struggle for her, even with Lillian to help her. Undaunted, Charlotte got dressed in her best and attended a performance. Afterward, Luce hurried back to Harris' dressing room. "I told her that Charlotte Greenwood was here, and wanted to thank her for the performance, but couldn't make it up the steps to the dressing room area. Julie said, 'I'll come to where she is!'"

Luce and Lillian helped Charlotte down the aisle to the lip of the stage, where Harris, still in her white dress from the performance, knelt down to Charlotte's eye level. Harris took Charlotte's hand and said, "Oh, I've always loved you." Remembers Luce: "And Charlotte, taking her cue, replied in a large voice that filled the Huntington Hartford, 'And I've always loved you.'"

Luce's last meeting with Charlotte was at the Westwood apartment, in December 1977. "I was running errands in Los Angeles before leaving the following Friday for South Africa," he says. "Our meeting was like others that followed Martin's death in 1971, with conversation about him. Her legs were so extremely bowed by arthritis, she moved only with great difficulty. She told me that a woman in church had said, 'My dear, we know that your arthritis can be healed.' Charlotte proudly described her reply to the woman. 'I don't know what you mean. Arthritis is *not* in a Christian Scientist's vocabulary.' She was like a ramrod, but that was part of a certain inflexibility that extended even to her work in theatre. Revisions were not in Charlotte's vocabulary."

That was December 13. Almost two weeks later, on December 28, 1977, Charlotte died. So total was her seclusion in her last years that the news of her death was unknown to most people until months later. The dismantling of the Rodeo Drive house had already begun, and now in earnest, since Charlotte had directed that the house and belongings not bequeathed to specific heirs be sold upon her death. Shortly after it was sold, the house, one of the first to be built in Beverly Hills, and its noble Himalayan cedars were razed and the lot overtaken by a sprawling columned mansion.[3]

The New York Times ran a single column obituary on Valentine's Day 1978, along with a photo of Charlotte as Aunt Eller, the text of which contains the usual errors — Charlotte did not begin making films in 1930 (her first was in 1918); *So Long Letty* was made in 1929, not a year later; *Oklahoma!* premiered in 1955, not a year earlier. And the headline and first paragraph make it clear that the obit writer on staff at the *Times* knew only the rudiments of Charlotte's serious theatre and film work, describing her as "...Stage and Film Comedian Known for Her High Kick..." No mention of her dramatic stage successes as lauded by James Agate and Alexander Woollcott and Heywood Broun — her roles in *The Late Christopher Bean* or *I Remember Mama*; nothing in depth about her revelatory screen performance as Aunt Eller. This was one exit line that Charlotte, who loved to perform long after the show was over and could not bear that anything should escape her audience's notice, would gladly have proven wrong.[4]

Yet what Charlotte gave the greater world through her filmed kicks and clowning was not to be despised or displaced, even by the serious theatre roles witnessed by a comparative few of which she was so proud. She had decided for herself at the very start of her career that what she hoped most of all to give those who watched her performances, and those whom she hoped would read her never-published memoirs, was the one thing she had had since the beginning and the last thing at the end, that had kept her talent and her will alive: *inspiration*.

Writing the final lines of her book at her desk in her Beverly Hills study (July 1941), Charlotte mused:

> [I]t suddenly occurs to me that I have drifted far away from the original object of this volume. It first had form as a minor essay of an inspirational sort; it seems to have developed into a sort of biography. And yet it should not be accepted as such for that is my most remote object. I felt at the beginning that I might provide something helpful for the lonely child who felt that her size had condemned her to perpetual existence as a wallflower, as if height were a blight. I felt that I should tell her about the tall trees in the forest which never try to cringe but go on reaching toward the sky, a beacon and an inspiration to all lesser trees.
>
> On this desk in front of me is perhaps material enough for a half dozen books but, frankly — and I do not write in a spirit of false modesty — I do not think they would be worth either the trouble of writing or reading. Mine, in the final analysis, has been to date an interesting but scarcely an important life.... I can see myself now, eyes bright, face shining and eager ... Somehow I believe it was this eagerness and willingness to be part of the fun that eventually helped me to wiggle out of my predicament and capitalize on my shortcomings and, as the copybooks put it, forge ahead. I may have forged much but [then] I am a head above most folks.[5]

That desire to join and not just watch the parade had made a celebration of her own life. Few would not wish to cheer Charlotte Greenwood as she and all her high-flying colors passed them by.

END

Afterword
by William Luce

I WELCOME THIS EXCELLENT BIOGRAPHY of Charlotte Greenwood by Grant Hayter-Menzies. Charlotte's life story as written here is a consummation of shared hopes. For Charlotte, who entrusted to me her memoirs and journals before she died, it was her hope for being remembered. For me, the desire for this book was to honor the family-like love extended to me by Charlotte and her adored husband, Martin Broones. Lastly, through Grant, who met the private Charlotte through my eyes and heart — that very warm, very real woman — this biography has become more than shared hopes. Grant has made it a reality. Here at last is the true story of this ingenious, funny, original entertainer, brilliant in theater and film, a fine dramatic actress and a wonderful comedienne.

William Luce wrote the award winning Broadway play The Belle of Amherst *for actress Julie Harris. His works for theater, opera, film and concert have been performed by many artists, including Renée Fleming, Christopher Plummer, Claire Bloom, Zoe Caldwell and George C. Scott.*

Appendices

Cast lists are not complete. Many credits for Charlotte's early stage performances are not verified — and in some cases they are missing — in my main source outside of Charlotte's own memoirs, the Internet Broadway Database (IBDB).

Appendix A: Greenwood's Performance History

1905

The White Cat—Ned Wayburn, co-director with Herbert Gresham; produced by Klaw & Erlanger; music by Ludwig Englander; book by Arthur Collins and adapted by Harry B. Smith; New Amsterdam Theater. Seymour Brown (Migonet), Herbert Corthell (Prince Plump), Henriette Cropper (The Fairy Queen), Patrick Dawe (Knocko), Charlotte Greenwood (Chorus).

1905–1906

"Vacation tour" in summer with Max and Gertrude Hoffman, featuring the latter and the Dolly Sisters.

1907

The Rogers Brothers in Panama—The Rogers Brothers. Gus Rogers (Hugo Kisser), Max Rogers (A. Gustav Windt), Flo Hengler (Pequita), May Hengler (Nita), Alfred Hickman (Hunting Coyne), George Lydecker (Camillo Mendoza), Lottie Greenwood (Lola).

1908

Nearly a Hero— Sam Bernard, director Charlotte Greenwood... Chorus and stand-in for star Grace La Rue for one performance in the touring company. Eunice Burnham, another chorus member, joined Charlotte after the run of the show in a duo.

1909–1911

Duo vaudeville act, "Two Girls and a Piano" Charlotte Greenwood and Eunice Burnham.

1912

The Passing Show of 1912— produced by The Winter Garden Company; music by Louis A. Hirsch; Winter Garden, Charlotte Greenwood (Fanny Silly); Harem Maid; Fannie.

1913

The Man with Three Wives (operetta), Franz Lehár; J. C. Huffman and William J. Watson, co-directors; Lee and J.J. Shubert, producers; Weber & Fields Theater. Stewart Baird (Captain Adhemar), Sophye Barnard (Colette, instructress of ballet school), James Billings (Blix, a tourist), Dolly Castles (Olivia, proprietress of the Germanium Inn), Sydney Grant (Wendelin, a country bridegroom), Ida Jeanne (Suzette, Colette's maid), Charlotte Greenwood (Chorus, not listed as such on the Internet Broadway Database).

The Passing Show of 1913— produced by The Winter Garden Company; music by Jean Schwartz and Al. W. Brown; book by Harold Atteridge. (Charlotte left this show early in the 58-perform-

233

ance run, which may account for why she is not listed on IBDB).

1914

The Tik-Tok Man of Oz—Oliver Morosco, producer (touring production). Charlotte Greenwood (Queen Ann Soforth of Oogaboo).

    Pretty Mrs. Smith (musical)—book by Oliver Morosco, producer, and Elmer Harris; lyrics by Earl Carroll; music by Henry James and Alfred Robyn; Casino Theatre. Fritzi Scheff (Drucilla Smith), Charlotte Greenwood (Letitia Proudfoot), Sydney Grant (Bobby Jones), James A. Gleason (George).

1916 (opened in California 1915)

So Long Letty (musical)—Oliver Morosco, producer; music and lyrics by Earl Carroll; Shubert Theater. Charlotte Greenwood (Letty), May Boley, Sydney Grant, Percy Bronson.

1918

Jane (silent film)—Paramount/Famous Players-Lasky; Frank Lloyd, director. Charlotte Greenwood (Jane), Sydney Grant (William Tipson), Forrest Stanley (Charles Shackleton), Myrtle Stedman (Lucy Norton).

1919

Linger Longer Letty (musical)—play by Anne Nichols, produced by Oliver Morosco; music by Alfred Goodman; lyrics by Bernard Grosman; Fulton Theater. Frances Bendsten (Lazelle), Oscar Figman (Father), Charlotte Greenwood (Letty), Arthur Hartley (Walter), Olin Howland (Jim), Cyril Ring (Colonel).

1920

Let 'Er Go, Letty (musical)—Oliver Morosco, producer; opened and closed in New Haven.

1922

Letty Pepper (musical)—Oliver Morosco, producer and George Hobart, co-writers; music by Werner Janssen; Vanderbilt Theatre. William Balfour (Mack), Hallam Bosworth (Hutchinson), Paul Burns (Abe Greenbaum), Charlotte Greenwood (Letty Pepper).

1922

Music Box Revue—by Irving Berlin; Hassard Short, director; Music Box Theatre. Jobyna Howland,

Sydney Grant, Charlotte Greenwood, Trixie Friganza, Anna Wheaton, Shirley Kellogg.

1924

Hassard Short's Ritz Revue—Hassard Short, director; Ritz Theater. Charlotte Greenwood, Eddie Conrad, Raymond Hitchcock, Chester Hale, Leila Ricard, Albertina Vitak.

1926

Vaudeville tour of "Her Morning Bath" sketch from the Ritz Revue, which Charlotte bought from actress-playwright Norma Mitchell.

1927

Rufus Lemaire's Affairs—Rufus LeMaire, producer; Bud Murray, director; Martin Broones, composer; Ballard MacDonald, book and lyrics; Majestic Theater. Charlotte Greenwood (replacing Sophie Tucker), Ted Lewis, Lester Allen, Peggy Fears, Martin Broones.

1928

Baby Mine (silent film)—Metro-Goldwyn-Mayer; Robert Z. Leonard, director. Karl Dane (Oswald Hardy), George K. Arthur (Jimmy Hemingway), Charlotte Greenwood (Emma), Louise Lorraine (Helen).

1929

So Long Letty (film—Charlotte's first talkie)—Warner Brothers; Lloyd Bacon, director. Charlotte Greenwood (Letty Robbins), Claude Gillingwater (Uncle Claude), Grant Withers (Harry Miller), Patsy Ruth Miller (Grace Miller), Bert Roach (Tommy Robbins).

    She Couldn't Say No (play)—Henry Duffy, producer, El Capitan in Hollywood and Alcazar Theatre in SF; renamed *Mebbe* and opened in Chicago week before Easter 1930.

1930

Love Your Neighbor (short film)—Educational Films Corp.

1931

Girls Will Be Boys (short film)—Educational Films Corp.; William Watson, director. Charlotte Greenwood, Vernon Dent, Eddie Baker.

    The Christmas Party (short film)—Metro-

Goldwyn-Mayer; Charles Reisner, director. As herself, with Jackie Cooper, Norma Shearer, Louis B. Mayer and others.

Jackie Cooper's Birthday Party (short film) — Metro-Goldwyn-Mayer; Charles Reisner, director. As herself, with Jackie Cooper, Lionel Barrymore, Wallace Beery, Marion Davies, Marie Dressler, Jimmy Durante, Clark Gable, Harpo Marx, Ramon Novarro, Anita Page and Norma Shearer.

"Parlor, Bedroom and Bath" (play) — Play by Charles Bell and Mark Swan.

Parlor, Bedroom and Bath (film) — Metro-Goldwyn-Mayer; Edward Sedgwick, director. Buster Keaton (Reginald Irving), Charlotte Greenwood (Polly Hathaway), Reginald Denny (Jeffrey Hathaway), Dorothy Christie (Angelica Embrey), Sally Eilers (Virginia Embrey), Art Direction: Cedric Gibbons, Costumes: René Hubert.

Stepping Out (film) — Metro-Goldwyn-Mayer; Charles Reisner, director. Charlotte Greenwood (Sally), Reginald Denny (Tom), Leila Hyams (Eve), Lillian Bond (Cleo), Cliff Edwards (Paul).

The Man in Possession (film) — Metro-Goldwyn-Mayer; Sam Wood, director. Raymond Dabney (Robert Montgomery), Clara (Charlotte Greenwood), Crystal Wetherby (Irene Purcell), Claude Dabney (Reginald Owen), Mr. Dabney (C. Aubrey Smith), Mrs. Dabney (Beryl Mercer), Sir Charles Cartwright (Alan Mowbray).

Flying High (film) — Metro-Goldwyn-Mayer; Charles Reisner, director. Bert Lahr (Rusty Krouse), Charlotte Greenwood (Pansy Potts), Pat O'Brien (Sport Wardell), Kathryn Crawford (Eileen Smith), Charles Winninger (Dr. Brown), Hedda Hopper (Mrs. Smith), Art Direction: Cedric Gibbons, Costumes: Adrian Dances: Busby Berkeley.

Palmy Days (film) — United Artists; A. Edward Sutherland, director. Eddie Cantor (Eddie Simpson), Charlotte Greenwood (Helen Martin), Barbara Weeks (Joan Clark), Charles Middleton (Yolando), George Raft (Yolando's Henchman), Costumes: Coco Chanel and Alice O'Neill.

1932

Cheaters at Play (film) — Twentieth Century; Hamilton McFadden, director. Thomas Meighan (Michael Lanyard), Charlotte Greenwood (Mrs. Crozier), William Bakewell (Maurice Perry), Ralph Morgan (Freddy Isquith), Barbara Weeks (Fenno Crozer).

Wild Violets (musical comedy) — Louis Dreyfus, producer; Robert Stolz, composer; Bruno Hardt-Warden's German libretto as translated and adapted by Hassard Short, director, Desmond Carter and Reginald Purdell; Theatre Royal, Drury Lane, Jerry Verno (Hans Katzen), Charlotte Greenwood (Augusta), Irene Potter (Greta), Louis Hayward (Carl Hoffman), John Garrick (Paul Hoffman), Wilfred Watson (Henriche), Esmond Knight (Otto Bergmann), Jean Cadell (Madam Hoffman), Adele Dixon (Liesl).

1933

The Late Christopher Bean (play) — Henry Duffy, producer; Russell Fillmore, staging and direction. Raymond Brown (Dr. Haggett), Marion Clayton (Susan Haggett), Charlotte Greenwood (Abby), Sarah Edwards (Mrs. Haggett), Adele Carples (Ada Haggett), William Carey (Warren Creamer), Emmett Vogan (Tallant), Craufurd Kent (Rosen), Reginald Mason (Davenport).

1934

Orders Is Orders (British film) — Gaumont-British; Walter Forde, director. Charlotte Greenwood (Wanda), James Gleason (Ed Waggermeyer), Cyril Maude (Colonel Bellamy), Finlay Currie (Dave), Ray Milland (Dashwood), Sir Cedric Hardwicke (Brigadier).

Three Sisters (operetta) — Jerome Kern and Oscar Hammerstein II; Theatre Royal, Drury Lane. Charlotte Greenwood (Tiny Barbour), Adele Dixon, Esmond Knight, Victoria Hopper, Eliot Makeham (Mr. Barbour).

Hollywood Party (film) — Metro-Goldwyn-Mayer, Jane (uncredited) in "Schnarzan" sequence with Jimmy Durante as "Schnarzan."

1935

Gay Deceivers (musical comedy) — Reginald Arkell, Martin Broones and Moises Simon; Gaiety Theatre, London. Clifford Mollison (Pat Russell), David Hutcheson (Bob Ferris), Charlotte Greenwood (Isabel Ferris), Gina Malo (Vivienne), Walter Williams (Horace Lavelle), Clare Luce (Maricousa Lavelle), Dances and Ensembles: Frederick Lord.

1935–1939

Leaning on Letty (play) — Henry Duffy, producer. First toured US, then taken on world tour, reached Australia before the outbreak of war cancelled remaining engagements.

1940

Star Dust (film) — Twentieth Century Fox; Walter Lang, director. Linda Darnell (Carolyn Sayres),

John Payne (Ambrose Fillmore aka Bud Borden), Roland Young (Thomas Brooke), Charlotte Greenwood (Lola Langdon), William Gargan (Dane Wharton), Mary Healy (Mary Andrews), Donald Meek (Sam Wellman), George Montgomery (Ronnie).

Young People (film) — Twentieth Century Fox; Allan Dwan, director. Shirley Temple (Wendy Ballantine), Jack Oakie (Joe Ballantine), Charlotte Greenwood (Kit Ballantine), Arleen Whelan (Judith), George Montgomery (Mike Shea), Kathleen Howard (Hester Appleby).

Down Argentine Way (film) — Twentieth Century Fox; Irving Cummings, director. Don Ameche (Ricardo Quintana), Betty Grable (Glenda Crawford), Carmen Miranda (Herself), Charlotte Greenwood (Binnie Crawford), Leonid Kinskey (Tito Acuna).

1941

Tall, Dark and Handsome (film) — Twentieth Century Fox; H. Bruce Humberstone, director. Cesar Romero (Shep Morrison), Virginia Gilmore (Judy), Charlotte Greenwood (Winnie), Milton Berle (Frosty).

Moon Over Miami (film) — Twentieth Century Fox; Walter Lang, director. Don Ameche (Phil O'Neill), Betty Grable (Kathryn Latimer), Robert Cummings (Jeffrey Boulton), Carole Landis (Barbara Latimer), Jack Haley (Jack O'Hara), Charlotte Greenwod (Susan Latimer), Costumes: Travis Banton.

The Perfect Snob (film) — Twentieth Century Fox; Ray McCarey, director. Charles Ruggles (Dr. Mason), Charlotte Greenwood (Martha Mason), Lynn Bari (Chris Mason), Cornel Wilde (Mike Lord). Anthony Quinn (Alex Moreno).

1942

Springtime in the Rockies (film) — Twentieth Century Fox; Irving Cummings, director. Betty Grable (Vicky Lane). Carmen Miranda (Rosita Murphy), John Payne (Dan Christy), Cesar Romero (Victor Prince), Charlotte Greenwood (Phoebe Gray), Edward Everett Horton (MacTavish).

1943

Leaning on Letty (play) — Henry Duffy, producer; Wilson Theater (opened Jan. 24, 1943).

Dixie Dugan (film) — Twentieth Century Fox; Otto Brower, director. James Ellison (Roger Hudson), Charlotte Greenwood (Mrs. Gladys Dugan), Charles Ruggles (Pa Dugan), Lois Andrews (Dixie Dugan).

The Gang's All Here (film) — Twentieth Century Fox; Busby Berkeley, director/dance director. Alice Faye (Edie Allen), Carmen Miranda (Dorita), Phil Baker (Himself), Benny Goodman (Himself), Eugene Pallette (Andrew Mason Sr.), Charlotte Greenwood (Mrs. Peyton Potter aka Buttercup Murphy), Edward Everett Horton (Peyton Potter).

1944

Up in Mabel's Room (film) — Edward Small Productions, producer; United Artists, distributor; Allan Dwan, director. Marjorie Reynolds (Geraldine Ainsworth), Dennis O'Keefe (Gary Ainsworth), Gail Patrick (Mabel Essington), Mischa Auer (Boris), Charlotte Greenwood (Martha).

Home in Indiana (film) — Twentieth Century Fox; Henry Hathaway, director. Walter Brennan ("Thunder" Bolt), Lon McAllister (Sparke Thornton), Jeanne Crain (Char Bruce), June Haver (Cri-Cri Boole), Charlotte Greenwood (Penny Bolt), Ward Bond (Jed Bruce), George Reed (Tuppy).

1944–1946

The Charlotte Greenwood Show (radio). Starting as a stand-in for Bob Hope's Pepsodent Hour, Charlotte had a show of her own by the second season, sponsored by Hallmark Cards. A rumor persists, abetted by a flawed Internet Movie Database mini-bio by Bill Takacs, that during this period Charlotte was given a part in *Annie Get Your Gun*, a role eventually so decimated by a rapacious Ethel Merman's demands that Charlotte handed in her resignation. Merman biographer Brian Kellow dismisses this rumor, and a glance at Charlotte's radio, film and stage commitments for the 1946–1947 period during which *Annie Get Your Gun* was produced shows there was no time for her to have even considered taking part in the Broadway hit.

1946

Wake Up and Dream (film) — Walter Morosco, producer; Twentieth Century Fox; Lloyd Bacon, director. John Payne (Jeff Cairn), June Haver (Jenny), Charlotte Greenwood (Sara March), Connie Marshall (Nella Cairn), Clem Bevans (Henry Pecket).

1947

Driftwood (film) — Republic; Allan Dwan, director. Ruth Warrick (Susan Moore), Walter Brennan (Murph), Dean Jagger (Dr. Steve Webster), Charlotte Greenwood (Mathilda), Natalie Wood (Jenny Hollingsworth), H.B. Warner (Reverend Hollingsworth).

1947–1949

I Remember Mama (play) — Russell Lewis and Howard Young, producers; Russell Fillmore, director. National touring company. For this performance, Charlotte won the San Francisco Drama Critics Award. Katrin (Jean Ruth), Mama (Charlotte Greenwood), Papa (Grandon Rhodes), Dagmar (Mary Joan Bradley), Christine (Eleanor Lawson), Mr. Hyde (John Pimley), Nels (Raymond Roe), Aunt Trina (Marie Bainbridge), Aunt Sigrid (Elizabeth Roadman), Aunt Jenny (Ruth Lee), Uncle Chris (Kurt Katch), Designer: George Jenkins, Costumes: Lucinda Ballard

   The Great Dan Patch (film) — Twentieth Century Fox; Joseph M. Newman, director. Dennis O'Keefe (David Palmer), Gail Russell (Cissy Lathrop), Ruth Warrick (Ruth Treadwell), Charlotte Greenwood (Aunt Netty), Henry Hull (Dan Palmer).

1949

Oh You Beautiful Doll (film) — Twentieth Century Fox; John M. Stahl, director. Mark Stevens (Larry Kelly), June Haver (Doris Fisher), S.Z. Sakall (Alfred Breitenbach/Fred Fisher), Charlotte Greenwood (Anna Breitenbach), Gail Robbins (Marie Carle), Jay C. Flippen (Lippy Branigan).

1950

Peggy (film) — Universal Pictures; Fred de Cordova, director. Diana Lynn (Peggy Brookfield), Charles Coburn (Professor Brookfield), Charlotte Greenwood (Mrs. Emilia Fielding), Barbara Lawrence (Susan Brookfield), Charles Drake (Tom Fielding), Rock Hudson (Johnny Higgins),

   Out of This World (musical) — Cole Porter, music and lyrics; Arnold Saint-Subber and Lemuel Ayers, producers; Agnes de Mille, director; New Century Theatre, NYC; Charlotte Greenwood (Juno), George Jongeyans, aka George Gaynes (Jupiter), William Redfield (Mercury), Priscilla Gillette (Helen), William Eythe (Art O'Malley), Peggy Rea (Vulcania), David Burns

(Niki Skolianos), Janet Collins (Night), Choreography: Hanya Holm. Settings and Costumes: Lemuel Ayers. Orchestrations: Robert Russell Bennett.

1953

Dangerous When Wet (film) — Metro-Goldwyn-Mayer; Charles Walters, director. Esther Williams (Katie Higgins), Fernando Lamas (André Lanet), Jack Carson (Windy Weebe), Charlotte Greenwood (Ma Higgins), William Demarest (Pa Higgins).

1955

Oklahoma! (musical film) — Rodgers & Hammerstein Pictures, Inc. (using Metro-Goldwyn-Mayer facilities); Richard Rodgers and Oscar Hammerstein II, music and lyrics; Fred Zinnemann, director. Gordon McRae (Curly McLain), Gloria Grahame (Ado Annie Carnes), Gene Nelson (Will Parker), Charlotte Greenwood (Aunt Eller Murphy), Shirley Jones (Laurey Williams), Eddie Albert (Ali Hakkim), James Whitmore (James Carnes), Rod Steiger (Jud Fry), Barbara Lawrence (Gertie Cummings), Jay C. Flippen (Ike Skidmore).

   Glory (film) — RKO; David Butler, director. Margaret O'Brien (Clarabel Tilby), Walter Brennan (Ned Otis), Charlotte Greenwood (Agnes Tilby), John Lupton (Chad Chadburn).

1956

The Opposite Sex (film) — Metro-Goldwyn-Mayer; David Miller, director. June Allyson (Kay Hilliard), Joan Collins (Crystal Allen), Dolores Gray (Sylvia Fowler), Ann Sheridan (Amanda Penrose), Ann Miller (Gloria Dell), Leslie Nielsen (Steve Hilliard), Agnes Morehead (Countess de Brion), Charlotte Greenwood (Lucy), Joan Blondell (Edith Potter).

1957

Charlotte starred in the pilot for a series to be called *The Enchanted Forest*; it was never produced. (Internet Movie Database).

1961

The Thompsons of Thunder Ridge, "Best of the Post," Episode: #1.25, April 22, 1961 (TV) — Guest appearance. Jay C. Flippen, Charlotte Greenwood.

Appendix B: Known Vocal Recordings of Greenwood

- July 30, 1928, New York City — vocal, accompanist unknown
- May 3, 1935, London — Vic test, song "Too Tall" (Martin Broones), accompanied by studio orchestra, BE-123
- 1935, London — Two songs from *The Gay Deceivers* (Martin Broones), accompanied by studio orchestra, HMV B-8324
- 1950, New York City — Original cast recording from *Out of This World*, Columbia Records, A-980

Appendix C: Lyrics Credited to Greenwood

- "Campus Capers," to music of Martin Broones in the film *So This Is College* (1929). Source: Internet Movie Database and Charlotte Greenwood papers, USC
- Other songs Martin set to music: "Gorgeous," "Blue Bird Blues," "Love's Merry Go Round," "Lovers Are Like Harmonies," "Blue Boy Blues," and two songs listed as used in the Marion Davies 1929 musical *Marianne*: "Here I Am Where I Don't Want To Be" and "Locked In My Heart." Neither appears in the final list of musical numbers from the film.
- 1937–38 — "When I Walk With You (In The Cool of The Evening)," credited to Martin Broones and Charlotte Greenwood, vocal Phyllis Kenny, Jerry Blaine and his Stream Line Rhythm, B-7445-B

Appendix D: Shows with Songs or Scores by Martin Broones

- *Park Theatre Review* (no date or theatre)
- *The Blue Pearl* (songs) Longacre Theatre, Broadway 1918
- *Charlot's Revue* (songs) Prince of Wales Theatre, London 1924
- *The Odd Spot* (*Dion Titheradge's Vaudeville Theatre Revue*) (songs), Vaudeville Theatre, London 1924
- *Hassard Short's Ritz Revue* (songs for Charlotte), Broadway 1924
- *Rufus LeMaire's Affairs* (score and songs), Broadway 1927
- *Give Me A Ring* (score and songs) London Hippodrome, London 1933 (lyrics by Graham John, book by Guy Bolton and Weston and Lee)
- *Seeing Stars* (score and songs) Gaiety Theatre, London 1935 (book by Guy Bolton and Fred Thomson, lyrics by Graham John)
- *Gay Deceivers* (score and songs) Gaiety Theatre and then Coliseum, London 1935 (from the French of Henri Duvernois and Maubon Chamfleury, by Reginald Arkell; co-composer was Moise Simons)
- *Swing Along* (score and songs) Gaiety Theatre, London 1936 (book by Guy Bolton, Fred Thomson and Douglas Furber, lyrics by Graham John)

Sources for all the above: The Guide to Musical Theatre (*www.nodanw.com/*) and programs and sheet music of Martin Broones.

Appendix E: Martin Broones Filmography

- *The Mating Call* (1928) ("The Mating Call") (uncredited); Caddo Company, produced by Howard Hughes and distributed by Paramount;
- *Wonder of Women* (1929) ("At Close of Day" and "Liebeslied: Ich liebe dich"); Metro-Goldwyn-Mayer
- *The Hollywood Revue of 1929* ("For I'm the Queen", sung by Marie Dressler); Metro-Goldwyn-Mayer

- *The Mysterious Island* (1929), score; with Lionel Barrymore as Count Dakkar; Metro-Goldwyn-Mayer;
- *So This Is College* (1929) ("College Days," "Until the End," "Campus Capers" and "I Don't Want Your Kisses If I Can't Have Your Love") (titles uncredited); with Cliff Edwards, Polly Moran and Robert Montgomery; Charlotte is alleged to have contributed lyrics to one of Martin's songs for this film; Metro-Goldwyn-Mayer
- *Laughing Sinners* (1931) ("What Can I Do? I Love That Man") (uncredited); with Joan Crawford and Clark Gable; Metro-Goldwyn-Mayer
- *The Great Dan Patch* (1949) ("Can't Get You Then — Can't Get You Now"); with Charlotte Greenwood, Dennis O'Keefe and Ruth Warrick; Twentieth Century Fox

Source for all the above: Internet Movie Database.

Appendix F: Known Piano Recordings of Martin Broones

- March 16, 1933, London — "Love's Roses," music Martin Broones, words Frances Ring, Miss Gwen McCormack accompanied by Martin Broones (private recording in the author's possession), The Gramophone Company, Ltd.
- September 7, 1933, London — "Love's Roses," music Martin Broones, words Frances Ring, John McCormack accompanied by Martin Broones, HMV OB 5307–1 (unpublished) and OB 5307–2 (30–1170 78 rpm) DA 1341, re-released on LP Pearl 274

Appendix G: GUPPA (Greenwood's Unusual Painless Pound Annihilator)

As Charlotte Greenwood's filmwork attests, even when past middle age she was a dancer of youthful elasticity and energy. This activity, over her long career, came at a heavy price — Charlotte suffered from severe arthritis in her later years. While she was able to do so, however, she followed a disciplined course of exercise, developed by herself, which she called "the Guppa Guide": *Greenwood's Unusual Painless Pound Annihilator.* She was devoted enough to this exercise regimen to include it in several drafts of her memoirs — and some of the exercises even sound like choreographic shorthand of Charlotte's more memorable dance routines: "a sort of combination of a windmill at work and a corkscrew at ease." The Guppa Guide is given here without cuts, as an example of how one of the 20th century's most famous physical comediennes (who as a gymnasium instructor tied Eddie Cantor in knots in *Palmy Days*) kept herself in tone and in good humor.

✳ ✳ ✳

So here, for the first time in print, is the Guppa — Greenwood's Unusual Painless Pound Anihilator. It is very, very simple:

First, put on a warm sweater and socks — I'm assuming, of course, that you are out of bed. In the event that you are not, then first is, get up. Now that you are up and dressed, if not entirely awake, tune some music on the radio or place a musical record on the phonograph and prepare for work. The first week, take it easy; do each exercise only eight times; in the second week, increase the dose to sixteen; after that let your conscience be your guide. You're on your own!

Here we go with the Guppa Guide:

1. Reach up — alternate arms — eight forward, eight backward. It's easy enough to reach forward; reaching backward is something else again. It should be easy for politicians who are popularly supposed to have their hands out behind their backs most of the time.
2. Bend forward touching the toes; then raise up with arms straight overhead. This sounds extraor-

dinary, but it is merely a stiff arm swing. At first you may not be able to touch your toes. You'll do it in time.

3. Standing — arms abreast. Turn body so right hand is in front and left hand behind; then return to front position; then swing around without stopping. This is a sort of combination of a windmill at work and a corkscrew at ease. It stretches your back muscles, if you really want to know. Nothing like a good stretch for the back muscles — loosens up the torso, makes the old frame supple and pliant, puts elasticity in the stride — oh, ever so many things.

4. Feet front, slightly apart; arms down at each side (if you can get both arms down on one side, you're a better gymnast than I am); raise right arm over head and proceed to touch the floor with the left side. Repeat this operation with the left arm and the right side. If the telephone rings, don't try to answer it before you get yourself untangled.

5. Arms overhead — stretch up on your toes — bend knees while remaining on toes. If Albertina Rasch [Russian ballerina/choreographer] comes rushing in to offer you a life contract, sign it at once! If not, balance four times, then get up on toes, then down — and arms also. At this time Martha Graham, Busby Berkeley, Hermes Pan and Veloz and Yolanda will probably try to sign you. Take the best offer.

6. Bend body left with right arm over head, left arm stretched down left side — then swing left arm over to right side — right arm down right leg. What, you don't get it? It's as easy as falling off a log. You haven't a log? Well have you a sawhorse? Oh, for goodness sake.... Bend body left and so on. Now then all together — eight times.

7. Arms over head so, that's it — legs apart — swing arms through legs touching floor as far back of you as possible. In this movement be sure that there are no pigs in the house. It will be very disconcerting if a pig decides to run through your legs when you are about ready for the giant swing — *very*.

8. Arms down at sides, feet together — jump — land with your feet apart — clap your hands over your head — jump again and land with your feet together — slap arms down at side. If you bruise easily, don't slap too hard! When you jump, don't forget to come down. If you're really tall, don't jump too high. There's a scar on the top of my head where the chandelier made contact once.

9. Hands on hips — jump with right foot forward; then jump with left foot forward. Make believe you are doing a footrace; say the hundred yard hurdles. Make believe you are winning. Why not, it doesn't cost any more!

10. Lie on the floor. Ah! This is more like it. Don't go to sleep there. Bend up and touch your toes to the floor back of your head. Perhaps you won't make it the first couple of days. You might not even make it the first couple of months, weeks or years, but perseverance will get you there in the end.

11. As long as you're there, remain on the floor. You probably won't be able to get up for a minute or two anyway. Get your legs up in the air and do a scissors movement. Imagine you're cutting out that new dress, or your neighbor's throat. On second thought, stick to the dressmaking. If you do these exercises you'll need a new dress — a nice slim model and your neighbor will be as jealous as all get-out. You can snub her on account she's hippy, and you're not. This will be fun — now go on ahead with the scissors business!

12. Now get yourself into a sort of spread eagle position — arms out flat on the floor. Bring your left foot up until you can touch the palm of your right hand with a left toe — any toe will do. Repeat the process in reverse — right toe to left palm. This is what is known as the never-let-your-left-toe-know exercise.

13. Get on your back. Stretch out — lift your feet an inch from the floor. Well an inch and a half or two inches if you insist. Let's not quibble over this thing. I haven't time to be hunting for a tape measure and you're certainly in no position to be looking for one. You're on your back, remember, and your feet are a teensy-weensy bit off the floor. Now then, spread them as far as possible, then bring them back to center. Do this coming and going — eight times and don't let your heels drag. Let the moths make tracks on the carpet. You tend to your knitting or exercising.

14. Get back flat on the floor and then lift yourself up on your shoulders, so your legs are straight in the air. Make like you're riding a bicycle for a hundred times. If you can't count to a hundred, at least you'll see a lot of cobwebs on the ceiling. Pick out a spider and count its swings

like Robert the Bruce. Do not stop to get a dust mop.

15. Bend forward, touching leg, first right, then left, then floor in center. This is a variation of the old patty cake business. You are, for a moment, the baker's man. Don't start thinking what you'll have for breakfast. That will come in good time.

16. Guppa sit — that is, get into a sitting position; then lean forward and grasp your ankles firmly. Be sure to keep the legs stretched out flat. Now then, roll backward; then forward; then backward; then forward; then sideways — see, I fooled you. Well I'm sorry if you bumped your head! Keep rolling from one side to the other; never let go of your ankles; never let your knees bend. Just keep rolling along — like Old Man River, maybe!

17. Turn over on your stomach and rock gently back and forth. Bet you haven't been on your stomach since you were a baby. Don't look as if you had the colic; and don't go to sleep either. Fun, isn't it? Isn't it! All right. Get up on your feet.

18. Now hold your arms rigid and walk, lifting your feet to touch your hands — right, left, right, left — eight times.

19. Go into a split — oh, of course you can't at first; but there's nothing particularly difficult about it. Give it a try! Then call for a derrick! That's it!

20. Start kicking — not about the exercise — I mean kicking, as hard as you can.

21. Stand up and swing your legs. Imagine you're a crane. Cranes don't swing their legs? Well, maybe they don't. Am I an ornithologist? Swing your legs like a pendulum — swing along.

22. March — lifting your knees as high as possible — and don't march back to bed; march to the shower — a cold shower. By this time you should be bathed in perspiration and ready for either a shower or the isolation ward. Tomorrow morning at this same hour, do the exercises again. You'll be surprised how you loosen up. If you don't I'll be surprised. In that event you are privileged to send me a very stern letter signed "Former Admirer."

— Charlotte Greenwood

Appendix H: Greenwood's Family Circle

Blanche Ring,
comic actress
m. **Charles Winninger,**
comic actor

Frances Ring, actress
m. **Thomas Meighan,**
actor

Cyril Ring, comic supporting actor
m. I ***Charlotte Greenwood,***
Stage and screen actress →

m. II ***Martin Broones,***
composer, producer
First music director
of MGM Studios
One of his most popular
songs was a setting of
Frances Ring's poem
"Love's Roses"

Blanche m. 2 more times

Cyril was uncle to:

James Meighan,
who played The
Falcon on radio
from 1945–1947

m. II Molly Green, Ziegfeld
Follies dancer

A. Edward Sutherland,
film director, who directed
Charlotte's 1931 film,
Palmy Days with
Eddie Cantor
m. **Louise Brooks**

Chapter Notes

Introduction

1. Zinnemann, p. 138
2. Ibid., p. 146.
3. *Getting To Know Him,* p. 316–319 [hereafter GTKH].

Chapter 1

1. Baroness Ravensdale first sat in the House of Lords in 1958.
2. *The Funsters* [hereafter TF], p. 278.
3. *Never Too Tall* [hereafter NTT]; TF, p. 275.
4. NTT, p. 2; Jaquett genealogy, pp. 104–113; also Roberta Phillips DeMott papers.
5. NTT, pp. 2 and 5. Charlotte misremembered or was misinformed about her descent from the Jaquetts. The connection comes not through Rodney's wife, Anne, but through his mother, Martha Jaquett Murry, daughter of John Murry and Isabelle/Sabrina Jaquett. The sickly lady she was told about was not her great-grandmother, Martha Higgins, who lived to a ripe old age, but her grandmother Anne, about whom we know little more than her first name.
6. CG's personal notes [hereafter CGPN]; Frank Greenwood's sisters: undated draft of letter to Hedda Hopper in the Charlotte Greenwood papers at USC
7. CGPN and NTT

Chapter 2

1. NTT, p. 4. The technical term for scrofula is tuberculous adenitis; earlier known as "the King's Evil," which the touch of a king was believed to cure. It is a tubercular condition of the lymph nodes, spread by the drinking of unpasteurized milk or by unsanitary conditions in the home. The bacteria can spread throughout the body. In CG's pre-penicillin childhood, complications from this disease could have proved fatal or at the least physically scarring.
2. Ibid., p. 4.
3. Ibid., p. 8.
4. Ibid., p. 9.
5. Ibid., p. 10.
6. Ibid., p. 11.
7. Ibid., p. 12.
8. Ibid., p. 12.
9. Ibid., pp. 12–13.
10. Ibid., p. 13.

Chapter 3

1. See *www.nhrhta.org/htdocs/ssta.htm.*
2. NTT, pp. 15.
3. Ibid., pp. 15–16.
4. Ibid., pp. 16.
5. CGPN, which deals with the accident in greater detail.
6. NTT, pp. 18–19.
7. Ibid., pp. 21–23.
8. Ibid., pp. 23–24.
9. Ibid., pp. 24–25.
10. Ibid., p. 26.
11. Ibid., pp. 26–27.
12. Ibid., p. 27.

Chapter 4

1. NTT, pp. 28.
2. Ibid., p. 29.
3. Ibid., p. 30.
4. Ibid., p. 31.
5. Ibid., p. 32.
6. Ibid., p. 37.
7. Ibid., p. 38.
8. *Pictorial History of the American Theatre* [hereafter PHAT], p. 73.
9. PHAT, pp. 87–91; *The Voice of the City* [hereafter TVC], p. 87.
10. NTT, p. 38.
11. Ibid., pp. 40–41; TVC, pp. 149–151.
12. NTT, p. 41; and CGPN.
13. CGPN.
14. CGPN.
15. NTT, pp. 43–44.
16. Ibid., p. 43.
17. Ibid., p. 44.
18. CGPN.
19. Ibid. This first contract of Charlotte's is now pasted into one of her scrapbooks in the Charlotte

Greenwood papers at USC, along with her early contracts from Klaw & Erlanger and the Shubert brothers.

Chapter 5

1. NTT, pp. 42–43; early version of NTT and handwritten notes.
2. *The Art of Stage Dancing*, p. 25.
3. NTT, pp. 45–47.
4. Ibid., pp. 47–48 and CGPN; and TF, p. 276.

Chapter 6

1. NTT, p. 49.
2. Ibid., pp. 53–54.
3. NTT, pp. 108–110.
4. "Coon shouting" refers to ragtime and minstrelsy-based songs with a strong African American influence; they were often sung in blackface, as Sophie Tucker did early in her career. The genre was popularized by vaudeville comedienne May Irwin [1862–1938].
5. NTT, pp. 55–56.
6. Internet Broadway Database [hereafter IBDB].
7. NTT, p. 55. Scrapbook photograph referred to is in the Charlotte Greenwood collection at USC.
8. *My Life Is In Your Hands*, pp. 34, 123, 285.
9. The author owns Charlotte's autographed copy of *Operatic Anthology: Celebrated Arias Selected from Operas by Old and Modern Composers*, Schirmer's 1903, in which Charlotte has marked up several arias. Along with the Bizet selections, Charlotte worked on "Connais-tu le pays?" from Ambroise Thomas' *Mignon*, "Ah! Mon fils!" from Meyerbeer's *Le prophète* and "My heart is weary" from Goring-Thomas' *Nadeschda*. There are further indications she worked on "Mon coeur s'ouvre à ta voix" from Saint-Saëns' *Samson et Dalila*. Charlotte's autographed copy of Brahms *Lieder*, also in the author's possession, similarly shows that she worked on several of these songs.
10. CGPN and *Collier's*, Jan. 15, 1938, "Lady Longlegs."
11. NTT, pp. 57–58.
12. Ibid., p. 58 and CGPN, p. 11a.
13. NTT, pp. 59–61.

Chapter 7

1. CGPN, pp. 11d; NTT, p. 62.
2. Ibid., p. 11h.
3. Ibid., p. 11d.
4. NTT, pp. 64–66.
5. Ibid., p. 69 and CGPN.
6. CGPN.
7. NTT, pp. 71–72. Eunice ended up very much a part of Charlotte's life for many years after the breakup of the duo, serving as a sort of permanent housesitter for Charlotte's residence on Long Island for the many years during which Charlotte was in London or on the road, and later coming out to California to fulfill the same function. She was married, per Charlotte's handwritten notes, to a Dr. Lewis. She appeared in at least one silent film, *Sham*, in 1921, and died in 1966. See the *Internet Movie Database*.
8. NTT, pp. 71–72.
9. Ibid.

Chapter 8

1. NTT, p. 73.
2. *American Musical Theatre: A Chronicle*, p. 277 [hereafter Bordman].
3. Passing Show of 1912 program, CG's personal copy.
4. Bordman, pp. 128–129.
5. Ibid., p. 277–78; and Passing Show program.
6. Passing Show program.
7. *San Francisco Chronicle*, full page feature, Feb. 25, 1912, saved in Charlotte's scrapbooks at USC.
8. Stanislavsky, *Sobranie sochiney*, Vol. VI, p. 256, quoted Benedetti, 1988, p. 246, from Antony Beevor's *The Mystery of Olga Chekhova*, p. 92.
9. Bordman, p. 277.
10. NTT, pp. 73–76.
11. Ibid., p. 76.
12. CGPN: list of reviews.
13. NTT, p. 78.
14. Ibid., p. 79. Jobyna Howland is alleged to have had a long-term affair with another of Charlotte's friends, playwright Zoe Akins. Mrs. Patrick Campbell was also a friend of Charlotte's — she, Akins and Charlotte are described (by Elsa Lanchester, rumored to be a lesbian) as hanging out together at the Garden of Allah in Sheilah Graham's book about Alla Nazimova's Hollywood estate-turned-hotel. (Nazimova also was a known lesbian.) As the originator of the famed quote, "Does it really matter what these affectionate people do? So long as they don't do it in the streets and frighten the horses!" we may assume Mrs. Pat, though not gay herself, was tolerant toward the sexuality of Akins and other lesbians of her circle. See *The Garden of Allah*, p. 66.

Chapter 9

1. In one version of her memoirs Charlotte describes these as the steps to the White House, but as there are not 200 steps to reach that building she clearly meant the Capitol complex.
2. NTT, pp. 86–87.
3. *The Oracle of Broadway*, pp. 13–27 [hereafter *Oracle*].
4. *The Night Is Large*, "The Royal Historian of Oz," pp. 329–347 [hereafter TNIL].
5. *Oracle*, p. 228 and p. 259.
6. TNIL, p. 343.
7. NTT, pp. 89–90.
8. *Oracle*, pp. 259–261.
9. NTT, p. 90.
10 NYT, Sep. 22, 1914
11. Bordman, p. 300; re: friendship between Fritzi Scheff and Charlotte Greenwood, see letters in Charlotte's scrapbooks at USC
12 NTT, p. 97.

Chapter 10

1. NTT, p. 105.
2. Ibid., pp. 100–101.
3. Ibid., pp. 102–103.
4. CGPN for her "firsts," pp. 3–4.
5. TF, p. 278.
6. NYT, July 25, 1915.
7. *Morning Oregonian*, Friday, Aug. 20, 1920.

8. From reviews CG provided in typed excerpts in her personal papers, without dates.

Chapter 11

1. NTT, p. 104.
2. *Off With Their Heads!: A Serio-Comic Tale of Hollywood*, p. 4
3. Ibid., p. 14.
4. TF, p. 277.
5. Ibid., p. 277.
6. NYT, April 11, 1922.
7. IBDB.
8. Miles Kreuger interview with the author. Because the 1920 census would show whether or not Charlotte and Cyril were still married, the author searched for any record for either person. No trace could be found. They may have been on tour when the census taker came to call.
9. *As Thousands Cheer: The Life of Irving Berlin*, pp. 174–175.
10. Bordman, p. 365.
11. NTT, p. 112.
12. Ibid., pp. 112–113.
13. Bordman, pp. 374–375; 1924 tour program of the second Music Box Revue.
14. *American Days*, p. 7.
15. NYT, Oct. 18, 1924.
16. Ibid.
17. CGPN.
18. NYT, Oct. 30, 1924.
19. NYT, Jan. 20, 1924.

Chapter 12

1. William Luce interviews with the author; 1920 Census. Luce remembers Martin telling him that his elderly mother, Erma Broones, who spent many years living at the famous Beaux Arts Ansonia Apartments in Manhattan, died in front of her television set, laughing at a sitcom — "A great way to go," he told Luce. Joseph Broones seems to have died before 1920, as he does not appear in the census for that year or for 1930.
2. Joseffy obituary from *The Etude*, 1915. He died of ptomaine poisoning on July 25, 1915. He was a pupil of Brauer, Liszt, Moscheles and Werzer.
3. William Luce interview with the author; and Martin Broones lecture, published in the Christian Science Monitor 21 Sep. 1970; and *Black Manhattan: Theatre and Dance Music of James Reese Europe, Will Marion Cook and Members of the Legendary Clef Club*, liner notes by Rick Benjamin (*http://sfx.library.nyu.edu/dram/note.cgi?id=24854*); and *Illustrated Sporting and Dramatic News* article in Charlotte Greenwood's scrapbooks at USC. I thank Dolly Sisters biographer Gary Chapman for clarifying the state of the cabaret in London and Martin's place in it during this period.
4. Bordman, p. 456.
5. *Spread a Little Happiness*, p. 41.
6. NTT, pp. 123–126.
7. B. Feldman & Co., London 1924, from MB's music collection.
8. Ibid., p. 126 and CG's personal notes.
9. William Luce interviews with the author.
10. *Collier's*, p. 43.
11. NTT, pp. 156–157; CGPN.
12. CGPN.

Chapter 13

1. NTT, p. 126; and TF, p. 277.
2. NTT, pp. 127–128.
3. TF, p. 277; Charlotte Greenwood papers, USC.
4. NTT, pp. 131–137; CGPN.
5. *The Chorus Lady*, p. 116.
6. NTT, p. 137.
7. Ibid., p. 139.
8. *Some of these Days*, p. 235.
9. Ibid., pp. 238–239.
10. NTT, p. 150.

Chapter 14

1. NTT, p. 150; TVC, pp. 66–67.
2. Bordman, p. 423.
3. *Merchant of Dreams: Louis B. Mayer, M.G.M. and the Secret Hollywood*, pp. 5–15.
4. Ibid., pp. 117–128.
5. NTT, p. 144.
6. Charlotte loved her cars: in 1912 she was reported as purchasing an EMF touring car (Everitt, Metzger and Flanders), a company later absorbed by Studebaker; and in 1929 she bought a princely Cadillac Imperial limousine "with a special Fleetwood body," one of the most expensive the maker offered. It is not known what happened to Bertha the Rolls Royce, but Charlotte does refer in her memoir notes to bringing her English chauffeur, Harris, and the car to New York after her return from London in the mid–1930s.
7. Ibid., pp. 145 and 157.
8. Ibid., pp. 145–146; *Hedda and Louella*, pp. 54–83.

Chapter 15

1. *The NYT Film Reviews, 1913–1931*.
2. Ibid.
3. *What Made Pistachio Nuts?*, pp. 274–275.
4. NTT, pp. 155–156.
5. Ibid., pp. 160–162.

Chapter 16

1. *Keaton*, p. 190.
2. Ibid., p. 191, pp. 197–198.
3. "American Days," p. 10.
4. *New York Times Film Reviews, 1913–1931*.
5. "American Days," p. 12.
6. Empire Theatre programme, 25 Sept. 1931.
7. *The Etude*, pp. 16–72.
8. NTT, pp. 163–164.

Chapter 17

1. *Everyone Was So Young*, p 192 and p. 230; NTT, p. 166.
2. NTT, p. 167.
3. Ibid.
4. Ibid., p. 168. An Austrian born in 1880, Robert Stolz was no friend of the Nazi regime and would leave Germany for his homeland in 1936, eventually escaping to France, where he was imprisoned in Colombe internment camp. A young Frenchwoman raised money to free him, married him, and they were in New York City by 1940. He eventually returned to Vienna and lived till

1975. See http://www.geocities.com/Vienna/Strasse/
1945/WSB/stolz.html.
    5. Ibid., p. 172.

Chapter 18

    1. NTT, p. 174.
    2. "American Days," p. 15.
    3. NTT, pp. 172–173 and *The Play Pictorial*, 1932.
    4. Ibid., p. 175.
    5. Ian Fox article as reproduced in NTT, pp. 176–177; a version appeared in *Film Weekly* on December 9, 1932 that is in some respects different. I have interpolated it into the version Charlotte reproduced in her memoirs.
    6. NTT, p. 173 and CGPN; for Flora Lion portrait information, see "Royal Academy Opens Exhibition" in NYT, April 29, 1933; and opening night program for *Three Sisters*, Theatre Royal Drury Lane.

Chapter 19

    1. CG's personal notes. Baillie had been a theatre goer most of his adult life and with his wife entertained actors, musicians, artists and various figures of note at the Deanery on a regular basis.
    2. Charlotte Greenwood papers, USC.
    3. NTT, pp. 179–180.
    4. Ibid., p. 180.
    5. Ibid., p. 180–181.
    6. Ibid., p. 184.
    7. Ibid., pp. 184–185.
    8. *Poor Little Rich Girl*, p. 89 [hereafter PLRG].
    9. NTT, pp. 184–185.
    10. Son of Emanuele Filiberto Prince of Savoy, Duke of Aosta and Hélène Princess of France; was married to Irene Princess of Greece and Denmark.
    11. NTT, p. 185; PLRG, pp. 90–91.
    12. NTT, p. 186.
    13. Tom Finch interview with the author.
    14. NTT, p. 188.

Chapter 20

    1. *The Late Christopher Bean*, 1933 edition, p. 8 & p. 17.
    2. NTT, pp. 190–191.
    3. Ibid, pp. 190–191. Martin also made himself part of the production: between Acts II and III were programmed his songs "I Don't Know How I Can Do Without You" and "Love's Roses." Even Letty invaded(the overture was made up of selections from *So Long Letty* and *Linger Longer Letty*.
    4. Ibid., pp. 192–193.
    5. GTKH, p. 126.
    6. Ibid., pp. 126–127.
    7. Ibid., pp. 127–128.

Chapter 21

    1. Martin seems to have worked very fast indeed: another of his shows, *Swing Along*, set on the *Train Bleu*, with book by Bolton, Thompson and Douglas Furber and lyrics by Graham John, also played the Gaiety later that year, in November 1936. Add to this his involvement with the management of the Gaiety itself and one wonders that he got any composing done at all.

    2. CGPN; NTT, p. 201.
    3. NTT, pp. 201–202.
    4. Ibid., p. 202.

Chapter 22

    1. NTT, p. 202.
    2. Ibid., p. 203.
    3. Ibid.
    4. Ibid, pp. 203–204 and CGPN.
    5. Ibid., pp. 204–205.
    6. Ibid., pp. 205–206.
    7. Ibid., p. 208.
    8. *London Illustrated News*, pp. 814–815; and *The Royal Record of Tree Planting, The Provision of Open Spaces, Recreation Grounds & Other Schemes Undertaken in the British Empire and Elsewhere, Especially in the United States of America, in Honour of The Coronation of His Majesty King George VI*, Cambridge University Press, 1939.
    9. *Don J. Ewan*, referencing p. 39 of Charlotte's inscribed copy from the poet. Martin set several of Wolfe's verses to music.
    10 NTT, pp. 207–208; William Luce interviews with the author. Excerpt from Charlotte's article for *The Tail-wagger Magazine*, Sept. 1948.
    11. Ibid., pp. 207–208.
    12. Ibid., pp. 209–210.
    13. Ibid., pp. 209–212.

Chapter 23

    1. NTT, p. 214.
    2. Ibid., p. 214.
    3. Ibid., pp. 214–215.
    4. Ibid., pp. 215–216.
    5. CGPN.
    6 NTT, pp. 217–218.
    7. Ibid., p. 218.
    8. NTT, pp. 220–221.
    9. Charlotte claimed her favorite authors were Shakespeare and Dickens, see *Funny Women*, p. 18.
    10. *Collier's*, p. 43.
    11. CGPN (including quote re: Winkie's British citizenship).
    12. NTT, pp. 225–227 and CGPN.

Chapter 24

    1. See *Kristallnacht* in the Jewish Virtual Library, *www.jewishvirtuallibrary.org*.
    2. *A History of the Second World War*, p. 15.
    3. NTT, pp. 228–229.
    4. CGPN.
    5. NTT, pp. 235–237.
    6. Ibid., pp. 242–243.
    7. Ibid., p. 243.

Chapter 25

    1. *When the Stars Went to War*, pp. 5–7 & p. 326 [hereafter WSWW].
    2. TVC, quoting Hal Leroy, p. 60.
    3. CGPN.
    4. WSWW, pp. 51–52

5 NTT, pp. 244–245.
6. *Child Star*, pp. 162–163 and 220–221 [hereafter CS].
7. NTT, p. 245.
8. NYT, May 4, 1940.
9. Ibid.

Chapter 26

1. CS, p. 310 and p. 312 and CGPN.
2. NTT, p. 245.
3. NYT, Oct. 18, 1940.
4. CGPN; *Western Family Magazine*, May 26, 1949, pp.4b-5b.
5. Charlotte Greenwood papers, USC.
6. Ibid.
7. CGPN.

Chapter 27

1. WSWW, p. 112.
2. Ibid., p. 113.
3. Note in the Charlotte Greenwood papers at USC.
4. *Cowardly Lion*, p. 214.
5. WSWW, p. 113.
6. Ibid., pp. 120–121; and note titled "Thoughts on War" in the Charlotte Greenwood papers at USC.
7. NYT, July 5, 1941.
8. NTT, pp. 254–255.
9. Included in the DVD *Hidden Hollywood: Treasures from the 20th Century Fox Archives*, 1997.
10. NYT, Dec. 23, 1943.
11. CGPN; and Hedda Hopper column preserved in Charlotte Greenwood scrapbooks at USC.

Chapter 28

1. Undated Edwin Schallert interview, preserved in Charlotte Greenwood's scrapbooks at USC. Also in these scrapbooks Charlotte carefully preserved the two pages of script containing this scene, writing in red pencil how long the take had been and how she had not needed further takes.
2. NYT, July 30, 1944.

Chapter 29

1. *Mrs. Eddy*, p. 146.
2. D. H. Johnson note, 2-14-1950.
3. *Science and Health*, viii.
4 Ibid., p. 63.

Chapter 30

1. TF, p. 283.
2. William Luce interviews with the author.
3. Ibid.
4. *Doris Day* [hereafter DD], pp. 149–150, in which she erroneously describes Charlotte as "that marvelous English [sic] comedienne."
5. Ibid., pp. 150–153; and *Science and Health*, Chapt. 13, p. 464.
6. DD, p. 161.
7. Ibid., p. 219.
8. Ibid., p. 257. Martin told William Luce in later years that he believed Melcher had allegedly suffered from a long-term venereal disease. Luce told the author of one strong case arguing for Martin's ability to heal, related by the composer-arranger Mel Henke. During his sessions with Martin, Henke told Luce, Martin would enter a state of silent prayer so intense he would grind his teeth and tremble — like a trance state, according to Henke. Henke told Luce he credited Martin with helping him cure his alclolholism. William Luce interview with the author.
9. William Luce interview with author.

Chapter 31

1. NYT interview, Dec. 17, 1950.
2. GTKH, p. 190; and *Green Grow The Lilacs* [hereafter GGTL], Scene Six.
3. NYT, July 21, 1950.
4. NYT Dec. 17, 1950.
5. *Not Since Carrie: Forty Years of Broadway Flops*, Mandelbaum, p. 102.
6. TF, p. 282; and Irene Dunne note in the Charlotte Greenwood papers, USC.
7. NYT, 12–17–50.
8. Ibid.
9. *The Life That Late He Led*, p. 264 [hereafter LLHL].
10. *Cole Porter*, p. 323.
11. Ibid., pp. 325–326.
12. Peggy Rea interview with the author.
13. George Gaynes interview with the author and the on-line recollections of Buddy Bregman, *http://www.buddybregman.com/stories2.html*.
14. *Cole Porter*, pp. 322–323.
15. Ibid., p. 324.
16. LLHL, p. 265, Selma Tamber quote.
17. Gaynes interview with the author and Selma Tamber in *Cole Porter*, p. 327.
18. LLHL, p. 266.
19. *Cole Porter*, p. 328; NYT review, Brooks Atkinson, Dec. 12, 1950; and NYT review, John Martin, January 14, 1951.
20. Peggy Rea interview with the author.

Chapter 32

1. NYT, Dec. 17, 1950.
12. Howard, *Harper's Weekly* 33, May 18, 1889, 391–94.
13. Albert Borowitz, "Pore Jud is Daid:" Violence and Lawlessness in the Plays of Lynn Riggs, Legal Studies Forum, Vol. 27, No. 1. [2003], pp. 157–184.
14. Jace Weaver, *The Cherokee Night and Other Plays*, xv [Foreword].
15. GGTL, Scene One.
16. *The Richard Rodgers Reader*, p. 113.
17. *Beautiful Mornin'*, pp. 70–79 [hereafter BM].
18. Helburn, pp. 281–282.
19. De Mille, 232–245.
10. BM, p. 71.
11. Helburn, pp. 281–290.

Chapter 33

1. GTKH, p. 314.
2. Ebert, quoted in *www.ebertfest/com/two/oklahoma_rev.htm*

3. Zinnemann, pp. 7–8.

4. Ibid., p. 136; GTKH, p. 315.

5. Aunt Eller's lines from the film *Oklahoma!*

6. James Mitchell letter to the author, April 8, 2005.

7. Shirley Jones interview with the author, June 7, 2006.

8. CGPN. Charlotte gave this lecture at the Upton Dramatic School in Philadelphia on Oct. 14, 1937.

9. NTT, p. 263.

Chapter 34

1. Martin told William Luce that Charlotte was offered the part of the Mother Superior, which Ham-merstein crafted for her, but that she turned it down because as a committed Christian Scientist she could not in good conscience don a Catholic nun's habit. William Luce interviews with the author.

Epilogue

1. William Luce interviews with the author.

2. Last will and testament of Charlotte Greenwood Broones, filed January 25, 1978, BK 2237, PC 1001, NEP 21238.

3. Ibid.

4. NYT obituary for Charlotte Greenwood, Feb. 13, 1978.

5. NTT, pp. 272–273, pp. 275–277.

Bibliography

Astaire, Fred. *Steps in Time*. New York: Harper & Row, 1959.

Baillie, Albert Victor, Dean of Windsor. *My First Eighty Years*, 1864–1944. London: John Murray, 1951.

Baral, Robert. *Revue: A Nostalgic Reprise of the Great Broadway Period*. New York: Fleet, 1962.

Bergreen, Laurence. *As Thousands Cheer: The Life of Irving Berlin*. New York: Viking Penguin, 1990.

Black, Shirley Temple. *Child Star: An Autobiography*. New York: McGraw-Hill, 1988.

Block, Geoffrey. *The Richard Rodgers Reader*. Oxford: Oxford University Press, 2002.

Blum, Daniel, enlarged by John Willis. *A Pictorial History of the American Theatre, 1860–1980*. New York: Crown, 1981.

Bordman, Gerald. *American Musical Theatre: A Chronicle*. Oxford: Oxford University Press, 1978.

Broones, Martin. "Is There a Way Out?" Lecture published in the *Christian Science Monitor*, Sept. 21, 1970. (Courtesy of Jon Finch, University of Central Oklahoma.)

Bull, Clarence, and Raymond Lee. *The Faces of Hollywood*. New York: A.S. Barnes, 1968.

Burke, Billie, with Cameron Shipp. *With a Feather on My Nose*. New York: Appleton-Century-Crofts, 1949.

Cantor, Eddie, with David Freedman and Jane Kesner Ardmore. *My Life Is in Your Hands* and *Take My Life*, (the autobiographies of Eddie Cantor). New York: Cooper Square Press, 2000.

Chevalier, Maurice, as told to Eileen and Robert Mason Pollock. *With Love*. Boston: Little, Brown, 1960.

Crowther, Bosley. *The Lion's Share: The Story of an Entertainment Empire*. New York: E. P. Dutton, 1957.

Csida, Joseph, and June Bundy Csida. *American Entertainment: A Unique History of Popular Show Business*. New York: Watson-Guptill, 1978.

Dakin, Edwin Franken. *Mrs. Eddy*. New York: Grosset & Dunlap, 1929.

Dardis, Tom. *Keaton: The Man Who Wouldn't Lie Down*. London: Andre Deutsch, 1979.

De La Haye, Amy, and Shelley Tobin. *Chanel: The Couturière at Work*. New York: Overlook Press, 1994.

Eddy, Mary Baker. *Science and Health with Key to the Scriptures*. Boston: First Church of Christ, Scientist, 1971.

Eells, George. *Hedda and Louella*. New York: G.P. Putnam's Sons, 1972.

_____. *The Life That Late He Led: A Biography of Cole Porter*. New York: G.P. Putnam's Sons, 1967.

Eyman, Scott. *The Lion of Hollywood: The Life and Legend of Louis B. Mayer*. New York: Simon and Schuster, 2005.

Forbes, James. *The Chorus Lady* (novelization of the play by John W. Harding). New York: G.W. Dillingham, 1908.

Forbes, Kathryn. *Mama's Bank Account*. New York: Harcourt, Brace, 1943. (From CG's library.)

Fordin, Hugh. *Getting to Know Him: A Biography of Oscar Hammerstein II*. New York: Da Capo Press, 1977.

Gardner, Martin. *The Night Is Large: Collected Essays 1939–1995*. New York: St. Martin's Griffin, 1996.

Gill, Gillian. *Mary Baker Eddy*. Cambridge, MA: Perseus Books, 1998.

Graham, Sheilah. *The Garden of Allah*. New York: Crown, 1970.

Green, Martin, and John Swan. *The Triumph of Pierrot: The Commedia dell'Arte and the Modern Imagination*. New York: Macmillan, 1986.

Green, Stanley, *The World of Musical Comedy: The Story of the Musical Stage as Told Through the Careers of Its Foremost Composers and Lyricists*. New York: Grosset & Dunlap, 1960.

Greenwood, Charlotte. "American Days." Article written in London, ca. 1932. William Luce collection.

_____. Miscellaneous notes and letters related to her memoirs. William Luce collection.

_____. *Never Too Tall*. Manuscript and notes, William Luce collection

_____. Papers in the archives of the Film and Television Library, University of Southern California, Los Angeles.

Gussow, Mel. *Don't Say Yes Until I Finish Talking: A Biography of Darryl F. Zanuck*. New York: Doubleday, 1971.

Hart, B.H. Liddell. *A History of the Second World War*. New York: G. P. Putnam's Sons, 1970.

Helburn, Theresa. *A Wayward Quest*. Boston: Little, Brown, 1960.

Higham, Charles. *Merchant of Dreams: Louis B. Mayer, M.G.M. and the Secret Hollywood*. New York: Donald I. Fine, 1993.

Hoopes, Roy. *When the Stars Went to War: Hollywood and World War II*. New York: Random House, 1994.

Hope, Bob, with Melville Shavelson. *Don't Shoot, It's Only Me: Bob Hope's Comedy History of the United States*. New York: G.P. Putnam's Sons, 1990.

Hopper, Hedda. *From Under My Hat*. Doubleday, 1952.

_____, with James Brough. *The Whole Truth and Nothing But*. New York: Doubleday, 1962.

Hotchner, A.E., with Doris Day. *Doris Day: Her Own Story*. London: W.H. Allen, 1977.

Howard, Sidney. *The Late Christopher Bean* (after *Prenez garde à la peinture* by René Fauchois). New York: Samuel French, 1933.

Ilyin, Natalia. *Blonde Like Me: The Roots of the Blonde Myth in Our Culture*. New York: Touchstone Books, 2000.

Jacobs, Lewis. *The Rise of the American Film*. New York: Harcourt, Brace, 1939.

Jenkins, Henry. *What Made Pistachio Nuts? Early Sound Comedy and the Vaudeville Aesthetic*. New York: Columbia University Press, 1992.

Jessel, George. *So Help Me: The Autobiography of George Jessel*. New York: Random House, 1943.

Katkov, Norman. *The Fabulous Fanny: The Story of Fanny Brice*. New York: Alfred A. Knopf, 1953.

Lahr, John. *Notes on a Cowardly Lion: The Biography of Bert Lahr*. Los Angeles: University of California Press, 2000.

Laskey, Jesse L., with Don Weldon. *I Blow My Own Horn*. New York: Doubleday, 1957.

Levant, Oscar. *A Smattering of Ignorance*. New York: Doubleday, Doran, 1940. (From CG's library.)

Marion, Frances. *Off with Their Heads! A Serio-Comic Tale of Hollywood*. New York: Macmillan, 1972.

Mauclair, Camille. *Au Soleil de Provence*. Grenoble: Editions J. Rey, 1931. (From CG's library.)

McBrien, William. *Cole Porter: A Biography*. New York: Alfred A. Knopf, 1998.

Mordden, Ethan. *Beautiful Mornin': The Broadway Musical in the 1940's*. Oxford: Oxford University Press, 1999.

_____. *Coming Up Roses: The American Musical in the 1950's*. Oxford: Oxford University Press 1998.

Morley, Sheridan. *Spread a Little Happiness: The First Hundred Years of the British Musical*. London: Thames and Hudson, 1987.

Morosco, Oliver, with Helen M. Morosco and Leonard Paul Dugger. *The Oracle of Broadway*. Caldwell, ID: Caxton Printers, 1944.

Nolan, Frederick. *The Sound of Their Music: The Story of Rodgers and Hammerstein*. New York: Walker, 1978.

O'Brien, Pat. *The Wind at My Back: The Life and Times of Pat O'Brien*. New York: Doubleday, 1964.

Parish, James Robert, and William T. Leonard. *The Funsters*. New York: Arlington House Publishers, 1979.

Ravensdale, Baroness Irene. *In Many Rhythms: An Autobiography*. London: Weidenfeld & Nicholson, 1953.

Rensselaer, Philip van. *Million Dollar Baby: An Intimate Portrait of Barbara Hutton*. New York: G. P. Putnam's Sons, 1979.

Riggs, Lynn, with a foreword by Jace Weaver. *The Cherokee Night and Other Plays*. Norman: University of Oklahoma Press, 2003.

Rosenstein, Jake. *Hollywood Leg Man*. Los Angeles: Madison Press, 1950.

Sellers, Edwin Jaquett. *Genealogy of the Jaquett Family*. Philadelphia, 1907.

Shirer, William L. *The Rise and Fall of the Third Reich: A History of Nazi Germany*. New York: Simon and Schuster, 1960.

Smith, Catherine Parsons. *William Grant Still: A Study in Contradictions*. Berkeley: University of California Press, 2000.

Snyder, Robert W. *The Voice of the City: Vaudeville and Popular Culture in New York*. Chicago: Ivan R. Dee, 1989.

Stuart, Sandra Lee. *The Pink Palace: Behind Closed Doors at the Beverly Hills Hotel*. New Jeresy: Lyle Stuart, 1978.

Suskin, Steven. *Opening Night on Broadway: A Critical Quotebook of the Golden Era of the Musical Theatre (1943–1964)*. New York: Schirmer Books, 1990.

Swanson, Gloria. *Swanson on Swanson*. New York: Random House, 1980.

Tucker, Sophie, with Dorothy Giles. *Some of These Days: The Autobiography of Sophie Tucker*. Garden City, NY: Doubleday, Doran, 1945.

Twomey, Alfred E., and Arthur F. McClure. *The Versatiles: A Study of Supporting Character Actors and Actresses in the American Motion Picture, 1930–1955*. New York: Castle Books, 1969.

Unterbrink, Mary. *Funny Women: American Comediennes, 1860–1985*. Jefferson, NC: McFarland, 1987.

Vaill, Amanda. *Everybody Was So Young: Gerald and Sara Murphy, A Lost Generation Love Story*. Boston: Houghton Mifflin, 1998.

Wayburn, Ned. *The Art of Stage Dancing: The Story of a Beautiful and Profitable Profession*. New York: Ned Wayburn Studios of Stage Dancing, 1925.

Windsor, Duchess of. *The Heart Has Its Reasons*. New York: David McKay, 1956.

Wolfe, Humbert. *Don J. Ewan*. London: Arthur Barker, 1937.

Woollcott, Alexander. *Enchanted Aisles*. New York: G.P. Putnam's Sons, 1924.

_____, edited by Beatrice Kaufman and Joseph Hennessy. *The Letters of Alexander Woollcott*. New York: Viking, 1944.

Zinnemann, Fred. *Fred Zinnemann: An Autobiography*. London: Bloomsbury, 1992.

Newspapers and Magazines

Collier's, Jan. 15, 1938.
The Etude, Jan. 1931.
Film Weekly, London, Dec. 9, 1932.
Harper's Weekly 33, May 18, 1889.
Hollywood Daily Citizen, 1931.
London Illustrated News, May 1937.
Morning Oregonian, Aug. 20, 1920.
New York Times, 1912–1978.
Play Pictorial, London, July 1935, Vol. LXVII, no. 399.
The Playgoer magazine, "Charlotte Greenwood in 'She Couldn't Say No,'" January 12, 1930.
San Francisco Chronicle, Feb. 1912.
Western Family Magazine, May 26, 1949.

Vital Statistics

U.S. Census records for 1870, 1880, 1890, 1900, 1910, 1920 and 1930; U.S. draft card for Cyril Ring, 1917; U.S. Social Security application for Charlotte G. Broones, 12/4/1934; deed of trust for 806 North Rodeo Drive, Beverly Hills, CA, 1943; obituaries for Annabelle Greenwood and Erma Schermann Broones, *New York Times*; death certificates for Martin Broones and Charlotte Greenwood Broones, last will and testament of Charlotte Greenwood Broones, California State Department of Health and Human Services; obituary for Charlotte Greenwood, *New York Times*.

Interviews

George Gaynes interview, February 2003. Peggy Rea interview, March 2003. Miles Kreuger interview, September 2003. Tom Finch interview, July 2005. William Luce interviews, July-August 2005. Shirley Jones interview, June 2006.

Index

Numbers in *bold italics* represent pages with photographs.